The Indian Army was the largest volunteer army during the Second World War. Indian Army divisions fought in the Middle East, North and East Africa, Italy – and went to make up the overwhelming majority of the troops in South East Asia. Over two million personnel served in the Indian Army – and India provided the base for supplies for the Middle Eastern and South East Asian theatres. This monograph is a modern historical interpretation of the Indian Army as a holistic organisation during the Second World War. It will look at training in India – charting how the Indian Army developed a more comprehensive training structure than any other Commonwealth country. This was achieved through both the dissemination of doctrine and the professionalism of a small coterie of Indian Army officers who brought about a military culture within the Indian Army – starting in the 1930s – that came to fruition during the Second World War, which informed the formal learning process.

The book will illustrate that the Indian Army was reorganised after experiences of the First World War. Then during the interwar period, the army developed training and doctrine for both fighting on the North West Frontier, and as an aid to civil power. With the outbreak of the Second World War, in addition to these roles, the army had to expand and adapt to fighting modern professional armies in the difficult terrains of desert, jungle and mountain warfare. This was addressed by the Directorate of Military Training with training pamphlets produced for fighting in these terrains. The doctrine developed through experience and was assimilated into later editions of the training pamphlets and memoranda. This training material formed the basis of training instructions that were produced in nearly every Indian Army division fighting in all theatres. Similarly the training instructions were updated after exercises and battle experience and the lessons were also disseminated back to the Military Training Directorate. A clear development of doctrine and training can be seen, with many pamphlets being produced by GHQ India that were, in turn, used to formulate training within formations and then used in divisional, brigade and unit training instructions – thus a clear line of process can be seen not only from GHQ India down to brigade and battalion level, but also upwards from battalion and brigade level based on experience in battle that was absorbed into new training instructions. Together with the added impetus for education in the army, by 1945 the Indian Army had become a modern, professional and national army.

Dr Alan Jeffreys is Head of Equipment and Uniform at the National Army Museum and a visiting research fellow at the University of Greenwich. He is also a series editor of Helion's War and Military Culture in South Asia, 1757-1947.

APPROACH TO BATTLE

War and Military Culture in South Asia, 1757-1947
www.helion.co.uk/warandmilitarycultureinsouthasia

Series Editors
Professor Emeritus Raymond Callahan, University of Delaware
Alan Jeffreys, National Army Museum
Professor Daniel Marston, Australian National University

Editorial Advisory Board
Squadron Leader (Retired) Rana Chhina, Centre of Armed Forces Historical Research, United Service Institution of India
Professor Anirudh Deshpande, University of Delhi
Professor Ashley Jackson, King's College London
Dr Robert Johnson, Oxford University
Lieutenant Commander Dr Kalesh Mohanan, Naval History Division, Ministry of Defence, India
Dr Tim Moreman
Dr David Omissi, University of Hull
Professor Peter Stanley, University of New South Wales, Canberra
Dr Erica Wald, Goldsmiths, University of London

Submissions
The publishers would be pleased to receive submissions for this series. Please contact us via email info@helion.co.uk

Titles
1 *'Swords Trembling In Their Scabbards'. The Changing Status of Indian Officers in the Indian Army 1757–1947* Michael Creese (ISBN 978-1-909982-81-9)
2 *'Discipline, System and Style'. The Sixteenth Lancers and British Soldiering in India 1822-1846* John H. Rumsby (ISBN 978-1-909982-91-8)
3 *Die in Battle, Do not Despair. The Indians on Gallipoli, 1915* Peter Stanley (ISBN 978-1-914059-14-8)
4 *Brave as a Lion. The Life and Times of Field Marshal Hugh Gough, 1st Viscount Gough* Christopher Brice (ISBN 978-1-910294-61-1)
5 *Approach to Battle. Training the Indian Army during the Second World War* Alan Jeffreys (hardback 978-1-911096-51-1, paperback 978-1-804514-74-0)
6 *The Indian Army in The First World War: New Perspectives* Edited by Alan Jeffreys (hardback 978-1-911512-78-3, paperback 978-1-804510-49-0)
7 *War without Pity in the South Indian Peninsula 1798–1813: The Letter Book of Lieutenant-Colonel Valentine Blacker* Edited and with introductory notes by David Howell (ISBN 978-1-912390-86-1)
8 *Of Islands, Ports and Sea Lanes: Africa and the Indian Ocean in the Second World War* Ashley Jackson (ISBN 978-1-912390-74-8)
9 *Ceylon at War 1939-45* Ashley Jackson (ISBN 978-1-912390-65-6)
10 *For The Honour of My House: The Contribution of the Indian Princely States to the First World War* Tony McClenaghan (ISBN 978-1-912390-87-8)
11 *'Terriers in India: British Territorials, 1914–1919* Peter Stanley (ISBN 978-1-804510-51-3)

Approach to Battle

Training the Indian Army during the Second World War

War and Military Culture in South Asia, 1757-1947 No 5

Alan Jeffreys

Helion & Company Limited
Unit 8 Amherst Business Centre
Budbrooke Road
Warwick
CV34 5WE
England
Tel. 01926 499 619
Email: info@helion.co.uk
Website: www.helion.co.uk
Twitter: @helionbooks
Visit our blog at blog.helion.co.uk

Published by Helion & Company 2017. Reprinted in paperback 2024
Designed and typeset by Mach 3 Solutions Ltd (www.mach3solutions.co.uk)
Cover designed by Paul Hewitt, Battlefield Design (www.battlefield-design.co.uk)

Text © Alan Jeffreys 2016
Maps drawn by George Anderson © Helion & Company 2016

Every reasonable effort has been made to trace copyright holders and to obtain their permission for the use of copyright material. The author and publisher apologize for any errors or omissions in this work, and would be grateful if notified of any corrections that should be incorporated in future reprints or editions of this book.

ISBN 978-1-804514-74-0

British Library Cataloguing-in-Publication Data.
A catalogue record for this book is available from the British Library.

All rights reserved. No part of this publication may be reproduced, stored in a retrieval system, or transmitted, in any form, or by any means, electronic, mechanical, photocopying, recording or otherwise, without the express written consent of Helion & Company Limited.

For details of other military history titles published by Helion & Company Limited contact the above address, or visit our website: http://www.helion.co.uk.

We always welcome receiving book proposals from prospective authors.

For Lorraine and Michael

Contents

List of Maps	x
List of Abbreviations	xi
Foreword	xiii
Acknowledgements	xv
Ranks in the Indian Army	xviii
Introduction	xix
1 The Indian Army prior to 1939	27
2 Training in India at the beginning of the Second World War	55
3 Mechanisation and Desert Warfare	81
4 Mountain Warfare	109
5 Jungle Warfare: Malaya 1941-42	130
6 Jungle Warfare: Burma, 1942-44	148
7 Training in India at the end of the Second World War	181
Conclusion	209
Biographical Notes	213
Bibliography	219
Index	241

List of Maps

1	Battle of Sidi Barrani, 9-11 December 1940.	91
2	18th Indian Infantry Brigade at Deir-el-Shein, 28 June-2 July 1942.	100
3	Final Battle of Keren, 15-27 March 1941.	113
4	Battle of Slim River, 7 January 1942.	141
5	The Counter-offensive at Kohima and Imphal, June-July 1944.	176
6	Training areas in Southern Army, 1944-45.	184

List of Abbreviations

A & MT	Animal & Motor Transport
AA/AT	Anti-Aircraft and Anti-Tank
ABDA	American British Dutch Australian
ACOTS	Armoured Corps Officers' Training School
ADC	*aides-de-camp*
AEC	Army Education Corps
AFV	Armoured Fighting Vehicles
AHQ	Army Headquarters
AITM	Army in India Training Memorandum
AT	Animal Transport
AWM	Australian War Memorial
BGS	Brigadier General Staff
BL	British Library
BMP	Burma Military Police
Bn	Battalion
BT	British Troops
CAC	Churchill Archives Centre
CGS	Chief of the General Staff
CIGS	Chief of the Imperial General Staff
C-in-C	Commander-in-Chief
CO	Commanding Officer
CRA	Commander Royal Artillery
Coy	Company
CUP	Cambridge University Press
DMT	Director of Military Training
ECO	Emergency Commissioned Officer
FOO	Forward Observation Officer
GHQ	General Headquarters
GOC	General Officer Commanding
GSO1	General Staff Officer Grade 1
GSO2	General Staff Officer Grade 2
HMIS	Her Majesty's Indian Ship
HMSO	Her Majesty's Stationery Office

HQ	Headquarters
IAC	Indian Armoured Corps
IACTC	Indian Armoured Corps Training Centre
IAF	Indian Air Force
IAOC	Indian Army Ordnance Corps
ICC	Imperial Cadet Corps
ICO	Indian Commissioned Officer
IDC	Imperial Defence College
IJA	Imperial Japanese Army
IMA	Indian Military Academy
IOR	India Office Record
ISF	Indian State Forces
IT	Indian Troops
IWM	Imperial War Museum
JRSC	John Rylands Special Collections
JUSII	Journal of the United Service Institution of India
LAA	Light Anti-Aircraft
L of C	Lines of Communication
MT	Motor Transport
MTP	Military Training Pamphlet
NAI	National Archives of India
NAM	National Army Museum
NCO	Non-Commissioned Officers
nd	not dated
NWF	North West Frontier
OCTU	Officer Cadet Training Unit
OTS	Officer Training School
OUP	Oxford University Press
RA	Royal Artillery
RAC	Royal Armoured Corps
RAF	Royal Air Force
RIASC	Royal Indian Army Service Corps
RIN	Royal Indian Navy
Regt	Regiment
RTC	Regimental Training Centre
S & M	Sappers & Miners
SEAC	South East Asia Command
TEWT	Tactical Exercise without Troops
TNA	The National Archives, Kew
VCO	Viceroy Commissioned Officer
WAC (I)	Women's Auxiliary Corps (India)
WT	Wireless Telegraphy

Foreword

The series in which this work appears is dedicated to filling in the gaps – and there are a very large number of them – the history of perhaps the most remarkable institution created by Britain during its long imperial adventure. To understand how the Indian Army worked and what it did is not an exercise in nostalgia. It is the study of an institution vital to the empire's existence. Field Marshal Lord Alanbrooke told his diary in 1946, as twilight deepened over the Raj, that the loss of the Indian Army would be fatal to the whole edifice of empire. He was, as so often, perceptive. Only twenty years later, the whole astounding imperial structure was either gone or going fast. The reasons for this unravelling were, of course, multiple, but the loss of the empire's cheap strategic reserve, garrison and police force, must be high on any list. How the Indian Army was built, how it worked, how, nearly wrecked in 1941/42, it rebuilt itself to give Britain a last imperial victory in Asia – these are the things this series will illuminate, and in doing so, help the readers of its volumes to understand an institution as important to imperial Britain as the legions were to Rome.

Military history has, in recent years broadened greatly as subjects remote from the battlefield, but nonetheless crucial to what happens there, have begun to be carefully explored. Of these one is the subject of Alan Jeffreys' very important work on the training of the Indian Army in the Second World War. Nearly four decades ago, as I wrote a brief survey of the 1942-45 Burma campaign, it quickly became apparent that there had been a sea change in that army in 1943-44. It was abundantly clear that the Indian units that fought in Malaya (1941-42), Burma 1942) and the first Arakan campaign (1942-43) – a textbook example of how not to run an operation – had been poorly and incompletely trained, and for the wrong war: the desert, not the jungle. It was equally plain that Slim's XIVth Army was a very different organisation. The question was obvious – what had happened between the onset of the monsoon in May 1943, closing the shambolic Arakan operations, and the "Admin Box" battle in February 1944, to transform what one of Slim's staff officers described at the end of the Arakan fighting as "a rather unwilling band of raw levies" into what Chris Bayly and Tim Harper in their splendid *Forgotten Armies* called a "cold, efficient killing machine". The official histories, surprisingly, shed little light on how this transformation happened; Slim's *Defeat Into Victory* rather more. Correspondence with the late Sir Reginald Savory, the Indian Army's Director of Infantry, 1943-45, was helpful but there I had to leave the matter. I always hoped that someone would go into it in depth because clearly it was the great question about the evolution of the Indian Army during the war. Now that question has finally been comprehensively answered, an answer based on massive research, by Alan Jeffreys. The work of the Indian Army's Military Training Directorate, its patient collation of the very painful lessons learned in 1941-43; its distillation of that knowledge into the memoranda, pamphlets and manuals that guided new and relevant training, was the core of the story. The new training norms became army-wide doctrine; effective feedback loops kept the training machine in touch with the new lessons being learned and new requirements being forged at the front. Slim said he wanted his soldiers to be able to go anywhere and do anything. By 1944 that was a very apt description of XIVth Army. Claude Auchinleck, as Commander-in-Chief, India, from mid 1943 presided over what amounted to an institutional revolution in the Indian Army; Reginald Savory saw that the impetus of that change never slackened; dozens of others in the training directorate and at training establishments throughout India were the foot soldiers of that revolution. Bill Slim used the finished product brilliantly. In this book Alan Jeffreys supplies the long missing key chapter in the story of how bitter defeat turned into stunning victory. I'm very glad that, forty years on, I'm here to read it.

Professor Emeritus Raymond Callahan, University of Delaware

Acknowledgements

I am very grateful to Squadron Leader Rana Chhina and the United Service Institution of India, Delhi for the award of a General Palit Military Studies Trust that enabled me to undertake research in Delhi in 2014, as well as appointing me a Senior Research Fellow for 2014-15. I am also grateful to my old school, Douai, and the Old Dowegian Society for the award of a bursary that meant I could travel to Washington DC to research the archive of Professor Stephen Cohen at the Brookings Institution in October 2013, as well as attend the 'Re-newing the Military History of Colonial South Asia symposium', held at Jadavpur University, Kolkata in January 2014. Many thanks to Steve Cohen for his generosity in allowing use of his interviews with senior Indian Army officers.

Thanks are due to the staff at the British Library, the Centre for South Asian Studies Archive, Cambridge; the Churchill Archives Centre, Churchill College, Cambridge; the Gurkha Museum, the Imperial War Museum, the Liddell Hart Archive, King's College London, the National Archives, the National Archives of India, the John Rylands Library, University of Manchester, the National Army Museum, the Nehru Museum and Memorial Library and the United Services Institution of India Library. I would like to thank the copyright holders of the Private Papers held at these institutions who kindly gave copyright permission. At the IWM, thanks are due to all my colleagues in the former Exhibits and Documents sections, particularly Jane Furlong, Maeve Underwood, Martin Boswell, Tony Richards and Stephen Walton.

Many thanks to the following historians for all their help and support: Jo Bandy and David Mason of the Army Historical Branch, Dr Tarak Barkawi, Tim Bean, Dr Jonathan Boff, Professor Raymond Callahan, Field Marshal Sir John Chapple, Squadron Leader Rana Chhina, Professor Stephen Cohen, Dr Michael Creese, Dr Anirudh Deshpande, Tom Donovan, Vipul Dutta, Nicola Evans, Dr Jonathan Fennell, Mark Frost, Tim Hicks, Professor Glyn Harper, Professor Ashley Jackson, Dr Karl James of the Australian War Memorial, Dr Indivar Kamtekar, Emma Kay, Professor Daniel Marston, Tony McClenaghan, Lieutenant Commander Dr Kalesh Mohanan, Dr Tim Moreman, Dr Joseph Moretz, Professor Douglas Porch, Dr Roger Pearson, Dr Gavin Rand, Pete Robinson, Dr Patrick Rose, Professor Peter Stanley, Dr Andrew Stewart, Professor Ian van der Wagg, Jerry White, Dr Cat Wilson, Alex Wilson, Dr Graham Winton and Colonel Denis Wood.

I am particularly grateful to Colonel Denis Wood who generously wrote up his time in the Indian Army, as well as a piece on the Gurkha Regimental Training Centres and in a very fruitful trip to the Gurkha Museum he translated a number of Gurkha training pamphlets. He also put me in touch with fellow Indian Army officer cadets and Gurkha officers, as did Colonel John Cross. Thanks to all with whom I corresponded or met including Lieutenant Colonel Edward Gopsill, Major Tim Healy, Harold James, Desmond McDougall, Dr Roger Pearson, Lieutenant Colonel Alastair Rose and Major Jim Vickers. Similarly I'm grateful to Mike Taylor, Tom Davis and Bob Wyatt for lending training pamphlets from their extensive libraries. Also many thanks to all those who have kindly given me relevant books including: Dr John Bullen, Field Marshal Sir John Chapple, Terry Charman, Squadron Leader Rana Chhina, the late Diana Condell, Phil Dutton, Dr Bryn Hammond, Peter Hart, Mike Hibberd, Emma Kay, Brad King, Chris McCarthy, Dr Simon Robbins, the late Martin Taylor, Mike Taylor, Denis Wood and Bob Wyatt. Thanks to Rana also for the use of the cover image.

My thoughts have developed much since I first started this project in 2009 with a paper on training at the British Empire at War Research Group workshop in Oxford and at a conference held at the IWM, later published in *Global War Studies* (2010) and the edited volume, *The Indian Army, 1939-1947* (2012) respectively, as well as a chapter in Kaushik Roy's *The Indian Army in the Two World Wars* (2012). Earlier versions of the second parts of chapters 3 and 4 appeared in Jill Edwards' *El Alamein and the Struggle for North Africa* (2012) and in Andrew Hargreaves et al., *Allied Fighting Effectiveness in North Africa and Italy, 1942-1945* (2014) respectively. Similarly an earlier version of chapter 5 was in Rob Johnson's *The British Indian Army* (2014) and some of the material on education will appear in *Military Education and Empire, 1854-1950* (forthcoming) edited by Doug Delaney and Rob Engen. I have been lucky enough to cover some of the ground that this study looks at. My wife, Lorraine, drove me around whilst I followed the path of 12th and 28th Indian Infantry Brigades at the Battle of Slim River, whilst on holiday in Malaysia. Aldino Bondesan led Glyn Harper, Peter Stanley and myself on a marvellous one day tour of the El Alamein battlefield including Deir-el-Shein where 18th Indian Infantry Brigade stopped Rommel's advance. More recently, Lt. Cols. Dave Marshall and Mark Kingston invited me along on the 1st (UK) Division's and 77th Brigade's tours of Myanmar.

In particular I would like to thank my good friends, and fellow series editors, Ray Callahan and Dan Marston who have not only been very supportive of the series but have also read my research, coming back with the most helpful of suggestions. It is always a pleasure to meet up with them and their families whenever they are in London. Another good friend, Kalesh Mohanan generously shared his research at the National Archives with me. Thanks also to Andrew Stewart who kindly read through the chapter on mountain warfare, Gavin Rand gave helpful writing up advice and Anirudh Deshpande made some useful comments. Many thanks to Tarak Barkawi who diligently read through the manuscript making some very helpful suggestions. I also acknowledge the support of the editorial board of the series, the members of the

'Curry Club' held quarterly at the Oriental Club, Steve Crump, as well as the generosity and good nature of my friend and publisher, Duncan Rogers of Helion.

On a personal note this book is also dedicated to the memory of my grandparents who lived and worked throughout the period of this book. My paternal grandmother Rachel (Nain) taught mathematics at the 'Gram', the Queen Elizabeth Grammar School for Boys, in Carmarthen during the war. She was the first female teacher in the school. My grandfather Huw (Taid) served as a codebreaker in the RAF in the Middle East. My maternal grandmother, Yvonne, and her family were lucky enough to escape from Malaya to Australia after the Japanese invasion and then served with No. 5 Observer Group, in the Royal Australian Air Force at Perth Control Centre. She was on one of the first ships to go through the re-opened Suez Canal in 1944 en route to marry my grandfather, Michael, then training to be a doctor who had been working in Lewisham Hospital during the Blitz. They had met through family at my old school Douai, where there seemed to have been quite a Malayan connection, having their first date in the Angel Hotel in Woolhampton before the war and keeping in touch before getting married in 1944. They all encouraged my interest in history, particularly my grandfathers.

I am very grateful to my own parents and sister for their support, especially my mother who gave me the laptop on which most of this book and the research for it was typed up on. I also appreciate the interest of my parents-in-law and friends, Ges, Ian, Niall, Pete and the late and much missed Anna.

Most importantly, I would like to thank my wife Lorraine and son Michael for their encouragement and support, help with reading drafts and correcting grammar, tolerating absences in both mind and body whilst researching and writing this volume, and lastly for putting up with the 'Indian Army' for the last six years.

Ranks in the Indian Army

Cavalry Officers	**Infantry**	**Rank badges**
Risaldar Major	Subadar Major	A crown
Risaldar	Subadar	Two stars
Jemadar	Jemadar	One star
Other ranks		
Duffardar Major	Havildar Major	Royal Arms
Duffardar	Havildar	Three stripes
Lance Duffardar	Naik	Two stripes
	Lance Naik	One stripe

A sowar is a trooper in the cavalry and a sepoy or jawan a private in the infantry. The book will use the names of places used at the time rather than the current nomenclature. For example, Burma instead of Myanmar and Calcutta instead of Kolkata.

Introduction

> If the approach to battle is good, then the battle will be easy.

Lieutenant General Sir Francis 'Gertie' Tuker, who commanded 4th Indian Division from 1942-44, repeated this phrase in his study of the Eighth Army. It was his take on Generalissimus Suvorov's axiom 'Train hard: fight easy'.[1] Tuker realised at an early stage of his career in the Indian Army that training, in particular training infantry, was an essential part to the approach to battle.[2] This monograph will concentrate on all aspects of training within India and chart the training undertaken by Indian Army formations in the Mediterranean, Middle Eastern and South East Asian theatres during the Second World War. It will examine the dissemination of doctrine through the training manuals produced by GHQ India and the training instructions issued by Indian Army formations. It differs from recent studies by examining the experience of the Indian Army as a whole in India, North and East Africa, Italy as well as the Burma campaign; presenting a complete picture for the first time of how the Indian Army learnt operational lessons and turned them into effective training across these different theatres.

The Indian Army was the largest volunteer army during the Second World War. Indeed two and a half million personnel served in the Indian Armed Forces and India provided the base for supplies for the Middle East and South East Asia. Until recently there was very little academic study on India during the Second World War. As most historians have concentrated on the nationalist narrative. This has now been remedied both internationally and within India with articles by Indivar Kamtekar, Andrew Buchanan and Sanjoy Bhattacharya, as well as the more recent books of

---

1   Lieutenant General Sir Francis Tuker, *Approach to Battle* (London: Cassell, 1963), pp. 3, 6, 85, 366.
2   See Major General F. S. Tuker, 'The Preparation of Infantry for Battle', *The Army Quarterly*, Vol. XLIX, No. 1, October 1944, pp. 74-83. Reprinted in India in March 1945 which Tuker states: 'This pamphlet contains a lecture given by me to the Infantry School in England, in October, 1943. It is on broad lines and is the pith of one's experience in more than 30 years of soldiering in peace and war from the command of a platoon to a Division', Papers of Lieutenant General Sir Francis Tuker, *Tuker Mss.*, IWM, 71/21/16.

Yasmin Khan and Srinath Raghavan.[3] Indeed in his excellent one volume of the war in India, Srinath Raghavan has argued that the war is 'central to understanding the country's rise on the world stage'.[4] There have been a number of academic studies of the Indian Army published in recent years, with chapters devoted to the Second World War, that include Kaushik Roy's *The Oxford Companion to Modern Warfare in India* and *A Military History of India and South Asia* edited by Daniel Marston and Chandar Sundaram.[5] Kaushik Roy has edited two collections that include essays on the Indian Army in the Second World War.[6] He has also written three articles covering the expansion, deployment, morale and loyalty of the Indian Army during the war and a recent book on the armed forces and society in India.[7] However, there are very few monographs on the Indian Army during the Second World War since the unfinished history of the Indian Army with the first volume of Compton Mackenzie's Eastern

3   See Indivar Kamtekar, 'A Different War Dance: State and Class in India 1939-1945', *Past and Present*, No. 176, pp. 187-221, Andrew N. Buchanan, 'The War Crisis and the Decolonization of India, December 1941- September 1942: A Political and Military Dilemma', *Global War Studies*, Vol. 8, No. 2, 2011, pp. 5-31 and Sanjoy Bhattacharya, 'British Military Information Management Techniques and the South Asian Soldier: Eastern India during the Second World War', *Modern Asian Studies*, Vol. 34, No. 2, May 2000, pp. 483-510. See also Yasmin Khan, *The Raj at War: A People's History of India's Second World War* (London: Bodley Head, 2015) and Srinath Raghavan, *India's War: The Making of Modern South Asia 1939-1945* (London: Allen Lane, 2016). Although Johannes H. Voigt's, *India in the Second World War* (New Jersey: Humanities Press, 1988) remains useful and Christopher Bayly and Tim Harper's *Forgotten Armies: The Fall of British Asia, 1941-1945* (London: Allen Lane, 2004) is an excellent political and social history of the British Empire in South and South East Asia during the war. See also Anirudh Deshpande, *British Military Policy in India, 1900-1945: Colonial Constraints and Declining Power* (New Delhi: Manohar, 2005) and Steven I. Wilkinson, *Army and Nation: The Military and Indian Democracy since Independence* (Cambridge, Massachusetts: Harvard University Press, 2015), chapters 1 & 2.
4   Raghavan, *India's War*, p. 6.
5   See Kaushik Roy, *The Oxford Companion to Modern Warfare in India* (New Delhi: OUP, 2009), pp. 169-178 and Daniel Marston, 'A Force Transformed: The Indian Army and Second World War' in Daniel Marston and Chandar Sundaram (eds.), *A Military History of India and South Asia* (Westport: Praeger, 2007), pp. 102-122.
6   See Kaushik Roy (ed.), *War and Society 1807-1945* (New Delhi: OUP, 2006) and in particular Raymond Callahan, 'Were the 'Sepoy Generals' Any Good? A Reappraisal of the British-Indian Army's High Command in the Second World War', pp. 305-329 and Kaushik Roy, *The Indian Army in the Two World Wars* (Leiden, Brill, 2012). See also the seminal work: Raymond Callahan, *Churchill and his Generals* (Lawrence, Kansas: Kansas University Press, 2007).
7   See Kaushik Roy, 'Expansion and deployment of the Indian Army during World War II: 1939-45', *Journal of the Society for Army Historical Research*, Vol. 88, No. 355, Autumn 2010, pp. 248-268; 'Discipline and Morale of the African, British and Indian Army units in Burma and India during World War II: July 1943 to August 1945', *Modern Asian Studies*, Vol. 44, No. 6, April 2010, pp. 1255-1282 and 'Military Loyalty in the Colonial Context: A Case Study of the Indian Army during World War II', *Journal of Military History*, Vol. 73, No. 2, April 2009, pp. 497-529. See also *India and World War II: War, Armed Forces, and Society, 1939-45* (New Delhi: OUP, 2016).

Epic produced in 1951, Major General Elliott's A Roll of Honour (1965) and the volumes official history of the Indian Armed Forces, all published during the 1950s and 1960s.[8] The Indian Historical Section was originally established in 1943 under Major General Tom Corbett, but little was achieved before Independence in 1947 when responsibility for the official histories came under the Combined Inter-Services Historical Section (India and Pakistan). It was then administered by the Ministry of Defence, India with expenditure being shared with Pakistan on a 70:30 ratio. Dr Bisheshwar Prasad was appointed director of the section in 1948. The director and the historians were all civilians, although the editors were army officers but few could be attached to the section due to staffing shortages in the Indian Army. Liaison officers were also based in the UK. Although, the Cabinet Office and Major General Stanley Woodburn Kirby, the British official historian of the War Against Japan volumes, in particular criticised the Indian official historians for their inaccuracy and their criticism of British officers. This view was hampered by the fact that Dr Prasad never visited London once while the series was being written. Kirby commented on the drafts on the Defence of India volume, in which he had been involved during the War:

> I find it almost impossible to submit any constructive comments on this rambling and extremely badly constructed narrative… The whole thing is in line in my opinion with the Indian campaign histories published to date, which we found to be hopelessly inaccurate and which our volumes II and III constantly contradict. I am left with the impression that the papers have been picked with one object, viz. to show that the British planners and staff had not the least idea of what they were doing, which is very far from the truth but which fits nicely with political views and an anti-British outlook.[9]

This was exacerbated by the fact that Dr Prasad spent some time in Moscow during the 1950s which made the British very suspicious of him during the climate of the Cold War. However, they remain very useful histories of the Indian Armed Forces particularly at the tactical level. Unfortunately, the monograph on training referred to in one of the Indian official histories cannot be traced.[10]

---

8   See Major General J. G. Elliott, *A Roll of Honour 1939-1945* (London: Cassell, 1965); Compton Mackenzie, *Eastern Epic* (London: Chatto & Windus, 1951) and Bisheshwar Prasad, *The Official History of the Indian Armed Forces in the Second World War 1939-45* (India & Pakistan: Combined Inter-Services Historical Section, 1956-1965). Eight of which were reprinted in 2012 and four more in 2014 by Pentagon Press on behalf of the Ministry of Defence, Government of India.
9   Quoted in Jeffrey Grey, *A Commonwealth of Histories: The Official Histories of the Second World War in the United States, Britain and the Commonwealth* (London: Sir Robert Menzies Centre for Australian Studies, 1998), p. 14.
10 See Sri Nandan Prasad, *Expansion of the Armed Forces and Defence Organization 1939-45* (New Delhi: Pentagon Press, 2012), footnote on p. 27.

This book will build on the work of Daniel Marston and Tim Moreman who have expertly covered the Indian Army in Burma and Malaya.[11] Other recent studies of the Burma campaign include those by Tarak Barkawi and Graham Dunlop which look at the culture of the Indian Army and logistics respectively.[12] Thus, a modern historical interpretation of the Indian Army as a holistic organisation learning at the tactical level during the Second World War is long overdue.

This interest in the Indian Army has been mirrored in academic conferences held at the Imperial War Museum in 2009, a British Commission for Military History Conference on the Indian Armies held in Oxford in 2011 and a workshop sponsored by the British Empire at War Research Group on 'India and the Second World War' in 2012, also in Oxford.[13] In 2013-14, Gavin Rand and Kaushik Roy set up the initiative of 'Renewing the Military History of Colonial South Asia' with the aim of reinvigorating the 'The New Military History of South Asia' from a conference that was held in Cambridge in 1997 and that has 'remained only partially realised… with the historiographical and methodological difficulties involved in navigating between cultural and military histories persist'.[14] Two symposia were organised at the University of Greenwich, London and Jadavpur University in Kolkata.[15] In addition to the conferences, two academic book series have been founded in Britain and India, entitled 'War and Military Culture in South Asia, 1757-1947' and 'Warfare and Society in South Asia' respectively.[16]

---

11   See Daniel Marston, *Phoenix from the Ashes* (Westport, Connecticut: Praeger, 2003) and Tim Moreman, *The Jungle, the Japanese and the British Commonwealth Armies at War, 1941-45* (London: Frank Cass, 2005). See also Alan Warren, 'The Indian Army and the Fall of Singapore' in Brian Farrell & Sandy Hunter (eds.), *Sixty Years on: The Fall of Singapore Revisited* (Singapore: Eastern Universities Press, 2003), pp. 270-289 and Alan Jeffreys, *The British Army in the Far East 1941-45* (Oxford: Osprey, 2005).
12   See Tarak Barkawi, 'Culture and Combat in the Colonies: The Indian Army in the Second World War', *Journal of Contemporary History*, Vol. 14, No. 2, April 2006, pp. 325-355 and Tarak Barkawi, 'Peoples, Homelands, and Wars? Ethnicity, the Military, and Battle among British Imperial Forces in the War against Japan', *Comparative Studies in Society and History*, Vol. 46, No. 1, 2004, pp. 134-163; Graham Dunlop, *Military Economics, Culture and Logistics in the Burma Campaign, 1941-1945* (London: Pickering & Chatto, 2009). See also Tarak Barkawi's forthcoming *Soldiers of Empire* (Cambridge: CUP, 2017) that the author has kindly shared a draft copy.
13   The IWM conference was published as Alan Jeffreys and Patrick Rose (eds.), *The Indian Army, 1939-47: Experience and Development* (Farnham: Ashgate, 2012) and the BCMH one as Rob Johnson (ed.), *The British Indian Army: Virtue and Necessity* (Newcastle: Cambridge Scholars Publishing, 2014).
14   See conference flyer for 'Renewing the Military History of Colonial South Asia'.
15   The proceedings of which are to be published by Routledge India.
16   The 'War and Military Culture in South Asia, 1757-1947' series is published by Helion with series editors: Professor Raymond Callahan, Professor Daniel Marston and Alan Jeffreys. The 'Warfare and Society in South Asia' is published by Routledge India, edited by Professor Kaushik Roy, Dr Gavin Rand and Professor Douglas Peers.

Doctrine and training has been simply defined by John Gooch as: '...doctrine is the glue which holds everything together, and training is the instrument through which it is imparted', the bridge between thought and war.[17] They have become increasingly important topics to study in the recent historiography of military history.[18] Surprisingly with the large amount of academic research that has been undertaken into the British Army during the First World War there is no monograph on Major-General Arthur Solly-Flood, General Sir Charles Bonham-Carter and the training branch at GHQ in the British Expeditionary Force.[19] However this has been remedied for the interwar period and the Second World War. Studies of the American, French and German armies have been produced for the interwar period, along with a number of important studies of the British Army and one on the Royal Navy during the Second World War that examine training.[20] As Tim Harrison Place has rightly commented, it is difficult to gauge how widely read

---

17 Timothy Harrison Place, *Military Training in the British Army, 1940-1944* (London: Frank Cass, 2000), p. vii. See also John Gooch, 'Military Doctrine and Military History' in John Gooch (ed.), *The Orgins of Contemporary Doctrine* (Camberley: Strategic & Combat Studies Institute, 1997), pp. 5-6.

18 For the importance of training and lessons learned for fighting efficiency see Richard Overy, *Why the Allies Won* (London: Pimlico, 1995), p. 6.

19 See Alistair Geddes, 'Major General Arthur Solly-Flood, GHQ, and Tactical Training in the BEF, 1916-1918' (University of Birmingham: MA dissertation, 2007). See also Gary Sheffield, *The Chief: Douglas Haig and the British Army* (London: Aurum Press, 2011), pp. 209-211. There are many studies of training within individual British Army formations, see for example: Mark Cook, 'Evaluating the Learning Curve: The 38th (Welsh) Division on the Western Front 1916-1918', (University of Birmingham: MPhil thesis, 2005) and at army level Jonathan Boff's *Winning and Losing on the Western Front: The British Third Army and the Death of Germany in 1918* (Cambridge: CUP, 2012), pp. 39-73.

20 See R. A. Doughty, *The Seeds of Disaster: The Development of French Army Doctrine, 1919-1939* (Mechanicsburg, PA: Stackpole Books, 2014); Robert M. Citino, *The Path to Blitzkrieg: Doctrine and Training in the German Army, 1920-1939* (Mechanicsburg, PA: Stackpole Books, 2008); Matthias Strohn, *The German Army and the Defence of the Reich: Military Doctrine and the Conduct of the Defensive Battle 1918-1939* (Cambridge: CUP, 2011); William O. Odom, *After the Trenches: The Transformation of the U.S. Army, 1918-1939* (Texas A&M University Press, 2008); Peter J. Schifferle, *America's School for War: Fort Leavenworth, Officer Education, and Victory in World War II* (Lawrence: University Press of Kansas, 2010); David French, *Raising Churchill's Army: The British Army and the War against Germany 1919-1945* (Oxford: OUP, 2000), pp. 12-47; David French, 'Doctrine and Organization in the British Army, 1919-1932', *Historical Journal*, Vol. 44, No. 2, 2002, pp. 497-515; Harrison Place, *Military Training*; John Buckley, *Monty's Men: The British Army and the Liberation of Europe, 1944-45* (New Haven: Yale University Press, 2014), pp. 19-21, 43-44. See also John Buckley and Gary Sheffield, 'The British Army in the era of Haig and Montgomery', *Journal of the Royal United Service Institution*, Vol. 159, No. 4, 2014, pp. 26-35; Edward Smalley, *The British Expeditionary Force, 1939-40* (Basingstoke: Palgrave Macmillan, 2015), pp. 37-83 and Brian Lavery, *Hostilities Only: Training the Wartime Royal Navy* (London: National Maritime Museum, 2004).

the training literature was in the British Army.[21] Indeed Major General Lewis Owen Lyne recounted an anecdote about General Montgomery speaking at the Senior Officers' School in 1942 in his autobiography. An officer commented that Montgomery's talk was the opposite to what was written in the military training pamphlet that he was brandishing, with Montgomery's reply asking who wrote the pamphlet and he looked forward to reading all the pamphlets produced by the War Office after the war was over.[22]

An important article by Hew Strachan in the *Journal of Contemporary History* has shown the importance of training and how it is essential to build up morale through drill, making actions automatic and in turn making the trained soldiers thoroughly professional. He states that training counters boredom, engenders professional pride and unit cohesion, by assimilating tactical thinking through drill and mastering new technological advances. It can also have psychological benefits in assisting the trained soldier to face adversity through instinctive reactions learnt in battle drills. Lastly it trains soldiers to kill, against the norms of society.[23] This has been further explored by Anthony King in his work on tactics and cohesion where he states that drills and training were critical to performance during the First World War, when they were enhanced by specific rehearsals.[24] Training is now taken as an essential factor in any study of combat performance, as well as cohesion. In a professional army as opposed to a citizen army, all soldiers are trained to a high level to perform a common set of drills, thus making the army professional.[25]

By the end of 1943 F. W. Perry highlighted that India had developed a more comprehensive training structure than any other country geared towards jungle warfare.[26] However, this book will argue that this training structure was in place long before 1943 and jungle warfare training was built upon this existing structure. A recent seminal article has defined how the British and German armies learned

---

21 Place, *Military Training*, p. 8.
22 See Major General Lewis Owen Lyne, 'Autobiography' (Unpublished Memoir), pp. 7-8, Papers of Major General Lewis Owen Lyne, *Lyne Mss.*, IWM 71/2/5.
23 See Hew Strachan, 'Training, Morale and Modern War' in *Journal of Contemporary History*, Vol. 41, No. 2, 2006, pp. 215-217. See also John Masters, *The Road Past Mandalay* (London: Michael Joseph, 1961), p. 45 and Barkawi, *Soldiers of Empire*, pp. 231-233.
24 See Anthony King, *The Combat Soldier: Infantry Tactics and Cohesion in the Twentieth and Twenty-First Centuries* (Oxford: OUP, 2014), p. 157.
25 See ibid., pp. 263, 266-337, 374.
26 F. W. Perry, *The Commonwealth Armies* (Manchester: Manchester University Press, 1988), p. 111. However this monograph will not look at jungle warfare training undertaken by the Chindits as only a few Gurkha battalions were involved and the experience was completely outside the rest of the Indian Army. Major General Orde Wingate and the Chindits have produced a large bibliography from both supporters and detractors. The latest publication is Simon Anglim's *Orde Wingate and the British Army, 1922-1944* (London: Pickering & Chatto, 2010).

lessons in the First World War through both formal and non-formal learning.[27] This monograph will demonstrate the former through the dissemination of doctrine and the latter through a small coterie of Indian Army officers who brought about a professional military culture within the Indian Army. This started during the 1930s and came to fruition during the Second World War, at the same time this group of officers informed the formal learning process.

Finally the book will demonstrate that once the Indian Army was reorganised after experiences of the First World War, it developed training and doctrine for both fighting on the North West Frontier and as aid to civil power. At the same time education of the army became an integral part of training. With the outbreak of the Second World War, in addition to these roles, the army had to expand and adapt to fighting modern professional armies in the difficult terrains of desert, jungle and mountain warfare. In contrast to the British Army there was a tradition of battle drill in the Indian Army. A clear development of doctrine can be seen with many training pamphlets being produced by GHQ India that were in turn used to formulate training within formations and then used in divisional, brigade and unit training instructions. Thus a clear line of doctrine can not only be seen from GHQ India down to brigade and battalion level but also upwards from battalion and brigade level, based on experience in battle that were promulgated into new training instructions. That the Army was able to adapt in a relatively short period of time was due to the advances in doctrinal thinking, at GHQ India and within the Indian Army formations in all theatres, from an early stage of the Second World War, resulting in suitable training for all eventualities.

---

27   See Robert T. Foley, 'Dumb donkeys or cunning foxes? Learning in the British and German armies during the Great War', *International Affairs*, Vol. 90, No. 2, 2014, pp. 279-298.

1

The Indian Army prior to 1939

Traditionally the Indian Army has been seen as an anachronistic organisation in the period in between the World Wars. The research undertaken in this period has been largely dominated by the Indianisation debate. This chapter will demonstrate that the army underwent reforms in organisation after the First World War and that training adapted from the 1930s onwards. Concurrently an important group of progressive Indian Army officers during this period were instrumental in bringing the army up to a professional level. This meant the army could adapt and build on the structure that was already in place by 1939.

The Indian Army has existed on the Indian subcontinent, present-day India, Pakistan and Bangladesh, since the 1740s with its origins of guarding the 'factories' of the East India Company in the seventeenth century. British India was ruled through the three presidencies of Bombay, Madras and Bengal, each with their own army. The majority of the armies comprised Indian sepoys, regular troops commanded by British officers, although there were a small number of European units.[1] The armies increased rapidly in size, in 1763 the Bengal, Madras and Bombay Armies numbered 6,680, 9,000 and 2,550 respectively escalating to 64,000 for the Bengal and Madras Armies and 26,5000 for the Bombay Army in 1805.[2] By the time of the Mutiny or Rebellion of 1857-58, also known as the First War of Independence, there were about 200,000 Indian troops of the East India Company and 40,000 European troops.[3] As a result of the Mutiny, that cast a long shadow over the Indian Army for the remainder of the nineteenth century and well into the twentieth century, the Company came under the control of the Crown. The Presidency armies were combined in 1895 and then reorganised by Lord Kitchener in 1903, the then C-in-C India, when he abolished

---

1   For the British regiments, see Peter Stanley, *White Mutiny: British Military Culture in India 1825-1875* (London: Hurst, 1998).
2   See Raymond Callahan, *The East India Company and Army Reform, 1783-1798* (Cambridge, Massachusetts: Harvard University Press, 1972), p. 6.
3   See T. A. Heathcote, 'The Army of British India' in David Chandler (ed.), *The Oxford Illustrated History of the British Army* (Oxford: OUP, 1994), pp. 380-381.

the Indian Staff Corps and re-numbered all the Indian Army regiments, dropping all reference to previous presidency affiliations. He reorganised the army into two tactical formations for the first time, namely Northern and Southern Armies, in order to prepare against the perceived Russian threat in Central Asia.[4]

The army was largely officered by members of the British middle classes, as unlike the British Army no private income was required, and increasingly throughout the late nineteenth and early twentieth century they were public school educated.[5] Both British and Indian families had traditions of serving in the Indian Army from the earliest days of the East India Company up until 1947 which continues for Indian families to the present day. For example, the Barrow and Jacob families both had three generations serving in the Indian Army. Major General Joseph Lyons Barrow served with the Royal Artillery in India and was present at the time of the Mutiny. His son, General Sir Edmund Barrow joined the Indian Army, followed by his son, Major R. E. Barrow, who served in the 38th Dogra Regiment throughout the Great War. His son Major B. E. Barrow joined the Scinde Horse during the 1930s and served throughout the Second World War until Independence.[6]

The Jacob family served in India from 1817 until 1926, beginning with William Jacob, who retired as a Lieutenant Colonel in 1849. His brother also joined the Indian Army but transferred to the Political Department, retiring as a Major General in 1861. Their cousins, Herbert, John and W. S. Jacob all served in the Indian Army with John Jacob becoming the most distinguished as he formed the irregular unit Jacob's Horse. Their sons served in India either in the army or the civil service. Claud William Jacob, grandson of William Jacob, went on to become a Corps Commander in France during the First World War and retired as a Field Marshal in 1930. Both Generals Barrow and Jacob narrowly missed becoming C-in-C India. Claud William Jacob advised his son Ian Jacob not to join the Indian Army, as it made family life very difficult.[7]

---

4 See John Gaylor, *Sons of John Company: The Indian & Pakistan Armies 1903-1991* (Tunbridge Wells: Parapress, 1996), p. 3. See also Keith Jeffrey, 'An English Barrack in the Oriental Seas? India in the Aftermath of the Great War', *Modern Asian Studies*, Vol. 15, No. 3, 1981, pp. 369-370.
5 See P. E. Razzell, 'Social Origins of Officers in the Indian and British Home Army: 1758-1962', *British Journal of Sociology*, Vol. 14, No. 3, September 1963, pp. 248-260. See also Brian Montgomery, 'Change: The Indian Army before the Demise of our Indian Empire in 1947', *Imperial War Museum Review*, No. 3, 1988, p. 106.
6 See Papers of Major B. E. Barrow, passed to the author by his daughter with a copy deposited in the IWM.
7 See Raymond Callahan, 'Servants of the Raj: The Jacob Family in India, 1817-1926', *Journal of the Society of Army Historical Research*, Vol. 56, No. 225, Spring 1978, pp. 4-24. Ian Jacob joined the Royal Engineers in 1918 and went on to become a Lieutenant General, serving as Military Assistant Secretary to Churchill's war cabinet during the Second World War, as well as Director General of the BBC after retirement from the British Army.

Similarly, numerous generations of Indian soldiers served in the Indian Army from the 1750s onwards. Three generations of the Muhiyal family served in Hodson's Horse. The four sons of Mehta Divan Chand all served in the regiment. The first transferred to the Guides Cavalry and was killed during the Mutiny and his son enlisted in the 2nd Punjab Cavalry. Mehta's second son served with the regiment for 34 years with three of his four sons all joining Hodson's Horse. The third son rose to the rank of Daffadar, with his son also joining the regiment and Mehta's fourth son served for 28 years retiring with a jagir (a grant of land).[8] Furthermore, the last C-in-C India, Field Marshal Sir Claude Auchinleck, described the army as a family: 'It was a family because… son followed father and nephew followed uncle in that way'. He remarked that for the Indian soldier, '…his loyalty was to his regiment, undoubtedly… the regiment was his home, he was loyal to this, really, and to his officers, but it was very much a family affair'. Although this can be perceived in paternalistic terms it was believed both by Auchinleck and many of those who served under him.[9] In a short article on his Indian Army career, Colonel Brian Montgomery stated that he joined for both family and financial reasons and this reflected the experience of the majority of officers and men.[10] General Sir Frank Messervy reiterated the financial aspect as well as sporting opportunities for joining the Indian Army, although he noted that there were less opportunities for the British officers after the First World War due to the uncertainty of the political future of India.[11]

Prior to the First World War, Indian Army officers were increasingly seen as only interested in sport and regimental duties.[12] Thus a need for professionalism was highlighted within the officer corps by Army Headquarters (AHQ). This was begun by the formation of the Indian Staff College at Quetta in 1907 and together with the establishment of a General Staff in 1909, overseen by Lieutenant General Sir Douglas Haig, which brought AHQ in line with the War Office organisation. The new Directorate of Staff Duties and Military Training was made responsible for the education of officers, training, tactical schemes and the organisation of various schools. More importantly was the policy to standardise training in India along the lines of

---

8 See Mehta Gyan Chan, *The Muhiyal Family of Hodson's Horse* cited in Michael Creese, '*Swords Trembling in their Scabbards': The Changing Status of Indian Officers within the Indian Army, 1757-1947* (Solihull: Helion, 2015), pp. 34-35.
9 Interview with Field Marshal Sir Claude Auchinleck by Charles Allen for the BBC, 1974, IWM SA 4902.
10 See Montgomery, 'Change: The Indian Army before the Demise of our Indian Empire in 1947', p. 106.
11 See the transcript of Professor Stephen Cohen's interview with General Sir Frank Messervy, 28 November 1963.
12 See Simon Robbins, 'The right way to play the game: the ethos of the British High Command in the First World War', *Imperial War Museum Review*, No. 6, p. 46. See for example, General Sir James Willcocks, *The Romance of Soldiering and Sport* (London: Cassell, 1925).

the British Army when War Office manuals such as the *Field Service Pocket Book* and *Field Service Regulations* became standard doctrine in India.[13]

The Re-organisation of the Indian Army after the First World War

At the outbreak of the First World War the Indian Army numbered 239, 561 men which increased to 1,440,437 by the end of the war.[14] The war demonstrated the problems of recruitment, reinforcement and training in the Indian Army for conventional warfare, particularly with the huge distances involved with troops serving on the Western Front, in East Africa, Gallipoli, Egypt, Mesopotamia and Palestine.[15] For example in 1886, single infantry battalion regiments had been linked together in groups of two to five units, with just one regimental centre responsible for recruitment, training and reinforcements. In times of war the system had to be abandoned, as otherwise those fully trained at the regimental centre, which amounted to about a third of the strength of the Indian Infantry, would not be available for active service.[16] Thus, the system broke down during the First World War and the 115 battalions serving overseas had their own individual depots that were all trying to recruit, train and reinforce in isolation. As recent historians have noted, the Indian Army was essential as the imperial reserve both at the beginning of the First World War on the Western Front and at the end in the Palestine campaign.[17] Indeed, James Kitchen has argued that the Indian Army at the Battle of Megiddo in 1918 stands alongside the all arms co-operation performance of the Indian Army in Burma in 1944-45.[18] This was due to the fact that Indian units were training along the same lines as British Army units and formations since before the First World War and thus could easily

---

13 See Tim Moreman, 'Lord Kitchener, the General Staff and the Army in India, 1902-14' in David French & Brian Holden Reid (eds.), *The British General Staff: Reform and Innovation c. 1890-1939* (London: Frank Cass, 2002), pp. 57-74. See also Patrick Rose, 'Indian Army Command Culture and the North West Frontier, 1919-1939' in Jeffreys and Rose (eds.), *The Indian Army 1939-47: Experience and Development*, pp. 41-45 and George Morton-Jack, *The Indian Army on the Western Front: India's Expeditionary Force to France and Belgium in the First World War* (Cambridge: CUP, 2014), pp. 96-97, 112-114.
14 See *Statistics of the Military Effort of the British Empire during the Great War 1914-1920* (London: HMSO, 1922), p. 777.
15 For a recent assessment of the Indian Army contribution to the Gallipoli campaign see Peter Stanley's *Die in Battle, Do not Despair: the Indians on Gallipoli, 1915* (Solihull: Helion, 2015).
16 See *The Army in India and its Evolution* (Calcutta: Superintendent Government Printing, India, 1924), p. 99, IOR, L/MIL/17/5/4288.
17 See Morton-Jack, *The Indian Army on the Western* Front, pp. 148-153 and James Kitchen, *The British Imperial Army in the Middle East: Morale and Military Identity in the Sinai and Palestine Campaigns* (London: Bloomsbury, 2014), p. 196.
18 See Kitchen, p. 213.

operate alongside troops from not only the British Army but also the Dominions.[19] In addition, the expansion of the Indian Army during the First World War has been seen as one of the great administrative achievements of the war. In contrast to the Second World War, it was mainly achieved by British service officers such as the new C-in-C India, General Sir Charles Monro who 'gathered around him a group of talented administrative officers with recent military experience in Egypt and at the Dardanelles, in a prime example of cross-campaign absorption of lessons learned'.[20] Colonel (later Brigadier General) William Villiers-Stuart, Commandant of the Mountain Warfare School from 1917-18, was rather forthright in his views of his predecessor as Inspector General of Infantry before he was appointed in October 1918:

> General Christian, British Service, had recently been made Inspector General of Infantry and as such had to tour the country and report on the standards of various units and assist them to improve where necessary. He was useless. He did not know anything of the Indian Army or the Gurkha Service; knew no detailed work at all, and despised the Territorials. So after a time he was persuaded to resign from the work…
>
> That none of this occurred to AHQ India was not surprising as they merely thought that all kinds of troops were the same except that of course the British troops must be the best. In their eyes all was well.[21]

In the *Indian Army List* for January 1917, out of the senior positions at AHQ in Delhi, only the Director of Military Operations, Brigadier General Andrew Skeen, was Indian Army. The C-in-C, India, the Chief of the General Staff, the Director of Staff Duties and the Inspector of Infantry were all British service, presumably Monro was instrumental in this predominance of British service officers. As the war progressed, several Indian Army officers were advanced including Villiers-Stuart who was appointed Inspector of Infantry, North in September 1918, as well as one future Indian Army general, Lieutenant W. J. Slim who was GSO3 in the Directorate of Military Operations in 1918, although he was with the West India Regiment at the time.[22] Similarly British service officers who had undertaken important training roles during the First World War, such as Major General Solly-Flood, were also instrumental for training in 1920s India. Solly-Flood was Major General Cavalry. His tenure in the role was noted for bringing uniformity of doctrine for the cavalry in

---

19   See Moreman, 'Lord Kitchener, the General Staff and the Army in India, 1902-14', p. 74. See also Kitchen, pp. 203-210.
20   Kristian Coates Ulrichsen, *The First World War in the Middle East* (London: Hurst, 2014), p. 138. See also C. T. Atkinson, 'The Expansion of the Indian Army' in Sir Charles Lucas (ed.), *The Empire at War* (London: Humphrey Milford & OUP, 1926), pp. 198-201.
21   R. M. Maxwell, *Villiers-Stuart goes to War* (Edinburgh: Pentland Press, 1990), pp. 193-194.
22   See *Indian Army Lists* for January and November 1918.

India with regards to reconnaissance, tactics and fighting in formations.[23] The expansion of the army continued after the war and provided troops for the campaigns in the Kuki-Chin rebellion in Burma 1917-19, the Third Afghan War 1919-20 as well as troops for the Mesopotamian rebellion in 1920, with the Indian Army reverting to its role as the imperial military reserve.[24]

However, the Indian Army's reputation took quite a blow after the First World War in British society. In the interwar period, Indian Army officers were sometimes seen as the Colonel Blimp stereotype or Poona Colonels only interested in sport and little else.[25] Lieutenant Peter Cochrane, who served with the 2nd Queen's Own Cameron Highlanders in 11th Indian Infantry Brigade at the Battles of Sidi Barrani, Cassino and on the Gothic Line, wrote of his childhood:

> As a schoolboy in the thirties I had absorbed the conventional wisdom that the regular army was officered by a coterie of elderly blimps with a leaven of frivolous young O.T.C. and a week's camp every year didn't do anything to change the imagined picture; in any case we had all read Graves and Sassoon, Remarque and Brooke and Blunden, though I doubt if anyone at Loretto was reading Owen at the time.[26]

23 See 'A note on the Policy regarding higher training of the Cavalry in India' (1932), Papers of Lieutenant General Thomas Corbett, *Corbett Mss.*, Churchill Archives Centre (CAC), CORB 2/9.
24 See Keith Jeffrey, 'An English Barrack in the Oriental Seas?', pp. 372, 377-378; Keith Jeffrey, 'The Eastern Arc of Empire: A Strategic View 1850-1950', *Journal of Strategic Studies*, Vol. 5, No. 4, December 1982, pp. 531-545.
25 See Brian Bond, *British Military Policy between the Two World Wars* (Oxford: Clarendon Press, 1980), p. 62; George Orwell, 'The Lion and the Unicorn: Part 1: England Your England' in *Orwell's England* (London: Penguin, 2001), pp. 268-269. See also John Archibald Hislop, *A Soldier's Story: From the Khyber Pass to the Jungles of Burma: The Memoir of a British Officer in the Indian Army 1933-1947* (Newhaven, East Sussex: New Haven Publishing, 2010), p. 88; John Connell, *Auchinleck* (London: Cassell, 1959), p. 74. See also Cohen interview with General Sir Frank Messervy, 28 November 1963, David French, 'Colonel Blimp and the British Army: British Divisional Commanders in the War against Germany, 1939-1945', *English Historical Review*, Vol. 111, No. 444, November 1996, pp. 1183-1184 and John Masters, *The Road Past Mandalay* (London: Michael Joseph, 1961), p. 22.
26 Peter Cochrane, *Charlie Company: In Service with C Company 2nd Queen's Own Cameron Highlanders 1940-1944* (London: Chatto & Windus, 1977), p. 16. See Edmund Blunden, *Undertones of War* (London: Richard Cobden-Sanderson, 1928), *The Collected Poems of Rupert Brooke: With a Memoir* (London: Sidgwick & Jackson, 1918), Robert Graves, *Goodbye to All That* (London: Cassell, 1929), Erich Maria Remarque, *All Quiet on the Western Front* (London: Putnam, 1929) and Siegfried Sassoon, *Memoirs of an Infantry Officer* (London: Faber & Faber, 1930). For the historical debate about these authors see Modris Eksteins, *Rites of Spring: The Great War and the Birth of the Modern Age* (London: Bantam Press, 1989), Samuel Hynes, *A War Imagined: The First World War and English Culture* (London: Bodley Head, 1990), Brian Bond, 'British 'Anti-War Writers and Their

This equally applied to Indian Army officers although there was also a rather romantic image of fighting on the North West Frontier, fostered by story papers such as the *Boy's Own Paper*, the novels of Rudyard Kipling and the children's literature of G. A. Henty, F. S. Brereton, Percy Westerman and W.E. Johns.[27] As Ashley Jackson has commented: 'These publications, along with school history curricula, school drill, school Officer Training Corps' and the Boy Scouts, were effective recruiting sergeants for the military and the imperial idea'.[28] The earlier literature and influences continued to be widely available in the interwar years with the interest in the empire making a resurgence in this period, in contrast to the reaction to the First World War.[29] Films also played an integral part in this romanticism such as the *Lives of a Bengal Lancer* (1934), *The Drum* (1938) and *Gunga Din* (1939).[30]

The Army in India Committee of 1919-20, otherwise known as the Esher Committee, was formed not just 'to be consistent with the gradual approach of India towards Dominion Status' as a result of the service of the Indian Army during the First World War, but also to examine reforming the army due to its perceived setbacks during the war.[31] Rather than decentralizing control to the officer corps, the committee strengthened the position of the C-in-C India as the sole military adviser to the Government of India, as well as giving the Imperial General Staff a more influ-

Critics' in Hugh Cecil and Peter Liddle (eds.), *Facing Armageddon: The First World War Experienced* (London: Leo Cooper, 1996, pp. 817-830 and Brian Bond, *The Unquiet Western Front: Britain's Role in Literature and History* (Cambridge: Cambridge University Press, 2002), chapter 2. Loretto Public School is in Musselburgh, East Lothian, a large number of public schoolboys from this period would have had read these books and held very similar opinions, including the author's grandfather at Douai School in the 1930s.

27 See Michael Paris, *Warrior Nation: Images of War in British Popular Culture, 1850-2000* (London: Reaktion Books, 2000), pp. 58-65, 92-95, 150-151 & 160-162. See also John M. Mackenzie, 'The Popular Culture of Empire in Britain' in Judith M. Brown & Wm. Roger Louis (eds.), *The Oxford History of the British Empire: Volume IV: The Twentieth Century* (Oxford: OUP, 1999), pp. 222-224.

28 Ashley Jackson, *Mad Dogs and Englishmen: A Grand Tour of the British Empire at its Height 1850-1950* (London: Quercus, 2009), p. 136.

29 See Paris, *Warrior Nation*, pp. 167-171. For the reaction to the First World War see Dan Todman, *The Great War: Myth and Memory* (London: Hambledon, 2005) and David Reynolds, *The Long Shadow: The Great War and the Twentieth Century* (London: Simon & Schuster, 2013), pp. 201-207, 217-224.

30 See Francis Yeats-Brown, *Bengal Lancer* (London: Anthony Mott, 1984). First published in 1930 on which the film is loosely based. *The Drum* was also a novella written specially for the screen in 1938 by A.E.W. Mason and *Gunga Din* was inspired by Rudyard Kipling's poem. See also Paris, *Warrior Nation*, p. 165, 170-171. Mackenzie, 'Popular Culture', pp. 225-229 and Jeffrey Richards, 'Boy's Own Empire: Feature Films and Imperialism in the 1930s' in John M. MacKenzie (eds.), *Imperialism and Popular Culture* (Manchester: Manchester University Press, 1986), pp. 140-164.

31 See the Committee appointed by the Secretary of State for India to enquire into the administration and organisation of the Army in India (1920), TNA, WO 106/1547. See also Deshpande, *British Military Policy in India*, p. 31.

ential role on the Indian Army.³² For instance, the committee recommended closer co-operation between the British and Indian Armies with regards to training, stating that one result of the war was closer assimilation. The committee recommended that this should continue with the interchange of officers as instructors at the Staff Colleges of Camberley and Quetta and other training establishments, with constant communication between the War Office and AHQ on training matters. It was now evident that the inferiority in training in comparison to the British Army was one of the factors that was responsible for the early setbacks of the Indian Army during the war and the subsequent drop in morale amongst Indian Army officers. In addition, the recent reluctance for Sandhurst cadets and their parents to select the Indian Army as their preference, even among families who had a tradition of serving in India such as the Jacob family, compounded the problem.³³ This was a result of the talks over the future of India in combination with the Indianisation debate which has tended to dominate military historical studies of the interwar period.³⁴ In 1920, due to the service of the Indian Army during the First World War, ten places at Sandhurst were reserved for Indian cadets. The following year the eight-unit scheme was introduced by the then C-in-C India, Field Marshal Henry Rawlinson, that earmarked eight units for gradual Indianisation of the officer corps.³⁵

The solution of the Committee was to increase the pay of officers in the Indian Army to give a greater incentive to officers joining the army, as those without private means could now for the first time, afford a career in the British Army after the First World War. They also recommended the importance of training and education across all ranks of the Indian Army.³⁶ As Sir Gupta Krishna commented in his minute: 'The admitted success of the Quetta Staff College and also of the Officers' College at

---

32   See Army in India Committee (1920), pp. 8, 56 and Deshpande, *British Military Policy in India*, p. 32.
33   See Army in India Committee, pp. 61-62.
34   The literature on Indianisation is extensive, see for example Philip Mason, *A Matter of Honour* (London: Jonathan Cape, 1974), pp. 453-466 ; Stephen Cohen, *The Indian Army* (Delhi: OUP, 1991), pp. 118-137; David Omissi, *The Sepoy and the Raj* (London: Macmillan, 1994), pp. 153-191; Lieutenant Colonel Gautam Sharma, *Nationalisation of the Indian Army* (New Delhi: Allied Publishers, 1996); Lieutenant General S. L. Menezes, *Fidelity and Honour* (Delhi: OUP, 1999), pp. 306-339 ; Pradeep Barua, *The Army Officer Corps and Military Modernisation in Later Colonial India* (Hull: University of Hull Press, 1999), Partha Saratha Gupta, 'The Debate on Indianisation 1918-1939' in Partha Saratha Gupta & Anirudh Deshpande (eds.), *The British Raj and the Armed Forces 1857-1939* (Delhi: OUP, 2002), pp. 228-269; Marston, *Phoenix from the Ashes*, pp. 15-24, 222-233; Marston, *Indian Army and the End of the Raj*, pp. 22-28.
35   Namely two cavalry regiments: the 7th and the 16th Light Cavalry and five infantry battalions: 2/1st Punjab Regiment, 5/5th Mahratta Light Infantry, 1/7th Rajput Regiment, 1/14th Punjab Regiment, the 4/19th Hyderabad Regiment and 2/1st Madras Pioneers.
36   See Army in India Committee, pp. 62, 85, 104.

Indore, shows that it is not a difficult matter to arrange training in India'.[37] Following the recommendations of the committee, the army was reorganised in 1921-22.[38] The cavalry was reduced from 39 to 21 regiments and the infantry and pioneers, which numbered 129 battalions in 1914, to 20 regiments. In order to alleviate the problems that surfaced during the war, the 1921 reorganisation introduced training battalions for the new infantry regiments that comprised a number of battalions. Each battalion had a training company within the training battalion, which meant that battalion commanders could concentrate on the training of their own battalion, rather than being responsible for recruiting and training recruits as well.

The two main roles of the army in the interwar period were internal security and policing the frontiers. The Garran Tribunal of 1933 divided the functions of the army into internal security, covering troops for the North West Frontier and the field army with the role of protecting the frontiers of India and act as the imperial reserve, stating 'Indeed, it is only the Indian Army which is readily available for any imperial purpose'.[39] By the mid-1930s, the army was proficient in fighting on the North West Frontier with a developing doctrine and *Esprit de Corps* developed by the 'endless round of regimental sport'.[40] Indeed sport was seen as an important component of training even in the interwar period.[41] However as Mark Jacobsen has indicated the Indian Army had shown little interest in modernisation from within, even without the financial restraints of the period.[42] The army was not ready to fight any army equipped with up-to-date weapons; British Army units going out to India had to be retrained in obsolete weapons.[43]

The Indian Army Modernisation Committee, known as the Auchinleck Committee, was established in 1938, comprising: the Deputy Chief of the General Staff, Major General Sir Claude Auchinleck, the Director of Staff Duties, Brigadier George Molesworth (Director of Military Intelligence in 1938) and the Director of Military Training, Colonel Eric Dorman-Smith. The resulting report noted that the Indian Army's most likely fight was an Asiatic war and it needed to be prepared for the five roles of frontier defence, coastal defence, external defence, internal security

---

37 Army in India Committee, p. 104.
38 See Mark H. Jacobsen, *The Modernization of the Indian Army, 1925-39* (Irvine: University of California, PhD Thesis, 1979), pp. 16-20.
39 Tribunal on Certain Questions in regard to Defence Expenditure in dispute between the Government of India, the War Office and the Air Ministry (1933), p. 55, See also pp. 46-47, TNA, WO 32/3864.
40 Alan Warren, *Waziristan, The Faqir of Ipi, and the Indian Army* (Karachi: OUP, 2000), p. 110.
41 See Lieutenant Colonel M. C. A. Henniker, *Memoirs of a Junior Officer* (London: Blackwoods, 1951), p. 223 and Spike Mays, *Fall Out the Officers* (London: Eyre & Spottiswoode, 1969), p. 198.
42 See Jacobsen, *The Modernization of the Indian Army*, p. 387.
43 See Report of the Expert Committee on the Defence of India, 1938-39, p. 49, TNA, T 162/993.

and a reserve force. Therefore it had to modernise accordingly, the report was later adopted by the Chatfield Committee.[44] Mechanisation was advocated by the Chatfield report with the reserve force having an 'element capable of producing a lightly mobile striking force' and the first installment of £200,000 for cavalry reorganisation paid by the beginning of the Second World War.[45] However it is important to note that this modernisation was for the defence of the North West Frontier and only one division for overseas service.[46]

A very important administrative change, which had a great impact on the readiness of the Indian Army at the beginning of the Second World War, was that until the end of the First World War orders were given in English in the Indian Army down to squadrons and companies and then translated into the languages of the battalion. This worked when the officers had served with the battalion in pre-war peacetime but when casualties mounted during war and officers were replaced by those who had little knowledge of the various languages used within the battalion, it resulted in much miscommunication. After the war it was decided that Urdu would become the *lingua franca* of the Indian Army. It had been in use in the army since the nineteenth century, but now was formalised as the language of the Indian Army as officers at the Indian Army School of Education at Belgaum further developed the Roman Urdu alphabet in order that training manuals could be translated into Urdu making it easier for officers to promulgate education and doctrine within the army.[47]

Another major factor in the Indian Army's lack of readiness for war was the fact that, from 1938 all Viceroy Commissioned Officers (VCOs) could no longer retire after thirty two years' service which meant, in combination with Indianisation, that there were dwindling numbers of VCOs, who were the backbone of the Indian Army and the vital link between the British officers and the Indian soldiers. VCOs now retired after differing lengths of service such as jemadars after twenty four years, subedars after twenty eight years and only the subedar majors after thirty two years which meant that just prior to the war there was a shortage of experienced VCOs.[48] In addition to this, discontent was widespread in the Indianised units due to platoonisation, as Indian Commissioned Officers (ICOs) were replacing VCOs as platoon

---

44 See Jacobsen, *Modernization of the Indian Army*, pp. 388-395. See also Sri Nandan Prasad, *Official History of the Indian Armed Forces in the Second World War: Expansion of the Armed Forces and Defence Organisation 1939-45* (India & Pakistan: Combined Inter-Services Historical Section, 1956), pp. 20-26.
45 Report of the Expert Committee, p. 54. See also Typescript of the Historical Section (India)'s history 'India at War 1939-1945', pp. 10-11, *Corbett Mss.*, CAC, CORB 3/28.
46 See Mackenzie, *Eastern Epic*, p. 3.
47 See Col. A. C. T. White, *The Story of Army Education 1643-1963* (London: Harrap, 1963), p. 66. See also Leslie Wayper, *Mars and Minerva: A History of Army Education* (Winchester: Royal Army Educational Corps Association, 2004), pp. 108-109.
48 See Hislop, *A Soldier's Story*, pp. 85-86.

commanders. Consequently ICOs felt that their status was diminished and VCOs could no longer command platoons, and NCOs in turn could not become VCOs.[49]

At the same time, there was a shortage of British officers due to the Retrenchment scheme, proposed in 1934, to reduce the officer corps by about nine hundred officers who had enlisted or transferred to the Indian Army during the First World War and immediately afterwards.[50] They were encouraged to look to other parts of the Empire for employment such as Africa, Australia and New Zealand or be pensioned off between 1934 and 1938. As a result there was a shortage of experienced officers generally in the build up to the Second World War.[51]

In the late 1930s the Indian Army acted as 'External Defence Troops' to protect interests in the eastern parts of the Empire and by 1939 units and formations were already stationed in Malaya, Singapore, Persian Gulf, the Red Sea, Burma, Egypt and Hong Kong.[52] India was the only place in the Empire that had a supply of trained troops at the beginning of the war and had sufficient space for training purposes although the armed forces were under-equipped for their main role of the defence of India or to fight a modern army.[53] The Indian Army was much smaller at this stage than perhaps generally imagined, numbering 194,373 men, with just 1,912 British officers and 344 Indian officers before the beginning of the Second World War.[54]

Training, Doctrine and Organisation

The pre-war training structure comprised: four training centres or schools for the Artillery; three for the Engineers; two for Signals and the Veterinary Corps; one each for the Royal Indian Army Service Corps and the Indian Army Ordnance Corps. Following the 1921-22 reorganisation, infantry training was carried out by the 10th (training) battalion of each regiment. The training battalion's main role was the

---

49 See Mohammad Musa, *Jawan to General: Recollections of a Pakistani Soldier* (Karachi: East & West Publishing Company, 1984) p. 45; Major General Partap Narain, *Subedar to Field Marshal* (New Delhi, Manas Publications, 1999), pp. 74-75 and Sharma, *Nationalisation*, pp. 157-159. See also Prasad, *Expansion*, p. 180 and Marston, *The Indian Army and the End of the Raj*, pp. 31-32.
50 See 'Indian Army Officers: Retrenchment Scheme', *The Manchester Guardian*, 17 October 1934.
51 See AHQ Information Bureau, *A Summary of Information for the Benefit of War Block and other Officers of the Indian Army* (Simla: Government of India Press, 1936), 3rd Edition, 15 March 1936. See also Hislop, *A Soldier's Story*, p. 93.
52 See Prasad, *Expansion*, pp.12-13. See also Perry, *Commonwealth Armies*, p. 101.
53 See 'India at War', pp. 4, 10, *Corbett Mss.*, CAC CORB 3/28 and Bisheshwar Prasad, *Defence of India: Policy and Plans* (India and Pakistan: Combined Inter-Services Historical Section, 1963), p. 12.
54 See Establishment of the Indian Army Officer Cadre, Annexure A, IOR, L/WS/1/924 and Chris Kempton, *'Loyalty & Honour': The Indian Army September 1939-August 1947: Part III* (Milton Keynes: The Military Press, 2003), p. 104.

training of recruits for the reinforcement of the active battalions in the regiment.[55] The battalion would also act as the permanent regimental depot for the regiment as the historian of the changes has noted:

> One great advantage of the system is the permanency of location of the training battalion, which thus provides a permanent home as well as a nursery for all the active battalions with which it is associated. The constant interchange of personnel between different active battalions and their training companies, and their association together in the training battalion for specified periods, create the most intimate relations between the active battalions and their training battalion, and with each other.[56]

The new training battalions consisted of four training companies and a headquarters company, with an establishment of nine British officers, thirteen VCOs and 637 other ranks. 256 of the other ranks would be training or administrative staff with the remaining 481 being recruits under training. The number of training units was based on the predicted casualties in a future war, from the statistics compiled from the experience of the Indian Army during the First World War. It was estimated that there needed to be enough reinforcements for the first eight months of a war as it took this long to train new recruits.[57] As Lieutenant Colonel Scott wrote in an article in the *Journal of the United Service Institution of India* in 1926:

> Most soldiers will agree that the experience we have reaped during the War has enabled us to evolve a higher standard of training than obtained up to 1914. This standard is marked by a development of individual training, an improved armament and technique and an understanding and cohesion between the various parts of the military machine which show that our evolution is progressing in the right direction.[58]

By 1931 training lasted eight months in peacetime and six during war. The *Training Battalion Manual* regarded the battalion as the nursery of the regiment and essential 'for its efficiency and esprit-de-corps, and for its traditions'. The regiment depended 'largely on the success with which the training battalion carries out its role'.[59] Although when Major Reginald Savory was posted to the training battalion of the

---

55 See *Training Battalion Manual*, 1931, p. 1, IOR, L/MIL/17/5/2216.
56 *The Army in India and its Evolution*, p. 101, IOR L/MIL/17/5/4283.
57 See Army Department General Staff Branch Notes Organization, No. 2809, pp. 34, 38, National Archives of India (NAI), Military Dept. Misc. February 1921 Proceedings B File No. 139.
58 Lieutenant Colonel G. B. Scott, 'The Training of a Battalion in the Indian Army', *Journal of the United Service Institution of India (JUSII)*, Vol. LVI, No. 243, April 1926, p. 83.
59 Training Battalion Manual, p. 1.

Sikh Regiment, based at Nowshera, he found the job 'rather narrow and very dull'.[60] Instructors needed to have recently undertaken courses at an army school of instruction even though units were loath to part with their best personnel.[61] The syllabus consisted mainly of physical education, drill, weapon training and general education. In the infantry battalions, training cadres were set up under the command of the adjutant. Instructors, along with a VCO, were responsible for passing on their knowledge acquired in the various army schools. This system in turn could be replicated by training cadres at company level when needed. From this, a grading system was introduced with two grades for NCOs and three for sepoys: the first grade meant the men would make good NCOs, second indicated normal merit and third deemed inefficient.[62]

The 1921-22 changes meant that the 21 cavalry regiments were divided up into seven groups of three regiments, with a permanent group centre for each of the groups where one regiment would also be based in an internal security role. In peace time the regiments trained their own recruits. The group centre was only responsible for the training of reservists for the whole group. In times of war it was envisaged that the group centre would become the depot for the group and would then train recruits and provide reinforcements for the cavalry regiments. However, this meant that regimental commanders were concentrating on training recruits, rather than training their units for war, and there would be much duplication of effort in the crossover period on mobilisation. Thus from 1937, the cavalry was divided up into three groups of six active regiments with three regiments set apart as training regiments for each group: Sam Browne's Cavalry, 15th Lancers and the 20th Lancers. These training regiments were responsible for providing trained men for the active regiments in the group, with instructors being provided by the active regiments, with each of the three squadrons in the training regiment being affiliated to two regiments of the group.[63] The Field Artillery Training Centre at Muttra was established in 1935.[64] Other training schools included ones for equitation, weapon training, small arms, physical training, education, chemical warfare and cookery.[65] The Indian Army School of Education, originally established in 1921, was amalgamated with the Army School of Education in 1924 to form Indian and British wings. The object of the Indian Wing was to train

---

60 'The Indian Wing of the Army School of Education, Belgaum, India', Papers of Lieutenant General Sir Reginald Savory, *Savory Mss*, NAM, 7603-93-29.
61 See Courses of Instruction (India) 1932, p. 1, IOR, L/MIL/17/5/2200. See also *Army Headquarters (AHQ) Training Memorandum No. 1: Individual Training Period, 1930*, p. 23, IOR, L/MIL/17/5/2199.
62 See Scott, 'The Training of a Battalion in the Indian Army', pp. 84-86.
63 See Major B. H. Chappel, 'Indian Cavalry Reorganization, 1937' in *JUSII*, Vol. LXVII, No. 287, April 1937, pp. 160-166.
64 See Menezes, *Fidelity and Honour*, p. 325.
65 See Prasad, *Expansion*, pp. 27-28. See also *The Army in India and its Evolution*, pp. 169-173.

selected VCOs and NCOs as unit instructors. Savory was appointed an instructor at the school after his brief sojourn at the Sikh Regimental Training Battalion. He noted that due to mechanisation, Indian recruits needed to be better educated. The students at the school were VCOs and NCOs who studied very hard, particularly at the wide-ranging syllabus with English as the main subject. Savory remarked on their diligence and intelligence with the aim of passing on their knowledge when they returned to their units. He wrote that these students were essential for the modernisation and mechanisation of the Indian Army at the beginning of the Second World War, commenting: 'The Indian Wing of the Army School of Education was as important a milestone in the development of the Indian Army as the Indian Military Academy was later to become; possibly even more so'.[66]

Education for Indian soldiers was considered an essential part of military training from the 1930s onwards. VCOs and NCOs needed to be able to understand training manuals and apply the principles within them, as well as read and write signal messages, understand map reading and be capable of instructing their soldiers in the use of weapons, minor tactics and be responsible for their training. English was also needed by VCOs and NCOs to communicate with British units serving in the Army of India. The Indian soldier was not divorced from civilian society and education vastly improved prospects after leaving the army. Instruction within units was both taught and self-directed. Within each unit education was supervised by a British officer, with a VCO as the unit education officer who had attended a course at the Indian Wing of the Army School of Education. His role was to teach instructors in the central unit school and help other VCOs to attend the Army Education School. The school also included a qualified NCO who assisted in educational training. Subjects taught in the central unit school included *Esprit de Corps*, regimental history, geography, history, Roman Urdu, English, maths, map reading, physical training, games, hygiene and sanitation.[67] In addition citizenship was seen as an essential subject: 'To assist students to form a sound judgement on current affairs and to realise their responsibilities in the respect of the army and on return to civil life'.[68] This was underpinned by a book on citizenship written by Captain Cannon, an Army Education Corps officer.[69]

During the interwar wars, training was divided up by collective and individual training. Collective training was from company up to brigade level, with exercises in the plains and as columns on the North West Frontier. It took place in the cold

---

66 'The Indian Wing of the Army School of Education, Belgaum, India', *Savory Mss.*, NAM, 7603-93-29. See also Scott, 'The Training of a Battalion in the Indian Army', pp. 87-88; Captain C. W. Toovey, 'The Training of the Indian Platoon Commander', *JUSII*, Vol. LVII, No. 247, April 1927, p. 30 and Wayper, *Mars and Minerva*, pp. 106-108.
67 *Educational Training Indian Army 1932* (Calcutta: Government of India Central Publication Branch, 1932), pp. 1-2, 5-7, 13-15, IOR, L/MIL/17/5/2272.
68 *Educational Training* (1932), p. 18.
69 Ibid., p. 90. See also Captain Philip Spencer Cannon AEC, *Citizenship in India* (Bombay: OUP, 1923).

weather and all battalion officers were meant to be present. Conversely individual training took place in the hot weather where all ranks could concentrate on such matters as weapon training and drill but many officers were absent on leave in the hill stations on hunting, shooting or fishing expeditions or on furlough in Britain. A series of *Training Memorandum* were produced by AHQ during the 1930s. Two were issued per year: one for individual training and the other for the collective period. The training pamphlet for the individual training period had sections: on officer training; historical campaigns to study; Staff College entrance examinations; the various arms of cavalry, artillery, tanks, signals; as well as on internal security duties; weapon training; anti-gas; field works; physical training; education; language study, co-operation with RAF; riding instruction; Indian Army officers attending demonstrations in Britain; vocational training; training publications and reservist training. At the end of the pamphlet were sections on the individual schools such as the Senior Officers' School, Equitation School, Small Arms School (Ahmednagar & Pachmarhi wings), School of Education (British & Indian wings), Army School of Physical Training, Signal School and the King George's Royal Indian Military Schools at Jhelum, Jullundur and Ajmer where young Indians were educated with the prospect of joining the Indian Army. Copies of the manual were also produced in Roman Urdu.[70] The training manual for the collective training period during 1930-31 concentrated on more tactical matters such as training for internal security, mountain warfare and co-operation with the RAF. The pamphlet also stated that the training policy for the Indian Army was not only to train for expeditions against frontier tribes and maintain internal peace but also train for larger operations against a 'moderately well equipped army', in contrast to the British Army in India who needed to be prepared to defend the Empire in any part of the world.[71] As the number of British officers in the Indian Army was much less than in the British Army, initiative was encouraged as an important part of collective training. As well as fighting during both night and day, fighting patrol skills were seen to be particularly useful for teaching the basis of infiltration tactics.[72] However, as Captain H. C. Duncan of the 13th Frontier Force Rifles noted, training had become more complex and some units were more efficient than before the First World War whereas other units had got it fundamentally wrong as they did not take into account the principles of training. He summarised the principles as the importance of the object, mutual co-operation, simplicity, uniformity, continuity, decentralization, economy of effort and elasticity. His article in the *Journal of the United Service Institution of India*, quoted extensively from the War Office training

---

70 See *AHQ Training Memorandum No. 1: Individual Training Period 1930*, IOR, L/MIL/17/5/2199. See also Captain T. H. L. Stebbing, 'King George's Royal Indian Military Schools' in *JUSII*, Vol. LXVI, No. 282, January 1936, pp. 24-34.
71 See *AHQ Training Memorandum No. 2: Collective Training Period 1930-31*, IOR, L/MIL/17/5/2199.
72 See *AHQ Training Memorandum No. 6: Collective Training Period 1932-33*, p. 8, IOR, L/MIL/17/5/2199.

pamphlet *Infantry Training* Vol. 1 Section II. He remarked that too often the training took over from the actual object of the training and emphasised it needed to be clearly apparent what the lessons of the training actually were.[73] This was just one of a number of articles published in the *Journal of the United Service Institution of India* during the interwar years that showed serious debate about training was occurring at the time. This debate indicated that not just the lessons of the First World War and the Third Afghan War, 1919-20 were being put into practice, but also the fact that units needed to be more efficient and adaptive to changing circumstances.[74]

Training developed during the 1930s as lessons drawn from the Mohmand operations of 1935 and Waziristan 1935-36 were assimilated.[75] At the same time the role of the Army in India slightly changed, as did the resulting training policy. The army needed to be able to face an enemy with more up to date weapons than those used by the frontier tribes and future exercises needed to assume that the enemy used aircraft, artillery and machine guns. The updated policy stated:

> The primary duty of the Army in India is to train for war against an enemy whose armed forces are inferior to those of the leading military powers in respect of organisation, training and equipment. At the same time officers must be kept in touch with the most up-to-date equipment and armament, and the latest doctrines evolved for their employment.[76]

An understanding of the organisation, equipment, armament and tactics of the British Army at the home was necessary, as well as other European and Asiatic armies. Thus War Office training pamphlets were to be more widely distributed in India, along with AHQ training memoranda to deal with issues that directly affected India. Training pamphlets were analysed in the *Journal of the United Service Institution of India*. Captain Gompertz commented that the new *Infantry Training* Vol. II was 'a model of simplicity and lucidity of expression' collating material from other training pamphlets, such as *Field Service Regulations* Vol. II, and was better arranged in precise

---

73 See Captain H. C. Duncan, 'The Principles of Training', *JUSII*, Vol. LX, No. 260, July 1930, pp. 339-345.
74 See for example Major N. I. Mitchell-Carruthers, 'Annual Training', *JUSII*, Vol. LVII, No. 253, October 1928, pp. 754-761; Major A. L. Skinner, 'Annual Training – Another View', *JUSII*, Vol. LX, No. 258, January 1930, pp. 22-28; "An Infantry Soldier", 'Collective Training in a Battalion', *JUSII*, Vol. LX, No. 259, April 1930, pp. 126-132 and "Beknut", 'Collective Training in a Battalion – A Criticism', *JUSII*, Vol. LX, No. 261, October 1930, pp. 484-486.
75 See *AHQ India Training Memorandum* No. 12, pp. 2-8 and *AHQ India Training Memorandum* No. 14, pp. 8-12, IOR, L/MIL/17/5/2199. See also Tim Moreman, *The Army in India and the Development of Frontier Warfare, 1849-1947* (Basingstoke: Macmillan, 1998), pp. 150-172.
76 *AHQ India Training Memorandum* No. 12: *Notes on Collective Training Period 1935-36*, p. 8, IOR, L/MIL/17/5/2199.

English as well as including new material.[77] Similarly, infantry training in India was to follow the War Office pamphlet *Infantry Training 1937*, except with the absence of equipment such as mortars, machine guns and other supporting arms and weapons. This perennial lack of equipment in the Indian Army continued throughout the Second World War until the end of 1943. Thus the Indian Army had to develop their firepower and tactics in both day and night fighting in order to compensate for the lack of equipment. Indeed the standard of individual and unit training in the Indian Army was high, particularly after service on the North West Frontier.[78]

Officer Training

Traditionally, officers were trained at the East India Company military seminary at Addiscombe, Surrey and the short-lived one at Barasat, Calcutta.[79] However when the Company came under government control in 1858, officer cadets attended the Royal Military College at Sandhurst where they underwent eighteen months training just like their British Army counterparts. A further failed attempt to organise officer training was the largely political Imperial Cadet Corps (ICC), set up by Lord Curzon in 1903, for Indian gentry and nobility. These aristocratic graduates were granted commissions in His Majesty's Native Land Forces but were subordinate to the most junior British officer. Their role, if they remained in the Indian Army rather than the States Forces, was for ceremonial purposes at the various Durbars and acting as *aides-de-camp* (ADC) on the staffs of general officers. For example, Amar Singh who graduated from the ICC in 1905 and was ADC to General O'Moore Creagh until 1914. He was eventually commissioned as a King's Commissioned Officers into the Indian Army, along with eight fellow ICC graduates in 1917 due to increasing political pressure. Amar Singh did eventually see active service in the Waziristan campaign and commanded his regiment for a short period in 1920. However he only really found fulfillment when he formed and commanded an Indian State Forces unit, the Jaipur Lancers in 1923, becoming Commander of all the Jaipur States forces and retiring as a major general in 1936.[80] During the First World War, there were four

---

77 See Captain M. C. T. Gompertz, 'The New Infantry Training, Vol. II', *JUSII*, Vol. LXII, No. 267, April 1932, p. 240.
78 See 'India at War', p. 26, *Corbett Mss.*, CAC, CORB 3/28. See also Lieutenant Colonel E. R. S. Dons, 'The New Infantry Training, 1937', *JUSII*, Vol. LXVIII, No. 293, October 1938, pp. 424-430.
79 See J. M. Bourne, 'The East India Company's military seminary, Addiscombe, 1809-1858', *Journal of the Society for Army Historical Research*, Vol. LVII, No. 323, Winter 1979, pp. 206-222. See also H. M. Vibart, *Addiscombe: Its Heroes and Men of Note* (London, 1894); Callahan, *East India Company*, p. 19 and Chandar Sundaram, '"Treated with Scant Attention": The Imperial Cadet Corps, Indian Nobles, and Anglo-Indian Policy, 1897-1917', *Journal of Military History*, Vol. 77, January 2013, p. 43.
80 See Sundaram, "Treated with Scant Attention", pp. 41-70. See also S. H. Rudolph, L. I. Rudolph with Mohan Singh Kanota, *Reversing the Gaze: Amar Singh's Diary, A Colonial*

officer schools set up for temporary commissions at Amabala, Sabathu, Bangalore and Nasik, with Quetta and Wellington for regular commissions. A temporary school for Indian cadets was established at Daly College in Indore but only one batch passed out in 1920; although this did include Kodandera Madappa 'Kipper' Cariappa, the future Commander-in-Chief in post-Partition India and Ajit Anil 'Jick' Rudra who became a major general.[81]

Despite the initial fall in prospective officer cadets for the Indian Army at the end of the First World War, prestige for the Indian Army increased during the interwar period. As Alan Warren has succinctly noted, there was no shortage of British volunteers for the Indian Army as 'The adventure, higher responsibilities and economical lifestyle of India assured there was no shortage of applications'.[82] Competition was fierce John Prendergast commented that 'by my time the Indian Army was held in universal respect and indeed only the top thirty-five or so of those who passed out of Sandhurst were considered fit for it'.[83] One cadet who passed out of Sandhurst highly enough to join the Indian Army, remarked that a British Army officer was a 'failed Indian Army officer' resulting in much distrust and envy between officers of the British and Indian Armies. The Indian Army was more popular with many of the cadets due to the quicker promotion prospects, more responsibility and 'was also much admired because of the glamour and prospects of seeing active service on the North West Frontier'.[84] Cadets all had to pass the school certificate before sitting the entrance examination for Sandhurst and the subsequent interview board. Cadets came from a cross-section of British society as well as from the Empire and around the world.[85] Generally, cadet officer training for those joining the Indian army at Sandhurst seems to be remembered more for humorous anecdotes rather than the actual training, demonstrated by the autobiographies of Francis Ingall, Geoffrey Beyts and John Masters.[86] Although Tony Mains' memoir is rather more matter of fact, he

Subject's Narrative of Imperial India (Boulder, Colorado: Westview Press, 2002), DeWitt C. Ellinwood, Jr., *Between Two Worlds: A Rajput Officer in the Indian Army, 1905-1921: Based on the Diary of Amar Singh of Jaipur* (Lanham, Maryland: Hamilton Books, 2005) and Michael Crease, *'Swords Trembling in their Scabbards': The Changing Status of Indian officers in the Indian Army 1757-1947* (Solihull: Helion, 2015).

81   See Alan Jeffreys, 'The Expansion of the Indian Army Officer Corps during the First World War' in Alan Jeffreys (ed.), *The Indian Army in the First World War* (Solihull: Helion, forthcoming 2017).
82   Warren, *Waziristan*, p. 109.
83   John Prendergast, *Prender's Progress: A Soldier in India, 1931-1947* (London: Cassell, 1979), p. 41.
84   Hislop, *A Soldier's Story*, pp. 26-27.
85   See Hislop, *A Soldier's Story*, pp. 19-22.
86   See Francis Ingall, *The Last of the Bengal Lancers* (London: Leo Cooper, 1988), pp. 10-16; John Masters, *Bugles and a Tiger* (London: Michael Joseph, 1956), pp. 41-70 and Geoffrey Beyts, *The King's Salt* (Privately published, 1996), pp. 6-7.

attended Sandhurst at the same time as fellow Indian Army officers: John Masters, Walter Walker (later General Sir), Mohammad Usman and Pran Nath Narang.[87]

Contrastingly Indian officer cadets at Sandhurst prior to 1932, experienced a vastly different culture to anything they had previously encountered, tended not to remember Sandhurst with such affection. Lieutenant General S. D. Verma commented in his memoir that: 'The eighteen months at the RMC were pleasant enough on the whole. I settled down to the routine after a couple of initial frights'.[88] Nearly all Indian Gentlemen Cadets experienced racial discrimination often from civilians.[89] The future General Kodandera Subayya 'Timmy' Thimayya was one of the first pupils to attend the Prince of Wales Royal Indian Military College in Dehra Dun that had been opened in 1922 along the lines of a British Public School. It had been set up to help train Indian cadets for Sandhurst. Once at Sandhurst, he did encounter prejudice from his guardian, a British colonel, but of the six Indian cadets he joined with in 1924, four of them passed out on 4 February 1926.[90] Similarly, Lieutenant General B. M. Kaul experienced much prejudice at Sandhurst but commented 'I learnt a code of conduct, a sense of discipline and the significance of honour'.[91] In contrast, his fellow cadet Major General Sher Ali Pataudi commented: 'My stay at Sandhurst was very pleasant. One didn't learn much in the way of soldiering'.[92]

Further officer training included the Senior Officers' School at Belgaum, which was for senior majors before getting command of their battalions.[93] The course lasted three months with the tactical aim to ensure 'uniformity of method in their application throughout the Army'.[94] Instruction was through lectures, conferences and tactical exercises without troops (TEWTS), based on published training manuals such as *Artillery Training* Vol. III, *Manual of Operations on North West Frontier, Armoured Car and Tank Training (War), Manual of Map Reading and Field Sketching* and *Training and Manoeuvre Regulations*.[95] As previously discussed, the Staff College at Quetta had

---

87 See Lieutenant Colonel Tony Mains, *Sandhurst to the Khyber 1932-1940: Pre-war Service with Gurkhas* (Durham: The Memoir Club, 1999), pp. 12-13, 17.
88 Lieutenant General S. D. Verma, *To Serve with Honour: My Memoirs* (Privately published, 1988), pp. 6, 8.
89 See Apurba Kundu, *Militarism in India: The Army and Civil Society in Consensus* (London: I.B.Tauris, 1998), pp. 18-19 and Barkawi, *Soldiers of Empire*, pp. 142-143.
90 See Major General V. K. Singh, *Leadership in the Indian Army* (New Delhi: Sage, 2005), pp. 89-91.
91 Lieutenant General B. M. Kaul, *The Untold Story* (Bombay: Allied Publishers, 1967), pp. 23-25, 30 and Cohen interview with Lt. Gen. B. M. Kaul, 19 December 1964.
92 See Major General Sher Ali Pataudi, *The Story of Soldiering and Politics in India and Pakistan* (Pakistan: Syed Mobin Mahmud & Co., 1988), p. 18.
93 See Prasad, *Expansion,* pp. 16, 27-28.
94 Courses of Instruction (India) 1932, p. 11, IOR, L/MIL/17/5/2200.
95 See ibid., p. 14.

been established in 1907 and rapidly produced badly needed staff officers.[96] Similarly to the Staff College at Camberley it was closed during the First World War, but in the interwar period Quetta was on an equal level to Camberley, teaching a similar syllabus and preparing for the mechanisation of the army.[97]

Indian Military Academy

On the recommendation of the Skeen Committee, the Indian Military Academy (IMA) at Dehra Dun was founded in 1932 for Indian cadet officers. Officers spent 30 months at the IMA with the course mirroring Sandhurst, except in the length. There were 40 officer cadets on the twice-yearly IMA course: fifteen civilians through open competition; fifteen from the Army; ten from the Indian State Forces; divided into two companies of twenty cadets each. General Mohammed Musa, who later became C-in-C Pakistan Army, was one of the first batch of cadets. He remembered how hard they worked and that extremely high standards were demanded.[98] According to evidence proffered to the Indianisation committee, Indian officers graduating from the IMA were considered to better trained than their contemporaries at Sandhurst with very thorough tactical training. The instructors at the IMA included nineteen British officers, two Indian officers and eight British warrant officers, such as Brigadier Lionel Peter Collins, Major Reginald Savory, Major David 'Punch' Cowan and Major Le Fleming, as well as Royal Army Education Corps officers transferred from Sandhurst.[99] Savory wrote to his parents:

> I have been selected as a staff officer at the new Indian Sandhurst; and it will be up to me among a few others to see if we cannot make a howling success of the young Indian cadet and Indianisation in general. It is a big thing. The future of the Indian Army will be largely in our hands; and as you can imagine, the interest and responsibility will be great. I feel very flattered at being one of two selected.[100]

---

96   See Tim Moreman, 'Lord Kitchener, the General Staff and the Army in India, 1902-14', pp. 57-74.
97   See Patrick Rose, 'British Army Command Culture 1939-1945: A Comparative Study of British Eighth and Fourteenth Armies' (PhD thesis, KCL University, 2008), p. 67 and Callahan, *Churchill and his Generals*, p. 65.
98   See Musa, *Jawan to General*, p. 25. See also Singh, *Leadership in the Indian Army*, p. 186.
99   See Brigadier L. P. Collins, 'The Indian Military Academy', *JUSII*, Vol. LXIV, No. 277, October 1934, pp. 517-526. See also Prasad, *Expansion*, p. 179; Marston, *Phoenix*, pp. 20-21; Cohen, *Indian Army*, pp. 118-119, 121, 131; Musa, *Jawan to General*, p. 25-26 and Mains, *Sandhurst to the Khyber*, p. 12.
100 Letter from Major Savory to his parents, 9 January 1932, *Savory Mss.*, NAM, 7603-93-34.

The other officer was 'Punch' Cowan. They were given seven months to prepare for the new intake at the academy in October 1932. Savory and Cowan argued successfully that the object of the academy was to create trained executive officers rather than recreate an academic establishment in the mould of an English Public School.[101] The first Commandant, Peter Collins, wrote to Savory in 1934 congratulating him for his work in setting up the Academy. He commented 'I count the Academy very fortunate in having yourself & Cowan as its first GSOs II and no one realises better than I do the contribution you have made towards its success &, what is far more important, towards establishing it on sound lines'.[102] As one of the IMA cadets, the future Lieutenant General Harbakhsh Singh, commented in his memoirs:

> The staff for the newly started Academy were the pick of the Indian Army, and included those who were sympathetic to the Indians for there is no doubt that the British wanted to make this experiment of Indianisation, however small, a success.[103]

He was in A Company under the tutelage of Savory, who he regarded as exceptional and the primary reason he had applied to join the 5th/11th Sikhs was that Savory had been in the 1st/11th Sikhs. He was later transferred to C Company under Major Le Fleming, from whom he also learnt a great deal.[104] Harbakhsh Singh and the first batch of cadets at the IMA were called 'The Pioneers'. This also included the future Field Marshal Sam Manekshaw, General Mohammed Musa and General Smith Dun who all rose to command armies in India, Pakistan and Burma respectively.[105] The establishment of the IMA was a landmark for the professionalism of the Indian officer corps from 1934 until the beginning of the Second World War. After the war, as Vipul Dutta has argued, the IMA also spurred the development of other military institutions. These new institutions, such as the National Defence Academy, were as much a product of the war and the campaigns of 'Indianisation' as the growth of professionalism, modernisation and institutionalised training framework that was evident from the 1930s onwards.[106]

---

101 See Savory's diary entries for 31 May and 10 June 1932, *Savory Mss.*, NAM, 7603-93-35. See also Collins, 'The Indian Military Academy', p. 520.
102 Letter to Savory from L. P. Collins, 30 December 1934, *Savory Mss.*, NAM, 7603-93-35.
103 Lieutenant General Harbakhsh Singh, *In the Line of Duty: A Soldier Remembers* (Delhi: Lancer Publications, 2000), p. 31. See also Major General Partap Narain, *Subedar to Field Marshal* (New Delhi: Manas Publications, 1999), p. 74.
104 See ibid., p. 40 and Musa, *Jawan to General*, pp. 25-26. See also Marston, *Indian Army and the End of the Raj*, pp. 29-30.
105 See Singh, *Leadership in the Indian Army*, p. 186.
106 I am grateful to Vipul Dutta for sharing his unpublished paper 'The Making and 'Unmaking' of Indian Armed Forces Institutions, 1940-1950' presented at the India and the Second World War Workshop at Kellogg College, University of Oxford on 17 January 2013 as part of the British Empire at War Research Group.

Both Indian and British officer cadets, for cavalry and infantry arms, would then spend a year with a British regiment or battalion in India before joining their Indian unit. Often little was learnt in the year and prowess in sport seemed to predominate.[107] It was noted in India that more attention was paid to an officer's general education at Sandhurst than to weapon training and tactics.[108] Thus the year with the British battalion was meant to improve the young officers' weapon training, make them a competent commander of the platoon with knowledge of minor tactics and continue their Urdu studies. This was further helped in 1932 by officers of the Indian Army Unattached List being posted in batches of four to British battalions to help the battalion organise their training.[109] Artillery officers were attached to a British battery for 16 months and attended a course at the School of Artillery at Kakul, Engineer officers went to Thomason Engineering College, Roorkee, for two-and-a-half years. By 1939, sixty Indian officers and one hundred and twenty British officers were commissioned each year into the Indian Army.

New Generation of Indian Army officers

During the late 1930s, some Indian Army officers such as Lieutenant Colonels Thomas Corbett, Reginald Savory and Francis 'Gertie' Tuker took training very seriously. When Tuker took over command of the 1st Battalion, 2nd King Edward VII's Own Gurkha Rifles (The Sirmoor Rifles) in 1936, he immediately instigated a new training regime for the battalion, as standards had dropped and operations in Waziristan had further impeded progress. The regimental historian commented: 'His contribution to his regiment and to the Indian Army was in effect the replacement of offensive for defensive thinking'.[110] In his 1934 paper on training infantry Tuker remarked that 'All is most certainly not well with the training of our infantryman'.[111] Within the battalion he issued training circulars, training orders and training instructions. In Training Circular No. 50, Tuker noted:

---

107 See Musa, *Jawan to General*, p. 29 and Verma, *To Serve with Honour*, pp. 13, 16. See also the Papers of Major B. E. Barrow sent to the author by his daughter. He spent his U.L.I.A. with the 2nd Battalion, the Oxfordshire and Buckinghamshire Light Infantry in that year he played polo, rugby and went pigsticking. When he joined the Scinde Horse, he continued to play polo and go hunting and shooting. This was common practice in both Indian cavalry and infantry regiments. See also Barkawi, *Soldiers of Empire*, pp. 145-146.
108 See for example Mains, *Sandhurst to the Khyber*, pp. 18-19.
109 See *AHQ Training Memorandum* No.3, p. 2, *AHQ Training Memorandum* No. 5, p. 1 and *AHQ Training Memorandum*, No. 7, p. 11, IOR, L/MIL/17/5/2199. See also Colonel H. R. C. Pettigrew, '"It seems very ordinary": Memoirs of Sixteen Years in the Indian Army 1932-1947' (Unpublished Memoir), p. 11, IWM, 84/29/1 and Mains, *Sandhurst to the Khyber*, p. 26.
110 Lieutenant Colonel G. R. Stevens, *History of the 2nd King Edward VII's Own Goorkha Rifles (The Sirmoor Rifles) Volume III 1921-1948* (Aldershot: Gale & Polden, 1952), p. 27.
111 The Training of Infantry 1934, *Tuker Mss*, IWM, 71/21/2.

The training that our men (and all men of the I.A. and B.A. for that matter) have had for years has been static. No man has been allowed to progress in his training beyond his first year as a trained man.

In early 1937 we made a beginning by putting about 100 riflemen through a higher rifleman's cadre, devoted mainly to map reading, minor tactics, application of fire, visual training, use of ground. The results were most encouraging and undoubtedly had an excellent effect on our minor tactics in Waziristan.[112]

Some of his ideas on infantry training were assimilated into Indian Army doctrine. For example, *AHQ Training Memorandum* No. 17 published in 1938 copied Tuker's ideas word for word.[113] The battalion trained for night work, patrolling and forest fighting. As a result of his thorough training of the battalion, Tuker came to the attention of GHQ India and was made Deputy Director of Staff Duties, GSO1 in 1939.[114] He was moved to the training directorate in October 1939. Tuker also realised that education was an essential element of training and made sure that all riflemen worked towards their 1st, 2nd or 3rd class certificates within the battalion, aided by central unit school staff who had been trained at the Army School of Education.[115] A Training Instruction on education was issued in 1939 stating that: 'The modernization of the Army in India necessitates aiming at a higher standard of Education that has yet been attained by this Battalion'.[116] Thus the battalion education system needed revising through improving the quality of the instructors. Education became the top priority over all other demands. Tuker's measures meant that there was a forty percent increase in the number of riflemen who achieved 2nd class certificates. His ideas were taken up by AHQ and also included in *Training Memorandum* No. 17 *Notes on Individual Training Period 1938*. Progressive education was based on the principle that there must be an incentive to become fully trained and disciplined through both privileges and responsibilities that developed character simultaneously. Basically a soldier's tactical training advanced as rapidly as his education permitted and the two were interdependent. In the collective training period, soldiers were trained in pairs. This ensured that a soldier learnt from a fully trained man, a continuation of what the regimental historian of the 2nd King Edward VII's Own Gurkha Rifles called the 'Sirmoor System'.[117]

---

112 Training Circular No. 50, *Tuker Mss.*, IWM, 71/21/5.
113 See *AHQ Training Memorandum* No. 17: *Notes on Individual training period 1938*, pp. 15-17, *Tuker Mss.*, IWM, 71/21/5 and IOR, L/MIL/17/5/2199.
114 See Stevens, *History of the 2nd King Edward VII's Own Goorkha Rifles*, p. 34.
115 See Individual Training – 1938, Training Circular No. 50, Appendix C Education 1938-39, *Tuker Mss.*, IWM, 71/21/5.
116 Training Instruction No. 1 on Education, 24 February 1939, *Tuker Mss.*, IWM, 71/21/5.
117 See AHQ India, *Training Memorandum* No. 17 *Notes on Individual Training Period 1938*, pp. 5, 15, *Tuker Mss.*, IWM, 71/21/5. and Stevens, *History of the 2nd King Edward VII's Own Goorkha Rifles*, p. 29.

Savory was another officer who took training very seriously, in 1939 he commanded the 1st/11th Sikhs. All battalions underwent an annual inspection. Brigadier H. R. C. Lane of the 10th (Jubbalpore) Infantry Brigade commented that the battalion was 'A very fine battalion. Under Lt. Col. Savory the previous high standard has been set even higher. He is well backed up by capable officers and his Indian officers are energetic, active and well abreast of their work'.[118] Lane observed the high tactical efficiency of the battalion with training undertaken in aid to civil power, scouting, intelligence work, concealment and camouflage, night operations, inter-communication and anti-gas training.

Similarly, Corbett issued training memoranda when he commanded the 2nd Lancers (Gardner's Horse). His 'Collective Training Report for 1934-35' was based on *AHQ Training Memorandum* No. 8 and Northern Command's Training Instruction No. 3. In his training regime, he advocated raising the standards of junior leadership, encouraging initiative and giving more responsibility for training to sub-unit commanders. He also ensured the tightening up of promotion exams and greater flexibility in tactics. He made sure his regiment trained for night operations and river crossings, concluding that, 'Troop commanders have realised the importance of studying their profession and are vastly improved instructors'.[119] Corbett was an advocate of mechanisation and went on to become an instructor at Quetta. In his opening address to the Senior Division, in the Spring term of 1937, Corbett discussed the issue of training. He commented that it lacked inspiration, that the modernisation of the Indian Army would be accelerated by first class training based on a common doctrine and that it should be developed by the new generation of officers attending the course.[120] A précis of his notes, for two lectures on formation training and the preparation of training exercises, stated that training was necessary to prepare an army for war. He described the object of training as: 'The aim in training must be to produce efficient leaders, a well trained staff, units well disciplined, hardy and skilled in the use of their weapons, and administrative services familiar with their war responsibilities'. This would be achieved through training pamphlets such as *AHQ Training Memoranda*, adapting to local conditions for the probable fighting commitments in India and within the Empire. He suggested that training should be varied and adaptable so to encourage initiative with each formation laying down its own

---

118 Extract form the Annual Inspection Report of the Battalion for the year 1938-39 – 1st Bn. 11th Sikh Regiment, Papers of Lieutenant General Sir Lewis Heath, *Heath Mss.*, IWM, P441, LM2.
119 Collective Training Report 1934-35 for 2nd Lancers (Gardner's Horse), 5 March 1935, *Corbett Mss.*, CAC, CORB 1/17. See also Alexander Wilson, 'Mechanisation and the Test of Battle: The Indian Cavalry, 1939-41' in Rob Johnson (ed.), *The British Indian Army: Virtue and Necessity* (Newcastle upon Tyne: Cambridge Scholars Publishing, 2014), p. 140 for training in this period in Skinner's Horse and the Central India Horse.
120 See Notes for Opening Address Spring Term Senior Division 1937, *Corbett Mss.*, CAC, CORB 2/29.

training objectives through training memoranda, conferences and exercises. Exercises would include TEWTS, model exercises, training with troops partially represented and war games. Corbett concluded that: 'the art is to direct without interfering' in organising training.[121] He also noted the need for a common doctrine but not at the expense of initiative and vision. He stated: 'It is not the intention to turn out from this institution standardised, stereotyped, mind changed officers, slaves of doctrine which in the very nature of things must be ever changing'.[122] This would be based on the training pamphlets, he remarked:

> Our manuals are intended to stimulate thought and imagination. The best way to achieve this is to have first class training. Many British officers appear to think the manuals are designed to obviate the necessity of any thinking on their part. Our training should make constant improvement, new thinking. The driving force for this must come from men like yourselves.[123]

Although in 1938, out of 41 training manuals issued in India, only seven were specific editions for India or War Office manuals reprinted in India.[124] Thus Corbett, Cowan, Savory and Tuker along with fellow officers, such as Major Michael Roberts and Captain Henry 'Taffy' Davies, took their careers very seriously, producing articles on such matters as intelligence, tactical matters and their experience at the Senior Officers' School in the *Journal of the United Services Institution of India*.[125] In 1934 Lieutenant Colonel Thomas 'Pete' Rees told the young subaltern B. M. Kaul on finding him reading a novel, that he had been studying military history and tactics for nineteen years and suggested that he would need to apply himself if he wanted to get anywhere.[126]

Indian Army officers also benefitted from the British Armed Forces interwar experience with two officers attending the Imperial Defence College (IDC) every year.[127]

---

121 Precis of two lectures – Formation Training & Preparation of training Exercises, Staff College Quetta, Senior Division, 1937, *Corbett Mss.*, CAC, CORB 2/22.
122 Notes for the Opening Address Spring Term Senior Division 1937, p. 2, *Corbett Mss.*, CAC, CORB 2/29.
123 Ibid., p. 13.
124 See *AHQ Training Memorandum* No. 17, *Notes on Individual Training Period 1938*, pp. 17-18, IOR, L/MIL/17/5/2199.
125 See for example Captain H. L. Davies, 'Military Intelligence in Tribal Warfare on the North West Frontier of India' and Auspex (pseudonym for Tuker), 'A Matrimonial Tangle (or Mountains and Machine Guns)' both in *JUSII*, Vol. LXII, No. 272, July 1933, pp. 289-330, 367-374; Major M. R. Roberts, 'Object!!' in *JUSII*, Vol. LXVII, No, 288, July 1937, pp. 322-324.
126 Cohen interview with Lt. Gen. B. M. Kaul, 19 December 1964.
127 For instance Auchinleck attended in 1927, Lieutenant Colonel Alan Hartley in 1931, Lieutenant Colonel George Molesworth in 1935, Colonel Roland Inskip in 1936, and the Gurkha officers: Lieutenant Colonel William Slim in 1937, Lieutenant Colonel Geoffrey

Additionally, an Indian Army officer was included on the directing staff at Camberley, hence both the instructor learnt from his time there, as did British service officers who had not served in India.[128] For example, during this period Slim spent four years at AHQ, two as an instructor at Camberley, a year at the IDC, with some regimental duties interspersed and then became Commandant of the Senior Officers' School as well as immersing himself in military history.[129]

Conclusion

A few years before the beginning of the Second World War, a blueprint was in place for training Indian Army units and formations with the use of training instructions, conferences and exercises based on a common doctrine. This ethos was promulgated throughout the pre-war Indian Army, as most regular officers spent a period of time at one of the training establishments in India or as an instructor at one, and were inculcated with the ideas of forward-thinking officers such as Corbett, Cowan, Savory and Tuker. All these officers knew each other and their ideas about training, tactics and the organisation of the Indian Army permeated throughout the army being a relatively small network of senior professional officers in 1939.[130] Thus in contrast to Field Marshal Sir Philip Chetwode's comment on retiring as C-in-C India in 1935, 'The longer I remain in Service, the more wooden and the more regulation-bound do I find the average British officer to be', there was now a coterie of very professional officers who laid the foundation for the transformation of the expanded Indian Army during the Second World War. This was perhaps contrary to the British Army, a professionalism that was not frowned upon by fellow officers.[131] This was in contrast to an earlier

---

 Scoones in 1938 and Lieutenant Colonel John Bruce in 1939 respectively. I am grateful to Dr Joseph Moretz for sharing his research on the IDC.
128 See Joseph Moretz, *Thinking Wisely, Planning Boldly: The Higher Education and Training of Royal Navy Officers, 1919-1939* (Solihull: Helion, 2015), p. 306.
129 See Ronald Lewin, *Slim the Standardbearer* (Ware: Wordsworth, 1999), p. 49. See also Duncan Anderson, 'The Very Model of a Modern Manoeuvrist General: William Slim and the Exercise of High Command in Burma' in Gary Sheffield and Geoffrey Till (eds.), *Challenges of High Command in the Twentieth Century* (Camberley: Strategic and Combat Studies Institute, 1999), p. 64 and Moretz, *Thinking Wisely*, pp. 308-309.
130 For the importance of networks see Ashley Jackson's chapter, '"A Prodigy of Skill and Organization': British Imperial Networks and the Second World War' in *Distant Drums: The Role of Colonies in British Imperial Warfare* (Brighton: Sussex Academic Press, 2010), pp. 242-261.
131 Quoted in Brian Bond, *British Military Policy between the Two World Wars* (Oxford: Clarendon Press, 1980), p. 68. See also Anderson, 'The Very Model of a Modern Manoeuvrist', p. 64 where he writes of Slim: 'Slim managed to take his profession seriously; he deepened and broadened his knowledge without being ostracized by his mess as a *'military shit'*, the fate that befell many intellectual officers in the 1920s and 1930s. None of these attributes, of course, was unique to Slim. They were shared to a great extent by officers like 'Punch' Cowan, Bruce Scott, 'Pete' Rees and hundreds more in the

generation of senior Indian Army officers who were routed in the pre-1914 period and wanted little change after the First World War. According to Douglas Gracey, who later commanded 20th Indian Division, they seemed 'to get stuck in a groove and be inundated by details which should have been left to their subordinates'.[132] Similarly, as Patrick Rose has eloquently pointed out, the Indian Army 'command culture' in this period due to fewer numbers of British officers meant that there was an informal decentralised mission command-oriented culture at higher and regimental command that was reinforced by service on the North West Frontier.[133]

Although not all British officers of this generation were quite so 'enlightened', as Brigadier C.J.C. Molony phrased it. For example Brigadier Alan McPherson, was a firm believer in the 'Martial Races' before the war and dropped two Indianised battalions from his command in 1937 due to the problems of replacing the Indian officers within the units.[134] In addition, Indian Army officers often got immersed at regimental level with undue respect for their particular regiment such as the cavalry regiments, the Garwhal Regiment, the Sikh Regiment and the Gurkha Regiments, in particular, that has been termed 'Gurkhaitis'.[135]

An article in a post-war issue of the *JUSII* posed the question: 'Was Our Pre-War Training Wrong?' The author commented that the lessons from the Second World War showed the importance of schools for mountain, jungle, desert warfare and street fighting for the future. However, he concluded with quotations from the War Office pamphlet *Infantry Training for War 1937* stating that the aim of training for the individual was to produce:

> A formidable fighting man like an expert hunter, always alert and seeking an opportunity of striking at his quarry or watching his movements with a view to future opportunities, confident and expert in the use of weapons, skilled in the use of ground and able to stand fatigue without undue loss of efficiency.

It followed that the aim of the unit was: 'Control and flexibility like a good machine each part working smoothly and in harmony with the remainder to achieve the object of the commander'.[136] These attributes were taught in the training establishments

---

British and Indian Armies'. See also Cohen interview with FM Sir Claude Auchinleck, 7 December 1963.
132   Letter from Douglas Gracey to Professor Stephen Cohen, 12 November 1963.
133   See Rose, 'Indian Army Command Culture and the North West Frontier, 1919-1939', pp. 30-55.
134   Cohen interviews with Brigadier C. J. C. Molony, 14 September 1963 and Brigadier Alan McPherson, 18 November 1963.
135   Cohen interview with Brigadier John Stephenson, 3 December 1963. See also Rose, 'Indian Army Command Culture and the North West Frontier, 1919-1939', p. 40.
136   Lieutenant Colonel W. H. Huelin, 'Was Our Pre-War Training Wrong?', *JUSII*, Vol. LXXVI, No. 325, October 1946, p. 389.

before the war, reinforcing the fact that the Indian Army was not only well-trained for the roles it undertook before the Second World War, but there was a training structure in place that could be built on in times of war. However in 1939, the Indian Army was implementing the recommendations of the Chatfield Committee. This involved a reduction in the army in order to undertake modernisation that was to be spread over a four year period. Therefore at the beginning of the Second World War, the army was actually reduced in size but also undertaking reorganisation for modernisation of the army. Units were subsequently weaker than the Indian Army of the earlier period of the 1930s and the officer cadre was also below strength.[137]

---

137 See undated typescript 'Since 1939', Papers of General Sir Rob Lockhart, *Lockhart Mss.*, NAM, 8310-154-25. See also Prasad, *Expansion*, p. 54.

2

Training in India at the beginning of the Second World War

India declared war on Germany on 3 September 1939. It had been the sole decision of the Viceroy, Lord Linlithgow, without consultation with his Executive Council and more importantly without the Central Legislative Assembly, a decision that was even criticised in the House of Commons.[1] The leaders of Indian public opinion were divided with Muhammad Ali Jinnah and the Muslim League, supporting the decision that ultimately helped increase the support base of his political party by the end of the war.[2] Whereas the Congress Party, which had generally been indifferent, if not displaying an aversion to the Indian Army, did not support the war effort. Although Mohandas K. Gandhi indicated to the Viceroy his moral support for the Allied cause.[3] Notwithstanding, the war had a far greater effect on India's population than during the First World War.[4] India was a huge source of manpower for the armed forces. It was also an important source for raw materials and manufacturing towards the war effort and became the main base for operations in the Middle East and the South East Asian theatre. As in the First World War, the Indian Army was largely paid for by the British government. It met the expenses for those fighting outside India's borders, as well as the expansion of the army (including the much needed modern equipment) for the duration of the war. This contrasted to the peacetime practice.[5] With the outbreak of the war the expansion of the Indian Army should have been essential, but due to

---

1   See R. J. Moore, *Churchill, Cripps, and India, 1939-1945* (Oxford: Clarendon Press, 1979), p. 7.
2   See Voigt, *India in the Second World War*, p. 38.
3   See Judith M. Brown, *Modern India: The Origins of an Asian Democracy* (Delhi: OUP, 1985), p. 346 and Voigt, *India in the Second World War*, pp. 19-20, 30. For a good overview of the political situation, see Raghavan, *India's War*, chapter 1.
4   See Brown, *Modern* India, p. 307.
5   See Voigt, *India in the Second World War*, pp. 9-10, 61-62.

the War Office's decision not to use the army, no expansion was deemed necessary for the first nine months.[6]

Expansion

The army belatedly embarked on a massive expansion programme in May 1940 to meet the requests for increased manpower due to the threat of hostilities with Russia and Afghanistan.[7] In a broadcast that was reported in the soldiers' newspaper, *Fauji Akhbar*, the Adjutant General, Major General Sir Roger Wilson, noted the importance of the lessons learnt in recruiting, training and organisation of recruits in the First World War. He remarked that:

> The last war taught us the need for a well organised system of maintenance of manpower and for the supply of reinforcements to units overseas, this lesson was studied during and after the war and during the intervening years of peace, recruiting and training and distribution of recruits was put on a firm basis.
>
> We, therefore, find ourselves today with fewer casualties to replace but with a thoroughly well oiled and smooth working machine with which to work.[8]

In eighteen months the army doubled in size, although it was very short of equipment.[9] To accomplish this, experienced NCOs, VCOs and officers were extracted from their units in order to bolster new and raw units. Expansion meant that a large number of the newly-enlisted Indian troops had little basic training, in direct contrast to the professional Indian Army of the pre-war period. When new units and formations were formed in 1940 *Fauji Akhbar* stated:

> Apart from the problem of equipment the absolute minimum period for transforming a raw recruit into even an elementary trained soldier is six to nine months. A special emergency procedure has been adopted to accelerate the process of training. The new formations will be built up on the existing army by obtaining a nucleus of trained men from units already in being.[10]

This process was called 'milking' and the newspaper went on to explain that from a regiment consisting of five battalions and one training battalion, the new battalion

---

6   See Personal Record, Folder No. 1, p. 11, *Tuker Mss.*, IWM, 71/21/9. See also Prasad, *Expansion*, p. 54.
7   See 'India at War', p. 27, *Corbett Mss.*, CAC, CORB 3/28. See also Voigt, *India in the Second World War*, p. 63 and Raghavan, *India's War*, chapter 2.
8   'India's Manpower': A Broadcast by Lt. General Sir R. C. Wilson, Adjutant General in India, *Fauji Akhbar*, Vol. XVII, No. 43, 28 October 1939, p. 15.
9   See Prasad, *Expansion*, pp. 53-73. See also Cohen, *Indian Army*, pp. 139-140.
10 *Fauji Akhbar*, Vol. XVIII, No. 32, 10 August 1940, p. 8.

would be formed by transferring one officer, three VCOs, six havildars, seven naiks, fourteen lance naiks and sixty sepoys from each battalion. The total strength of trained personnel in the new battalion would be about 450 men. The remainder would be made up of trained recruits from the training battalion, as well as replacing the losses in the original battalions.[11] For example, the 9th Battalion, 14th Punjab Regiment was formed at Jhansi on 1 April 1941. It was raised with drafts from the 1st, 4th, 5th, 6th and 7th Battalions of the 14th Punjab Regiment amounting to 240 all ranks. Recruits from the Regimental Centre then arrived in June and July bringing the battalion strength up to 690 all ranks.[12] However, some units were formed almost entirely of new recruits, of whom only some had passed through a training centre.

One result of expansion was the abandoning of the 25-unit Indianisation scheme with Indian officers being placed where there was the most need for them. By November 1940, few infantry battalions had more than three or four pre-war regular officers.[13] The lack of experienced officers and instructors in these battalions was remedied by the use of training teams. Additionally, trained infantry battalions were transferred from the Indian Territorial Force and by 1941 all the Territorial battalions had been converted into regular units. Pensioners and reservists were also called up to man garrison battalions.[14] The class composition of regiments was also relaxed during the war as expansion dictated that it was impossible to recruit solely from the traditional 'martial races' from the Punjab. Thus, large numbers of the supposedly non-martial classes, such as from Madras, were recruited into the field artillery, the RIASC and new regiments such as the Madras Regiment.[15]

The rapid expansion of the armed forces resulted in a shortage of experienced VCOs and NCOs. This was partially remedied by transferring infantry VCOs and NCOs to other arms that had previously been very small, such as the Indian Armoured Corps and the RIASC. Special training units were formed for men considered suitable for promotion as VCOs and NCOs. Together, with the call up of pensioners, reservists, the direct recruitment of educated recruits and the improved education of recruits during basic training determined that numbers of VCOs and NCOs steadily improved. The lack of education and suitable qualities amongst recruits equally applied

---

11 See *Fauji Akhbar*, Vol. XVIII, No. 32, 10 August 1940, p. 8. See also Prasad, *Expansion*, pp. 82-83 and Marston, *Phoenix from the Ashes*, pp. 42-47.
12 See Lieutenant Colonel J. R. Booth and Lieutenant Colonel J. B. Hobbs, *Ninth Battalion, Fourteenth Punjab Regiment* (Cardiff: Western Mail, 1948), p. 11.
13 See Prasad, *Expansion*, p. 100.
14 See Prasad, *Expansion*, p. 83. See also 'India's Manpower': A Broadcast by Lt. General Sir R. C. Wilson, Adjutant General in India, *Fauji Akhbar*, Vol. XVII, 28 October 1939, p. 15.
15 See Prasad, *Expansion*, p. 85, Marston, *Phoenix from the Ashes*, p. 50 and Marston, *Indian Army and the End of the Raj*, pp. 77-82. For a fuller explanation of the Indian Army continuing to recruit the martial races from the Punjab for frontline infantry battalions and the large numbers of men recruited from Southern India who largely served in auxiliary and support roles during the war, see Wilkinson, *Army and Nation*, pp. 69-74.

to British officers and other ranks for specialist corps, as many of those who applied for commissions in the Indian Army Ordnance Corps (IAOC) had failed to pass the required examination boards.[16]

Simultaneously the Indian Army was lacking the equipment and vehicles to accommodate expansion. For example, in 1939, the Indian Artillery comprised six mountain regiments and one Indian Field Regiment; that was not considered a success and there were no 25-pounders in India. However, within two years Indian Medium, Field, Anti-Aircraft, Anti-Tank and Coastal Defence units were established. These all used technical equipment manned by Indian personnel, as well as British and Indian officers. Similarly, production of new and repaired rifles in India numbered 1,647 at the beginning of the war and this had increased to 8,800 by August 1941.[17] This situation was remedied by the end of the war demonstrated by the Ishapore rifle factory near Calcutta which had built and repaired nearly 700, 000 rifles.[18]

Military Training Directorate

The training organisation at GHQ India originated from the 1930s but was intensified by the pressure of war. The Military Training Directorate was responsible for directing training. In 1939, it consisted of 12 officers divided into three sections: M.T.1 was responsible for the military training schools and establishments; M. T. 2 responsible for higher training and training publications; M. T. 3 looked after individual training and had control of training schools.[19] The original Director of Military Training (DMT) was the controversial Brigadier Eric Dorman-Smith, but he had requested a transfer to the Staff School at Haifa.[20] In July 1940, a Deputy Director, Military Training (GSO1) post was created along with another three officers that were brought into the directorate.[21]

In September 1940, Tuker was appointed Director alongside Deputy Director, 'Punch' Cowan, with another seven officers added to the directorate. Tuker was also Inspector of Infantry. Consequently there were now 16 officers in the directorate with nine attached officers advising on artillery, signals, education, physical training and the Indian States Forces. In addition, there were two training teams consisting of nine

---

16 See Prasad, *Expansion*, pp. 98-99.
17 See Colonel Emile Charles Victor Foucar, Modernisation and Mechanisation of the Armed Forces of India, 1939-1944, Part II, The Modernisation of the Army, pp. 15-18, 41, Papers of Lieutenant General Sir Thomas Hutton, *Hutton Mss.*, LHCMA, 3/22.
18 See David Egerton, *Britain's War Machine: Weapons, Resources and Experts in the Second World War* (London: Penguin, 2012), p. 61.
19 See Prasad, *Expansion*, pp. 305-306.
20 See Lavinia Green, *Chink: A Biography* (London: Macmillan, 1989), pp. 137-148. Although Tuker states that Dorman-Smith was not keen to go just as he was not keen to become DMT. See Personal Record Folder No. 1, p. 11, *Tuker Mss.*, IWM, 71/21/9.
21 See Prasad, *Expansion*, p. 306.

officers and the editorial team of the soldiers' newspaper, *Fauji Akhbar*.[22] As Tuker commented regarding his time as DMT: 'I set to work with a will to clean up the whole of the training system of the Indian Army, and I think I had some success'.[23] The directorate slowly expanded with another ten officers in post by the end of 1941, as well as the upgrade of the director and his deputy to major general and brigadier respectively. By January 1942, the numbers had increased to twenty eight officers in addition to the training teams and the editorial staff.[24] In September 1942, a GSO1 was appointed to visit and co-ordinate the training centres. This was later upgraded to the Inspector of Training Centres with the rank of brigadier in July 1943. Thus, the awareness of the importance of the directorate was made more apparent by the increasing workforce and upgrading of the various ranks within the department.

Training Pamphlets for use in India

In the first two years of the war, under Tuker's tutelage, the directorate produced a large amount of training pamphlets. For instance, the doctrine for the traditional roles of aid to civil power and for the North West Frontier were formalised. A considerable amount was based on existing experience. For example, a doctrine was finally produced for internal security with the publication of *Military Training Pamphlet* (*MTP*) No. 11 (India), *Notes on training for duties in aid of the civil power, 1941*.[25] The *MTP* (India) series of manuals covered tactical situations that were not necessarily well covered in the War Office *MTP* series but frequently occurred in India such as internal security. Ever since the Amritsar Massacre of 1919, the Indian Army had espoused a policy of minimum force, together with deterrence and civil-military co-operation.[26] This was enshrined in the various editions of *Internal Security Instructions*, produced during the 1930s, that developed through training.[27] Together with Charles Gwynn's

---

22 See *Indian Army List*, April 1941, pp. 8-8A.
23 Personal Record, Folder No. 1, p. 26, *Tuker Mss.*, IWM, 71/21/9.
24 See *Indian Army List*, January 1942, pp. 10-11.
25 *See Military Training pamphlet* No. 11 (India), *Notes on training for duties in aid of the civil power, 1941* (Delhi: GSI, 1942), IOR, L/MIL/17/2252.
26 Recent and contrasting work on Dyer and the Amritsar Massacre include Nigel Collett, *The Butcher of Amritsar: General Reginald Dyer*, (London: Hambledon, 2005); Nick Lloyd, *The Amritsar Massacre: The Untold Story of the One Fateful Day*, (London: I. B. Tauris, 2011) and Nick Lloyd, 'The Amritsar Massacre and the minimum force debate', *Small Wars and Insugencies*, Vol. 21, No. 2, June 2010, pp. 382-403.
27 See Srinath Raghaven, 'Protecting the Raj: The Army in India and Internal Security, c. 1919-1939', *Small Wars and Insurgencies*, Vol. 16, No. 3, December 2005, pp. 254-257, 272-273. See also Gyanesh Kudaisya, ' "In Aid of Civil Power": The Colonial Army in Northern India, c. 1919-42', *Journal of Imperial and Commonwealth History*, Vol. 32, No. 1, January 2004, pp. 41-68; Simeon Shoul, 'Soldiers, Riot Control and Aid to the Civil Power in India, Egypt and Palestine, 1919-39', *Journal of the Society for Army Historical Research*, Vol. 86, No. 346, Summer 2008, pp. 131-134 and Marston, *The Indian Army and the End of the Raj*, pp. 39-42.

Imperial Policing which became prescribed reading, that looked at the experiences of Amritsar, the Moplah Rebellion of 1921, the Peshawar riots in 1930 and the Burmese Rebellion of 1930-32.[28] The new pamphlet collated all the previous training material from the 1920s onwards, and for the first time, a doctrine for internal security was available for British and Indian troops in India. Training was to encompass civil and police officers as well as the Army in India and included the dispersal of unlawful assemblies, co-operation with police, patrolling, disarming and dealing with acts of destruction, both by day and night. The training would be delivered through lectures, use of models, aerial photographs, TEWTS and demonstrations. Every officer had to carry a copy of Indian Army Form (IAF) D-908, an appendix to the training manual, which prescribed the law and gave instructions for dispersing unlawful assemblies.[29] In his book, *Unofficial History*, Slim commented that IAF D-908 'was a very serviceable handrail to steady one among the pitfalls of the law', further remarking 'unlike many army forms, [it] was a useful thing to have about one.'[30]

Similarly, the doctrine for the North West Frontier had already been encapsulated with the publication of *Frontier Warfare – India (Army and Royal Air Force)* in 1939.[31] It was the latest update of the *Manual of Operations on the North West Frontier of India* and had been drafted by the then Major General Claude Auchinleck. The manual was issued to British and Indian units and RAF squadrons and formed the basis for training until the end of the war. In the words of Tim Moreman: 'It provided the Army in India with a comprehensive and up-to-date formal written doctrine of frontier warfare upon which a comprehensive system of training was based'.[32] It was the culmination of many years of experience and literature on the Frontier, stretching back from Colonel Callwell's *Small Wars* to the more recent work of Colonel John Villiers-Stuart and General Sir Andrew Skeen's *Passing it On*.[33] This doctrine was further augmented during the war by *MTP* No. 6 (India) *The Support of Land Forces*

---

28 See Charles Gwynn, *Imperial Policing* (London: Macmillan, 1934) and *MTP*, No. 11, p. 31, IOR L/MIL/17/2252.
29 See *MTP*, No. 11, pp. 4-6, 28-30, IOR, L/MIL/17/2252.
30 Field Marshal Sir William Slim, *Unofficial History* (Barnsley: Pen & Sword reprint, 2008), p. 77.
31 See *Frontier Warfare – India (Army and Royal Air Force), 1939*, IOR, L/MIL/17/5/2220.
32 T. R. Moreman, *The Army in India and the Development of Frontier Warfare, 1849-1947* (Basingstoke: Macmillan, 1998), p. 171.
33 See *Frontier Warfare*, p. 162, IOR, L/MIL/17/5/2220. See also Colonel C. E. Callwell, *Small Wars: A Tactical Textbook for* Imperial *Soldiers* (London, HMSO, 1896), 2nd ed. 1899, 3rd ed. 1906, reprinted by Greenhill Books, 1990, pp. 286-347; Colonel J. P. Villiers-Stuart (brother of Brigadier General William Villiers-Stuart, another trainer of note), *Letters of a Once Punjab Frontier Force Officer to his Nephew giving his Ideas on Fighting on the North West Frontier and in Afghanistan* (London: Sifton Praed, 1925) and General Sir Andrew Skeen, *Passing it On: Short Talks on Tribal Fighting on the North West Frontier of India* (Aldershot: Gale & Polden, 1932), 2nd ed. 1932, 3rd ed. 1934, 4th ed. 1939, recently reprinted as *Lessons in Imperial Rule: Instructions for British Infantrymen on the Indian Frontier* (Barnsley: Frontline Books, 2008). For a fuller explanation of the tactical

by Aircraft in Tribal Warfare on the Western Frontier of India 1940, with an updated edition in March 1941, as well as two editions of *MTP* No. 16 (India) *Platoon Leading in Frontier Warfare*, published in 1941 and 1942 respectively.[34] *MTP* No. 16 (India) was based on *Frontier Warfare – India*, with the manual stating that the principles of frontier warfare did not differ from other types of warfare but that experience showed that special techniques were needed for the terrain and tribal warfare. The second edition doubled in circulation with extra material on picqueting and signalling, and was issued to those battalions earmarked for the North West Frontier.[35] Colonel Brian Montgomery, brother of Field Marshal Sir Bernard Montgomery, commented on training for the North West Frontier Province (NWFP) before the war:

> My immediately preceding reflection leads me to emphasise that training for war in the Indian Army was long, continuous and hard. It is also true that our training for the NWFP generally had the first priority; the reasons for this was that those (NWFP) operations meant actual training with live ammunition; against well armed and skilled tribesmen intent on shooting you and your men. Death or serious wounds incurred on Frontier operations were certainly not infrequent; furthermore your reputation at all levels of command and action, could depend on your NWFP service.[36]

Thus by 1939, most Indian Army units, particularly Gurkha and Frontier Force regiments, had through tradition, training and experience become highly skilled in frontier warfare. The North West Frontier continued to engage large numbers of troops during the war. In 1943, fifty seven British and Indian infantry battalions and four armoured car regiments were based on the North West Frontier. Regiments based in Northern Command continued to train for frontier warfare and the Army School of Frontier Warfare was set up at Kakul in March 1941, with Colonel Frank Le Marchand as Commandant.[37]

Other existing training literature included the *Field Service Pocket Book* (*FSPB*) which was issued to all officers on arrival in India. The various pamphlets in the *FSPB* had been produced in the British Army by the War Office since the First World War. Some pamphlets were reprinted in India, *Field Service Pocket Book (India)*, to include information

---

development of frontier warfare see Moreman's *The Army in India and the Development of Frontier Warfare.*
34 See *Military Training Pamphlet* No. 6 (India). *The Support of Land Forces by Aircraft in Tribal Warfare on the Western Frontier of India, 1940* IWM and 2nd ed. March 1941, IOR, L/MIL/17/5/2247. See also *MTP* No. 16 (India) *Platoon Leading Frontier Warfare*, 1st ed. 1941, IWM and 2nd ed. 1942 IOR, L/MIL/17/5/2258.
35 See *MTP* No. 16 (India) 1942 *Platoon Leading in Frontier Warfare*, pp. 1, 41-88.
36 Montgomery, 'Change: The Indian Army before the Demise of our Indian Empire in 1947', p. 107.
37 See Moreman, *Army in India and the Development of Frontier Warfare*, pp. 174, 179, 181.

on local conditions as they generally covered administrative detail such as a glossary of military terms and abbreviations of military units.³⁸ The pamphlets also included instructions for more practical matters such as *FSPB(I)* Part 1 – Pamphlet No. 13 *Discipline, office work and burial parties*. The Indian version of this pamphlet differed from the War Office one as Indian Army officers were governed by Indian military law. Hence VCOs needed to be included as there was no equivalent in the British Army and the religious practices of Hindu, Muslim and Sikh soldiers needed to be taken into account.³⁹

War Office *Military Training Pamphlets* (*MTPs*) were usually reprinted in India and *MTPs* (India) were only produced if there was a specific need for the Indian Army. For example, infantry training was based upon the various parts of War Office pamphlet *MTP* No. 23 such as *Operations*, Part II, *The Infantry Division in the Defence* (23 March 1942) and *Operations*, Part IX, *The Infantry Division in Attack* (21 July 1941), which were reprinted by GHQ India in July 1942 and November 1941 respectively.⁴⁰ These training manuals contained the latest ideas on subjects dealt with in *Field Service Regulations* Volume II (1935). Important War Office *MTPs* were translated into Roman Urdu such as *MTP* No. 33 *Training in Field Craft and Elementary Tactics*.⁴¹ As Timothy Harrison Place has pointed out in his thorough treatise on training in the British Army, the *MTP* series covered the specialisms of the army ranging from motorcycling to minor tactics. They were issued under the auspices of CIGS by the Directorate of Military Training rather than the pre-war cumbersome committee-based Army Council training manuals, although *MTP* No. 23, on the infantry division in attack, still took fifteen months in preparation.⁴²

Training Pamphlets produced for fighting in other theatres

MTPs India were now being produced in large numbers and quickly to cover not only the traditional roles of aid to civil power and fighting on the North West Frontier but also subjects such as armoured units in the field and supply.⁴³ The publication

---

38 See for example *Field Service Pocket Book (India)* Part I – Pamphlet No. 1, *Glossary of Military Terms* (1944) which superseded *FSPB(I)* Pamphlet No. I, 1940 and *FSPB(I)* Part I – Pamphlet No. 3, *Abbreviations* (1944), Author's collection.
39 See *FSPB(I)* Part I – Pamphlet No. 13, *Discipline, office work and burial parties* (1944), pp. 1, 3, 7, 35.
40 See *MTP* No. 23 *Operations* Part II *The Infantry Division in the Defence* (1942), reprinted in India in July 1942 and *Operations* Part IX *The Infantry Division in the Attack* (1941) reprinted in India in November 1941, IWM.
41 See *MTP* No, 33 *Training in Fieldcraft and Elementary Tactics* 1940 that was translated and issued by the General Staff in India together with Modifications for India No. 1 in 1941, IWM.
42 See Harrison Place, *Training*, p. 9.
43 See *MTP* No. 1 (India) *Armoured Units in the field. Parts 1–12*, IOR, L/MIL/17/5/2244 and *MTP* No. 4 (India) *Supply in the field in Eastern Theatres of war, 1939*, IOR, L/MIL/17/5/2246.

of *Military Training Pamphlet*, No. 9 (India), *Notes on Forest warfare*, October 1940, demonstrated that the problems of jungle warfare were taken seriously enough in GHQ India to warrant issuing a training pamphlet. It was written under the direction of Tuker with copies dispatched to Malaya.[44] It was based on Tuker's experience in Assam in 1919 and training with the 2nd Gurkhas in 1933, as well as acting as a corrective to Malaya Command's training pamphlet that noted the difficulty of operating in the jungle and suggested keeping to tracks and roads.[45] The training manual encouraged the use of the forest rather than roads and was written to examine the tactics in jungle, as the *Field Service Regulations* Vol. II only discussed engaging with a primitive enemy, whereas in Malaya the threat was of a modern army.[46] The foreword stated:

> These notes amplify the instructions in Field Service Regulations and consider warfare against a modern enemy. It must be remembered always that forest warfare lends itself more than any other form of warfare, to ingenuity. Small active parties, skillfully playing upon the enemy's fears, can exert an influence on operations out of all proportion to their strength. A commander must examine every local factor and turn each to his advantage or the enemy's disadvantage. Written instructions can only serve to guide the commander's imagination and guile in the right directions. That is all these Notes attempt.[47]

The manual was eleven pages long and therefore only gave general guidelines for jungle warfare in an eastern theatre of war. It emphasised the use of mobility in forest warfare and how this was developed by constant training. *MTP* No. 9 concentrated on the importance of infantry, mobility and the use of particular equipment such as machetes, sub-machine guns and 3-inch mortars for close support in jungle combat.[48] Tactics for attack, defence and the counter attack were explained; outflanking, patrolling, specialised equipment, all-round defence, mobile reserves, security against enemy penetration and the speed and support of counter-attack were all examined. In withdrawal, the training manual noted that a retreating force will always be in fear of being outflanked but this can be counteracted 'by skilful patrol activity wide

---

44 See letter from Tuker to the editor of the Daily Telegraph, 15 March 1967, *Tuker Mss.*, IWM, 71/21/7/4 and 'Personal Record', Folder No. 1, pp. 28-29, *Tuker Mss.*, IWM, 71/21/9.
45 See Attack on Aihang village, Assam, May 1918, *Tuker Mss*, IWM, 71/21/2/1 and a Letter from Tuker to Lieutenant-Colonel A. E. Cocksedge, Defence Department, Combined Inter Services Historical Section, Simla, dated 26 July 1947, *Tuker Mss.*, IWM, 71/21/4/5. See also General Staff, Malaya Command, *Tactical Notes for Malaya 1940* (1941) Reprinted by the General Staff, India, AWM.
46 See *Field Service Regulations* Vol II, (1935), pp. 183-185.
47 *MTP* No. 9 (India), *Notes on Forest Warfare* (1940), p. ii, IWM.
48 See *MTP* No. 9, pp. 1-2.

to the flanks' and varying the direction of withdrawal.[49] Tactically the pamphlet recommended the use of patrols. It laid out battle drills for platoon actions against the enemy, with a pair of scouts preceding each section off the main track and the infantry moving on a wide front. It also noted that training in the jungle was essential, mentioning night training and remarking that 'patrol training and the inculcation of the inquisitive and aggressive spirit are essential'.[50] However, it is most difficult to gauge how widely read the pamphlet actually was in Malaya and whether it received a similar fate to the forgotten pamphlets on anti-tank warfare found in a General Staff cupboard.[51]

Another manual produced in the early days of the Directorate was *MTP* No. 5 (India) *Notes on Training for Extensive Warfare 1940*, published on 16 May 1940, in an edition of 14,000 copies. Extensive warfare was defined as mobile warfare where armies had scope for movement and manoeuvre and where small and mobile forces could operate at great distances, with long lines of communication and less prominence of heavier weapons. The main areas for this type of warfare was the Middle East but the training pamphlet also remarked that it would equally be applicable to the mountains of the North West Frontier and the jungles of Burma and Malaya. Recent examples of this type of warfare were the opening phases of the Mesopotamian campaign, with the greatest success seen as the latter stages of the campaign in Palestine during the First World War. Modern armies would be more adept due to mechanised cavalry with Light Armoured Groups and motor regiments in the Indian Army. Infantry, artillery, engineers and air support needed to be coordinated with the mobile arm. In attack, the importance of infiltration was acknowledged but at this early stage of the war, the lack of equipment was a limiting factor.[52]

Following on from this pamphlet was *MTP* No. 7 (India) *Extensive Warfare (Notes on Warfare in Mountainous Country between Modern Forces in Eastern Theatres) 1940* as it was deemed necessary to learn the lessons after the Norwegian Campaign. Mountain warfare was clearly defined as separate from 'frontier warfare', tribal warfare on the North West Frontier, and although large sections of the Indian Army were natural mountaineers, there had been no training specifically for tactical operations in snow and ice in such areas as Italian East Africa. As with *MTP* No. 5, mobility was emphasised along with air support. The problems of defence, attack, counter-attack, withdrawal, transport and operations in a hostile country were explored. The pamphlet concluded that strong leadership and the use of initiative were essential. It also emphasised the value of patrolling, and even suggested the transportation of

---

49 *MTP* No. 9, p. 6.
50 Ibid., p. 8.
51 See Ivan Simson, *Singapore: Too Little, Too Late: Some Aspects of the Malayan Disaster in 1942* (London: Leo Cooper, 1970), p. 56. See also the Second Supplement to *The London Gazette* of Friday 20 February, Operations of Malaya Command, from 8 December 1941 to 15 February 1942, by Lieutenant General A. E. Percival, p. 1259.
52 See *MTP* No. 5 (India) *Notes on Training for Extensive Warfare 1940*, pp. 2-4, 7, 19, IWM.

3.7 inch howitzers as a form of mobile light artillery. In training terms, the manual advocated the need for physical fitness of troops that could operate at night, in forests as well as in mountain warfare. Infantry needed to cope with the element of surprise, undertake patrol work, use initiative and self-reliance in attack and be mindful of ammunition supply, rations and water, as well as care of the wounded. Once again the pamphlet noted the importance of co-operation with the different arms as well as the RAF.[53] It concluded:

> Above all things an instructor must so train his leaders and men that each is confident that he is better at arms than any of the enemy. They must be skilled at mountain craft and be proud of it. Instill the spirit of shikari who is all out to make a bag and a big one.[54]

Perhaps betraying a slightly amateur ethos, the pamphlet was updated and revised the following year, stating that the armament and equipment mentioned was not possessed by the Indian Army. Examples were given from recent operations in Norway, Greece and Eritrea where 4th and 5th Indian Divisions had been fighting. For instance, it was noted that in defence, the Italian forces evacuated the crests of mountains during the bombardment until it stopped and then moved back to shower hand grenades on the attacking infantry.[55]

One particularly important pamphlet was *MTP* No. 14 (India) on *Infantry Section Leading*, published in 1940 with a reprint and amendments produced in October 1942. The training manual was divided up into three parts covering leadership, organisation, weapons and training, with the last and largest section dealing with tactics. In the words of Auchinleck, it was 'an attempt to widen the outlook of the section leader' and cover all the aspects of the job. It was designed to be used in collaboration with other training manuals, such as *MTP* No. 33 on fieldcraft, and the various pamphlets on small arms training. It emphasised the importance of training men both as individuals and as a team and the need for section leaders to explain, demonstrate, execute and repeat in practical instruction. Part II covered command, control, communication and intelligence and the need to look after the welfare of the troops. Part III heeded the importance of patrolling, action against tanks, air attack and tactics for attack, defence and fighting in towns and villages. It also included chapters on jungle and mountain warfare based on *MTP* Nos. 9 and 7 (India) respectively.[56]

---

53   *MTP* No. 7 (India) *Extensive Warfare (Notes on Warfare in Mountainous Country between Modern Forces in Eastern Theatres)* 1940, pp. 1-10, 12-16, IWM.
54   Ibid., p. 16.
55   See *MTP* No. 7 (India) *Extensive Warfare (Notes on Warfare in Mountainous Country between Modern Forces in Eastern Theatres)*, (1941), pp. 3, 5 & 9, IOR, L/MIL/17/5/2248.
56   See *Military Training Pamphlet* No. 14 (India), *Infantry Section Leading 1941*, pp. xi, 4-5, 8-14, 82-153, IWM.

These training pamphlets were not meant to be the last word on the subject and were often revised in light of further experience. As Tuker noted in the DMT's address of 23 September 1941:

> It has always been our object on the training side to try and get everybody under one hat. We do not wish this so as to control them but to get their help in order to devise our various tactical doctrines, and in order that they may be able to spread the news abroad whenever we have built up new methods and produced new ideas.[57]

In the same address Tuker advocated the importance of all arms co-operation, called combined arms at the time, providing Iraq as an example and stating '…we are not only up with other people but well ahead in tactical doctrine and training'.[58] As Tuker continued, the Indian Army had had to accept the equipment it was given but there was no reason why the army had to be organised in the same way as other armies, stating that: 'There is no manner of doubt that the doctrine of warfare comes before anything else in the Army's make-up'.[59]

The Directorate produced *Army in India Training Memoranda* (*AITMs*), a development of the pre-war *AHQ Training Memoranda*, with the first one appearing in May 1940. They were originally designed to complement the War Office *Army Training Memoranda* (*ATM*) but in order to cut down the amount of bumpf that officers were meant to read important lessons from the *ATMs* were copied in *AITMs*.[60] Both dealt 'with all aspects of military training carried out by all arms of service'.[61] The second *AITM*, published in November 1940, clearly showed the importance of patrolling and 'infiltration' for infantry, a lesson that had to be repeatedly learnt in most theatres of war throughout the Second World War. It also demonstrated why training was proving difficult at this early stage of the war due to the large number of inexperienced officers, warrant officers and NCOs in the Indian Army, together with the reorganisation, mechanisation and change of tactical methods within the army, as well as the added problem of the further expansion.[62] *AITM* No. 3 listed all the various training material available in 1940, amounting to twenty one War Office *MTPs* and eight Indian *MTPs* stating that *MTPs* (India) 'cover special subjects and forms of war, on which no other guidance is readily available'.[63] With regards to the War Office *ATMs*, these showed the progress made in the UK, stating much was applicable to the Indian Army suggesting that *ATMs* Nos. 25-29 and 35 were worthy of reading. The *AITMs*

---

57 DMT's Address of 23 September, 1941, p. 1, *Tuker Mss.*, IWM. 71/21/2
58 Ibid., p. 4.
59 Ibid., p. 9. See also Barua, *Army Officer Corps*, pp. 125-126.
60 *AITM* No. 3, p. 1, IOR, L/MIL/17/5/2240.
61 *List of GS Training publications 1945*, p. 1, IOR, L/MIL/17/5/2197.
62 See *AITM* No. 2, pp. 17, 25. IOR, L/MIL/17/5/2240.
63 *AITM* No. 3, p. 22, IOR, L/MIL/17/5/2240.

were essential for disseminating the development of doctrine in the army. As Tuker remarked:

> I used to spend most of my time on tour, having a thundering good staff up at GHQ to look after my affairs. I kept in close touch with them, and I always left them plenty of outline instructions and policies on which they were to work and so they did work. They were an excellent staff. I think there were only a dozen of them and that I made the thirteenth, but they produced, under my guidance, a training memorandum every month, and I look back upon those training memoranda, which I have still with me, as something really of great value to the Army, as the Army was not hesitant in telling me at the time, and they worked like beavers on expansion and getting into practical shape my training policies…'[64]

Tuker compared his Military Training Directorate with the equivalent at the War Office, summarising both his time as DMT and the inertia of the Military Training Directorate at the War Office:

> The War Office had 79 officers and I had a dozen, or thirteen…we had produced numbers of training memoranda and some training pamphlets, very vital ones, and they produced none: furthermore, we were training and organizing and bringing up to a modern standard a multilingual army which was hardly educated at all in the beginning, and had, in most cases, never seen anything that went faster than a bullock cart.[65]

The British army had different series of training memoranda including *Current Reports from Overseas*, *Notes from Theatres of War* and *Army Training Instructions*. None were distributed in India, nor even mentioned in the Indian training material. However, lessons learnt from all theatres, including North West Europe, were mentioned in the *AITMs*. Thus in India, the *MTPs* encapsulated the doctrine at the time of publication with the *AITMs* adding to this doctrine from both practical experience and learning the lessons in different campaigns.

Officer Training

Expansion of the army meant there was a desperate need for trained officers in India. The officer training structure and organisation adapted immediately in 1939, the Officer Training School (OTS) at Belgaum being established in October. It replaced the Senior Officers' School which was closed. Captain Kendall attended the second course at Belgaum in January 1940 with many of cadets coming from the British

---

64 Personal Record, Folder No. 1, p. 29, *Tuker Mss.*, IWM, 71/21/9.
65 Personal Record, Folder No. 1, p. 35, *Tuker Mss.*, IWM, 71/21/9.

business community domiciled across India. The rigorous training course consisted of TEWTS, courses on leadership and map reading amongst other subjects.[66] The Belgaum OTS took 300 British cadets and continued to take only British cadets throughout the war, whilst the IMA shortened the regular course and took fifty Indian cadet officers and later some British cadets for wartime commissions. The cadets, once commissioned, were termed Emergency Commissioned Officers (ECOs) as they were only given temporary rather than regular commissions. In May 1940, OTS Bangalore for British officers and OTS Mhow for Indian officers were established.[67] Bangalore and Mhow began to take both British and Indian cadet officers, except officer cadets for the Indian Engineers and the IAOC, who went to the Officer Cadet Training Units at Bangalore, Kirkee and Roorkee and the IAOC Training Centre, Jubbulpore. By November 1941, Mhow and Bangalore had expanded to 800 and 1200 cadets respectively.[68] In July 1940, *Fauji Akhbar* noted the amount of work needing to be undertaken in order to get suitable candidates for the new OTS at Mhow, commenting:

> The future recruitment and training of Indian Commissioned Officers to the Army is governed by the number of suitable candidates forthcoming and by the training capacity of the Military Training Directorate. The recruitment of candidates from all over India is in itself an immense undertaking. For every single cadet selected many thousands are interviewed by District Commanders, who send the selected candidates for examination by a Central Board. The Central Board itself will have to go through several hundred candidates to choose the first batch of 100 to be trained at the new centre to be established.[69]

Up to July 1940, 381 officers had been recruited from the Indian Regular Reserve of Officers, recalled mostly from the UK. As well as Army in India Reserve of Officers, civilians working in India who carried out two weeks annual training, and through transfer from the Indian Territorial Force (Auxiliary Force India) as well as those cadets who had passed out from the IMA were commissioned in this period. In addition, there were a number of specialist officers who had been directly recruited into

---

66 See Captain Peter Gordon Kendall, 'The War Years 1939-1945' (Unpublished Memoir), pp. 24-25, IWM, 02/32/1.
67 See Prasad, *Expansion*, pp. 99-100.
68 See Notes for the benefit of volunteers arriving in India from overseas for appointment in India as officers in his Majesty's land forces after training as cadets in an officers' training school, 30 December 1941, p. 7, IOR, L/MIL/17/2287. See also Lt. Col. R.S.M. Calder, 'From Sloth belt to Springboard being a brief account of the activities of Southern Command India during World War II', p. 25, NAM, 8209-14.
69 *Fauji Akhbar*, Vol. XVIII, No. 28, 13 July 1940, p. 7. See also Calder, 'From Sloth belt to Springboard' p. 25, NAM, 8209-14.

such regiments as the Indian Medical Service.[70] Cadets also arrived from Britain, with little knowledge of India and no family tradition of service in the Indian Army. They were issued with a pamphlet entitled *Four Lectures by a Commanding Officer for Officers joining the Indian Army* aimed at explaining Indian culture, the organisation of the army and the importance of leadership through personal example. It stated:

> It is a big thing, this personal example, and it counts for a lot. It is true in any army, but it is a hundred times more important in the Indian Army. Your own integrity must be beyond reproach. You must be honest with yourself and others. Your men must have confidence in you and you have to got to earn, and deserve that confidence.[71]

The pamphlet finished with the ten commandments for aspiring officers that were: learning the language; knowing your job; do what you ask your men to do; be firm and impartial; don't lose your temper; know your men's country and customs; be accessible; be sympathetic; don't introduce reforms into a unit until settled in and make them seem to come from within rather than imposed; and finally, 'Work hard, play hard, fight hard, and when necessary, die hard'.[72]

The Indian Military Academy virtually became another OTS, with 49 'war courses' being held at the Academy, with eight courses being for schoolboy cadets and the remainder for British and Indian cadets, culminating in 3,887 commissions.[73] The editor of the IMA Journal commented on the Academy in June 1942: 'The Public School atmosphere has been blown away and replaced by an air of toughness, a more intense programme…'.[74] By 1941 OTS Belgaum already had a good reputation with both students and instructors. Captain E. L. G. Stones wrote that 'The instruction I found extremely good', commenting that in contrast to the British Army the 'drill was simpler, their whole attitude more reasonable, and for those of us who a few months before had been impatient about fussiness, this was a great tonic. The lectures, too, were, on the whole, admirable'. He described his company commander Colonel Pettigrew as 'remarkably lucid, rational and convincing'.[75] Although it was noticeable that equipment was lacking in India and attitudes towards the experience differed

---

70 See ibid.
71 *Four lectures by a Commanding Officer for Officers joining the Indian Army* (Delhi, GSI, 1942), p. 25, IOR, L/MIL/17/5/2225.
72 Ibid, p. 30.
73 See Barua, *Army Officer Corps*, p. 50. See also B. P. N. Sinha & Sunil Chandra, *Valour and Wisdom: Genesis and Growth of the Indian Military Academy* (New Delhi: Oxford & IBH Publishing Co., 1992), p. 155.
74 Sinha & Chandra, *Valour and Wisdom*, quoted on p. 159.
75 Captain E. L. G. Stones, 'Indian Reminiscences of Professor E. L. G. Stones, as a cadet and then an officer in the Royal Corps of Signals (1941-45)' (Unpublished Memoir), p. 15, IWM, 85/52/1.

between regular Indian Army officers and ECOs, Captain Stones noted: 'Generally speaking the staff at Belgaum had come to India in peacetime, of their own accord; most of us were there only because of Hitler, and did not want to stay any longer than we had to'.[76] Colonel Pettigrew said of his time as a company commander and instructor at Belgaum:

> I was one of four company commanders and a good ten years younger than the others. Each of us had a hundred officer cadets at a time, with sixteen weeks in which to turn them into officers fit to join an Indian cavalry regiment or infantry battalion. To help us we had a good British company sergeant major and four experienced British sergeants. All the weapon training, physical training, map reading and Urdu instruction were centralised under specialist staff. So my particular responsibilities were, drill and discipline, individual field skills, section and platoon training, and all the general administration and military education of my 'boys'.[77]

In late 1941, the instruction was based on a mixture of War Office and GHQ India pamphlets namely: *Infantry Section Leading*, *Infantry Training*; *Frontier Warfare India*; and *Field Service Regulations* Vol. II.[78] The syllabus developed with time and by 1943 the fundamentals of jungle warfare were being taught at the OTS and the IMA, with lectures being continually updated.[79] The routine was much remembered by the ECO cadets as being in contrast to austerity measures in the UK. For example, at OTS Bangalore, the day began at 6am with *Chota Hazri* (Little breakfast of tea and biscuit), then parade and two hours exercise such as an assault course. This was followed by breakfast with a morning of instruction on organisation and administration, Urdu lessons, weapon training, drill or map reading. After lunch more training, with compulsory sport after tea time, followed by dinner in the Mess. There was a demonstration platoon from an Indian regiment, such as one of the Gurkha Regiments and the course finished with a day and night exercise.[80]

Lengths of OTS courses varied according to arm of service. For example, infantry underwent four months instruction. Those joining the Royal Indian Artillery

---

76 Stones, 'Indian Reminiscences', p. 19, IWM, 85/51/1.
77 Pettigrew, "It seemed very ordinary", p. 115, IWM, 84/29/1.
78 See Officers' Training School, Mhow, Instructions to Cadets for Outdoor Work in the Papers of Captain V. P. Sams, IWM, 05/2/1.
79 See Indian Military Academy Precis Book, Papers of Lieutenant J. R. Cottle, IWM, 67/289/1.
80 See Notes for the Benefit of Volunteers arriving in India from overseas for appointment as officers in his Majesty's Land Forces after training as cadets in an officers' training school, p. 7, IOR, L/MIL/2287. See also Robin Sharp, *The Life of an E.C.O. in India* (Durham: Pentland Press, 1994), pp. 11, 14, Gerald Elliot, *A Memoir of India* (self-published, 2014), pp. 10-13 and Capt. J. E. King, 'Memoirs of a "Reluctant" Infantry Officer' (Unpublished Memoir), p. 9, IWM, 85/6/1.

attended the School of Artillery (India) and Cadet Wing at Deolali for a further month. Engineers underwent six months training.[81] Officers for the Royal Indian Army Service Corps spent three months at the OTS followed by three months at the RIASC School at Kakul. Prior to the war, officers would spend a few years in infantry regiments before transferring to the RIASC, but during the war officers were commissioned directly into the Corps.[82]

The training and assimilation of recently commissioned officers, as in the pre-1939 Indian Army, continued once they joined their units under the tutelage of their fellow officers and VCOs. As the war continued, the OTS adapted to the changing circumstances with those officer cadets with no previous military experience undergoing pre-commission training of a month, before undertaking the normal period of training depending on which arm of service they intended to join. Those cadets aged between 35 and 44 were able to undertake two months training at OTS Bangalore in the organisation and administration of the Indian Army and military law, in order that they could become administrative and staff officers.[83]

The OTS and the officer corps adapted quickly and produced a large number of trained officers. Although the British officers were not as proficient in Urdu or the language of their unit as previously in the Indian Army due to the shorter training time.[84] By September 1941, 5,000 officers had been trained in the four OTS establishments. Mhow and Bangalore OTS increased their capacity by 25% in 1942 with over 2,600 officers passing out per annum.[85]

Training Battalions

The training battalions introduced for infantry regiments in the 1921-22 reforms were essential in wartime and like the organisation for officer training they also adapted during the Second World War. This was realised by General Auchinleck who was appointed the new C-in-C India in January 1941. He provided a new stimulus to the transformation of the Indian Army. He was empathetic to the Indian soldiers and officers, ultimately improving pay and conditions and removing prejudice within the army, resulting in greater cohesion of the army particularly amongst British and

---

81 See Notes for the information of British other ranks proceeding to India for training at an Officers' Training School, issued March 1943, p. 9, IOR, L/MIL/17/5/2288. See also *Fauji Akhbar* Vol. XX, No. 7, 14 February 1942, p. 19.
82 See Notes for the Benefit of Volunteers arriving in India from overseas for appointment as officers in his Majesty's Land Forces after training as cadets in an officers' training school, p. 7, IOR, L/MIL/2287. See also Brigadier V. J. Moharir, *History of the Army Service Corps (1939-1945)* (New Delhi: Sterling Publishers, 1979), p. 137.
83 See *Fauji Akhbar*, Vol. XX, No. 30, 25 July 1942, p. 12.
84 See Barkawi, *Soldiers of Empire*, pp. 52-59.
85 See 'Expansion of Army Training Schools', *Fauji Akhbar*, Vol. XX, No. 7, 14 February 1942, p. 19.

Indian officers.[86] Major General Henry 'Taffy' Davies served as Brigade Major under Auchinleck in the 1930s. He wrote in his memoir, 'Small Green Men':

> My commander was Brigadier Auchinleck, now generally known to everyone as the 'Auk'. The time that I spent as staff officer to this great man was one of the happiest and most interesting periods of my life. I learned a great deal from him about soldiering, particularly as, during my time with the Peshawar Brigade, the Mohmand campaign of 1933 took place. I do not recollect ever meeting a commander who was so highly regarded by both his officers and men as the 'Auk'. They trusted his judgement implicitly, they loved and admired him as a commander and they were all fully aware that his first consideration was invariably for the safety and well-being of his men. Maneouvres and exercises carried out by the Peshawar Brigade were realistic and constructive to a degree. They were also tough. During these exercises the troops were expected to put up with all the hardships and fatigue that is synonymous with active service. But there was no grousing. The men appreciated that this was real worthwhile training and they delighted in having their metal proved. I have always found this about training. The tougher it is the more the men like it, provided always that they know what it is all about and what they are doing. The one thing that kills in training is boredom and that applies to everyone from the humble private soldier to the Major-General.[87]

Auchinleck also learnt from his experience serving with the British Army from 1939 until 1940. Under his auspices, the first of many pamphlets on leadership and man management were produced for officers in India, entitled *The Handling of Men*. It was a copy of an address by Brigadier A. de L. Cazenove, who had served under his command in Britain. As Auchinleck commented in the foreword: 'The remarks represent so closely my own ideas on the subject that I have had them printed as I feel that they may be of great help to you when you begin your career as an officer'.[88] The pamphlet promoted competence of the role, integrity, leading by example, fairness, looking after the needs of those under one's command and the importance of drill, concluding:

> Smartness produces self-respect in a man, and individual self-respect soon develops into Unit pride. Unit pride produces efficiency, and efficiency, in its turn, produces happiness amongst men. Men are much happier in a strict and

---

86 See Voigt, *India in the Second World War*, pp. 65-66. See also Marston, *Phoenix from the Ashes*, pp. 219-226.
87 Major General H. L. Davies, '"Small Green Men": An Autobiography' (Unpublished Memoir), p. 84, IWM, 08/120/1.
88 *The Handling of Men* (New Delhi, General Staff, India, 1941), foreword, IWM.

well-run unit, in spite of the extra work involved, than they are in one which is slovenly and incompetently run. Smartness, efficiency and happiness go hand in hand.[89]

Auchinleck noted that the training of infantry was the most difficult of all training as the other combatant arms were only really required to achieve higher technical skill, with tactical application being the smaller part of the necessary training. Whereas infantry training needed the technical skill in a number of weapons, the larger part of training was in the tactical application of the weapons by day, night, in differing terrain and both up close and distant from the enemy. Thus trained infantrymen and officers needed to be the most highly skilled of all arms.[90]

As mentioned, training was undertaken within the infantry regiments by the 10th (Training) Battalion of each regiment but the pressure on the training battalions increased dramatically with the onset of the war. The organisation was flexible enough to increase the number of recruits through the battalion and decrease the length of the courses. Before the war about 400 recruits were trained in the 10th (Training) Battalion of the 2nd Punjab Regiment. This more than doubled in size in 1940 with 987 recruits leaving the battalion and further increased to 2,467 in 1941.[91] In the Gurkha regiments, recruits were trained independently by their own parent battalions. In the 2nd King Edward's Own Gurkha Rifles, the Regimental Centre was set up in 1940 from combining the two Training Companies of the 1st and 2nd Battalions and had increased to 3,000 recruits within three months.[92] Initially, often officers without battle experience were instructors. For example, Lieutenant Donald Lear was commissioned from the OTS at Bangalore and was made adjutant for the Regimental Training Depot for the 16th Punjab Regiment at Sialkot. He was only twenty years old and was mainly told what to do by his jemadar, who was about ten years his senior and had experienced battle. The routine consisted of early morning physical training, breakfast and office work until lunchtime, when the officers slept in the afternoon due to the heat and with the evening spent on the range.[93]

---

89   Ibid., pp. 1-3.
90   See 'The Training of Infantry' by General C. Auchinleck, 19 March 1942, *Lockhart Mss.*, NAM, 8310-154-25.
91   See Lieutenant-Colonel Sir Geoffrey Betham and Major H. V. R. Geary, *The Golden Galley: The Story of the Second Punjab Regiment 1761-1947* (Oxford: 2nd Punjab Regiment Officers' Association, 1956), p. 301.
92   See Colonel D. R. Wood, 'The Indian Army Officer Corps and the training of the Indian Army 1939-47', 2 April 2011, given to the author, p. 5.
93   See Lieutenant Colonel Donald Jeffrey Lear, IWM SA 23225, reel 2. See also Captain Peter Kendall, 'The War Years 1939-1945', pp. 27-28, IWM, 02/32/1. He spent four months in 1940 at the training battalion 10th/17th Dogra Regiment at Jullunder.

Corps centres were also set up, such as the Indian Army Veterinary Corps Centre, which was formed on 1 December 1942 at Ambala and trained 11,256 all ranks by the end of 1943. Training consisted of ten weeks basic training followed by six weeks technical training.[94] The situation was not quite so organised in all the Corps. The RIASC was responsible to two directorates for training. The Military Training Directorate directed general military training, whilst technical training came under the Director of Supplies and Transport. Prior to the war, the RIASC had a similar set up to the infantry with training units within the corps: a training wing for the Supply Personnel Depot; the Animal Transport (AT) training companies; the Motor Transport (MT) training battalion; and the RIASC School where officers and NCOs were trained. All RIASC units were required to submit training reports and commanding officers kept training diaries, with all units following the doctrine laid down in *Royal Indian Army Service Corps Training. Volume 1. Training and War* published in 1938.[95] However the situation had deteriorated by the start of the war. As the RIASC historian has commented: training 'was a question of *ad hoc* development as the demands increased. The basic cause of the haphazard approach was that control and direction in the matter of training were somewhat vague and too decentralised'.[96] In practice, training was initially set by RIASC officers taken from limited resources, as units were sent to Egypt and Force K-6 to France in 1939 and 1940 respectively, leaving few officers to either raise new units or provide instructors for the training schools. Although, instruction in the training battalions did slowly develop with a syllabus being produced.[97]

Infantry recruit training developed from the beginning of the war until 1941, when *MTP* No. 19 (India), *Notes on the training of the infantry recruit* was produced based on experimentation in training. The training manual not only gathered together all the developments into one volume but also acted as a basis for further study and future development. As the pamphlet stated, the 'aim is simply to crystallize thought at one point in a growing system of training'. It was noted that there would need to be improvements and the General Staff were open to suggestions, even welcoming constructive criticism.[98] The importance of fieldcraft was noted and it advocated the eradication of 'parrot-mindedness', stating certain drill could be discontinued. Indeed the training manual commented:

---

94 See Alan Harfield, 'The IAVC Centre, Ambala during World War II', *Durbar: Journal of the Indian Military Historical Society*, Vol. 12, No. 2, Summer 1995, pp. 46-51.

95 See *Royal Indian Army Service Corps Training. Volume 1. Training and War* (1938), pp. xv, 1-21, IOR, L/MIL/17/5/2187.

96 Brigadier V. J. Moharir, *History of the Army Service Corps (1939-1945)* (New Delhi: Sterling Publishers, 1979), p. 121.

97 See for example No. 6, M.T. Training Battalion, RIASC. Advanced Training Recruits Course: Lectures and Instructions, private collection.

98 *MTP* No. 19 (India). *Notes on the training of the infantry recruit, 1941*, p. 1, IOR, L/MIL/17/5/2261.

The object of recruit drill is to instill discipline, orderliness and self-respect. Some barrack-square drill is essential, but the hours at present allotted must be reduced. Fieldcraft, provided imagination is used in its teaching, can largely replace drill in achieving the object.[99]

Educational training was prioritised as well as weapon training based on the Small Arms Training Pamphlets and *MTP* No. 33 produced by the War Office. The training manual impressed upon the need for signal training, training in morse, driving and maintenance, organised team games and that the 'recruit should be training tactically from the start'.[100] Similar to Tuker's ideas of the education of his Gurkha battalion during the 1930s, education and the training of soldiers in pairs were most prominent in 1941.[101] Tuker as DMT was instrumental in developing his ideas from his military service and training a Gurkha battalion in the 1930s to training the Indian Army in the first couple of years of the war. Training manuals, schools and training battalions all adapted for fighting in the Middle East and Mediterranean theatre of war.

Education

Education was generally promoted for Indian troops by pamphlets issued on educational training and instruction methods that stated that educational training remained an integral part of military training. The officers of the Army Education Corps were to advise along with warrant officers and sergeants in teaching English to VCOs and other ranks, as well as British troops. For the Indian Army, soldiers were aiming to achieve the first class English certificate and the special certificate of education in all subjects including geography, Indian history, Roman Urdu, English, maths, map-reading, hygiene and sanitation and citizenship. A supernumerary list of VCOs, once they had passed the senior course at the Army School of Education aided by the AEC officers, helped with candidates for the special certificate examination and 1st and 2nd Class English certificate exams. The standard of the 1st class exam was advanced and determined that the candidate could enter for the Special Certificate of Education and for the IMA. The 2nd class exam required a knowledge of reading and writing and 3rd class featured an oral review with the candidate required to ask and answer questions.[102] The first subject to be taught to new recruits was the importance of conduct, regimental identity and history. As *Educational Training 1939* stated: 'The primary objects of teaching regimental history are to develop *Esprit de Corps* and to help the soldier to understand the duties which the

---

99   *MTP* No. 19, p. 5.
100 *MTP* No, 19, p. 11. See also pp. 5-7 13-36.
101 See *MTP* No. 19, pp. 4-5. See also chapter 1.
102 See *Educational Training, Indian Army 1939*, (1940), pp. 1-2, 4, 6-9, IOR, L/MIL/17/5/2272. See also Wayper, *Mars and Minerva*, pp. 108-109.

Indian Army is called upon to perform'.[103] In *Notes on Instructional Methods: For Use in the Indian Army with special reference to Educational Training 1940*, the manual advocated the importance of reading and encouraged self-directed learning, with sections on teaching, giving lectures, methods of teaching Roman Urdu, reading and writing, as well as advice on particular subjects such as geography, citizenship, mathematics and map reading. For example, the main drive in citizenship was to prepare the soldier for the return to civilian life and as the majority of soldiers were farmers or landowners, most of the lectures were on rural reconstruction and the work of co-operative societies.[104] However due to the rapid expansion of the army at the beginning of the war the syllabi for the recruits' test, and the 2nd and 3rd class certificates of education, were simplified and only the essential subjects such as Maths, Urdu and map reading were retained.

Junior NCO Courses in 1941 were almost entirely run by VCOs and included drill, weapon training and field craft were taught as well as physical training, anti-gas, organisation, administrative, discipline and quartermaster duties, with educational lectures.[105] Even the military schools for children expanded in August 1941, the King George's Royal Indian Military School at Jullundur taking an extra one hundred students. The three military schools at Jhelum, Jullundur and Ajmer had been founded to educate the sons of serving and retired Indian officers, NCOs and men. They were organised along the lines of the British Public School system with houses named after Kitchener, Rawlinson and Wavell, with sport very much to the fore. They prepared students for the army as candidates for early promotion as NCOs and VCOs, but also provided opportunity of joining one of the OTS.[106] A Pre-Officer Cadet School was also establsihed for the Indian State Forces at Indore in October 1941 in order to improve the education standards for eligibility to the OTS.[107] Education was essential with the increasing mechanisation of the army. Thus, the educational infrastructure was developed from the beginning of the war, building upon the existing arrangement.

---

103 Ibid., p. 6.
104 See *Notes on Instructional Methods: For use in the Indian Army with special reference to Educational Training*, September 1940, pp. 18, 28, Gurkha Museum.
105 See Junior NCOs' Course, 1941, private collection.
106 See *Fauji Akhbar*, Vol. XX, No. 7, 14 February 1942, pp. 24-26.
107 See Calder, 'From Sloth Belt to Springboard', p. 25, NAM, 8209-14. See also Richard Head and Tony McClenaghan, *The Maharaja's Paltans: A History of the Indian State Forces (1888-1948)* (New Delhi, Manohar, 2013), pp. 29-31. The training organisation within the Indian Army was mirrored in the State Forces, who not only set up an officers' cadet school, there was also a wing in the Indian Army Armoured Car School at Ferozepore, a training battery at the Mountain Artillery Training Centre at Ambala, a wing with the Royal Indian Artillery at Chhindwara, a training unit within 39th (Training) Division, a training battalion for Sappers and Miners and the West India Circle Training School for elementary training for pre-Indian Army schools.

Southern Command

During the first two years of the Second World War, the number of the main training establishments differed little to that before the war.[108] Although new schools were being established, the Tactical School was formed in 1941. This expanded later in the year to include a Junior Wing that took 160 students, who trained potential company commanders for six weeks. A special wing was formed to run two week courses for brigadiers, commanding officers, staff officers and instructors of other schools.

Tuker and GHQ India decided to concentrate all the training schools in Southern Command that contained the districts of Deccan, Bombay and Madras and the Jubbulpore (Independent) Area.[109] As a large numbers of schools and training establishments were already based in Southern Command.[110] Some schools were vacated to enable formation of other schools, such as the Small Arms School formed at Saugor in the accommodation vacated by the Education School. In order to allow the Mahratta Light Infantry Regimental Centre to expand, the Chemical Warfare School and the Army School of Education were moved to the accommodation vacated by the School of Weapon Training and Mechanisation at Pachmarhi. Other new schools that were established in the first two years of the war included the Engineers OTS in May 1940, formed alongside the Madras Sappers and Miners Depot at Bangalore, the Junior Commanders School at Deccan College in Poona that became the Tactical School in April 1941 and the School of Artillery at Deolali and the Signals Training Centre at Mhow which were opened in September 1940. The numbers attending these schools increased dramatically during this period. For instance, at the IAOC Centre in Jubbulpore, a pre-war attendance of 700 recruits had increased to 4,000 by January 1941. Military labour, as in all wars, was increasingly needed as the Second World War progressed. In August 1940, the Labour Corps was formed with the

---

108 See *Regulations for the Army in India. Instructions by His Excellency the Commander-in-Chief* (New Delhi: Government of India Press, 1942), pp. 82-85, IWM. The School of Artillery (India) was located at Kakul, the Equitation School at Saugor, the Army Signal School at Poona, the Small Arms School (India) at Pachmarhi, the Army School of Physical Training at Amabala and Kasauli, the Royal Tank Corps School (India) at Ahmednagar, the Army School of Education (India) at Belgaum, the Army School of Cookery at Poona, two Army Veterinary Schools at Ambala and Poona, the RIASC School and MT Training Battalion at Chaklala, the RIASC Bakery School at Quetta, the IAOC Training Centre at Jubbulpore as well as the IMA and the three OTS.
109 See DMT's Address, 23 September 1941, p. 9, *Tuker Mss.*, IWM, 71/21/2/5.
110 For example the headquarters and depots of both the QVO Madras Sappers and Miners at Bangalore and the Royal Bombay Sappers and Miners at Kirkee, the Signal Training Centre at Jubbulpore, the Regimental Centre of the Bombay Grenadiers at Nasirabad, the Regimental Centre of the Mahratta Light Infantry, IAOC School at Jubbulpore, Army Veterinary School at Poona, Senior Officers' School, Chemical Warfare School and Army School of Education all at Belgaum, the Army Signal School, Army School of Cookery at Poona and the Equitation School at Saugor.

headquarters and depot at Auranggabad. It was later renamed the Auxiliary Pioneer Corps and subsequently the Indian Pioneer Corps, finally proving the largest corps in the Indian Army.

Combined operations training was commenced in Southern Command from rather humble origins, by a band of staff officers who were amateur yachtsman. Training began at Karakvasla, where due to training grants, mock-ups, scrambling nets and boats were purchased. In June 1941, the first combined operations exercise was undertaken at Dhond by 19th Indian Infantry Brigade, 8th Indian Division before rejoining its parent division in Iraq. However, little combined operations doctrine actually originated in India and tended to be based on War Office pamphlets on combined operations reprinted in India.[111]

One training innovation introduced in Southern Command during this early period of the war was an umpires' course held at Secunderabad, under the auspices of 19th Indian Division. It was thought that the standard of umpiring and directing exercises had decreased due to the large numbers of new officers in the Indian Army. The course was run by No. 2 Training Team and attended by officers of 17th and 19th Indian Divisions. It was held again by 19th Indian Division and by HQ Southern Army in August 1942. The standards of umpiring were raised by the courses that essentially made the exercises more realistic.

Training areas such as No. 1 Training Area between Poona and Dhond were set aside for desert warfare formation training, although it was only actually used by 17th Indian Division from October 1941 for two months before their departure to Burma and Malaya. Returning officers from North Africa taught desert warfare to the brigades of the newly formed divisions, who were also trained by two training teams consisting of two or three GHQ officers, first loaned to Southern Command in April 1941. No 1 Training Team was based at Poona and No. 2 at Secunderabad. The teams set TEWTS, war games and model exercises during the early training of formations and prepared exercises for brigade and higher training.[112] According to Lieutenant Colonel Calder, the teams were made up of experts: 'They were experts in modern battle technique and tactical methods and were very useful to the divisional commanders whose staffs they freed from a great deal of work in connection with higher forms of training'.[113] The training teams continued to be used throughout the war, as the evacuated Argyll and Sutherland officers from Malaya joined the teams in 1942, to teach jungle warfare to units and formations throughout India.

---

111 See for example *Combined Operations: Memorandum on Opposed Landings for Unit Commanders [Provisional] 1940* (London: War Office, 1940) reprinted in India by the Manager of Publications, Delhi in 1940, IWM.
112 For the above sections see Calder, 'From Sloth Belt to Springboard', pp. 10-20, 25-33, NAM 8209-14.
113 Ibid., p. 26.

Conclusion

Southern Command was at the heart of training for the Indian Army until the establishment of Central Command in April 1942. The new command led by Lieutenant General Henry 'Ulysses' Willcox, relieved the Army Commanders in the front line of training and internal security duties. The reorganisation of South Command to form Southern Army took three months, commanded by Lieutenant General Sir Noel Beresford-Peirse, with Central Command taking over many of the training and administrative establishments.[114] Willcox was reported in *Fauji Akhbar* as: 'Describing the functions of his command, he said that the Central Command was primarily a training command. Practically all the recruit training in India to-day was carried out there'.[115] This included artillery training and training of the Corps of Indian Electrical and Mechanical Engineers, Royal Indian Army Service Corps, Indian Army Ordnance Corps, the medical services and the Army Remount Depot, all of which needed large numbers of highly skilled technicians, as well as eventually including the Women's Auxiliary Corps (India) (WAC(I)) and the training divisions.[116]

Similarly, in Northern Command, comprising 1st Armoured Division and 7th Indian Division, the impetus for training changed between the issue of the first and second training instructions of April and July 1940. Training for 'extensive warfare' was the new priority with Training Instruction No. 2 stating: ' "Intensive" warfare in Europe is for the present at an end, whereas new theatres of operations in which "extensive" warfare predominates, have sprung into being. It is these theatres in which the Army in India is likely to be employed'.[117] Nevertheless, training for the NWF continued based upon the doctrine of *Frontier Warfare – India (Army and Royal Air Force)* and *MTP* No. 6 (India), *The Support of Land Forces by Aircraft in Tribal Warfare on the Western Frontier of India*.[118] There was a severe shortage of equipment and weapons, but one way of compensating for this deficiency was thorough training for night operations.[119] The 7th Indian Divisional history remarked that, by November, 'training was in full swing, or as near to full swing as it is possible to be when a large proportion of one's equipment is imaginary or dummy'.[120] Training at this period continued along the lines of the pre-war *AHQ Training Memorandum* series. The

---

114 See Field Marshal Viscount Wavell, 'Operations in Eastern Theatre based on India, from March 1942 to December 31, 1942', *Supplement to the London Gazette*, 17 September 1946, p. 4668.
115 'Central Command – Primarily a Training Command', *Fauji Akhbar*, Vol. XXII, No. 45, 7 November 1944, p. 10.
116 Ibid. pp. 10, 20.
117 Northern Command Training Instruction No. 2, Training Year 1, 1 April 1940 – 30 April 1941, 17 July 1940, p. 1, Corbett Mss., CAC, CORB 3-6.
118 See ibid., p. 3.
119 See ibid., p. 7.
120 Brigadier M. R. Roberts, *Golden Arrow: The Story of the 7th Indian Division* (Aldershot: Gale & Polden, 1952), p. 2.

shortage of officers was a major problem therefore every officer, warrant officer and NCO was instructed to train an understudy at the same time. It was also noted that Gurkha battalions needed to make more use of their Gurkha officers as their efficiency had been witnessed in both times of peace and war. Training Instruction No. 2 was issued to the formations under command, but also copies were sent to the DMT. Thus co-ordination amongst formations across India was beginning to be put into effect.[121]

During the first couple of years of the Second World War, after an initial period of inactivity due to the delay in expansion, the Indian Army developed the existing pre-war training structure under the direction of Tuker and the Military Training Directorate. Primarily in Southern Command, but also across India, new schools were established, training pamphlets were produced and the rapidly expanded units and formations underwent training. This training organisation within India disseminated the doctrine for Frontier, aid to civil power and open warfare, as well as producing early training pamphlets on jungle and mountain warfare. The Directorate was therefore becoming paramount to India's war effort in the first years of the war.

---

121 See Northern Command Training Instruction No. 2, pp. 7, 12, *Corbett Mss.*, CAC, CORB 3-6.

3

Mechanisation and Desert Warfare

This chapter will discuss training for mechanisation and the problems that were encountered due to the lack of equipment, culminating in the fact that only one Indian armoured division was raised during the war.[1] Secondly, it will examine open warfare in the desert for the infantry fighting in North Africa and how essential training was in this theatre.

At the beginning of the Second World War, Indian Army infantry divisions usually consisted of three brigades: one battalion in each brigade would usually be British and the other two, Indian or Gurkha. As Major General Henry 'Taffy' Davies, who later commanded 25th Indian Division, commented in his memoir:

> The Division, as all soldiers know, is the basic fighting formation in practically every army in the world. It is large and powerful enough with its establishment of about 17,000 men, to effect a decisive influence in any military operation, irrespective of the scale of the campaign. At the same time, it is sufficiently compact to enable its commander to exercise a personal leadership and control and to permit its functioning as a well co-ordinated team. In the British Army, during two world wars, the Divisional spirit has been something which has been fostered and nourished as an important matter of principle.[2]

The artillery units in the division were usually all British, with the exception of the Indian Mountain Batteries. The sappers were Indian, as were the signals and other administrative services, with British NCOs in technical appointments. Indian Army formations shared a similar organisation to the British Army and therefore

---

1   Although 2nd Indian Armoured Division was formed in 1941 and later amalgamated with elements of 43rd Armoured Division in 1943 to form 44th Indian Armoured Division. All three of these formations were short-lived. Armour was represented in the Indian Army at brigade level during the war – see Kempton, *Loyalty & Honour: Part II Brigades*, pp. 1-8.
2   Davies, 'Small Green Men', p. 126, IWM, 66/82/1.

regular units were able to fight alongside British Army units with little disruption. At the beginning of the war, Middle East Command requested three infantry divisions and one armoured division from GHQ India. In the expansion programme one armoured division was to be formed in 1940 and a further two the following year. They were to comprise two light armoured regiments, one field regiment, one anti-aircraft regiment, one anti-tank regiment, two field squadrons and two motorised battalions. Expansion was limiting across the entire army and particularly in the Indian Armoured Corps due to the poor supply of equipment, provision of workshops and the lack of sufficient officers.[3]

Mechanisation

Training in mechanisation was already under way before the war. As Major General Davies commented:

> There had long been controversy over the possibility or otherwise of mechanising the Indian Army. Many diehards considered that the peasant classes from which the Indian Army was recruited and which had been on a bullock cart basis throughout history, would not prove sufficiently machine-minded to warrant mechanisation. The idea of a Rajput or Mahratta cultivator being put in charge of a modern tank appalled them. These diehards were, of course quite wrong and the Indian soldier took to mechanisation like a duck to water. Nevertheless, the earlier stages of their training with motor vehicles certainly had its moments.[4]

The Armoured Fighting Vehicles School was established at Ahmednagar in 1938, replacing the Machine Gun School. There was a British and an Indian Wing established to train officers, VCOs and NCOs to drive, maintain and gun fighting vehicles. The first two regiments to mechanise were the Scinde Horse (14th Prince Of Wales's Own Cavalry) and the 13th Duke of Connaught's Own Bombay Lancers. The regiments sent two officers, four VCOs and eight NCOs each to the Driving and Maintenance Wing and one officer, one VCO and seven NCOs to the Armament Wing of the AFV School to be trained as instructors. In October 1938, Lieutenant Barrow, a squadron commander in Scinde Horse, commented: 'I first had to go on a three months Driving & Maintenance Course, and from then on it was all out training to make the Squadron fit for active service in the autumn'.[5] In August 1939, the regiment moved to Peshawar for technical and tactical training with the Royal Tank Corps. The final training period was deployment to Waziristan where Lieutenant Barrow commanded the first Indian tank squadron on active service. The

3 See Expansion 1941, meeting held 17 July 1940, *Corbett Mss.*, CAC, CORB 3-6.
4 Davies, 'Small Green Men', p. 90.
5 *Barrow Mss.*, IWM.

unit remained in Waziristan for the next two years mainly supporting infantry operations.[6] It also sent 48 drivers from the Scinde Horse to the 48th Motor Transport Training Battalion, RIASC. Thus by April 1939 the regiment had 294 personnel trained in driving and maintenance and 208 in gunnery.[7] In the same year, the training regiments responsible for recruit training were converted into the 1st and 2nd Indian Cavalry Training Centres, at Ferozepore and Lucknow respectively.[8] The School of Weapon Training and Mechanisation at Pachmarhi was split in December 1939 into the Fighting Vehicles School and the Small Arms School. The AFV School trained tank and armoured car crews and also taught driver mechanics of all arms in Ahmednagar. Thus GHQ India did concentrate on training for mechanised warfare from the start of the war, but the lack of equipment hampered success as there were only 216 light tanks in India in 1940.[9] However mock-ups were made to represent tanks which 'have been made for 30-cwt. Lorries and 15-cwt. Trucks, at a cost of only Rs. 25 per vehicle'.[10] The designations of the two Cavalry Training Centres were changed to 1st and 2nd Indian Armoured Corps Training Centres (IACTC) in August 1940. The Indian Armoured Corps was formed on 1 May 1941 with new regiments 42nd to 48th Cavalry raised. A third Indian Armoured Corps Training Centre was established at Lucknow and was shortly afterwards relocated to Babina. The training centres became responsible for all training of recruits.

In January 1940, Corbett was appointed Brigadier Cavalry to oversee mechanisation within the Indian Army cavalry regiments, with a remit for training the arm in full co-operation with the Military Training Directorate.[11] He embarked on a training programme across the cavalry, although individual training was also organised within the regiments such as in the Central India Horse and Skinner's Horse, once a cadre of officers, VCOs and NCOs had been sent to the AFV School.[12] The pre-war professionalism of officers such as Corbett, who brought his experience from training a cavalry regiment in the interwar period and teaching at Quetta, meant that he was in a great position to direct training for mechanisation. This he could do centrally from within the Military Training Directorate rather than leaving it to the regiments to adapt by themselves. From the beginning he was asked his opinion on the first training instruction produced by the 6th Duke of Connaught's Own Lancers

6   See ibid.
7   See Major General Gurcharn Singh Sandu, *The Indian Armour: History of the Indian Armoured Corps (1941-1971)* (New Delhi: Vision Books, 1987), p. 23.
8   See Sandu, *Indian Armour*, p. 25.
9   See Foucar, Modernisation and Mechanisation of the Armed Forces of India, 1939-1944, chapter II, p. 26, *Hutton Mss.*, LCHMA, 3/22.
10 *AITM* No. 5, p. 1, IOR, L/MIL/17/5/2240.
11 See Brigadier, Cavalry, confidential note, Cavalry representative at AHQ, 14 February 1940, *Corbett Mss.*, CAC, CORB 3-5.
12 See Wilson, 'Mechanisation and the Test of Battle: The Indian Cavalry, 1939-41', pp. 143-145 and Sandu, *Indian Armour*, p. 24.

in December 1939, as the commanding officer was keen to prepare for mechanisation.[13] The training instruction highlighted the need to adapt, with the likely changes being an increase of trained signallers, machine gunners and MT drivers, as well as noting the need for greater education within the regiment that now the majority of the regiment would be required to obtain the 2nd Class certificate as a minimum.[14] Corbett realised the problems that expansion of the Indian Cavalry Training Centre would engender such as the increase of accommodation, instructors and vehicles. He suggested the pooling of instructors and resources and the subsequent 'milking' of personnel from already mechanised units. Hence the six months needed to train, prepare and receive vehicles could be reduced by about a month. However, the training period for a new recruit was ten months, and even five months for reservists.[15]

As Brigadier Cavalry, Corbett tried to prevent cavalry officers from being appointed outside the arm during expansion of the army.[16] He composed a memo on the problems of a cavalry adviser at Army Headquarters, stating that the evolution and training of the cavalry could not progress under the present arrangements, indicating the need for co-ordination across the arm and at the Training Directorate. He suggested that a major general post be created for the Indian Armoured Corps, who was responsible for 'Co-ordination of training and training of higher formations, theoretically and practically in conjunction with the DMT and RAF'.[17] The post would also include supervision of the IACTC with support from a GSO1 and staff captain. In addition a GSO2 would be attached to the MT Directorate to help co-ordinate training, IACTC and other schools. Additionally, he produced a paper on cavalry training citing the importance of fieldcraft, night training and anti-gas training, taking his source material from War Office publications *MTP* No. 23 *Operations*, Part I, *General Principles, Fighting Troops and their Characteristics* and *Army Training Memoranda* No. 24.[18] He understood the importance of junior leadership stating that: 'Minor tactics play an increasingly important part in cavalry operations owing to the range and speed of movement and dispersion. Success depends largely on the initiative, tactical sense and cohesion of junior leaders'.[19] He suggested the use of tactical exercises and floor models for officers and NCOs, also stressing the importance of intercommunication, including wireless silence. Rather than learn the hard way, the primary focus for Light

13 See letter from CO 6th DCO Lancers to Corbett, 16 February 1940, *Corbett Mss.*, CAC, CORB 3-3.
14 See DCO Lancers Individual Training Instruction No. 1, December 1939, *Corbett Mss.*, CAC, CORB 3-3.
15 See Note from Brigadier, Cavalry, 22 May 1940, *Corbett Mss.*, CAC, CORB 3-4.
16 See Note from Brigadier, Cavalry, 22 April 1940, *Corbett Mss.*, CAC, CORB 3-4.
17 Note from Brigadier, Cavalry re. Cavalry Adviser at AHQ, 29 May 1940, *Corbett Mss.*, CAC, CORB 3-5.
18 See *MTP* No. 23 *Operations*, Part I, *General Principles, Fighting Troops and their Characteristics*, Septembr 1939, and *ATM* No. 24, September 1939, pp. 6-9, IWM.
19 Cavalry Training Summer 1940, p. 1, *Corbett Mss.*, CAC, CORB 3-3.

Tank Regiments, for example, was to learn from the experience of the British regiments which 'will save much waste of time in trial and error, also unnecessary wear and tear of equipment'.[20] Much was still in a process of evolution, such as the role and organisation of motor regiments, whereas armoured regiments could learn from frontier operations. Although, there was still a section for horsed cavalry and the need for it in enclosed country.[21] Corbett concluded that there should be a timetable for troop and squadron training, ending with night and two day exercises, as he commented: 'There has been as tendency in cavalry tactical training to leave situations half done'.[22]

From August 1940 all cavalry were to start mechanisation, with only a few vehicles each. The plan was to mechanise the 3rd Cavalry, 7th Light Cavalry, 8th King George V's Own Light Cavalry, 16th Light Cavalry, 17th Queen Victoria's Own Poona Horse and 19th King George V's Own Lancers, as well as raise another six or seven units and a new Indian Cavalry Training Centre at Muttra with up to six wings of 300 recruits. Reservists were called up with the formation of the 1st Armoured Division in September 1940, consisting of two light armoured regiments, two armoured brigades and two infantry battalions. Tactics were based on highly mobile forces with a wide circuit of action and the ability to fight mounted, as well as learn the lessons from the co-operation of the RAF and armoured forces in the European theatre.[23] A training directive was immediately produced for 1st Armoured Division to be read in conjunction with AHQ training notes, including *MTP* No. 5 (India) *Training for Extensive Warfare, 1940*. Nevertheless, it was only possible at this early stage to issue training instructions which anticipate likely scenarios, as the development of divisional organisation and equipment was at a very early stage. However, the division was to train for warfare in the Middle Eastern and North African theatres with the main roles of action against enemy mobile forces, delaying actions, fighting with mobile infantry formations and a counter offensive role. All commanding officers down to section level needed to be trained in WT. Machine gunners in motor regiments trained to fire from a moving vehicle, artillery officers through TEWTS and attachments needed to operate alongside the armoured division so co-operation could develop. Within the division, a training programme for trained units was drawn up with individual training and driving and maintenance, whereas half-trained and recently formed units also underwent WT and weapon training. All units underwent regimental tactical exercises for officers and junior leaders throughout the Summer of 1940, then training was increased to

20 Ibid., p. 3.
21 See ibid., pp. 3-5.
22 Ibid., p. 6.
23 See re. Expansion & Mechanization sent to all Commandants of Cavalry Regiments, 23 August 1940, *Corbett Mss.*, CAC, CORB 3-3.

regimental and brigade level with battle practice and live firing, as well as brigade and divisional TEWTS, and formation HQ training up until March 1941.[24]

On 1 September 1940, Corbett became the commanding officer of 1st Indian Armoured Division based at Sialkot. He immediately started organising training for the division through the issue of training instructions. These training instructions were used by the majority of formations of the Indian Army across all the different theatres during the war. They used the latest doctrine from GHQ India, in the form of the published *MTPs* and *AITMs*, and looked at the particular training and drill that the formation needed to undertake for its next operation or role as well as covering lessons learned from exercises and battle experience. In contrast, British Army formations were forbidden to issue training instructions.[25] Training Instruction No. 1 for 1st Indian Armoured Division suggested an hour every day for tactics that 'will enable COs to decentralize tactical training and yet control doctrine'.[26] The importance of understudies was reiterated.[27]

Training Instruction No. 3 was an appreciation of the tactical exercises undertaken during the Winter months of 1940-41. It emphasised the need for planning, use of initiative, flexibility of control, the use of independent armoured detachments and that the initial concentration of armoured formations for every operation, was of the utmost importance. Lessons were also learnt from the experience of the Battle of Sidi Barrani, stressing the 'Practical benefit of the all-important factor of psychology is achieved by the commander who deliberately establishes moral superiority over his enemy and gauges by progressive encounters the fighting qualities of the enemy….'.[28] The instruction promoted the significance of training in night operations, especially as the enemy was disinclined to undertake night operations. Lastly it demonstrated the importance of artillery, engineers, infantry as well as armour, fighting together.[29] This demonstrated that the training instructions issued in the armoured division used both exercises and battle experience in order to keep doctrine and training as current and up to date as possible.

Training Instruction No. 5 stated that the essential foundations for the efficiency of the formation during the war was teamwork, hence vehicle crews needed to be efficient in field craft, driving and maintenance and in weapon systems, as well as

---

24 See Training Direction No. 1 for 1st Armoured Division by Brigadier Cavalry, August 1940, *Corbett Mss.*, CAC, CORB 3-4.
25 See *ATM* No. 25, p. 16, IWM. For an explanation of the dissemination of doctrine in the British Army see Harrison Place, *Military Training in the British Army, 1940-1944*, chapter 2.
26 1st Armoured Division Training Instruction No. 2, 7 November 1940, p. 2, *Corbett Mss.*, CAC, CORB 3-15.
27 Ibid.
28 1st Armoured Division Training Instruction No. 3, 27 March 1941, p. 3, *Corbett Mss.*, CAC CORB 3-6.
29 See ibid., pp. 2, 4, 6.

proficient in communication, battle drill, map reading, anti-gas measures, crew drill, field works, observation, concealment and camouflage and finally, cooking and first aid. Officers and NCOs needed to have tactical soundness, be vigilant, know the principles of fire and movement, use initiative, make concise orders, lead battle drill, keep up morale, as well as fire control, having speed of decision and action, and co-ordination with other arms. The instruction included a summary of lessons learnt and mistakes issued at the end of an exercise disseminated to all subordinate commanders.[30] Traditionally the Indian Army officer put the welfare of his men before himself and this was recognised as 'The care of their men is a deep rooted tradition in British officers'.[31] Training progressed through theoretical means of tactical exercises with maps and models, formulating a doctrine for armoured warfare that would continue until the end of 1941, when new equipment would be available and the division could take the final leap to become a fully-fledged and trained armoured division, with later training instructions concentrating on weapons training.[32] Training instructions were issued to units within the formation, detailing the need for training to be based on the divisional training instructions and *AITMs* Nos. 3-13, *MTPs* (India) and War Office training pamphlets.[33] The experience of the division directly informed the training pamphlets produced by the Military Training Directorate at GHQ India, as Corbett was involved in drafting sections on tactical principles for armoured battle in *MTP* No. 1 (India) Part 4 *Armoured Battle, 1941*.[34]

In May 1941, the 1st Armoured Division became the 31st Armoured Division, in order to avoid confusion with British Armoured Divisions. It moved to Iraq in June 1942 but the issuing of training instructions had ceased when Corbett left the division in January 1942 to become CGS to Auchinleck as C-in-C Middle East. Although training continued in Iraq with the newly acquired Grant tanks, as Lieutenant General S. D. Verma noted in his memoir, 'by then the men were pretty confident of being able to handle their equipment'.[35] An Indian Armoured Corps Training and Reinforcement camp was also set up near Cairo in May 1941 and the wing of the Royal Armoured Corps School at Abbasia was designated the Middle East Indian

---

30 See 1st Armoured Division Training Instruction No. 5, 2 May 1941, pp. 1-2, 4, *Corbett Mss.*, CAC, CORB 3-15.
31 1st Armoured Division Training Instruction No. 6, 1 July 1941, pp. 2-3, *Corbett Mss.*, CAC CORB 3-15.
32 See 1st Armoured Division Training Instruction No. 7, 20 August 1941, p. 2, CORB 3-6 and 1st Armoured Division Training Instruction No. 9, 4 September 1941, *Corbett Mss.*, CAC, CORB 3-15.
33 See 1st Support Group Training Instruction No. 1, nd., *Corbett Mss.*, CAC, CORB 3-15.
34 See Draft copy of a Military Training Pamphlet on the handling of Armoured and Light Armoured Units in the Field (based on a draft of Military Training Pamphlet No. 1 (India), received from GHQ India), *Corbett Mss.*, CAC, CORB 3-17 and Military Training Pamphlet No. 1 (India). Armoured Units in the field. Part 4. Armoured Battle, 1941, IOR, L/MIL/17/5/2244.
35 Verma, *To Serve with Honour*, p. 40.

Armoured Corps Training Centre. Officers were trained at the RAC School, whereas VCOs and NCOs were instructed at the IAC Training Centre. The principal instruction centred around the equipment that was used in the Middle East.[36] Not all Indian divisions produced training instructions. For example, 10th Indian Division who served in Iraq under the command of Major General 'Bill' Slim did not produce any training instructions most likely due to the adhoc nature of the division coming together and the lack of time for training.[37] The division was instrumental in the capture of Basra and the battle for the British air base at Habbaniya, consisting of No. 4 Service Flying Training School, RAF.[38]

Tuker conducted a tour of the Middle East in 1941 as DMT and gained valuable insight as to how useful the training material produced by the directorate had proved. The Indian troops in this theatre were regarded as well-trained. However, during his tour he became convinced that: 'Training is the main thing that wins battles, for it is the only thing that makes soldiers out of common citizens. GHQ India as a whole has yet to realise this and that we will never reach a standard that is high enough for today'.[39] For instance, Tuker interviewed an officer of the 2nd Queen's Own Cameron Highlanders who remarked that standards fell whenever the training had lapsed or was unsuitable giving the example of Halfaya and Keren respectively.[40] *MTPs* (India) were seen to be most useful in the Middle East evidenced by the commandant of the Staff School at Haifa stating: '…he believed Indian Infantry to be the best soldiers in the Empire. He said he constantly reminded all his students to try and get hold of every GHQ India training memorandum and pamphlet they could lay hands on'.[41] *MTP's* Nos. 13 ad 14 proved very popular on *Navigation by the Stars* and *Infantry Section Leading* respectively and Tuker promised to distribute more training pamphlets.[42] Middle East Command asked for 5,000 copies of *MTP* No. 14 on section leading.[43] Thus, training pamphlets from GHQ India were undoubtedly in demand.

---

36 See Sandu, *Indian Armour*, pp. 31-34.
37 See 10th Indian Division, GS Branch, War Diary 1 April – 31 December 1941, TNA, WO 169/3326.
38 See Dharm Pal, *Campaign in Western Asia* (New Delhi: Pentagon Press, 2012), chapters 8 & 9. The most recent history is Robert Lyman, *First Victory: Britain's Forgotten Struggle in the Middle East, 1941* (London: Constable, 2006), chapter 3.
39 DMT's tour of the Middle East, Note C, *Tuker Mss.*, IWM, 71/21/2/6.
40 See DMT's tour of the Middle East Note C, p. 8, *Tuker Mss.*, IWM, 71/21/2/6.
41 DMT's tour of the Middle East, Note F, *Tuker Mss.* IWM, 71/21/2.
42 See *Military training pamphlet* No. 13 (India). *Navigation by the stars* (1941), IOR L/MIL/17/5/2255 and *Military training pamphlet* No. 14 (India). *Infantry section leading, 1941* (1941), IOR, L/MIL/17/5/2256.
43 DMT's tour of the Middle East, Note E, p. 1, *Tuker Mss.*, IWM 71/21/2/6.

North African Campaign

Three Indian Divisions fought in North Africa, with 4th Indian Division almost fighting throughout the campaign, firstly with Western Desert Force and then in 8th and 1st Armies.[44] The 18th Indian Infantry Brigade of 8th Indian Division was instrumental in the delaying action at Deir-el-Shein during the First Battle of El Alamein and 3rd Indian Motor Brigade also fought briefly in North Africa. In addition, Indian Army officers such as General Sir Claude Auchinleck, C-in-C Middle East, and his Chief of General Staff (CGS), the aforementioned Lieutenant General Tom Corbett held important posts in theatre. However, unlike Dominion formations in North Africa, the Indian Army had no right of appeal to GHQ India. At the beginning of the North African Campaign, all Commonwealth formations were responsible for their own training with little central direction.[45] In both Western Desert Force and 8th Army, with the exception of 4th Indian Division and 7th Armoured Division in 1940, most British and Commonwealth formations had little opportunity to train together due to the ever-changing composition of formations, the expansion of the British and Commonwealth armies, the transfer of experienced troops to other theatres of war and mounting casualties.[46]

Battle of Sidi Barrani

Two Brigades, 5th and 11th Indian Brigades of K-4 Force, soon to be 4th Indian Division, left India for Egypt in 1939. Indian troops quickly adapted to the conditions in North Africa and immediately began training for desert warfare. Training pamphlets were issued and weekly training programmes for all units were instigated. The 11th Infantry Brigade concentrated on collective training whereas 5th Brigade embarked on individual training. Collective training was from company up to brigade level and individual training involved all ranks, concentrating on such matters as weapon training and drill. Troops underwent TEWTS and lectures on armoured divisions, desert warfare and the Egyptian Army and in the Italian opponents were organised. Exercises in the desert were planned as early as October and November 1939.[47]

The 4th Indian Division, along with 7th Armoured Division, were designated Western Desert Force and commanded by General Richard O'Connor, under the

---

44 The other divisions were 5th Indian Division and 10th Indian Division.
45 See Niall Barr, *Pendulum of War: The Three Battles of El Alamein* (London: Jonathan Cape, 2004), p. 46.
46 See Tim Moreman, 'From the Desert Sands to the Burmese Jungle: The Indian Army and the lessons of North Africa, September 1939-November 1942' in Roy (ed.), *Indian Army in Two World Wars*, pp. 231-232.
47 See 4th Indian Division Training Conference, 11 October 1939, TNA, WO 169/602.

overall command of General Archibald Wavell, C-in-C Middle East.[48] Neither formation was at full strength, with 7th Armoured Division consisting of two regiments in its brigades, instead of the usual three. The 4th Indian Division comprised two infantry brigades rather than three and lacked much of its artillery. However, both divisions had trained in the desert. As Lieutenant General Sir Geoffrey Evans, Brigade Major in 11th Indian Infantry Brigade at the time, commented: 'We were sent out into the desert in July 1940. Before and since then our training for desert warfare had been hard and continuous. We were fit, we were tough and we were ready for battle'.[49] Niall Barr compares both formations to the British Expeditionary Force of 1914 'in terms of quality, training and expertise'.[50]

On 13-16 September 1940 the Italian forces of 10th Army advanced to Sidi Barrani, 60 miles inside Egypt, under the command of Marshal Rodolfo Graziani. They were dispersed into fortified camps that were incapable of supporting each other. The plan for Operation Compass proposed that 4th Indian Division would advance through the 15 mile gap between the camps at Solfafi and Nibeiwa and then attack the Italian camps at Nibeiwa, Tummar East and Tummar West from the rear, supported by 7th Armoured Division with artillery support. According to 4th Indian Division Operational Order No. 2, written by Colonel Thomas 'Pete' Rees, GSO1 with 4th Indian Division, 'The Art[iller]y will produce concentrations of smoke and HE (high explosive) to cover the approach of the Tanks, and will keep their fire on the targets as long as possible'.[51] As the British official historian has commented on the plan: 'In short, quantity was going to be challenged by quality'.[52] A replica of Nibeiwa was set up in the desert. Exercise No. 1 took place on 25-26 November led by 4th Indian Division commanding officer, Major General Sir Noel Beresford-Peirse. He used tactics laid out in the training pamphlet 'The Division in the Attack' based on First World War experience.[53] The training consisted of attacks on dummy camps with live artillery and machine gun fire being used.[54] According to the subsequent training material, *Middle East Training Pamphlet* No. 10:

48 As well as Matruh Garrison and 7th Royal Tank Regiment.
49 Lieutenant General Sir Geoffrey Evans, *The Desert and the Jungle* (London: Kimber, 1962), p. 11. See also Lieutenant Colonel G. R. Stevens, *Fourth Indian Division* (Toronto: McLaren, nd), pp. 7, 10, 13 and Major General G. L. Verney, *The Desert Rats: The History of the 7th Armoured Division 1938 to 1945* (London: Hutchinson, 1954), p. 27.
50 Barr, *Pendulum of War*, p. 46.
51 4th Indian Divisional Operational Order No. 2, Papers of Major General T. W. Rees, *Rees Mss.*, BL, Mss Eur F 274/13.
52 Major General I. S. O. Playfair, *The Mediterranean and Middle East: Vol. I: The Early Successes against Italy* (London: HMSO, 1954), p. 260.
53 See Jim Beach (editor), 'SS 135 The Division in the Attack – 1918', reprinted as a Strategic Combat Studies Institute Occasional Paper No. 53, (Shrivenham: Strategic and Combat Studies Institute, 2008).
54 See 4th Indian Division Instructions Nos. 1 & 2 for WDF Exercise No. 1, November 1940, TNA, WO 169/602.

Mechanisation and Desert Warfare 91

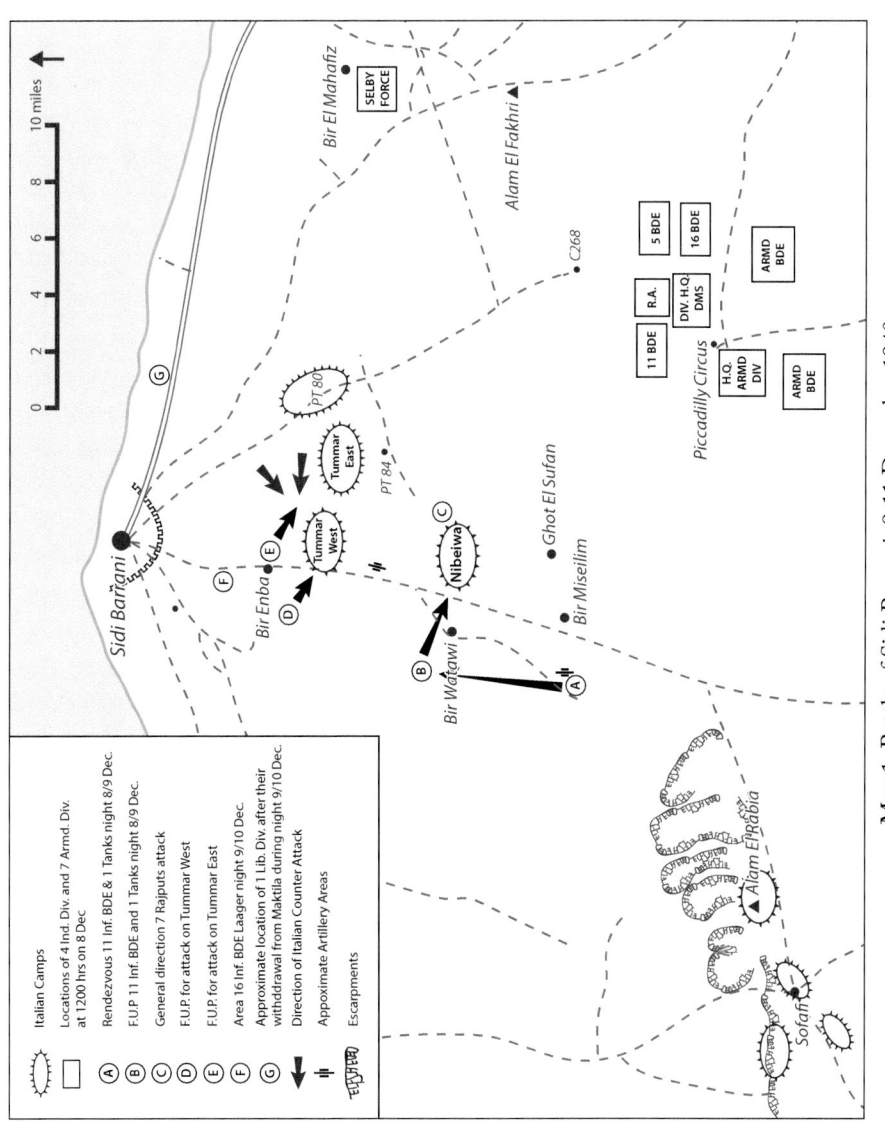

Map 1 Battle of Sidi Barrani, 9–11 December 1940.

> The exercise was of the greatest value. It showed clearly that alterations would have to be made in some tactical methods. As a result a training memorandum was issued, many of the methods advocated therein being adopted for the operations and later were proved to be sound.[55]

During training, the tanks advanced under artillery cover with the infantry twenty minutes behind. O'Connor and his commanding officers surmised the advance was too protracted and therefore added a diversionary attack by a battalion on the eastern face of Nibeiwa. Exercise No. 2 was the next planned training that, in fact, was the actual attack.[56]

On 9 December at 7am, the division crossed a hundred miles of desert undetected, 11th Indian Brigade led by Brigadier Reginald Savory, supported by 7th Royal Tank Regiment with 48 Matildas and 4th Indian Divisional Artillery with 72 guns, advanced in "desert formation" that Geoffrey Evans compared to 'a large fleet of small ships at sea'.[57] The formation slipped through the gap undetected and formed up around Nibeiwa. The diversionary attack on the eastern face was led by 4/7th Rajput Regiment and had begun at 5am. By 7am the primary attack on the camp included an artillery bombardment and tank advance on the Northwest entrance, followed by the 2nd Queen's Own Cameron Highlanders and the 6th Rajputana Rifles. The Italian anti-tank weapons were unable to penetrate the tanks but their artillery fought well. By 10.40 am 2,000 prisoners and 35 tanks had been taken for a loss of eight officers and 48 men.

Brigadier Wilfrid Lloyd, commanding 5th Indian Brigade again supported by 7th Royal Tank Regiment, attacked Tummar West. The artillery attack took place at 1.35pm and 22 tanks attacked at 1.50 pm with the 1st Battalion, Royal Fusiliers engaging twenty minutes later, followed by the 3/1st Punjab Regiment. No Italian tanks were encountered; only artillery on this occasion. Yet again the tanks proved immune and they took the gun positions with infantry support. The same tanks then attacked Tummar East, supported by 4th Battalion Rajputana Rifles. The Italians launched a counterattack on Tummar West but were caught by the machine gun fire of the Rajputana Rifles and the 1st Battalion, Royal Northumberland Fusiliers. There were some 400 Italian casualties in the ten minute action. 16th Brigade and 11th Indian Brigade isolated Sidi Barrani, finally marking the end of the thirty six hours of hostilities.

The attack went according to plan, facilitated by the fact that the Western Desert Force were pre-war regular soldiers who had properly trained in the desert, in close

---

55 *Middle East Training Pamphlet* No. 10, *Lessons of the Cyrenaica Campaign December 1940-February 1941*, p. 3, IWM.
56 See Cochrane, *Charlie Company*, p. 29.
57 Evans, *The Desert and the Jungle*, p. 15.

co-operation of infantry, tanks and artillery, as well as having naval and air support.[58] It proved what could be achieved with good training, intelligence, all arms co-operation, high morale and the fighting ability of the two regular army divisions, at a very early stage of the Second World War. At the Battle of Sidi Barrani the Italians lost 38,300 prisoners, 237 guns, 73 tanks and more than a thousand vehicles for British and Indian losses of 624 killed, wounded or missing. Training was of the utmost importance, in particular the training exercise. According to the battle report:

> In fact, the Exercise was an excellent full scale rehearsal for the forthcoming operations. From this exercise lessons were deduced and necessary tactical and administrative arrangements for the Exercise were studied, discussed and prearranged after considerate thought and discussion.[59]

Other lessons from the battle included successful secrecy surrounding the operation to the degree that the second training exercise was actually the real operation. In fact, 'The operations were favoured by good fortune. Generally speaking, everything went according to plan as far as 4 IND DIV was concerned; the enemy was undoubtedly surprised...'.[60] According to a report written by Savory the victory was due to high morale, the training exercise, reconnaissance, air support and the importance of night training. He stated: 'It is no exaggeration to say that the battalions could work as well by night as by day, either on foot or in M.T'.[61] Shortly after Sidi Barrani, 4th Indian Division was transferred to East Africa.

After the Battle of Keren, 4th Indian Division returned to North Africa but was short of men and equipment and was not prepared for battle. However, the division was designated for Operation 'Battleaxe'. Training for the desert was undertaken again as well as night training and the studying of German methods and organisation.[62] Western Desert Force, now under the command of Beresford-Peirse, was to seize the Halfaya Passes and secure the Bardia-Sollum-Capuzzo area. Both 4th Indian Division and 7th Armoured Division needed re-training, re-equipping and reorganisation. The plan was for 4th Armoured Brigade and 4th Indian Division, comprising

---

58   See Lucio Ceva, 'The North African Campaign 1940-43: A Reconsideration', *Journal of Strategic Studies*, Vol. 13, No. 1, 1990, p. 86.
59   Report on Capture by 4th Indian Division of Enemy positions at Nibeiwa, the Tummars, etc south of Sidi Barani culminating in the capture of Sidi Barrani itself 9, 10, 11 December 1940, p. 3, *Rees Mss*, BL, Mss Eur F 274/13. See also same report TNA, WO 169/602 and in the Papers of Major General Donald Bateman, *Bateman Mss.*, IWM, 72/117/2/1.
60   Ibid, p. 28.
61   An Account of the Operations carried out by the 11th Indian Infantry Brigade of the 4th Indian Division in the Western Desert of Egypt from 6th to 12th Dec. 1940, Appendix – Lessons from the Operation 6-12 December 1940, *Savory Mss.*, NAM, 7603-93-44.
62   See 11th Indian Infantry Brigade – Notes on Brigade Commander's Conference, 15 May 1941, TNA, WO 169/5351.

11th Indian Infantry Brigade and 22nd Guards Brigade, to attack the Halfaya-Sollum-Capuzzo-Bardia area on 15 June. Fort Capuzzo was seized and defended against German counter-attack and the barracks at Sollum were also captured but a German counterattack on 17 June determined that 4th Indian Division's commanding officer, Major General Frank Messervy, ordered a general retreat. The battle was the third successive defeat of British and Commonwealth forces by General Rommel. The late Paddy Griffiths commented that, Operation 'Battleaxe', 'stands as a classic early example of all those difficulties of reconnaissance, navigation and terrain analysis that proved such pitfalls for tacticians throughout the whole desert war'.[63] The problems of inadequate training time should also be acknowledged, particularly for reinforcements such as the 2nd Queen's Own Cameron Highlanders who received a draft of two hundred reinforcements on 12 June.[64]

Operation Crusader

Following the failure of 'Battleaxe' Wavell, C-in-C Middle East, was replaced by General Sir Claude Auchinleck, previously C-in-C India. Auchinleck and his Army Commander, General Alan Cunningham, after much harrying by Winston Churchill, instigated their first attack on Rommel's forces entitled Operation 'Crusader'. Western Desert Force was replaced by 8th Army in September 1941 with Western Defence Force HQ becoming XIII Corps, comprising 4th Indian Division and 7th Armoured Division. By October, 4th Indian Division was still in XIII Corps, along with the 2nd New Zealand Division and 1st Army Tank Brigade. Although 4th Indian Division was the most experienced infantry division in the desert, it was much depleted after Sidi Barrani, Keren and Operation 'Battleaxe'.[65] There had been an absence of divisional training since the division had returned from Eritrea, with most of the time taken up with the preparation of defences. The 7th Indian Brigade was the only formation that had actually carried out any formation training.[66] The main objectives of the operation were the recapture of Cyrenaica and the relief of Tobruk. The 4th Indian Division's role was to cover the Egyptian border from Sidi Omar to the coast: 11th Indian Infantry Brigade executed this holding role on the coastal sector but had sent patrols out into No Man's Land to establish ascendancy. The 4th Indian Division was also meant to cover the advance of 2nd New Zealand Division and 7th Indian Infantry Brigade, attacking the Omar position on 22 November. By 28 November 4th Indian Division had control of the area up to, and including, Bardia.

---

63 Paddy Griffiths, *World War II Desert Tactics* (Oxford: Osprey: 2008), pp. 29-30.
64 See Report by Commander 4th Indian Division on Operations in the Western Desert 15-18 June 1941, TNA, WO 169/3289.
65 See Michael Carver, *Dilemmas of the Desert War: The Libyan Campaign 1940-1942* (Staplehurst, Kent: Spellmount, 2002), p. 32.
66 See Account of Operations in Cyrenaica, 18 November to 28 February 1942, pp. 3- 4, *Bateman Mss.*, IWM, 72/117/2/6 and *Tuker Mss.*, IWM, 71/21/4/5.

On 1 December, 4th Indian Division took Omar. However, it was becoming evident that the standard of training within the division was dropping. On the night of 30 November, 3rd/1st Punjab Regiment attempted a night attack on Omar from the north, in which they made limited progress. The Report on 4th Indian Division's action during Operation 'Crusader' commented:

> With a trained and experienced battalion, this attack would in all probability have succeeded; but the battalion, through no fault of its own, lacked training and experienced leaders, with the result that fire was opened prematurely, and the enemy roused.[67]

The Division continued to fight as a complete formation at the Battles of El Gubi and Alam Hamza and then advanced towards Bengazi. The report concluded that the successful actions by 4th Indian Division were due to 'its high standard of training, and the very intimate teamwork and co-operation existing among all ranks'.[68] However, when the division was out of the line for rest and reorganisation in late December 1941, a report on operations and training noted that the success of the formation was down to the original standard of training and that this must be re-established.[69] Thus, it can be seen that although 4th Indian Division fought well at 'Crusader', it was becoming apparent that units were not as effective as previously, due to the lack of time for suitable training. The 'Crusader' battles were more important actions for the Indian Army than El Alamein, simply as they were more involved. Indeed, as Griffiths has concluded, this was an important series of battles often overlooked in modern historiography, arguing that: '…the 'Crusader' battles represented a British victory that in itself was as significant as Second Alamein in late 1942… But the key difference is that in 'Crusader' Eighth Army was unable to sustain its follow-up…'.[70]

Major General Tuker and 4th Indian Division

Until Operation 'Battleaxe, 4th Indian Division was a well-trained division when the lack of time for training and the assimilation of reinforcements into the units meant that standards had plummeted. However, the arrival of Major General Tuker brought a fresh impetus to training. On 30 December 1941, Tuker assumed command from Messervy, who was made commanding officer of 1st Armoured Division. Under Tuker's tutelage, 4th Indian Division issued training instructions and he, of course, sent copies back to the DMT India. Indeed, as DMT, he had sent copies of all GHQ

---

67 Account of Operations in Cyrenaica, p. 22.
68 Ibid., p. 90.
69 See Operations & Training, 4th Indian Division, 26 December 1941, TNA, WO 169/3289. See also Training Note by Brigadier Donald Bateman, 14 January 1942, *Tuker Mss.*, IWM, 71/21/2/7.
70 Griffiths, *Desert Tactics* p. 42. See also Callahan, *Churchill and his Generals*, p. 80.

India training material to Auchinleck as C-in-C Middle East.[71] Initially Tuker wrote the divisional training instructions. Training Instruction No. 2 was on desert fighting. It promulgated the drill, tactics and organisation for battle groups stating 'to operate successfully in the manner indicated in this Instruction requires the highest possible training of all arms'. The battle groups were organised mainly for defensive operations except for night attacks with battle drills of 'simplicity and speed'.[72] Tuker regarded the use of Jock Columns for all actions as tactically unsound, opining they were useful for harassing the enemy, raiding or establishing ascendancy in 'No Man's Land' but concentration of force was the only way to defeat the enemy, namely 'Concentration as opposed to "Swanning"'.[73]

Training Instruction No. 3 was clearly based on Tuker's experience with sections on mountain warfare from *MTP* No. 7 (India), infantry tank co-operation and night training; all subjects that he had been studying since the 1930s. Theatre training material was also adopted as the lessons learnt in *Middle East Training Pamphlet No. 5* were assimilated into this training instruction, as well as lessons from recent actions such as Operation 'Crusader'. The division had two months to retrain, in direct contrast to many British and Commonwealth divisions in North Africa.[74] Training Instruction No. 6 was the final instruction that Tuker personally wrote. It was entitled 'The Infantry Night Attack on a German Armoured Leaguer' prescribing the battle drill for a night attack on an armoured leaguer that he stated the division could perform this at any time from April 1942 onwards.[75]

Tuker's old battalion joined 4th Indian Division in April 1942 and Tuker wrote in a confidential note at the end of the war:

> By now I had a Goorkha Bn in 7 Bde for I had found when I took over the Division in Jan 42 that the infantry was not up to the standard to which I was accustomed. Frankly, I built the infantry of the Division round that Bn for it had

---

71 See Letter from Auchinleck to Tuker, 13 July 1941, *Tuker Mss.*, IWM, 71/21/1/8.
72 4th Indian Division Training Instruction No. 2, 2 May 1942, *Tuker Mss.*, IWM, 71/21/2/7.
73 Training, Infantry Tactics, 27 March 1942, TNA, CAB 106/776. See also Verney, *The Desert Rats*, p. 25. Jock Columns were named after Lieutenant Colonel J. C. Campbell, 4th Royal Horse Artillery. They were small columns of all arms that could attack the rear of the enemy as well as other suitable targets. According to Verney the 'Jock Columns' established 'moral superiority' over the Italian forces. See also Neal Dando, 'From 'Jock Column' to Armoured Column: Transformation and change in British and Commonwealth unit tactics, in the Western Desert, January 1941 to August 1942' in Michael LoCicero, Ross Mahoney and Stuart Mitchell (editors), *A Military Transformed? Adaptation and Innovation in the British Military, 1792-1945* (Solihull: Helion, 2104), pp. 189-206.
74 See 4th Indian Division Training Instruction No. 3, 29 April 1942, *Tuker Mss.*, IWM, 71/21/2/7.
75 See 4th Indian Division Training Instruction No. 6, 8 June 1942, and a letter from Tuker, 19 January 1961, *Tuker Mss.*, IWM, 71/21/2/7.

been mine and I had put into it the whole of my knowledge of training and war, and after me, Lovett, a very fine CO, took on my work and brought the Bn to the highest pitch of battle skill I have ever seen. With this new example the standard of British and Indian Infantry in the Division rapidly rose.[76]

The formation was withdrawn from the desert and split up, one brigade going to Cyprus, one to Palestine and the third to the Canal Zone, even though the division had trained as an infantry division in a mobile role to work with an armoured division for desert warfare.[77] Tuker encountered difficulties trying to keep his division together under the command of both Auchinleck and Montgomery. The Government of India acquiesced to the formations being broken up, in contrast to the governments of the Dominions who insisted that their formations fought together. In fact, in a letter written to Brigadier Glyn Gilbert, Commandant of the Infantry School, he commented that: 'As a Divisional Commander I have always found it a far greater trouble to fight for the keeping in existence of my Division as a Division and then for its equipping and opportunity to train that I have to fight the enemy'.[78] Although Montgomery had stated, on gaining command of 8th Army, that divisions would not be broken up and stressed the need for training and time to made available for training to take place.[79] In a letter to General Sir Alan Hartley, Tuker lamented the break up of all the Indian Army divisions:

> It was the most experienced Div[ision] in Mid[dle]-East and all it needed and asked for was to get out for 2 months as a Div.[ision] with about 4500 reinforcements and to train on certain new lines as a result of its experience of last winter's fighting. I asked for this and that we sh[oul]d be back in May for the fighting. You know the result. All our Ind Div[ision]s are fed up and feel a bit humiliated at the break up of their Div[ision]s and their squandering piecemeal. 10 Div[ision] has virtually ceased to exist; 5 Div[ision] has practically none of its art[iller]y left. I'm afraid the prestige of the Indian Div[ision]s has dropped sadly and the sorrow of it is that it wasn't their fault. They were taken from their Div[isional] Com[man]ds and sent here, there and everywhere. They'd no knowledge of this type of fighting. How could they have any? 5 & 10 Div[ision]s hadn't seen the Western Desert and the German armour. Its v.[ery] sad. It's a wearing game trying to get one's Div[ision] together. I've been at it since March. But we must do it and we've got to restore the name of the Ind Div[ision]s out here.[80]

---

76 Note by Major General F. S. Tuker, 6 October 1945, p. 12, *Tuker Mss.*, IWM, 71/21/1/6.
77 See Tuker, *Approach to Battle*, pp. 98-99.
78 Letter to Brigadier Glyn Gilbert, 7 Jan 1967, *Tuker Mss.*, 71/21/2/7 and Notes by Tuker for the History of 4th Indian Division, December 1943, *Tuker Mss.*, IWM, 71/21/2/9.
79 See ibid.
80 Letter to General Sir Alan Hartley, 27 August 1942, *Tuker Mss.*, IWM, 71/21/2/9.

Even though the division was dispersed, training instructions continued to be issued and relevant to the particular role. Two instructions were produced to cover the major and minor tactical problems of Cyprus.[81]

Battles of El Alamein

Indian Army formations played a much smaller part of the larger Empire forces in the Battles of El Alamein than in Operation 'Crusader'.[82] One of the first Indian divisions to produce training directives and instructions in the Middle East was 5th Indian Division on its arrival in North Africa in 1941 from Eritrea. Training Instruction No. 2 commented that, like mountain warfare, training for the desert 'is a specialist job but it is a job that can be learnt, if not mastered, by well trained troops quickly, if training is practical and intense'. The instruction had sections on learning desert navigation, night movement, dispersion, wireless communication and minefields.[83] The next training instruction was on the essential role of infantry/tank co-operation in desert warfare.[84] The 5th Indian Division was rushed to Iraq in August 1941. They returned to North Africa when Major General Harold Briggs took over as divisional commander but he had little time to retrain the division for desert warfare before being involved in the defeat at the Gazala Line and a defending role at Ruweisat Ridge during the Battle of El Alamein. As Anthony Brett-James remarked in his memoir, *Report My Signals*, reinforcement Sikh drivers were sent, but they could barely drive, impeded by Brett-James' lack of Urdu, and similarly, reinforcement telephone operators who barely spoke English were employed. He wrote: 'We had only time to give our new men the barest supervision and training'.[85] The formation returned to Iraq in late 1942 and began training for a new role as a 'mixed infantry and armour division'. The 5th Indian Division issued over 10 training instructions and revisions, together with General Briggs' GOC's training directives for this new role.[86]

---

81 See Training Instruction Nos. 9-10. Some Minor Tactical Problems of the Island of Cyprus and Major Tactical Problems of the Island of Cyprus respectively, 2 July 1942, *Tuker Mss.*, IWM, 71/21/2/7.
82 In July 1942 there were the British 7th Armoured and 50th Divisions, 4th and 5th Indian Divisions, 9th Australian Division, 1st South African Division and 2nd New Zealand Division. See for example Peter Stanley, '"The Part We Played in This Show": Australians and El Alamein' in Jill Edwards (ed.), *El Alamein and the Struggle for North Africa: International Perspectives from the Twenty-first Century* (Cairo: The American University in Cairo Press, 2012), p. 62.
83 5th Indian Division Training Instruction No. 2, 19 August 1941, TNA, WO 169/3301.
84 See 5th Indian Division Training Instruction No. 3, Some Principles regarding co-operation between infantry and 'I' tanks in desert warfare, 1 October 1941, TNA, WO 169/3301.
85 Anthony Brett-James, *Report My Signal* (London: Hennel Locke Ltd., 1948), pp. 19-20.
86 See 5th Indian Division War Diaries, TNA, WO 169/7541 and WO 172/1936. See also Antony Brett-James, *Ball of Fire* (Aldershot: Gale & Polden, 1951), pp. 244-247.

Other important actions by Indian formations included the delaying action at Deir el Shein by 18th Indian Infantry Brigade. Deir-el-Shein was saucer-shaped and its choice was largely dictated being the only place in the area that it was possible to dig in. It was four miles north west of Ruweisat Ridge, made of solid rock, and as a result was important to the defence of the Alamein position. The brigade was unprepared for desert warfare and had just arrived from Iraq, under the temporary command of Lieutenant Colonel C. E. Gray of 2/3rd Gurkhas. The remainder of the brigade consisted of 2/5th Essex Regiment and 4/11th Sikh Regiment. Gray had just spent a year in the Adjutant's Branch and the Essex battalion and Gurkhas had never been in action. The brigade had not even been able to train in the use of the 2-pounder anti-tank guns.

The brigade spent their first two days digging, wiring and mining. In addition, only dry rations had been delivered and water allowance was three-quarters of a gallon per day. A defensive 'box' might have been possible if there had been enough time to build it, but the compressors arrived too late to dig emplacements and the full quota of mines arrived too late to be laid. In addition, three different types of mines had been delivered but often without fuses, as there was no engineer officer in charge of issuing. According to Colonel Bamfield, Commanding Officer 4/11th Sikh Regiment:

> Guns did not exist when we first arrived but there were rumours of some coming from various sources. Eventually, the Commander, 121 Field Regiment RA arrived and after a reconnaissance sited the guns we expected. These were eighteen 25-pounders, sixteen 6-pounders and twenty 2-pounders A-tk. There was little time to dig them in and they later suffered accordingly.[87]

The brigade was without signal equipment, short of ammunition and the supporting artillery regiments, 79th and 121st Field Regiments, had fought all the way back from Tobruk. The 'box' itself was about 4000 by 2000 yards. The brigade took up positions, with the Sikhs on the north west side, the Essex on the north east side with the Gurkhas in a semi-circular front of about 6000 yards on the east and 66th Field Company, Sappers & Miners holding the south west. There were gaps in the perimeter due to the lack of mines. There were also four medium machine guns, manned by men of the Cheshire Regiment, and seven Matilda tanks with crews from 42nd Royal Tank Regiment. The 2-pounders were manned by South African units together with personnel from the Welch Regiment and the 6-pounders by various other units. The Advanced Dressing Station was from 32nd Field Ambulance and lastly, there were some South African sappers with compressors.

---

87 Major P. C. Bharucha, *Official History of the Indian Armed Forces in the Second World War 1939-1945: The North African Campaign 1940-43* (India & Pakistan: Combined Inter-Services Historical Section, 1956), p. 548.

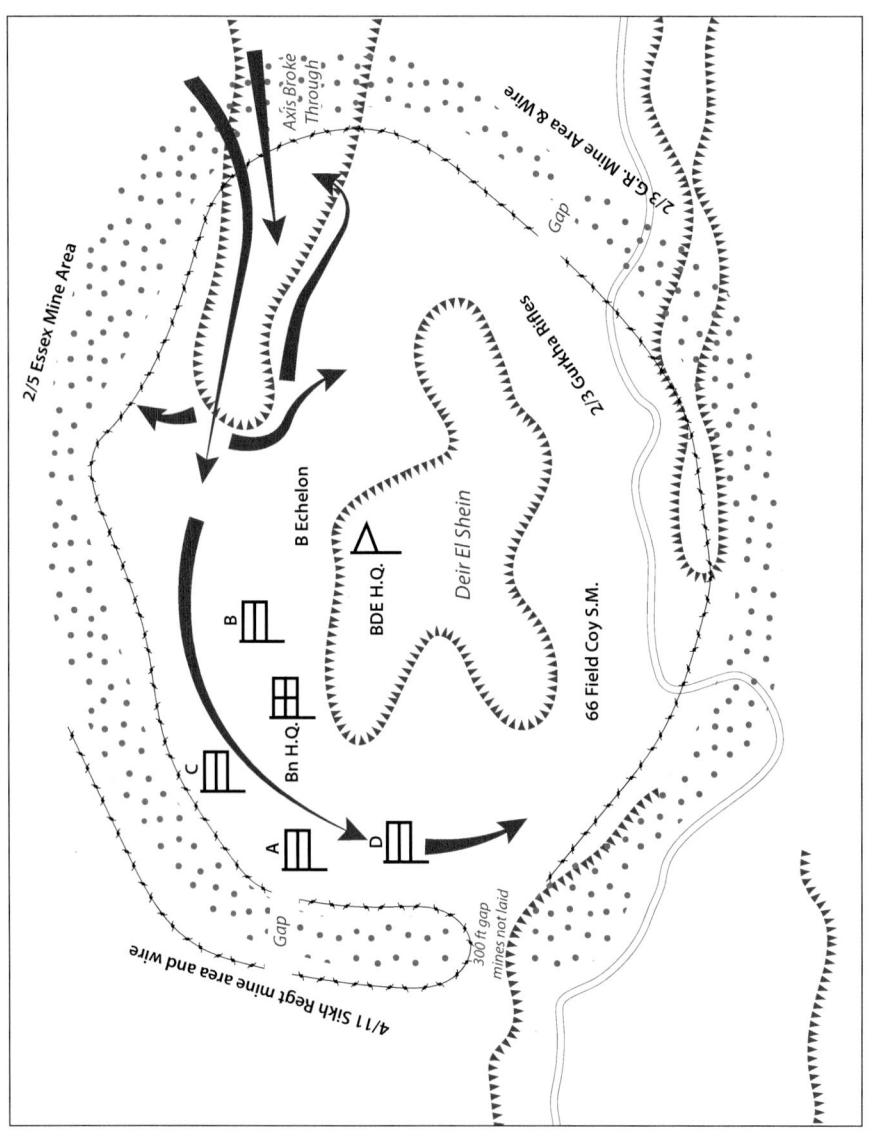

Map 2 18th Indian Infantry Brigade at Deir-el-Shein, 28 June–2 July 1942.

On the 1 July at 9am the German shelling began for an hour on the Essex positions and subsequently over the whole box. At 11.15am two men dressed as British prisoners were sent in to offer surrender terms that were refused. In the afternoon, under the cover of a heavy dust storm, the enemy advanced through the gap in the minefield and formed up behind the Essex and the Gurkhas. This was followed by twelve Mark IV tanks and some light tanks. The Essex anti-tank guns and 25-pounders accounted for two tanks before surrendering. The German tanks advanced towards the Sikhs, where a troop of 2-pounders destroyed two panzers. The tanks destroyed the four remaining 25-pounders. Some of the Sikhs managed to escape, but seven officers and 500 men were missing. The tanks then attacked the Gurkha positions who withdrew from the position, but two companies ran into a tank park. The Gurkhas and the Sikhs were the most heavily hit, with the Gurkhas losing twelve officers and 580 men and their CO was captured and the Sikhs losing three officers and 370 other ranks.

At the same time there was heavy shelling of brigade headquarters which was overrun by five tanks supported by infantry guns. The brigade CO was injured and the HQ captured, although some did manage to escape. At about 7pm, the battalion HQ of 2/3rd Gurkhas evacuated the area. A and C Companies were cut off but also managed to escape through a gap in the area, as did the remainder of the brigade, particularly after the diversion of an Allied bombardment. Most of the survivors managed to get to the El Alamein box. Due to the 'fog of war', support eventually came with 22nd Brigade and its eighteen tanks in the early evening and then withdrew after dark. The Brigade destroyed eight Panzers for the loss of four tanks. The New Zealand official historian commented on the importance of this delaying action:

> Contemporary records do not do justice to 18 Brigade. Auchinleck mentions its 'stalwart resistance' and that 'the stand made by the brigade certainly gained valuable time for the organisation of the Alamein Line generally' (Despatch, p. 364). Post-war revelations of all the facts show that the brigade did much more than this. Tactically and administratively insecure though it was, the brigade fought with a vigour that upset Rommel's battle plan. Just as the fighting in July marked the turn of Allied fortunes in the Middle East, so the action of 18 Brigade on 1 July may be said to have marked the turn of the battle on the Alamein Line. Had Eighth Army been able to avail itself of the opportunity created by the brigade, a crushing defeat might have been imposed on Rommel.[88]

This delaying action resulted in the destruction of 18th Indian Infantry Brigade, but due to this and similar defensive actions the Afrika Korps suffered significant losses in armour that meant any further advance was impossible. Lieutenant Colonel

---

88 Lieutenant Colonel J. L. Scoullar, *Official History of New Zealand in the Second World War 1939-45: Battle for Egypt: The Summer of 1942* (Wellington: War History Branch, 1955), p. 159.

K. F. May (CO 2nd /5th Battalion, Essex Regiment) reported, once he had escaped captivity, that if the Sikhs had fought, the brigade could have broken off the attack under cover of darkness. Thus was due to the lack of acclimatisation and training in desert warfare, the brigade was unable to break off from the action and the majority were captured.[89] Recent research by Jonathan Fennell suggests that during this period morale was low among all British and Commonwealth forces, including the Indian units.[90]

In contrast, 5th Indian Infantry Brigade was a seasoned desert-trained formation. However from June until September the brigade had come under four separate commands: firstly 5th Indian Division, then 10th Indian Division, back to 5th Indian Division before rejoining 4th Indian Division in September. In October 1942 it was to act as reserve to XXX Corps with 7th and 161st Brigades charged to hold the Alamein position and then placed under the command of 51st Highland Division on 3/4th November. The formation's role in Operation 'Supercharge' was to channel a pathway through the enemy minefields south of Tel el Aqqaqir. They speedily achieved their objective of the Rahman track helping the armoured divisions pass through and taking 351 prisoners for 80 casualties. On 7 November 1942 much to their chagrin, 4th Indian Division was withdrawn from offensive operations to conduct battlefield salvage.[91] The 5th Indian Infantry Brigade immediately learnt from this action with a training instruction produced in November on updating the drill for penetrating organised defences. The original drill had been laid out in 4th Indian Division's Training Instruction No. 16, which was not based on experience and was too detailed for practical application.[92] The new drill recommended sending in the minefield bridgehead force to clear the mines with the help of the close support armour, who also made sure the striking force armour had a clear pathway to the objective. Once the minefield bridgehead force had completed its task, the striking force armour would advance alongside supporting infantry with the close support armour going into reserve. For night actions, all armour would be used in the close support role, thus the drill for night only involved the minefield bridgehead force, close support armour and the final objective battalion.[93]

---

89 See Lt. Col. K. E. May, Report on action of 18th Indian Infantry Brigade at Deir-el-Shien, 1st July 1942 written 1 April 1944, TNA, WO 106/2233.
90 See Jonathan Fennell, *Combat and Morale in the North African Campaign* (Cambridge: CUP, 2011), p. 49.
91 See Stevens, *Fourth Indian Division*, p. 199.
92 See 4th Indian Division Training Instruction No. 16, 27 September 1942, *Tuker Mss.*, IWM, 71/21/2/7.
93 See 5th Indian Infantry Brigade Training Instruction No. 2, November 1942, TNA, WO 169/7611.

4th Indian Division within 8th Army and the Indian Army influence in theatre

The 4th Indian Division continued training after Alamein. Training Instruction No. 19 was issued on desert movement, giving basic formation for Brigade groups moving during the day that would be capable of all round defence against tank attack.[94] The 7th Indian Infantry Brigade acted upon these instructions in their training programme between November and December. The first week consisted of mobile training, the next couple of days concentrated on desert movement and the final couple of days on a training exercise prepared by GHQ Training Team No. 2, with both day and night formations.[95] This resulted in a further divisional training instruction on desert movement, issued on 16 December 1942, that stipulated 'the formations that will be adopted by units and Bdes. In order that attached arms can know their relative pos[itio]n in whatever formation they may be working…'. The instruction listed drills for attack and defence, as brigades could be detached as complete fighting groups. In attack, the units were already in position with minimal fuss and should never be beyond range of the supporting artillery. In defence, the drill was to squat, once intelligence of an enemy force had been received, suggesting a move to a shallow saucer impression with a rim such as at Deir-el-Shein, providing within easy reach and ensuring that the artillery was out of sight. The brigade would then halt and debus with little disruption, as it was already in position for all round defence.[96] Once again, training instructions were updated from both battle experience and training exercises.

In addition to infantry training and tactics, 4th Indian Division was innovative in its use of supporting artillery. For example, heavy artillery support was used in the second battle for Keren, but as at Alamein, the element of surprise was lost due to pre-battle ranging and excessive rigid control. The 4th Indian Division counteracted this by giving the Commander Royal Artillery (CRA) his own signal section, whereas other British divisions were still deploying the barrage and dispersion of fire power.[97] Brigadier Harry Dimoline was appointed CRA not long after Tuker became divisional CO. He followed Tuker's example and produced training instructions and memorandum for the divisional artillery. The first training memorandum was based

---

94 See 4th Indian Division Training Instruction No. 19, 12 November 1942, *Tuker Mss.*, IWM, 71/21/2/7. See also 4th Indian Division Artillery Training Instruction No.4, 14 November 1942, Papers of Brigadier H. K. Dimoline, *Dimoline Mss.*, IWM, 73/40/1.
95 See 7th Indian Infantry Brigade, Training Programme Nov-Dec 1942, Training Exercises 27-29 November, and Training – Drill for Desert Formation, 25 November 1942, Papers of Major General A. W. W. Holworthy, *Holworthy Mss.*, IWM, 91/40/2 AWWH 1/14-16 and AWWH 2/3-4.
96 See 4th Indian Division Training Instruction No. 25, 16 December 1942, *Tuker Mss.*, IWM, 71/21/2/7.
97 Royal Artillery – 4th Indian Division Note by Brigadier K. Dimoline, CRA, April 1946, *Tuker Mss.*, IWM, 71/21/2/7.

on the lessons learnt from 'Crusader', forming the basis for training and stating that 'We must at all times remain adaptable and be constantly on the alert to think out new tactics to deal with any new developments'.[98] The memorandum detailed that small mixed columns had proved unsatisfactory in the desert and were now replaced by brigade and battalion battle groups and small raiding parties. The groups would operate as mobile harbours that could act as bases from which armoured forces could operate from. The raiding parties were infantry detachments of two or three trucks, highly trained in Long Range Desert Group work, to operate behind enemy lines and destroy aircraft, MT and ammunition dumps. The instruction concentrated on co-operation with 'I' tanks and infantry in both close support work and as divisional artillery. For example, in close support the artillery would move with the tanks and then be sited in parallel to the tank attack, no more than 3000 yards from the objective. They would bring down high explosive and smoke shells on the point of the tank attack. Targets were selected by the tank commanders in co-operation with artillery Forward Observation Officers (FOOs) attached to each forward squadron. As divisional artillery, the guns were needed for counter battery work against the German 88's sited through aerial photographs and reconnaissance. The divisional artillery was additionally responsible for the fire plan of a battle with FOOs in the leading companies of infantry following the tanks; as the artillery was needed to move quickly forward into captured positions and for consolidation tasks.[99]

Artillery training for the desert was based upon Training Memorandum No. 1, Training Instructions Nos. 1 and 2, all produced within the division as well as *MTP No. 13 (India) Navigation by the Stars*.[100] Tactics were updated after experience. For example, after an objective was taken, artillery had to move to within 3000 yards of the objective in order to continue giving support if required.[101] Artillery was also vital for covering fire for the final 2000 yards of an advance. As Training Instruction No. 3 stated: 'An operation of this nature, requiring as it does intimate co-operation and detailed co-ordination should be rehearsed beforehand wherever possible'.[102] Alongside the use of understudies in 1st Armoured Division, the use of 'double-banking' key men in the artillery was evident, as was the ability to be able to execute operations at night.[103] Synonymous with the divisional training instructions being sent back to the DMT in India, the artillery instructions were also sent back to both the Major General Royal Artillery at GHQ India and the Middle East Staff School.

---

98 4th Indian Divisional Artillery Training Memorandum No.1, 1 April 1942, p. 1, *Dimoline Mss.*, IWM, 73/40/1.
99 See ibid. pp. 3-4.
100 See 4th Indian Division Artillery Training Instruction No. 2, 27 April 1942, *Dimoline Mss.*, IWM, 73/40/1.
101 See 4th Indian Division Artillery Training Instruction No. 3, 30 September 1942, p. 4, *Dimoline Mss.*, IWM, 73/40/1.
102 Ibid, p. 5.
103 Ibid., p. 9.

Lessons from the division and the artillery experience in particular were taken back to the UK. For instance, after the Tunisian Campaign, Tuker was sent to England to lecture to the Army Council and, Dimoline became an instructor at the Gunnery School at Larkhill, hence his methods were disseminated throughout the British and Indian Armies. He later became CRA in 7th Indian Division in the Burma Campaign in 1945.[104]

Tuker believed in the importance of training for a particular type of terrain, such as desert or jungle warfare. He wrote to General Sir Alan Hartley, Deputy C-in-C India, stating:

> No formation can come straight into the show and do well. 1st Armd has been written off twice in 12 months. Most of our Indian Bdes from Cyprus and Iraq were written off out here. The fact is that it is a different sort of fighting just as jungle fighting is different. I would not take 4 Div into Malaya or Burma as it is. It would need and I would need at least a months hard training in the jungle with some instructors who know their job.[105]

He also commented to Hartley that he brought his own defensive system out from India and this had now been adopted in the Middle East Tactical Schools, which he described as: 'Part of the mobile reserve and part of the unthreatened garrisons go to thicken up the threatened place or areas and to act offensively'.[106]

The Indian Army Divisions were not the only formations that underwent training programmes and issued training instructions. Commonwealth formations such as 9th Australian Division were a well-trained and battle-hardened division.[107] The 2nd New Zealand Division trained for six weeks through a series of exercises before 'Crusader' and were re-training again in September 1942, as nearly all the battalion commanders were new in post.[108] The 51st (Highland) Division underwent training exercises and issued training instructions as they had two months to train from September 1942. The 51st Highland Division Training Instruction No. 2 was issued on 13 September 1942, outlining training for breaking through prepared defences, night attacks, wireless

---

104 See unpublished biography of Tuker by John Smyth, p. 40, Papers of Brigadier Sir John Smyth, *Smyth Mss.*, IWM.
105 Letter to General Sir Alan Hartley, 16 October 1942, *Tuker Mss.*, IWM, 71/21/1/3.
106 Ibid.
107 See Allan Converse, *Armies of Empire: 9th Australian Division and 50th Division in Battle, 1939-1945* (Cambridge: CUP, 2011), pp. 101-103. For 6th Australian Division see Craig Stockings, 'An Abundance of Riches: Training & Sustaining the Second AIF in First Libyan Campaign, North Africa, 1940-41' in Peter Dennis & Jeffrey Grey (eds.), *Raise, Train and Sustain: Delivering Land Combat Power* (Canberra: Australian Military History Publications, 2010), pp. 93-107.
108 See Fennell, *Combat and Morale in the North African Campaign*, pp. 225, 238-239.

communication, co-operation with tanks and the RAF and navigation for desert operations for mobile operations, with assistance from 9th Australian Division.[109]

Niall Barr and David French have stressed the poor level of training of troops for the Middle East and that there was an informal approach to training with little uniformity of doctrine.[110] This problem was recognised by Auchinleck when he took over as C-in-C Middle East. He requested that a Director of Military Training Middle East at Major General level be appointed, whose primary role would encompass increasing co-operation between armour, artillery and infantry.[111] Major General John Harding was appointed DMT in January 1942. Auchinleck and Harding also wanted all the training establishments to be concentrated in Southern Palestine, such as in India where they had been concentrated in Southern Command. Harding made an appreciation of the training situation in the Middle East recommending the setting up of a Middle East War School, the expansion of the Junior Staff School as the tactical training of junior officers 'is the most important part of all training and is not, in my opinion, on a satisfactory basis'.[112] He remarked that time made available for training was short and that the wartime officers were not of the same standards as pre-war regulars and therefore recommended battle drill to cover the common circumstances in battle. He advocated that units and formations would be trained by two training teams, in designated training areas that could hold an entire division and that they could only go into battle once inspected by the DMT. Further ideas included the establishment of a senior staff college and that all instructors at training establishments needed to have battle experience. The Directorate was divided into two sections, as in India, with Military Training 1 (MT1) responsible for training pamphlets and MT2 in charge of the training schools. Another Indian Army officer, Brigadier Bateman, was appointed as the first Commandant of the Middle East Training Centre. He had been GSO1 in 4th Indian Division and had been responsible for writing some of the divisional training instructions issued, with the new centre also issuing training memoranda.[113] Thus Auchinleck and Harding, amongst others, began the reorganisation of training and the issue of training material with a common tactical doctrine for the Middle East theatre, before the great

---

109 See 51st Division Training Instruction No. 2, 13 September 1942 and 51st Highland Division Training Exercise No. 1, 26-27 November 1942, TNA, WO 169/4164. See also Fennell, *Combat and Morale*, p. 238 and Barr, *Pendulum of War*, pp. 262-264.
110 See Barr, pp. 50, 157-159 and French, *Raising Churchill's Armies*, pp. 232-235.
111 See Letter from Auchinleck to General Alan Brooke, 15 January 1942, Papers of Field Marshal Sir Claude Auchinleck, *Auchinleck Mss.*, John Rylands Special Collections (JRSC), AUC 640.
112 Major General A. F. Harding's appreciation of Training Situation, 28 February 1942, p. 2, *Corbett Mss.*, CAC, CORB 4/10.
113 See Letter from Auchinleck to Brooke, 2 June 1942, *Auchinleck Mss.*, JRSC, AUC 894. See also Despatch on Operations in the Middle East from 1st November 1941 to 15 August 1942, pp. 368-369. TNA, WO 32/10160.

trainer, General Montgomery, assumed command of 8th Army, immediately issuing Eighth Army Training Memorandum No. 1 on 30 August 1942.[114] Lessons were learnt from the later battles of El Alamein and published as 'Lessons from Operations Oct. And Nov. 1942', in *Middle East Training Memorandum* No. 7 and distributed throughout the army.[115] Lessons were also taken back to India, with returning officers such as Colonel D. W. Morrell giving a lecture on his experiences with 4th Indian Division in North Africa at the Indian Military Academy and was asked by the DMT to give the same lecture on a tour of the instructional schools. He went on to become the Assistant Commandant of Belgaum OTS until the end of the war.[116]

Conclusion

As Chris Mann has eloquently determined, 'The Indian Army in its approach to war differed somewhat to the Montgomery dominated British 8th Army'.[117] In North Africa, Indian Army formations were more successful when employed as a whole division, rather than brigades under differing commands. After the war, Tuker noted that the 'approach to battle', including training, had been incorrect in North Africa resulting in Indian Army divisions such as 5th Indian Division at the Battle of the Cauldron and 10th Indian Division in the retreat from Gazala being decimated. He noted that the officers and men were blamed as opposed to the Corps command commenting that 'Those were dark days for our Indian Army' although 'In Eritrea, Burmah and Italy those two divisions showed themselves to be outstanding divisions in any army'.[118] In conclusion, the Indian Army formations in Egypt and Libya were most effective when well-trained, such as at Sidi Barrani and 5th Indian Infantry Brigade in the breakthrough during Operation 'Supercharge'. When there was inadequate time for training, then the formations were not so successful such as during

---

114 See Eighth Army Training Memorandum No. 1, 30 August 1942, Papers of Major General Raymond Briggs, *Briggs Mss.*, IWM 99/1/2/5 and Notes on Five Months as CGS, MEF, *Corbett Mss.*, CAC, CORB 4/16.
115 See *METM No. 7 Lessons from Operations Oct. and Nov. 1942*, IWM.
116 See *The Sikh Brigade News Letter* No. 22, 1971, p. 24, Papers of Colonel D. W. Morrell, IWM, P488.
117 Chris Mann, 'The Battle of Wadi Akari, 6 April 1943: 4th Indian Division and its Place in 8th Army' in Jeffreys & Rose (eds), *The Indan Army 1939-47*, p. 108.
118 Lieutenant General Sir Francis Tuker, *The Pattern of War* (London: Cassell, 1948), pp. 88-89. For an example, Major General Rees, 10th Indian Division CO at Sollum, getting the blame by his Corps commander see Alan Jeffreys, 'Slim's Welsh General: Major-General 'Pete' Rees in the Burma Campaign', *Transactions of the Honourable Society of Cymmrodorion*, New series, Vol. 12, 2006, pp. 150-152 and Raymond Callahan, 'Were the "Sepoy Generals" Any Good? A Reappraisal of the British-Indian Army's High Command in the Second World War' in Kaushik Roy (ed.), *War and Society in Colonial India* (New Delhi: OUP, 2006), pp. 311-312.

Operation 'Battleaxe' and 18th Indian Infantry Brigade at Deir-el-Shein.[119] As General Wavell commented in the foreword of Training Memorandum No.11 in September 1941, 'The successes won by Indian troops in the Middle East were due as much to their high standard of training as to their fighting abilities'. He continued, that the well-trained infantryman was 'the most important factor in nearly all operations'.[120]

---

119 See for example Jonathan Fennell, 'Courage and Cowardice in the North African Campaign: The Eighth Army and Defeat in the Summer of 1942', *War in History*, Vol. 20, No. 1, 2013, p. 117.
120 Quoted in Archibald Wavell, *Speaking Generally* (London: Macmillan, 1946), p. 45.

4

Mountain Warfare

The Indian Army was well versed in mountain warfare due to the experience of fighting on the North West Frontier (NWF). Peter Cochrane commented in his memoir, *Charlie Company*, that 'Mountain Warfare is like fishing a strange loch. There is a daunting expanse of water, and one's flies look very insignificant. But one must start somewhere if trout are to be caught, and a blend of guesswork and experience tells one where to begin'.[1] This NWF experience was drawn upon during the early stages of the Second World War when twenty Indian Army officers were loaned as mountain warfare advisors for the Norwegian Campaign in 1940.[2] This chapter examines the Indian Army experience of mountain warfare in Eritrea and Italy. It will show how training and mountain warfare doctrine adapted during this period.

The available Indian Army training manuals included numerous offerings on mountain warfare in the North West Frontier, but only *MTP* No.7 (India) *Extensive warfare (notes on warfare in mountainous country between modern forces in Eastern theatres)* was aimed at conventional mountain warfare during the Second World War.[3] A second edition was produced in 1941 after the Norwegian Campaign to include the lessons learnt and remedy the lack of available doctrine. It clearly highlighted the similarities and differences between frontier and mountain warfare. For example, the importance of mobility in both was stressed, shown by the success of the Pathans on the North West Frontier by using higher mobility, whereas against a modern army, higher mobility was still needed but some might need to be sacrificed to increase firepower. The importance of air power was also notable in both stating: 'The air weapon is there to be used whenever it can effectively and economically be employed and not

---

1 Cochrane, *Charlie Company*, p. 53.
2 See Loan of Indian Army officers experienced in mountain warfare, 1940, IOR, L/WS/1/377. See also Prenderghast, *Prender's Progress*, pp. 115-140.
3 See *Military Training Pamphlet* No. 7 (India). *Extensive warfare (notes on warfare in mountainous country between modern forces in Eastern theatres*, (2nd edition, June 1941), IOR, L/MIL/17/5/2248.

only when land weapons cannot possibly perform the tasks'.⁴ There were sections on attack, defence, counter-attack and transport. The pamphlet asserted the importance of training: the need of physical fitness, surviving without transport for 48 hours, living on the hillside, night training, the importance of surprise and initiative, particularly for infantry.

This training pamphlet demonstrated how the Indian Army continued to learn lessons during the Second World War with regards to mountain warfare fought against a modern army. It clearly showed the differences of fighting on the North West Frontier but also of those skills honed on those renowned training grounds. The British Army, by contrast, produced their first training pamphlet on mountain warfare in 1943 namely *MTP* No. 56.

Battle of Keren

The first real test of conventional mountain warfare for the Indian Army during the war was in the Eritrean campaign of 1941. Together with 5th Indian Division, 4th Indian Division was instrumental in the defeat of another Italian force at the Battle of Keren. The East African Campaign, from July 1940-November 1941, truly is a forgotten war. The 70,000 British, Commonwealth and Allied force fought against 300,000 Italians. The Allies ultimately captured 50,000 prisoners, occupied 360,000 square miles at a cost of 500 casualties and 150 killed. It was very much a campaign fought by the military forces of the Empire with not only the Indian Army involved, but units such as the Somaliland Camel Corps, Sudan Defence Force, Royal West African Frontier Force, King's African Rifles, Rhodesian and South African volunteers and a Cypriot Mule Company all playing an important part.

Little has been written on the campaign since the Indian and South African official histories were produced.⁵ The first book to be written was Carel Birkby's *It's a Long Way to Addis* published as early as 1942. The author was a South African journalist and the book is mainly about the South African forces who advanced from Kenya and doesn't deal with the Indian Army formations at Keren. However, it was widely appreciated at the time and required reading for those undergoing jungle training in India in 1944 as it showed the speed of the troops in the campaign rather than

---

4   Ibid., p. 3.
5   See J. F. MacDonald, *Abyssinian Adventure* (London: Cassell, 1957), W. E. Crosskill, *The Two Thousand Mile War* (London: Robert Hale, 1980), Michael Glover, *An Improvised War: The Ethiopian War 1940-41* (London: Leo Cooper, 1987), A. J. Barker, *Eritrea 1941* (London: Faber and Faber, 1966), Neil Orpen, *East African & Abyssinian Campaigns* (Cape Town: Purnell, 1968) and Bishenhwar Prasad, *East African Campaign 1940-41* (India & Pakistan: Combined Inter Services Historical Section, 1963). The lack of a modern interpretation of the campaign has been recently remedied with the publication of Andrew Stewart, *The First Victory: The Second World War and the East African Campaign* (New Haven: Yale University Press, 2016).

anything about jungle warfare or the Indian Army.[6] The campaign is important as Andrew Stewart has commented: 'The British Commonwealth forces …proved far more adept at overcoming the resulting logistical challenges showing themselves time and again to be able to move over poor terrain at great speed and keep their opponent uncertain of their strategy'.[7] Overall command of the campaign resided with Wavell, Lieutenant General William Platt was responsible for the northern part with mainly regular forces under his command such as 4th and 5th Indian Division as well as the Sudan Defence Force and Free French forces that were to be used to capture the oldest Italian colony of Eritrea. The southern campaign from Kenya was led by Lieutenant General Alan Cunningham who was to advance into Italian Somaliland and support the irregular forces and Patriots under Colonel Dan Sandford and Major Orde Wingate supporting the return of Haile Selassie as Emperor of Ethiopia.

The Allied forces had some advantages over the enemy as 4th Indian Division had come straight from defeating Italian forces at Sidi Barrani and the RAF had air superiority. However, the Italian forces were numerically superior, had mules and mountain guns for mountain warfare whereas the Indian troops had been mechanised and were armed with 25-pounders that had low trajectories making them less useful for mountain warfare. They had also left their mule companies behind on the North West Frontier and carrying parties needed to be formed that meant that battalions were depleted by as much as a quarter of their strength. The hilly terrain was difficult to contend with that was compounded by the conditions which were very harsh for the troops with water shortages, very hot days and incessant flies followed by very cold nights. The military officer turned historian, Colonel Arthur Barker commented:

> Men who were at Keren, who served subsequently in other theatres of war on other battlefields, in Italy, Burma and Northwest Europe where conditions have been described as 'bloody', 'appalling' or just 'frightful' – have said that nothing – NOTHING – was worse than Keren. It was not just the fighting and the casualties, though twenty-five or thirty a day was gruesome enough, but conditions which went with it…[8]

One of the first Indian formations to learn early lessons in Eritrea was Gazelle Force that had been formed on 16 October 1940 as 5th Indian Division's mobile force, commanded by Colonel Frank Messervy. The unit was in action around Kassala on the Sudanese border and immediately learnt from these early encounters with the Italian forces. For example, Messervy noted that junior leaders in mechanised units

---

6   See Carel Birkby, *It's a Long Way to Addis* (London: Frederick Muller, 1942). See also Report 14 Indian Division Jul 1943-Nov 1945, pp. 16-17, Papers of Major General Alfred Curtis, *Curtis Mss.*, IWM, P140.
7   Andrew Stewart, ' "Speed and dash": The British Commonwealth's Campaign in East Africa, 1940-41', *Global War Studies*, Vol. 7, No. 2 2010, p. 161.
8   Barker, *Eritrea*, p. 124. See also Evans, *The Desert and the Jungle*, p. 28.

needed to be highly trained which brought self-confidence and initiative. This could be achieved through sending units out for two or three days leaving the junior officers to make all the tactical decisions. He also commented that 'The young British officer should be trained in the same way. There is a tendency to keep them at Sq[uadro]n HQ and leave all such tasks to the VCOs'.[9] Gazelle Force was transferred to 4th Indian Division in January 1941. It led the Indian force for the capture of Keren advancing two hundred miles in fifteen days but came to a standstill at the edge of the Keren escarpment due to the Italian engineers disabling the Ponte Mussolini bridge. The Italian forces were commanded by General Nicolangelo Carnimeo, a very experienced commander who had commanded a regiment in the Spanish Civil War. On the night of 2 February, the 2nd Battalion the Queen's Own Cameron Highlanders of 11th Indian Infantry Brigade, took Cameron Ridge but a counterattack forced them back to Mount Sanchil. The 3/4th Punjabis passed through the Camerons and took the west end of Brig's Peak and both units were bombarded continuously the next day. They were reinforced by 1/16th Rajputana Rifles and held off the Italian counterattacks. On 7 February, 5th Indian Infantry Brigade led by Brigadier Wilfrid Lloyd tried to capture a small path on Acqua Col that led into Keren. The attack was to be led by 4/16th Rajputana Rifles whose aim was to seize the entrance, followed up by 4/11th Sikhs whose objective was Mount Zeban with the 1st Royal Fusiliers going on into Keren, with one company in each battalion acting as porters. However, the Rajputana Rifles did not achieve the first objective.

On 10 February, 3/1st Punjabis supported by a heavy artillery concentration took Brig's Peak and the lower slopes of Sanchil but had to pull back from Sanchil due to the lack of reinforcements. On 12 February, the Rajputana Rifles and the Sikhs achieved their objectives on Acqua Col but were immediately counterattacked by the Italian forces during which 70 out of 87 of one Sikh Company were killed or wounded. The advance was over by 15 February and marked the end of the first phase of the battle of Keren. The 4th Indian Division lacked the right sort of equipment, had too few troops in the difficult terrain and the Italian defence was tenacious. According to Arthur Barker: 'Those who had scoffed at the Italian soldier were now revising their views'.[10] As Geoffrey Evans commented:

> The Italians, fully prepared for mountain warfare, had mule transport to keep their positions supplied. They also had the advantage of operating on the opposite side of the mountain from us where the slopes down to the Keren Plateau were not nearly so steep. And, of course, having had ample time for preparation,

---

9   HQ Gazelle. Training Lessons from Operations – Mechanised Units, 16 December 1940, TNA, WO 169/2818.
10 See Barker, *Eritrea*, p. 118.

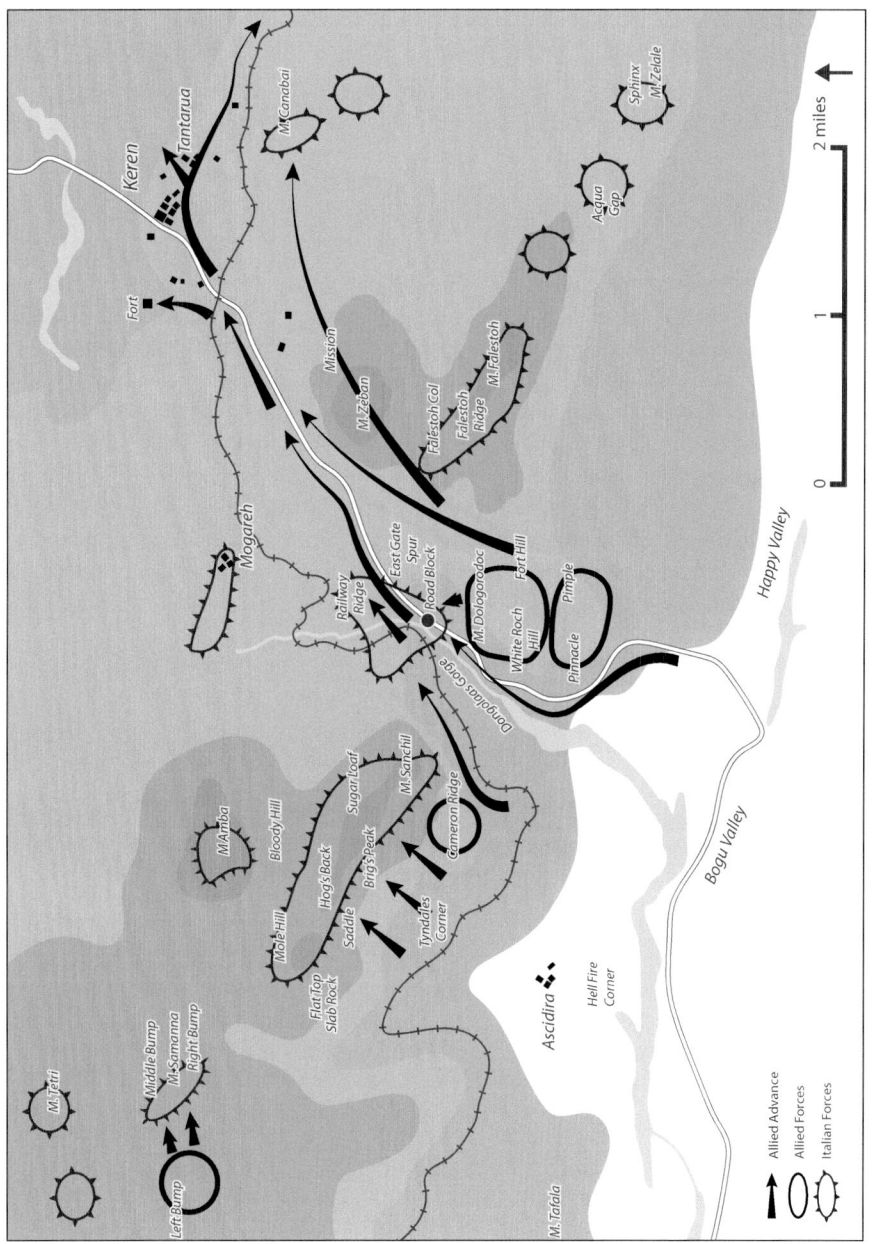

Map 3 Final Battle of Keren, 15–27 March 1941.

they had properly constructed defence positions, strongly fortified and protected by barbed wire. They even had a piped water-supply to Mount Sanchil.[11]

For all the recent fighting, 4th Division only held Cameron Ridge and Mount Zeban. Platt had concluded by mid-February that a full-scale frontal attack was needed. In the month-long lull in between battles, training in mountain warfare was undertaken by the individual brigades: 29th Indian Infantry Brigade trained at Tessani, 9th Indian Infantry Brigade at Agordat and 5th Indian Division at Kassala.[12] Also at Kassala, officers of both Indian divisions had briefings around a model of the Keren stronghold.[13] Messervy, now commanding 9th Indian Infantry Brigade, issued training instructions stating that: 'It is the problem of the last 400 yards when our men are tired, when our fire support problem becomes more difficult, and when the enemy will put in everything he can to stop us, which has to be satisfactorily solved'.[14] The two battalions who held Cameron Ridge were under immense pressure.

The plan in the second phase of the fighting for Keren which was intended to begin on 15 March, was for 4th Indian Division to keep the Italians busy on Sanchil and then for 5th Indian Division to take Dologorodoc, followed by Falestoh and Zedan, all with tactical air support. The 7th Indian Infantry Brigade, commanded by Brigadier Harold Briggs, designated North Force advanced on Keren from the north and established wireless communication with 4th Division so closer co-ordination was feasible for the second phase.

The 11th Indian Infantry Brigade was on Cameron Ridge and 5th Indian Infantry Brigade below Mount Samona when the Cameron's attacked Brig's Peak, but once again came up against fierce Italian defence. The 5th Indian Infantry Division's attack on Dologorodoc was equally unsuccessful. A new plan devised by Major General Lewis 'Piggy' Heath, 5th Indian Divisional Commander, and Messervy was for 5th Indian Infantry Division to take 'Pinnacle' and 'Pimple' hills with a night attack by 3/5th Mahrattas commanded by Lieutenant Colonel Denys Reid. The Mahrattas took Pinnacle; Pimple was taken by the West Yorkshires, Dogras and Sikhs which they managed to hold onto with supplies dropped by air and also carried overland by the Cypriot Mule Company. The 10th Indian Infantry Brigade, now commanded by Brigadier 'Pete' Rees, took over from 11th Indian Infantry Brigade making equally unsuccessful night attacks, as did 5th Indian Infantry Brigade against the series of hills from Mount Sanchil to Mount Samanna. However, Lieutenant Colonel Napier leading the 6/13th Frontier Force Rifles found that the road block was not as heavily defended as previously thought. Thus the new plan on 25 March was for 9th Indian

11   Evans, *The Desert and the Jungle*, p. 42.
12   See Barker, *Eritrea*, pp. 117, 127; Henry Maule, *Spearhead General: The Epic Story of General Sir Frank Messervy and his Men in Eritrea, North Africa and Burma* (London: Odhams Press, 1961), p. 69; Mackenzie, *Eastern Epic*, p. 56; Musa, *Jawan to General*, p. 53.
13   See Maule, *Spearhead General*, p. 75.
14   Quoted in Maule, *Spearhead General*, p. 75.

Infantry Brigade to attack along the slopes of Dologorodoc and 10th Indian Infantry Brigade attack on their left using the tunnel route to attack Railway Bumps with 4th Indian Division keeping the Italians busy on Cameron Ridge. Once 9th and 10th Indian Infantry Brigades were successful, Fletcher Force, comprising 14 tanks and 36 Bren gun carriers would advance along the road when the block was cleared. Progress was slow for the 9th but 10th Indian Infantry Brigade completely surprised the Italians. The engineers cleared the road and Fletcher Force got through. North Force was also very close to getting through and 'Piggy' Heath was one of the first to enter Keren.

It was the decisive battle in Eritrea. 586 Allied troops were killed and 3,229 wounded in contrast to 3,500 Italians killed, 4,500 wounded and 3,500 captured. The Italian defence was stout but the Indian troops were regular army soldiers, used to fighting in similar conditions such as the North West Frontier and were able to quickly adapt. They had undergone mountain warfare training prior to going into action and in the lull in fighting, and their use of night attacks proved decisive against a numerically-superior, better-equipped and well-supplied defending force. As the British official historian wrote:

> To General Wavell belongs the credit for allotting to the Eritrean front the two divisions most likely to adapt themselves quickly to the conditions and the best able to work in double harness. Many of the commanders and troops had had experience of mountain warfare, but not against an enemy who possessed aircraft and artillery and numerous mortars, machine-guns, and grenades.[15]

Major General James 'Jim' Elliott commented on the two divisions in his unpublished history of Keren that: 'They worked well in harness. Very much alike in composition and outlook, officers and men in the different battalions known to one another, – it all made for cooperation and flexibility in tactical and administrative planning'.[16]

Lessons were learnt from the campaign, for example 9th Indian Infantry Brigade produced a report for guidance in training in mountainous country: noting the importance of fitness and the problem of the last 400 yards in capturing a position when artillery support could be difficult. The solution was support from 3-inch mortars, medium machine guns, snipers or rifle grenades. Night operations were mentioned but the problem was the consolidation of the advance during the day. The need of artillery and air support was vital as was portage with one man being required to carry forward for three on the hill. Messervy, the brigade commander, wrote that he would hold a conference before an operation and issue orders personally, or by

---

15 Major-General I. S. O. Playfair, *The Mediterranean and Middle East: Volume I: The Early Successes against Italy (to May 1941)* (London: HMSO, 1954), p. 440.
16 Major General J. G. Elliott, 'Unpublished manuscript on the Battle of Keren', p. 214, IWM, Misc 952.

WT, stating that 'Written orders are useful as an exercise for Staff Officers and Adjutants, and for historical records'.[17] The 5th Indian Division, under the command of Major General Ashley Mayne, also learned lessons for training with the importance of porterage, mortars, night attacks with artillery support, the value of training with tanks, concluding 'Success may be achieved by a platoon in the early stages of contact which will be with difficulty equalled by employment of a brigade later on'.[18] A constant theme throughout the Second World War.

The Battle of Keren was a very important action for the development of the Indian Army. It showed the significance of the pre-war training of the Indian Army particularly as they were mainly regulars, trained and experienced in frontier warfare and night attacks as well as undergoing conventional mountain warfare training. This experience helped defeat a numerically superior opponent even though it was equipped as a mechanised force rather than for mountain warfare. The battle is an important link between 'a classic adventure of the British Empire' and the modern Indian Army of 1945, as Compton Mackenzie asked: 'Has any campaign in history lasting two months produced from two divisions a fighting army commander, two fighting corps commanders and seven fighting divisional commanders within four years?'[19] For example, Brigadier William 'Bill' Slim who had commanded 10th Indian Brigade went on to command 14th Army in Burma; Major General Lewis 'Piggy' Heath, CO 5th Indian Division commanded III Corps in Malaya; Brigadier Frank Messervy, CO Gazelle Force and 9th Indian Brigade, commanded 4th Indian Division and 7th Armoured Division in North Africa and 7th Indian Division and IV Corps in Burma; Brigadier Harold Briggs, CO 11th Indian Brigade commanded 5th Indian Division in the Middle East and Burma; Brigadier Wilfrid Lloyd, CO 5th Indian Brigade became commander of 14th Indian Division; Major Donald Bateman, Brigade Major in 5th Indian Brigade commanded 5th Indian Infantry Brigade from 1942-43 and became DMT in 1945; Lieutenant Colonel Dudley 'Pasha' Russell, GSO1 with 5th Indian Division became commander of 8th Indian Division; Brigadier Thomas 'Pete' Rees, CO 10th Indian Brigade commanded 19th Indian Division; Brigadier Reginald Savory, CO 11th Indian Brigade commanded 23rd Indian Division and then became Inspector of Infantry at GHQ India and Lieutenant Colonel Denys Reid, Battalion Commander of the 3rd Mahratta Light Infantry became divisional commander of 10th Indian Division in Italy. In contrast to the later campaigns in North Africa, the Indian divisions fought together learning from one another and were employed as complete divisions rather than as individual brigades under differing commands.

17 HQ 9th Infantry Brigade. Lessons of recent operations for guidance in training with special reference to operations in mountainous country, Papers of Brigadier Harold Charrington, *Charrington Mss.*, LCHMA, 3/2.
18 5th Indian Division Report on Operations of training value for the month ending 10th April 1941, *Charrington Mss.*, LCHMA, 3/1. I am grateful to Alex Wilson for the above two references.
19 Mackenzie, *Eastern Epic*, p. 63.

Lessons from East Africa were written up in the *AITMs*, such as the use of one comprehensive written order at the beginning of operations in Eritrea after which the formation relied on verbal orders.[20] They also emphasized how successful Indian troops were in the Middle East and how this was down to their high standard of training.[21]

After the battles of El Alamein, Tuker realised that 4th Indian Division would have to be retrained for mountain warfare with the onset of the Tunisian Campaign. In a letter to General Horrocks he stated that 4th Indian Division had 'more experience than most in this type of warfare' due to service on the North West Frontier and the fighting at Keren.[22] Training in mountain warfare started in January 1943 with the issue of Training Instruction No. 28 that needed a 'true appreciation of the tactical value of ground and features. It is an art which has become generally rusty as a result of much desert fighting'. The instruction included a lecture by the Commandant of Middle East Training Centre who noted that apart from the North West Frontier the other limited experience during the Second World War was at Keren. The directive stressed the importance of physical fitness, tactical awareness and training in mountain warfare as well as the importance of the initiative of junior leaders, of mobility, co-operation of all arms and inter-service, concentration of forces, security of the lines of communication and the element of surprise as 'in mountainous countries initial errors are not easy to rectify'.[23] Similarly training instructions were produced for the artillery noting the doctrine produced in *MTP* No. 7 (India) *Extensive Warfare (notes on warfare in mountainous country between modern forces in Eastern theatres)* and the recent experience in Eritrea.[24] The success of this mountain warfare training was demonstrated by the divisional night attacks on the Matmata mountains in March 1943 and the Battle of Wadi Akarit, the following month.[25] Montgomery did not rate 4th Indian Division highly or the Indian Army generally and he used them sparingly after he took over command of 8th Army. Tuker noted:

> Monty disliked Indian Div[ision]s Matmata and Akarit were a shock to him. Akarit w[a]s won by 4 Ind Div and no-one else. We'd licked the Axis army by

---

20 See *AITM* No. 9, p. 29, IOR, L/MIL/17/5/2240.
21 See *AITM* No. 11, p. iii, IOR, L/MIL/17/5/2240.
22 Stevens, *Fourth Indian Division*, p. 201.
23 4th Indian Division Training Instruction No. 28, Mountain Warfare, 16 January 1943, TNA, WO 169/14735. See also 4th Indian Division Artillery Training Instruction No. 6, 1 January 1943 and X Corps Training Instruction No. 2, January 1943, *Dimoline Mss.*, IWM 73/40/1.
24 4th Indian Division Artillery Training Instruction No. 2, 27 April 1942, *Dimoline Mss.*, IWM 73/40/1.
25 See Tuker, *Approach to Battle*, pp. 311-332. See also Mann, 'The Battle of Wadi Akarit, 6 April 1943: 4th Indian Division and its place in 8th Army', Jeffreys and Rose (eds.), *The Indian Army, 1939-47*, pp. 87-108.

0830 hours on 6 April completely and utterly, while other Div[ision]s were still struggling and fighting, and being driven back and attacking again.[26]

After these actions the division joined the 1st Army for the remainder of the campaign in North Africa. The 4th Indian Division was hugely successful at Medjez el Bab with their night approach, mountain warfare experience and all arms support. Tuker, along with Lieutenant General Charles Allfrey, V Corps Commander, accepted General Hans-Jurgen von Arnim's surrender in North Africa, taking more prisoners than the division had at Sidi Barrani but 'This time they were Germans and not Italians'.[27]

Italian Campaign

For the Allied formations fighting in Sicily there had been little time to train for the mountainous terrain following the Tunisian Campaign and the terrain had surprised even the most battle-hardened formations.[28] A few Indian Army battalions, such as the Indian State battalion, the Jodhpur Sardur Light Infantry, the 3/10th Baluchis and the 3rd Royal Battalion, Frontier Force Regiment were on beach-head duties during the Sicily landings and had undergone combined operations training.[29] But no Indian formations were involved in the fighting, three Indian divisions took part in the later campaigns on the Italian mainland. The 4th Indian Division arrived in Italy in December 1943. The 8th and 10th Indian Divisions had been involved in Persia and Iraq although the 10th had briefly been in North Africa. In 1943 the 8th was commanded by Major General Dudley 'Pasha' Russell and landed at Taranto in September 1943. The 10th had had a succession of commanders, including 'Bill' Slim and 'Pete' Rees, and when it arrived in Italy in March 1944 it was commanded by Major General Denys Reid.

Apart from the *Official History of the Indian Armed Forces* volume on the Italian campaign and some pocket divisional histories produced by the Director of Public Relations of the War Department in Delhi, there has been little research on the Indian Army formations in Italy.[30] Equally, the importance of training for mountain warfare seems to have been underestimated by the British High Command in Italy and thus

---

26   Letter to General Sir Alan Hartley, 21 February 1944, *Tuker Mss.*, IWM 71/21/2/9.
27   "Camel", 'Fourth Indian Division': A Short Record of the 4th Indian Division reproduced from the Journal of the United Service Institution of India, *Dimoline Mss.*, IWM 73/40/1.
28   See Ian Gooderson, *A Hard Way to Make a War: The Allied Campaign in Italy in the Second World War* (London: Conway, 2008), pp. 102-104.
29   See Major General Rafiuddib Ahmed, *History of the Baloch Regiment 1939-1956* (Uckfield, East Sussex: Naval & Military Press, nd.), pp. 90-91 and Brigadier W. E. H. Condon, *The Frontier Force Regiment* (Aldershot: Gale & Polden, 1962), pp. 271-277.
30   See D. Pal, *The Campaign in Italy, 1943*-45 (Delhi: Combined Inter-Services Historical Section, 1960). The exception is Patrick Rose, 'British Army Command Culture 1939-45'.

no doctrine ensued.[31] Indeed the British official historians lamented the lack of use of the Indian divisions for mountain warfare.[32] In contrast the German army was well aware of the need for mountain warfare training, Field Marshal Kesselring insisted that it was at the unit level, 'where mountain warfare was won or lost' and noticed that 'Allied junior leadership continued to lack initiative' in this type of warfare.[33]

The Italian campaign combined the need for adequate training for mountain warfare, fighting in the towns and villages and crossing water obstacles. Indian Army officers were instrumental in the Middle East Mountain Warfare Training Centre in the Lebanon. It was set up by Brigadier Alan Holworthy, a Gurkha officer mountain warfare specialist, in January 1943.[34] He spent six months there before taking over as GOC 4th Indian Division.[35] It was originally established to train troops for 'behind the lines' operations in the Balkans with the reconstituted 2/7th Gurkha Rifles which had undergone rock training, acting as the demonstration battalion.[36] With the start of the Italian campaign, the centre did however train troops for conventional mountain warfare.[37] The mountaineer wing produced a mountaineer battalion from two Gurkha battalions.[38] The final report of the ski wing recognised how adaptable Gurkhas were as mountaineers, when a platoon of the 7th Gurkha Rifles underwent two months training and only 2 out of 30 were unable to adapt.[39] Unsurprisingly, this very well trained battalion for mountain, rock and snow warfare was later specifically requested for action by 4th Indian Division.[40] Other Indian Army officers such as Brigadier Donald Bateman, who had been a staff officer in 4th Indian Division going on to command 5th Indian Infantry Brigade, lectured on mountain warfare at the Middle East Staff School in December 1942. His lecture was based on the experience of the division at Keren and the lessons learned.[41]

31   See Field Marshal Lord Alanbrooke (edited by Alex Danchev and Daniel Todman), *War Diaries 1939-1945* (London: Weidenfeld & Nicolson, 2001), p. 510.
32   See W. G. F. Jackson, *The Mediterranean and Middle East Vol. VI: Victory in the Mediterranean Part 1, 1st April to 4th June 1944* (London: HMSO, 1984), pp. 13-14. See also Douglas Porch, *Hitler's Mediterranean Gamble: The North African and the Mediterranean Campaigns in World War II* (Weidenfeld & Nicolson, 2004), p. 658.
33   Porch, ibid., p. 628.
34   See Stevens, *Fourth Indian Division*, p. 202. See also Bob Maslen-Jones, *Outrageous Fortune* (Caithness, Scotland: Whittles Publishing, 2006), p. 89.
35   See photograph albums, *Holworthy Mss.*, IWM, 91/40/2.
36   See Colonel J. N. Mackay, *History of 7th Duke of Edinburgh's Own Gurkha Rifles* (London: William Blackwood & Sons, 1962), p. 241 and Training Instructions Nos. 2-4, TNA, WO 169/15014.
37   See 'The M. E. Mountain Warfare Training Centre', *Fauji Akhbar*, Vol. XII, No. 2, 18 March 1944.
38   See Ralph Robert Griffith interview, IWM, SA 18467/2.
39   See Mountain Warfare Training Centre Ski Wing: Final report, p. 7, IWM, 19146.
40   See 4th Indian Division: organisation, equipment & movement, TNA, WO 204/7981.
41   M.E. Staff School lecture. Training for War – Mountainous Country, Papers of Major General D. R. E. R. Bateman, *Bateman Mss.*, IWM, 72/117/1/2/7.

In October 1943, mountain warfare training teams were offered to General Alexander and were to prove very useful to British troops as Major General Gerald Templer 'reported that they accomplished very useful results in subjects in which both officers and men had had little or no previous training'.[42] The expertise of Colonel Le Marchand, who had been the commandant of the Mountain Warfare School in India and was on loan from the Indian Army, was also offered in finding suitable training ground and preparing schemes.[43]

The 4th Indian Division underwent combined operations training and in Autumn 1943 it was established as a mountain division. The 7th Indian Infantry Brigade followed by 11th Indian Infantry Brigade underwent training at the Mountain Warfare School in Lebanon.[44] The principles in mountain warfare were reiterated on the eve of 4th Indian Division's landing in Italy when Training Instruction No. 40 commented:

> Division policy in mountain fighting has, ever since 1942, been one of obtaining penetration of the enemy-occupied areas as quickly as possible and of bursting through into his gun-areas and maintenance system and cutting his roads behind him. That is, only to fight to fight him if we cannot burst through without fighting. To keep highly mobile on our MT as long as we can and to seek everywhere for the road or track that will let us through.[45]

The training instruction continued: 'For this we have trained and will continue to train, – as our recent visit confirms this as the right policy'.[46] Added to this were three extra training requirements such as a motor transport attack on an unguarded position, an attack on a hill position near a main road and an attack on foot behind the enemy and the following defence against counterattack even by tanks. Observers from 4th Indian Division in Italy also noted a lack of initiative, the importance of the PIAT in 'tank hunting' and most importantly the need for all units of all arms to be trained for porterage work. This training instruction and those of the other Indian divisions were distributed to corps command, the other Indian divisions within theatre, the Director of Military Training India or GHQ India, the reinforcement camps and

---

42   Mountain Warfare Training Teams, TNA, WO 204/4200.
43   See ibid.
44   See Lt. Col. G. R. Stevens, *The 9th Gurkha Rifles Vol. 2 1937-1947* (9th Gurkha Rifles Regimental Association, 1953), pp. 58-59. See also Lt. Col. J. P. Lawford & Major W. E. Catto, *Solah Punjab: The History of the 16th Punjab Regiment* (Aldershot: Gale & Polden, 1967), p. 161 and Stevens, *History of the 2nd King Edward VII's Own Goorkha Rifles (The Sirmoor Rifles) Vol. III 1921-1948*, pp. 93-94 and Cochrane, *Charlie Company*, p. 107.
45   4th Indian Division Training Instruction No. 40, 10 December 1943, TNA, WO 169/14735.
46   Ibid.

affiliated battalions. Thus all training material and lessons learnt were disseminated amongst fellow Indian Army formations and GHQ India.

The 8th Indian Division was in a similar situation according to their Training Instruction No. 1 issued on 27th March 1943. The division had been using PAIFORCE and Tenth Army training instructions about which it stated: '...our past training has therefore obviously been on sound lines. The time which has elapsed since these instructions were published, however, and the number of new units who have joined the Division makes a further instruction now desirable as a more immediate guide'. This was the first training instruction issued to the division since Major General Russell had only taken over command of the division in January 1943, suggesting that he saw this as the best way of disseminating training information, following the example of 4th Indian Division where he had previously commanded 5th Indian Infantry Brigade. General observations included the importance of air support and of junior leadership. Differing from the 4th Indian Division training instructions it referred to specific British and Indian training pamphlets such as *MTP* No. 23 on river crossings, *MTP* (India) No. 25 *Battle Manoeuvre and a Drill for teaching it* and *AITM* No. 15 on 'Night Vision'. The importance of these training pamphlets were emphasised in the instruction: 'Training pamphlets appear from time to time. These are very carefully compiled after discussing the subject with officers who have had experience in operations. The pamphlets concerned with operations of war mentioned in this instruction will be carefully studied'. For future training the instruction noted the importance of training for river crossings, mountain warfare, battle drill and night training.[47] In May 1943 senior officers in the division attended a combined operations exercise, lectures were given to officers in the division and a brigade level combined operations exercise was undertaken. Officers and units attended both the Combined Training Centre at Kabrit and the Mountain Warfare Training Centre and by July 1943 Training Instruction No. 4 stated that: 'The Division appears to be the next to go into to bat, but we can all do with a little extra training at the nets'.[48] The same training instruction noted the importance of snipers, an immediate lesson from the fighting in Sicily, stating that: 'A good sniper can be an infernal nuisance to the enemy and is usually a source of valuable information, let the enemy come to know the snipers of 8th Indian Division as something infernal'.[49]

---

47 8th Indian Division Training Instruction No. 1, 27 March 1943, TNA, WO 169/4766.
48 See 8th Indian Division GS Branch War Diary and Training Instruction No. 4, July 1943, TNA, WO 169/4766. See also *History of the 5th Royal Gurkha Rifles (Frontier Force) Vol. II 1929-1947* (Aldershot: Gale & Polden, 1956), pp. 64-65; Condon, *The Frontier Force Regiment*, pp. 312-313; Lt. Col. M. G. Abhyankar, *Valour Enshrined: A History of the Maratha Light Infantry 1768-1947* (New Delhi: Orient Longman, 1971), pp. 315-316 and Major General Indar Jit Rikhye, *Trumpets and Tumults* (New Delhi: Manohar, 2004), p. 66.
49 8th Indian Division Training Instruction No. 4, July 1943, TNA, WO 169/4766. See also Gooderson, *A Hard Way to Make a War*, pp. 129-130.

Prior to arriving in Italy, 8th and 10th Indian Divisions trained together in Exercise Crocodile in Palestine in the use of assault boats and the establishing of bridgeheads.[50] 10th Indian Division underwent combined operations and mountain warfare training like 4th and 8th Indian divisions.[51] In Cyprus, Syria and Palestine most of their training had been for mountain warfare which was continued at Venafro. For example in Palestine, a battle school for 10th Indian Division was set up in December 1943 with the first courses starting the following January. These lasted three weeks which some officers found too strenuous due to unfitness, although Captain Richard Tolson, one of the instructors, thought the first course had 'gone tolerably well. I have been very fortunate in my section instructors and demonstration Platoon – they have all worked exceedingly hard. The students seem to have enjoyed the course, and I have learned a great deal'.[52] A series of training instructions were produced for 10th Indian Division. These again reiterated the lessons from Sicily and the experience of the Indian formations fighting on the mainland. The importance of patrolling was extolled. The different patrols were defined as Reconnaissance, Fighting and Battle patrols. Reconnaissance patrols comprised one to two men patrolling to obtain information and not engage the enemy. Fighting patrols were normally at platoon level to gain information by engaging the enemy. Battle patrols were a larger force to obtain information about the strength of an enemy attack and delay it. These patrols were now to be commanded by brigade and battalion patrol masters. This idea was adopted from 4th Indian Division at brigade level and both in the infantry battalions and the artillery regiments.[53] Similarly to 8th Indian Division, lessons learnt from Sicily included the importance of sniping; there were now to be eight snipers in a battalion, as well as two in each company under the control of the Battalion patrol master. The training instructions, as with 8th Indian Division, disseminated lessons from training manuals. In the case of patrolling, extracts were taken from *Army Training Memorandum* No. 46 showing the worth of patrolling to improve the battle experience of a battalion.[54]

The 4th Indian Division had had six months in Palestine for rest and training and assimilating the lessons from the North African Campaign. When it arrived in Italy

---

50 See 10th Indian Division War Diary April 1944, TNA, WO 169/18813 and Ray Hunting, 'War Signals', IWM, P339, p. 65.
51 See Lt. Gen. Sir Ralph B. Deedes, *Historical Record of the Royal Garwhal Rifles Vol. II 1923-1947* (Dehra Dun: Army Press, nd.), pp. 106-107 and Brigadier C. N. Barclay (editor), *The Regimental History of the 3rd Queen Alexandra's Own Gurkha Rifles Vol. II 1927-1947* (London: William Clowes & Sons, 1953), pp. 110-112. See also Richard Tolson, *A Soldier Poet: Letters and Poems of an English Officer 1938-1952* (Oxford: Tolson Publications, 2009), pp. 112-129.
52 Tolson, *A Soldier Poet*, p. 123.
53 See 4th Indian Division Artillery Training Instruction No. 8, 17 February 1943, *Dimoline Mss.*, IWM, 73/40/1. See also E. D. Smith, *Even the Brave Falter* (London: Robert Hale, 1978), pp. 28-65.
54 See 10th Indian Division Training Instruction No. 4, 4 April 1943, TNA, WO 169/18813.

commanded by General Tuker, they endeavoured to learn from the formations around them. All the Indian divisions learnt from other formations in the field such as the very successful French mountain divisions. 8th Indian Division noted that:

> When taking over from an ally whose methods of warfare differ from our own, the problem is greatly simplified if those methods are understood. We frequently capture a place with a Bn and hold it with a company: the French seem to go even further than this; capturing with a Brigade and holding with a platoon. There is a lot to be said for this method in the hilly country in which we are fighting.[55]

Similarly for fighting in towns and villages lessons were learned from the experience of the Canadians at Ortona with an important training instruction penned by 4th Indian Division concerning fighting in towns and villages.[56] After 4th Indian Division's major action at Cassino, Brigadier E. D. 'Birdie' Smith commented that 'there were many physical and mental "hills" around Cassino'.[57] After the battle his battalion had a month out of action and then undertook more mountain warfare training to refresh what the unit had learnt in the Mountain Warfare School in Lebanon. He remarked:

> There was talk about using us as high altitude troops which made sense as the Battalion had been trained for such a role during 1943. Several of us were sent on a mountaineering refresher course at Benevento run by the Americans. The intensive programme of rock-climbing tested nerves and aptitudes. No one from our Battalion failed probably because we knew as much about mountaineering as our instructors. It ended with us feeling outrageously fit.[58]

The 4th Indian Division continued training under their new GOC, Major General Holworthy, the mountain warfare specialist, who took over command on the 25 March 1944. Training instructions continued to be disseminated in the division. For instance, Training Instruction No. 45 was issued in April 1944 on counter mortar organisation. It was in response to the failure to counter the enemy mortars, the

---

55 8th Indian Division Training Instruction No. 8, 30 November 1944, TNA, WO 204/7570.
56 See 4th Indian Division Training Instruction No. 44, 5 January 1944, *Tuker Mss.*, IWM 71/21/2/7. See also Ian Gooderson, 'Assimilating Urban Battle Experience – The Canadians at Ortona', *Canadian Military Journal*, Winter 2007-08, pp. 64-73.
57 Smith, *Even the Brave Falter*, p. 25. See also Christopher Mann, 'Failures in Command and Control: The Experience of 4th Indian Division at the Second Battle of Cassino, February 1944', Andrew Hargreaves, Patrick Rose and Matthew Ford (eds.), *Allied Fighting Effectiveness in North Africa and Italy, 1942-1945* (Leiden: Brill, 2014), pp. 188-205.
58 Smith, ibid., pp. 66-67.

solution was to have counter mortar officers at brigade and battalion level.[59] Mountain warfare also meant that 149th Anti-Tank Regiment was converted to a pack regiment and underwent training for the conversion with the firing and maintenance of 3.7inch Howitzers, the loading and unloading of the ordnance onto mules and animal management with a six week period for this re-training.[60]

The 8th Indian Division's second major action was the crossing of the River Gari. The division along with 1st Canadian Armoured Brigade had three weeks training together before going into action, concentrating on river crossings, handling assault boats and infantry/armour co-operation.[61] Also prior to the action much reconnaissance was done at night. The plan was for the heavily camouflaged Canadian tanks to be deployed on the river bank to enable the infantry to cross by night. The tanks were also to launch three Bailey bridges. The barrage started at 11pm on 11 May, followed by the infantry attack 45 minutes later. The 17th Indian Infantry Brigade was to attack on the right supported by 11th (Ontario) Armoured Regiment with 19th Indian Infantry Brigade on the left supported by 14th (Calgary) Armoured Regiment. The 19th Indian Infantry Brigade were across the river by the morning and only the extreme left of their flank was not secure. Two of the three bridges were erected and the first tanks crossed the river in the morning. The German defenders in the small village of San Angelo managed to resist until the next day when it was taken by two companies of Gurkhas supported by heavy artillery fire followed by tank support. With San Angelo captured and the left flank secure the division was able to advance up the Liri Valley capturing the objective of Pignataro. Twenty four hours later the Polish division took Monastery Hill at Cassino and thus the Gustav Line was finally taken.[62] There were slight hitches as not enough time was given to allow for the infantry crossing, so they were not able to keep up with the barrage. The night reconnaissance and attack surprised the enemy who had not expected an advance in the Liri valley shown by the absence of mines and lack of anti-tank defences. Training Instruction No. 7 produced by General Russell, who saw the objective of these instructions as a way to record the knowledge acquired by the division, clearly showed the importance of the three arms training together before going into battle that was subsequently proven in the ensuing action. As it stated: 'Co-operation between the two assaulting brigades, their supporting armoured regiments and the Arty FOOs with the infantry

---

59 See 4th Indian Division Training Instruction No. 45, 13 April 1944, TNA, WO 169/18776.
60 See HQ RA 4th Indian Division, Movement and conversion to Pack Arty, 30 August 1943 and 4th Indian Division Artillery Training Instruction No. 9, 1 November 1943, p. 2, *Dimoline Mss.*, IWM, 73/40/1.
61 See Pal, *Campaign in Italy*, pp. 156-157 and Rose, 'British Army Command Culture 1939-1945', p. 19.
62 See Pal, *Campaign in Italy*, pp. 159-183 and *The Tiger Triumphs* (Delhi: HMSO for the Government of India, 1946), pp. 65-78 and *Current Reports from Overseas* No. 47, pp. 1-6, IWM.

was excellent, thanks to the training which they had done together'.[63] The conclusion reiterated the importance of training particularly before a set-piece attack, as well as the need for 'speed, dash and risk in more mobile operations'. Russell and his staff also noted the need of flexibility of the Division to work with any armour.[64]

All three divisions and 43rd (Gurkha) Lorried Brigade fought in the mountain campaigns of the Gothic line. The 8th Indian Division faced the Germans at Monte Veruca and Monte Citerna. The division's task was to take the three objectives of Femina Morta, La Saclette and Alpe di Vitigliano. The first objective was Monte Citerna which was captured by 21st Indian Infantry Brigade on 12 September with 1/5th Maratha Light Infantry taking M. Veruca and then took La Saclette on 14 September. The 3/15th Punjab Regiment took Alpe di Vitigliano on 15 September. The same day 17th Indian Infantry Brigade attacked Femina Morta which was secured two days later. This remarkably quick operation in the mountains pierced the Gothic Line in a particularly heavily defended German position.[65] After crossing the Arno, 12th Frontier Force Regiment successfully fought off a German counterattack where the 77 smoke grenade was the decisive factor. 8th Indian Division's Training Instruction No. 8 noted: 'This was the first time that its effect had been tested in the open. Its value in village fighting and against strong points is well known'.[66] Lessons learned included the use of smoke as artillery but could not be used due to the steepness of the hills. It was realised that although reconnaissance patrols brought back valuable information, fighting patrols did not kill many of the enemy so the formation decided to send fighting patrols of only two to three men to act as a nuisance which the division found more effective. Other administrative lessons included the carrying of seven man pack loads of ammunition with each rifle company going into action in case of counterattacks. 'Pasha' Russell concluded: 'In this hill-fighting, speed and dash by the leading troops pay a handsome dividend, but must be immediately backed up'.[67] Lessons were also instigated for future training. It was remarked that the division needed to overcome the 'tank & 88mm hoodoo'. Patrolling was once again stressed, suggesting that a patrol should consist of 2 PIAT men, 3 grenade men, 4 bayonet men, 4 'Tommy' gun or Bren gun men and a section commander and an NCO that should all be trained as a complete team with a drill laid down for differing conditions. Other training needs included such matters as minelaying, setting of booby traps, tightening of weapon security and all second in command's to command battalions in action.[68]

The 4th Indian Division was equally successful on the Gothic Line. On 29 August 1944, 5th Indian Infantry Brigade took Monte della Croce unopposed due to confusion among the defending German troops. The Brigade went on to take Monte Calvo

---

63   8th Indian Division Training Instructions No. 7, 30 July 1944, TNA, WO 204/7570.
64   Ibid.
65   See Jackson, *The Mediterranean and Middle East Vol. VI*, pp. 285-286.
66   8th Indian Division Training Instruction No. 8, 30 November 1944, TNA, WO 204/7570.
67   8th Indian Division Training Instruction No. 7, 30 July 1944, TNA, WO 169/18796.
68   See ibid.

with 3/10th Baluch Regiment being the first unit in 8th Army to breach the defensive position. The 11th Indian Infantry Brigade took Tavoleto on the night of 3/4 September whilst 7th Indian Infantry Brigade took Auditore on the 3 September and Poggio San Giovanni on 4 September. The Division fought for a further 26 days advancing more than 60 miles, the last 25 miles of which had been against constant German defence in mountain warfare before it was relieved by 10th Indian Division and earmarked for Greece. After Cassino, the thorough training under the leadership of General Holworthy reinvigorated the division for further mountainous warfare on the Gothic Line.

Early lessons learnt by 10th Indian Division in their initial actions included the importance of night advances particularly the need for training for an outflanking movement in night fighting. It was noticed that reconnaissance patrols needed to be backed up by adequate troops to take advantage of the situation otherwise they just gave notice of an impending operation. The need of portering by mules for the artillery was noted and by porters rather than mules for the infantry. Early successful actions were attributed to intensive training, fitness, adaptability and limited objectives. But there was room for improvement in intercommunication, the use of maximum force for objectives, improvement of traffic control, patrol technique, location of HQ's, the bringing forward of mortars and the concealment of objectives.[69]

After 10th Indian Division relieved 4th Indian Division on 3 October 1944, 20th Indian Infantry Brigade attacked Sogliano whilst 25th Indian Infantry Brigade attacked San Martino and both were taken the following day. As part of V Corps advance across the Fiumicino, 20th Indian Infantry Brigade attacked Monte Farnetto while 25th Indian Infantry Brigade attacked Monte Gattano with 10th Indian Infantry Brigade in reserve again once both positions were secured whilst 10th Indian Infantry Brigade supported by 43rd (Gurkha) Lorried Brigade took Monte Spaccato and Monte Codruzzo on 10 October. The division continued advancing until withdrawn for rest on 2 November. The historian of the Indian formations in Italy remarked that it was a mountaineer's battlefield and commented on 10th Indian Division's role:

> These operations among the eastern spurs of the Apennines revealed Tenth Indian Division in its most adept role. Concealment, unobtrusive infiltration, followed by a violent pounce upon enemies taken unawares – so ran attack after attack. General Reid's slogans inculcated his division with a dominant idea in terms sufficiently simple to be understood, sufficiently explicit to serve as a standing guide and instruction.[70]

---

69 See Narrative of 10th Indian Division, June-December 1944, Papers of Major General Denys Reid, *Reid Mss.*, IWM.
70 *The Tiger Triumphs*, p. 150.

For this later fighting, the divisional battle narrative noted that the hills were smaller and rivers were across the main line of advance with all the actions undertaken in pouring rain apart from two. The division also came up against village fighting which they had not encountered much up until this point but prior to going into action it had undertaken training in this as well as team work. Throughout this month of fighting, brigades passed through each other without slowing the momentum of advance. In addition, when taking over from a formation the division immediately went on the offensive as can be seen when they took over from 4th Indian Division and thus a continuity of action was possible. They used concealment in attack and crossed rivers by infiltration. Air and tank support were good but little used due to the weather. The narrative concluded with the success of patrolling commenting that: 'Patrolling was again excellent and the co-operation between Bdes [Brigades] and other arms reached a very high standard. To this may largely be attributed the success of these actions'.[71]

The lessons drawn from the division's first six months of action pinpointed much that had already been noted. Weapons were analysed for usefulness with the 2-pounder anti-tank gun shown to be fairly useless and the 6-pounder having been used little. The rum ration, particularly in atrocious weather conditions, was essential for the battle welfare of the troops, in addition to individual mess tins for mobile operations and light sleeping bags rather than heavier blankets. In patrolling, as with the other Indian divisions, it was noticed that 'For fighting patrols use of a smaller number of skilled men has produced better results than when organised on a platoon basis'.[72] Finally, with regards to the training of junior leaders a brigade training cadre was set up, 'To compete with the drain of battle casualties on junior leaders permanent Bde training cadres have been found necessary. These function continuously irrespective of whether the Bde is in or out of the line. Reliance on periods of rest from training is not sufficient'.[73] Thus, it can be seen that all three divisions together with the 43rd Lorried Brigade mounted successful operations on the mountainous Gothic Line underpinned by their training in mountain warfare.

Field Marshal Harold Alexander, Mediterranean Supreme Commander, thought the Indian divisions were not as good as the New Zealand forces or the French Expeditionary Corps, commenting that they were 'slow to get started and slow on exploitation but knew how to fight in the mountains'.[74] This begrudging comment also betrayed the traditional prejudice against the Indian Army by British service officers. The Indian formations started training for the Italian campaign in the Middle East

---

71 Narrative of 10th Indian Division, June–December 1944, *Reid Mss.*, IWM.
72 Ibid.
73 Ibid.
74 Field Marshal Harold Alexander, Answers to George Howe's questions for Alexander, Reel, Item 5007, p. 11, George C. Marshall Research Library, Lexington, Virginia, USA. I am grateful to Professor Glyn Harper for this quotation. See also Glyn Harper and John Tonkin-Covell, *The Battles of Monte Cassino: The Campaign and its controversies* (Auckland: Allen & Unwin, 2013), p. 241.

and continued to learn the lessons from their experience in Italy through the promulgation of training instructions across all three divisions. In contrast to the Brazilian Expeditionary Force where it was a case of learning on the job in Italy.[75]

Experience from the Italian Campaign was disseminated back to India with contributions to the *Army in India Training Memoranda* especially if they were applicable to the campaigns in Burma. *AITM* No. 27 which was produced in January 1945 had a section entitled "Notes by a Corps Commander in Italy" followed by "What the Brigadier Said". The corps commander noted the lessons learnt in river crossings stating the need for training, patrolling, mopping up, traffic control even to the level of use of ropes; as well as sections on counter mortar organisation, light scales of transport and traffic control. The brigadier noted lessons in mountain warfare such as the need for the tactical timetable to be subordinate to administrative requirements.[76] *AITM* No. 25 reprinted the administrative lessons from the Italian campaign from one of 8th Indian Division's training instructions.[77]

Conclusion

Mountain warfare was investigated by the War Office with the setting up of the Mountain Warfare Committee in late 1944. On the original three man committee were two Indian Army officers, namely Colonel Le Marchand, a mountain warfare expert, and Brigadier Donald Bateman who had commanded 5th Indian Infantry Brigade in Italy and went on to become Director Military Training, India in 1945. The object of the committee was 'To study experience gained so far in the tactical doctrine, organisation, equipment and training for the employment of troops in mountainous and snow conditions against a first-class enemy'. The committee looked at a variety of Allied sources, interviewing a large number of personnel including Major General Tuker and Brigadier Dimoline, CRA 4th Indian Division. The result of this committee was a viable doctrine in *MTP* No. 34 *Snow and Mountain Warfare* produced by the War Office in December 1944.[78]

Mountain warfare continued to be of importance in India. Training teams from 8th and 10th Indian Divisions were sent to the North West Frontier to lecture about

---

75 See Cesar Campiani Maximiano, 'Learning on the Job: Training the Brazilians for Combat in the Gothic Line', Hargreaves et al. (eds.), *Allied Fighting Effectiveness*, pp. 120-147.
76 See in *Army in India Training Memorandum* No. 27, January 1945, pp. 38-40, IOR, L/MIL/17/5/2240. See also Major General F. A. M. B. Jenkins, 'Some Lessons from the Italian Campaign', *JUSII*, Vol. LXXIV, No. 314, January 1944, pp. 8-17.
77 See in *Army in India Training Memorandum* No. 25, July 1944, pp. 21-25, IOR, L/MIL/17/5/2240.
78 See Snow and Mountain Warfare Committee on Training and Tactics 1944-45, TNA, WO 32/10993.

fighting with modern equipment in mountainous terrain.[79] The Frontier Warfare Committee was set up in 1944 under Tuker's chairmanship who thought traditional forms of 'frontier warfare' were now outdated and lessons from the experience of mountain warfare in the Italian campaign should be instigated. However, the proposals of the Committee were not acted upon due to Partition when responsibility for the region went to Pakistan.[80]

The Battle of Keren, along with the use of training instructions from material disseminated both by GHQ and in theatre, is the essential link in the development of the Indian Army from an Imperial policing force in 1939 to becoming a thoroughly professional force in 1945. The combination of training and fighting experience meant that the individual commanders and formations had fought alongside each other and could build upon that experience and then fight together in the Italian campaign as well as in Burma. In Italy, the 4th, 8th and 10th Indian Divisions trained for mountain warfare, fighting in towns and villages and river crossings that they successfully undertook. The successful actions along the Gothic Line, in particular, were underpinned by their continual training in mountain warfare.

---

79 See Report by General Sir Claude J. E. Auchinleck, Commander-in-Chief in India covering the period 1st January to 31st December 1945, 30th June 1947, p. 22, TNA, WO 203/2670.
80 See Moreman, *Army in India*, pp.182-185.

5

Jungle Warfare: Malaya 1941-42

This chapter will look at the doctrine, training, experience and lessons learned by Indian Army formations on the Malayan peninsula. There is a vast bibliography on the Malayan campaign and the Fall of Singapore but little has concentrated on the army that made up the bulk of the forces on the mainland, namely the Indian Army.[1] Prior to the Second World War, there were only two Indian Army battalions in Malaya in 12th Indian Infantry Brigade which was posted to Malaya as the strategic reserve in 1939. By 1941 six Indian brigades made up the bulk of the defence force on the Malayan peninsula comprising 9th and 11th Indian Divisions, albeit both with only two brigades.[2] They came under the command of III Indian Corps with Lieutenant General Sir Lewis 'Piggy' Heath in charge. Heath had commanded 5th Indian Division at the Battle of Keren and therefore had much recent battle experience. The General Officer Commanding (GOC) Malaya, Lieutenant General Arthur Percival, junior to Heath in date of rank, was British service with previous experience of Malaya as a staff officer. However he had had little experience of dealing with the Indian Army that probably helped to reinforce the existing prejudice of British service

---

1   See Justin J. Corfield, *A Bibliography of the Literature Relating to the Malayan Campaign and the Japanese Period in Malaya, Singapore and Northern Bormeo* (Hull: University of Hull, Centre for South-East Asian Studies, Bibliography and Literature Series Paper No. 5, 1988). More recent studies include: Brian P. Farrell, *The Defence and Fall of Singapore* (Stroud: Tempus, 2005), Tim Moreman, *The Jungle, the Japanese and the British Commonwealth at War 1941-45* (Abingdon: Frank Cass, 2005), chapter 1, Brian P. Farrell & Garth Pratten, *Malaya 1942* (Canberra: Army History Unit, 2009); Romen Bose, *Singapore at War* (Singapore: Marshall Cavendish, 2012); Justin and Robin Corfield, *The Fall of Singapore* (Richmond, Australia: Hardie Grant Books, 2012). The only recent work on the Indian Army is Alan Warren, 'The Indian Army and the Fall of Singapore' in Brian Farrell & Sandy Hunter (eds.), *Sixty Years On: The Fall of Singapore Revisited* (Singapore: Eastern Universities Press, 2003), pp. 270-289.
2   In late 1941 the breakdown for troops was: 37,000 Indian, 19,000 British, 17,000 Malay/Chinese and 15,000 Australian.

and Indian Army officers in theatre.³ Indeed, the historians Brian Farrell and Garth Pratten have remarked there were three distinct contingents, Australian, British and Indian within Malaya Command with no standard doctrine and the three contingents each trained slightly differently.⁴ The Indian Army formations in Malaya were a mixture of the regular units and newly formed battalions that continued to be 'milked' of officers, Viceroy Commissioned Officers and other specialists to form new battalions in India.

The defence of Malaya against a possible overland invasion emerged as a growing threat during the 1930s. This was the first indication that specialist knowledge of living, moving and fighting in the jungle might be required. But the War Office felt there was no need for landward defences as the jungle was seen as impenetrable and this remained the official policy until 1938. This view was challenged following the appointment of Major General William Dobbie as GOC Malaya Command in 1935. One of his officers, Lieutenant Colonel Stanley Woodburn Kirby who later became the official historian of the campaign, submitted a report in 1936 noting 'that the Back Door is at present being left unlocked'. Kirby was critical of infantry training in Singapore, believing it suffered due to the climate and terrain. He observed that most battalions' standards dropped after a tour there and recommended that all units needed to be sent where 'adequate training facilities exist'.⁵ Brigadier F. H. 'Jo' Vinden, who took up the post of GSOII Malaya in 1937 and worked for the Joint Intelligence Bureau of Malaya Command, challenged the idea that an invasion in the north of Malaya during the monsoon season was impossible. He sailed up the coast and found Chinese junks landing on the east coast in order to avoid Malaya's immigration quotas. This myth of the impenetrable jungle was also destroyed after an exercise by three British Battalions and the Johore Defence Force against an attacking battalion of Gordon Highlanders. The Commanding Officer of the Gordons had had jungle experience in West Africa, he attacked through the jungle and caught the defence in the rear. To counteract this threat Vinden suggested an increase in the number of troops who would need to be trained in jungle warfare.⁶ General Dobbie came to the same conclusion as his staff officers, based on their evidence and supported by lessons learnt from a number of exercises.⁷ Thus, by 1938, some officers in Malaya Command

---

3   See Raymond Callahan, *The Worst Disaster: The Fall of Singapore* (Newark: University of Delaware Press, 1977), p. 111. See also Warren, 'The Indian Army and the Fall of Singapore', p. 272.
4   See Farrell and Pratten, *Malaya 1942*, p. 128.
5   Lieutenant Colonel S. W. Kirby, 'Notes on Singapore', Papers of General Arthur Percival, *Percival Mss.*, IWM, P41. See also Ong Chit Chung, *Operation Matador* (Singapore: Times Academic Press, 1997), p. 54, n. 128.
6   See Brigadier F. H. Vinden, 'By Chance a Soldier' (Unpublished Memoir), pp. 71-72, 77, IWM, 96/36/1.
7   See Combined Operations Exercise 1938, Appendix E, *Percival Mss.*, P41.

understood there was a need for jungle training but appropriate training for specific local conditions was not implemented.

Doctrine

Experience of the jungle was generally lacking in the Indian Army with the exception of those officers who had been hunting, known as *shikar*, an activity often seen as one of the advantages of service in India.[8] Compared to the North West Frontier where most Indian Army officers spent a period of time, only officers attached to paramilitary forces such as the Assam Rifles and the Burma Military Police had encountered the jungle through imperial policing in such areas as the jungles of the North East Frontier of India and Burma.[9] The only source of tactical guidance for jungle warfare during the interwar period was the official doctrine used by all Commonwealth armies laid down in the 1935 edition of *Field Service Regulations* that devoted only two pages to the subject that focused on operations against uncivilised opponents.[10] Although lessons from Waziristan continued to be learnt by the Indian Army in the 1930s which showed fighting in thick scrub and jungle 'was just as unfavourable to the enemy, as it was to our own troops. The thick cover enable our troops to get to close quarters with the enemy, to envelop his flanks and to threaten his lines of withdrawal'.[11] Thus there was no established conventional doctrine of jungle warfare for Commonwealth units to draw upon when deployed in the jungles of northern Malaya, bar publications on imperial policing on the North East Frontier of India and the experiences in the East African Campaign during the First World War.[12] On arrival in Malaya in 1939, David Wilson, an officer in the 2nd Battalion of the Argyll and Sutherland Highlanders, remembered that:

> The British Army had not fought in any similar terrain, and there was no pamphlet of advice on how to operate in it. There *was* a pamphlet that had been written during the First World War, about fighting in scrub country against the formidable German General von Lettow Vorbeck, which advised the construction of

---

8 See General Staff, India, *Indian Military Almanac* (Delhi, 1929), pp. 98-104. See also Major-General J. G. Elliott, *Field Sports in India 1800-1947* (London: Gentry Books, 1973) and Tony Mason and Eliza Reidi, *Sport and the Military: The British Armed Forces 1880-1960* (Cambridge: CUP, 2010), p. 54.
9 See T. R. Moreman, ' "Small Wars' and 'Imperial Policing": The British Army and the Theory and Practice of Colonial Warfare in the British Empire, 1919-1939', *Journal of Strategic Studies*, Vol. 19, No. 4, December 1996, pp. 120-124 and Colonel L. W. Shakespear, *History of the Assam Rifles* (London: Macmillan, 1929).
10 See *Field Service Regulations*, Volume II (London, 1935), pp. 183-185, IWM. See also French, *Raising Churchill's Army*, p. 13.
11 *AHQ India Training Memorandum* No. 16, p. 6, IOR, L/MIL/17/5/2199.
12 See Moreman, '"Small Wars and Imperial Policing"', pp. 105-128.

zarebas (thorn fences) to protect one's position, but there were no thorns to be had in the Malayan jungle! We had to find out for ourselves the hard way.[13]

Troops could easily become bewildered, depressed and frightened in the jungle due to the strangeness of the terrain, emphasized by the limited visibility, the strange noises, the difficulty of movement and the sense of isolation in the jungle. This, in combination with the exhausting climate, made the conditions in Malaya extremely trying for the new troops. These difficulties had to be overcome, before coming into contact with the enemy, through training and experience.[14]

The growing garrison of Malaya was not left without guidance as two pamphlets on jungle warfare were produced in 1940, one issued by Malaya Command and the other by GHQ India.[15] Malaya Command's pamphlet, *Tactical Notes for Malaya*, was produced under the auspices of Lieutenant General Lionel Bond, GOC Malaya Command, based upon various exercises in Johore and Singapore at the beginning of the war.[16] It discussed the types of jungle in the country, the exhausting nature of the climate and noted the danger of malaria. The characteristics of the most likely enemy, the Imperial Japanese Army (IJA), were highlighted such as their high standards of training, great endurance, amphibious landing skills and it stressed their ruthlessness. Their weaknesses included little jungle training, poor minor tactics and the lack of initiative. Also listed under the weak points of the IJA was that they were trained to attack flanks, they were believed to be poor shots and were susceptible to malaria. The problems of jungle movement were investigated with the pamphlet suggesting that long moves would be by road, movement through rubber plantations by infantry and progress through the jungle was very slow and in single file. Although the training manual stressed, moreover, in capital letters that:

13   David Wilson, *The Sum of Things* (Staplehurst: Spellmount, 2001), p. 53. See also Angus Rose, *Who Dies Fighting* (London: Right Book Club, 1944), pp. 11-12. For the South African forces the lessons of the East African Campaign were encapsulated in Brigadier General John J. Collyer's *The South Africans with General Smuts in German East Africa 1916* (Pretoria: Gouvernement of South Africa, 1939). It was intended for instructional purposes at the South African Military College and used as a primer for jungle warfare. I'm grateful to Professor Ian van der Waag for alerting me to this publication and its purpose. See also Ian van der Waag, 'Contested Histories: Official History and the South African Militry in the Twentieth Century' in Jeffrey Grey (ed.), *The Last Word? Essays on Official History in the United States and British Commonwealth* (Westport, Connecticut: Praeger, 2003), pp. 34-36.
14   See *Notes from Theatres of War* No. 19 – *Burma, 1943/44*, p. 135, IWM.
15   See General Staff, Malaya Command, *Tactical Notes for Malaya* (Malaya, 1940). Reprinted by GHQ India in 1941 and *MTP* No. 9 (India). *Notes on Forest Warfare* (India, 1940), AWM. See also chapter 2.
16   See Moreman, *Jungle*, p. 17.

> TROOPS NEWLY ARRIVED IN MALAYA MUST TAKE EVERY OPPORTUNITY OF TRAINING ALL RANKS IN MOVING THROUGH JUNGLE. THE DIFFERENCE IN VALUE BETWEEN TRAINED AND UNTRAINED TROOPS IS IMMENSE.[17]

It was issued to all Commonwealth troops arriving in Malaya and reprinted in India. The pamphlet recommended high standards of leadership, surprise and the use of flanks in attack and offensive action in defence, recommending defence in depth rather than defence based on static positions. For perimeter camps the manual continued with the idea of building a 'zareba' from the East African experience but with cut saplings and creepers for trip wires.[18]

The 9th Indian Division was the first Indian Army formation to produce training instructions in April 1941. They were meant to help newly arrived officers adapt to conditions in Malaya and used material from Malaya Command Training Instructions, the *Field Service Pocket Book* (issued to all officers), *Military Training Pamphlet* No. 23 Part III and *AITM* Nos. 4 and 5. The instructions covered such matters as communications, chemical warfare, weapon training, fitness, unarmed combat, mines, traffic control but also noted the characteristics of the Japanese in their proficiency in fighting at night. The importance of patrolling was emphasized stating that: 'All troops must be trained in offensive patrolling in the jungle. In addition each bn. [battalion] will train at least two pls [platoons] in extensive jungle patrolling'.[19] The second Training Instruction noted the importance of moving both by day and night in the jungle and stated that this took a long time to perfect but that a reasonable degree of efficiency could be achieved in a short time as long as the practical rather than theoretical hard work was put in.[20]

Training

Matters were further complicated because the Army did not have a free hand in devising a coherent defence. Its deployment was constrained by the need to defend the airfields to a significant extent, about whose location they had not been consulted by the Royal Air Force. Furthermore, the only higher training undertaken by the reinforcing Indian Army formations had been for desert warfare in a mechanised role, therefore there had been no preparation for jungle warfare. As Kirby later wrote: 'The re-training of all arms on arrival in Malaya was thus of the utmost importance, in

---

17   Malaya Command, *Tactical Notes*, p. 6.
18   See ibid., pp. 3-5, 8- 9, 10-12.
19   9th Indian Division Training Instruction No.1, 21 April 1941, AWM, 54 553/5/22 Part 17.
20   See 9th Indian Division Training Instruction No. 2, 21 April 1942, AWM, 54 553/5/2/22 Part 17.

particular for the infantry, which in enclosed country, is the key arm in battle'.[21] There were also very real concerns about the basic quality of the reinforcements. As Denis Russell-Roberts remarked about his battalion in Malaya, the 5/11th Sikh Regiment, 'we had been milked to a dangerous extent'.[22] It arrived in Malaya with 460 recent recruits and 6 ECOs and was further 'milked' losing 30 officers and other ranks to form a new machine gun battalion.[23] Similarly the Indian Army units in 11th Indian Division were continually milked to bolster new battalions in India right up until the Japanese invasion with the divisional historian stating that in some battalions there were not more than two men per section with over two years' service.[24] F. W. Perry commented that 'milking', in combination with the training for the Middle East rather than for jungle warfare, was the reason for the poor performance of the Indian Army in Malaya.[25]

The actual progress being made in training by Indian troops between 1940-41 was delayed by the building of defences.[26] For instance, the 5/11th Sikhs arrived in Kuantan in April 1940 and immediately began defence work despite the fact the unit was in dire need of basic training. Prior to the Japanese invasion the battalion had only undergone some platoon and company training, three forty eight hour battalion schemes and no higher formation training had been attempted. It was poorly equipped with mortars, Thompson submachine guns were received only in September 1941 and training in these new weapons had yet to be undertaken.[27] Brigadier Berthold Key, CO 8th Indian Infantry Brigade, commented that the defence work at Kota Bahru was also at the expense of training. Permission was given to commence training only as late as November 1941. His brigade was very short of equipment and ammunition and forty percent of the officers, Viceroy Commissioned Officers and specialists were milked from each unit. When the Japanese attacked there were only three regular officers in each battalion, the remainder were Emergency Commissioned Officers just out from the Officer Training Schools in India and often not speaking the language of their soldiers. He concluded: 'further, if war came, there would be no question of breaking the troops in, they would be in the front line from the word "go"'.[28] Other

---

21 Major General S. Woodburn Kirby, *Singapore: The Chain of Disaster* (London: Cassell, 1971), p. 93.
22 Denis Russell-Roberts, *My Own War in Malaya* (Privately published, nd.), p. 133.
23 See Moreman, *Jungle*, pp. 20-21.
24 See A. M. L. Harrison, *History of the 11th Indian Division in Malaya* (Unpublished history), p. 16, IWM.
25 See Perry, *Commonwealth Armies*, p. 108.
26 See Simson, *Singapore*, pp. 30-40.
27 See Diary of the 5th Bn. (D.C.O.) The Sikh Regiment in the Malayan Campaign 8 Dec. 41-15 Feb. 42, *Heath Mss.*, IWM, LMH 4b. See also Russell-Roberts, *My Own War in Malaya*, p. 1 and Alan Warren, *Singapore 1942* (London: Hambledon, 2002), p. 45.
28 Brigadier B. W. Key, 'Brief History of the 8th Indian Infantry Brigade in Malaya, November 1940 – February 1942', pp. 2-3, IWM, P456. See also Lieutenant Colonel J. Frith, '2/10 Baluch in the Malayan Campaign', pp. 2, 8-9, NAM 7306-121.

Indian Army battalions' attempts at training were equally unsuccessful. Lieutenant Colonel B. K. Dymott of the 2/16th Punjab Regiment noted that training was handicapped by the avoidance of rubber plantations to avoid damage to the trees and night training prevented by the medical authorities due to fears of malaria.[29]

The amount of training that was actually carried out by Commonwealth units largely depended on their role and the initiative of the individual commanders rather than any action by Malaya Command. The most notable example was that of the 2nd Battalion Argyll and Sutherland Highlanders, under the command of Lieutenant-Colonel Hector Greenfield, with Major Ian Stewart as second in command. The unit was posted from India in 1939 and, together with the 4/19th Hyderabad Regiment and the 5/2nd Punjab Regiment, the Argylls formed 12th Indian Infantry Brigade. The whole brigade trained in jungle warfare, but the Argylls' experience has been the best documented.[30] The 5/2nd Punjabis started training in November 1939 under the direction of Lieutenant Colonel C. C. Deakin and continued in January 1940, sending officers such as Major Pierce to lecture on jungle warfare to 26th Squadron Royal Australian Air Force as part of Army/Air Force co-operation.[31] The Hyderabads' had also had considerable experience of bush warfare in East Africa during the First World War.[32]

Stewart assumed command of the Argylls in 1940 and took a keen interest in training to fight in the jungle. His far sighted approach was instrumental in developing innovative new ideas during early exercises in Johore after seeing the essential problems presented by jungle terrain, such as poor visibility, limited movement and the difficulties of command and control. The Argylls underwent two years of jungle training, mainly because their brigade was to act as the mobile reserve in the event of an invasion and therefore had to acquire experience of the jungle, and had the time and the opportunity to do so. Stewart believed that it took six months to get

---

29 See Lieutenant Colonel B. K. Dymott, 'I am Ready 2nd and 3rd Battalions 16th Punjab Regiment Malaya', p. 3, IWM, 67/264/1.
30 See Lieutenant Colonel Sir Geoffrey Betham and Major H. V. R. Geary, *The Golden Galley: The Story of the Second Punjab Regiment 1761-1947* (Oxford: 2nd Punjab Regiment Officers' Association, 1956), p. 223.
31 See War Diary of 12th Indian Infantry Brigade HQ, TNA, WO 172/112. See also Lieutenant Colonel C. C. Deakin and Major G. M. S. Webb, 'The Malayan Campaign, 1941-42: Accounts of the part played by the 5th Battalion, 2nd Punjab Regiment', (Unpublished Memoir), p. 2, NAM 6509-14.
32 See Mackenzie, *Eastern Epic*, p. 221 footnote. See also Brigadier Jasbir Singh, *Escape from Singapore* (New Delhi: Lancer Publications, 2010), pp. 20-23, Roy, *India & World War II*, p. 248, and Muhammad Ismail Khan interview, IWM, 117448 reel 1. Although Lieutenant-General Bond asked the C-in-C India if the 4/19th Hyderabads could be recalled to India and be replaced by a non-Indianised battalion due the seditious letter of Zahir-ud-Din and the resulting unrest in the battalion. See Chandar Sundaram, 'Seditious Letters and Steel Helmets: Disaffection among Indian Troops in Singapore and Hong Kong, 1940-1, and the Formation of the Indian National Army' in Kaushik Roy (ed.), *War and Society in Colonial India 1807-1945* (New Delhi. OUP, 2006), pp. 129-140.

a battalion fully acclimatised to the jungle. He understood that control of the roads was vital and this would be best maintained through operating in the surrounding jungle rather than in static defence. By developing tactics consisting of what he termed 'filleting' and the use of 'Tiger Patrols' that were practised in training until the jungle became 'a friend and not an enemy' to the Argylls. 'Filleting' consisted of an encircling attack to the rear of the enemy combined with a frontal attack that would split the enemy. 'Tiger Patrols' involved five men going behind enemy lines, also encircling the enemy.[33] Jonathan Moffat and Audrey McCormick in their study of the Argylls have remarked that: 'These patrols were not intended for reconnaissance; they were there to find the enemy, break his morale and destroy him'.[34] Stewart made sure that all troops in the battalion were integrated into his doctrine of jungle fighting, this included the pioneer and anti-aircraft platoons, and laid the foundation for them to become experts in this type of warfare.

The Argylls' methods and training attracted publicity. In particular, the march back to Singapore from Mersing, a distance of 61 miles, was achieved in three days and was widely reported in *The Straits Times*. At the same time battalions such as the 2nd Battalion, the Gordon Highlanders packed up work at noon which was standard in the pre-war routine of British Army battalions stationed in Malaya.[35] Stewart was dismissed as a crank by some in Malaya Command and was nicknamed 'Mad Stewart', an opinion reinforced by his abrasive character that alienated much support.[36] As a result Malaya Command did not act upon his innovative ideas on jungle warfare but his methods were recognised in other quarters. Four Argylls joined 101st Special Training School as instructors, for behind the lines work in the jungle, and two officers joined the Officer Cadet Training Unit as jungle warfare instructors. It must be noted that overall the Argylls were themselves by no means perfectly trained. One of the constraints the battalion faced when it went into action was the effects of 'milking', exacerbated by the fact that at any one time up to thirty Argylls were used by Malaya Command as orderlies, often for menial tasks.[37] According to Stewart, only a third of the battalion was jungle trained, a third partially trained and the remaining third had little or no experience of the jungle at the outbreak of hostilities.[38]

The appointment of Lieutenant General Arthur Percival as GOC Malaya Command in May 1941, selected by his mentor General Dill, the Chief of the Imperial General Staff, because of his previous experience in Malaya, led to an increase in the tempo

---

33 See Brigadier I. M. Stewart, *The Thin Red Line: 2nd Argylls in Malaya* (London: Nelson, 1947), pp. vii, 2-4.
34 Jonathan Moffatt & Audrey Holmes McCormack, *Moon over Malaya: A Tale of Argylls and Marines* (Glasgow: Coombe Publishing, 1999), p. 33.
35 See ibid., pp. 10, 18.
36 See Simson, p. 42. See also Murfett et al., p. 187 and Moffat and McCormack, p. 34.
37 See Moffatt and McCormack, pp. 36-37, 44.
38 Stewart, p. 7.

of training in Malaya following completion of the defence works. Percival had served during the interwar period with the Royal West African Frontier Force, one of the few regiments with a tradition of bush warfare both for internal security and fighting a conventional army during the First World War.[39] This experience, in combination with his time in Malaya Command in 1936-37, made him appear to be the ideal candidate to promote jungle training to meet a possible Japanese overland invasion. It would seem logical that, with Percival's previous experience and the existing training pamphlets, he would have ensured that Malaya Command instigated a thorough training programme for newly arrived troops. However, in his Despatch, Percival stated that 'no units had any training in bush warfare before reaching Malaya. Several of the units had in fact been specially trained for desert warfare' and went on to note that there needed to be a balance between time for training and the building of defence works.[40] He issued instructions that individual, sub-unit and unit training were to be instigated from July until November 1941 and where possible in jungle country and as the defences were completed, training could then be increased. He noted that 8th Australian Division and 12th Indian Infantry Brigade had been able to carry out some very profitable training in jungle warfare conditions in contrast to the troops in the north of Malaya who suffered from the 'milking' of the Indian Army.[41] In addition, Percival noted the availability of jungle warfare training manuals and the general War Office training manuals as well as directives that were issued to supplement the training manuals.[42] Thus, training was encouraged and training manuals were available but there was not enough time before the Japanese invasion to put it all into practice. Percival wrote that 'the war came before the training of the majority of even the smaller formations could be completed'.[43] Although it is worth noting that in Malaya Command, 'training was in the hands of a comparatively junior officer of the staff duties department'.[44] In fact there were no training centres apart from the Officers Cadet Training Unit at Changi.[45] In direct contrast to the Middle East where

---

39 See Major A. E. Percival, 'The West African Frontier Force', *The Army Quarterly*, Vol. XV, No. 1 (October, 1927), pp. 91-99. See also A. H. Clarke and W. Clarke, *History of the Royal West African Frontier Force* (Aldershot: Gale & Polden, 1964) and Sierra Leone Battalion Royal West African Frontier Force, *Bush Warfare* (Freetown: Sierra Leone Battalion, 1938).
40 Despatch on the Operations in Malaya, p. 26. *Percival Mss.*, IWM, P71. See also Second Supplement to *The London Gazette* of Friday 20 February 1948, Operations of Malaya Command, from 8 December 1941 to 15 February 1942, by Lieutenant General A. E. Percival, pp. 1258-1259.
41 See Farrell and Pratten, *Malaya 1942*, pp. 128-135.
42 See for example Malaya Command Training Instruction No. 5, 12 May 1941, AWM 54 553/5/22 Part 17.
43 Lieutenant-General A. E. Percival, *The War in Malaya* (London: Eyre & Spottiswoode, 1949), p. 69.
44 Ibid., p. 91.
45 See Wilson, *Sum of Things*, pp. 60-61. See also Despatch, p. 1259.

all newly arrived troops passed through desert warfare training centres before going into combat.[46]

Later arrivals were also able to train in the jungle, such as the 2/1st King George V's Own Gurkha Rifles and the 2/9th Gurkha Rifles of 28th Indian Infantry Brigade.[47] Both the battalions and the brigade started training on their arrival in Malaya in September – October 1941, although the regimental historian of the 9th Gurkha Rifles suggested that this was not the usual attitude in Malaya: 'Officers returning from courses or from attachment brought tales of an all-too-casual pace and of disconcerting unawareness of the imminence of war'.[48] Brigadier W. S. Carpendale, who commanded 28th Indian Infantry Brigade had fought in the jungle during the Malabar Rebellion (1921-22).[49] He made the time to instigate jungle training as his formation was going to be the corps reserve in north Malaya. In his report on the campaign, he noted that *Tactical Notes for Malaya* was the only available literature on jungle warfare but it contained little mention of minor tactics. The brigade was expected to come up with its own doctrine, yet he was informed that Stewart's ideas on jungle warfare and training were not condoned by Malaya Command. The brigade trained in thick jungle country and later exercises for control of the roads were undertaken at corps and divisional level. The 12th Indian Infantry Brigade also took part and Carpendale noted that his brigade and the Argylls in particular, had better motor transport discipline and speed of foot. In addition, a course in jungle lore was held where instruction included the use of parangs for cutting a pathway through the jungle, lighting fires without matches and survival in the jungle on rice alone. He wrote that by 8 December, after only two months' training, 'the men were in every way fit to meet the Japanese on equal terms'.[50] In contrast to Stewart's estimate of six months, Carpendale considered two months to be enough time to train troops for jungle warfare. However, it should be noted that this particular brigade did already have a high standard of basic training, with years of battle experience on the North West Frontier.[51]

Consequently training was delayed due the late arrival of equipment, the apparent disinterest in doctrine with pamphlets not being distributed and the building of defences.[52] This lack of interest in carrying out hard extensive training was also partly the result of the fact that the Imperial Japanese Army was underestimated by Malaya

---

46 Kirby, *Singapore*, p. 93.
47 See War Diary of 2/1 Gurkha Rifles, 9-12 September 1941, TNA, WO 172/136.
48 Stevens, *The 9th Gurkha Rifles*, p. 139.
49 See biographical portrait of Carpendale in Corfield, *The Fall of Singapore*, p. 52. See also Nick Lloyd, 'Colonial Counter-insurgency in Southern India: The Malabar Rebellion, 1921-1922' *Contemporary British History*, Vol. 29, No. 3, 2015, pp. 297-317.
50 Brigadier W. Carpendale, Report on Operations of 11th Indian Division in Kedah and Perak, IOR, L/WS/1/192. See also Roy, *Sepoys Against the Rising Sun*, pp. 77-78.
51 See Mackenzie, *Eastern Epic*, p. 229.
52 See Callahan, *Worst Disaster*, p. 177.

Command and the intelligence services. John Ferris even goes so far as to say that 'the authorities in Singapore were weeding material on the IJA to fit a preconceived notion'.[53] As the author of the 11th Indian Division's history has noted, the local view of the IJA was seen 'as lying somewhere between that of the Italian and Afghan Armies'. This view prevailed despite the fact that Lieutenant Colonel G. T. Wards, who had been Military Attache in Japan and was an expert on the Japanese Army, had informed senior officers that the Japanese Army was the equivalent of the 'unmilked' Indian Army of 1939.[54] However, the condescending viewpoint was the more widespread, heavily influenced by ethnocentrism, support being found in misperceptions of the Japanese performance against the Chinese and the Russian Armies.[55]

The Malayan Campaign

The Japanese 25th Army invaded the Malayan mainland at Kota Bahru on 8 December 1941, with unopposed landings in Thailand at Singora and Patani. Operation 'Matador', a British pre-emptive plan to forestall the Japanese landings, was not ordered in time.[56] The Japanese air forces quickly gained complete superiority over the obsolescent planes of the Royal Air Force and the Royal Australian Air Force. Henry Probert has remarked that 'after the first day the RAF virtually ceased to exist as a means of defence'.[57] This, in addition to the sinking of HMS Repulse and HMS Prince of Wales on 9 December, meant that after three days the defence of Malaya was the army's responsibility alone, without any significant support from the other two services. Percival's plan was for III Indian Corps, consisting of 9th and 11th Indian Divisions with 28th Indian Infantry Brigade, to be stationed in the north and east coast of Malaya to forestall the Japanese forces and provide time for reinforcements to arrive in theatre from overseas.

The first major land engagement of the Malayan Campaign was the Battle of Jitra on 11 December. The Japanese Army overran the fixed defences at Jitra in just fourteen hours using tanks, infiltration and encirclement, with the demoralised defenders abandoning valuable equipment and supplies. These losses could not be made up and were particularly damaging as 11th Indian Division was the best equipped formation

---

53   John Ferris, 'Worthy of some better enemy? : The British estimate of the Imperial Japanese Army, 1919-41, and the Fall of Singapore', *Canadian Journal of History*, Vol. XXVII, August 1993, p. 248.
54   See Harrison, History of the 11th Indian Division in Malaya, p. 5.
55   See Antony Best, 'This Probably Over -Valued Military Power: British Intelligence and Whitehall's Perception of Japan, 1939-1941', *Intelligence and National Security*, Vol. 12, No. 3, July 1997, p. 74.
56   See Ong Chit Chung, pp. 215-233. See also Sir Andrew Gilchrist, *Malaya 1941: The Fall of a Fighting Empire* (London: Robert Hale, 1992).
57   H. Probert, *The Forgotten Air Force: The Royal Air Force in the War against Japan, 1941-1945* (London: Brassey's, 1995), p. 43.

Jungle Warfare: Malaya 1941-1942 141

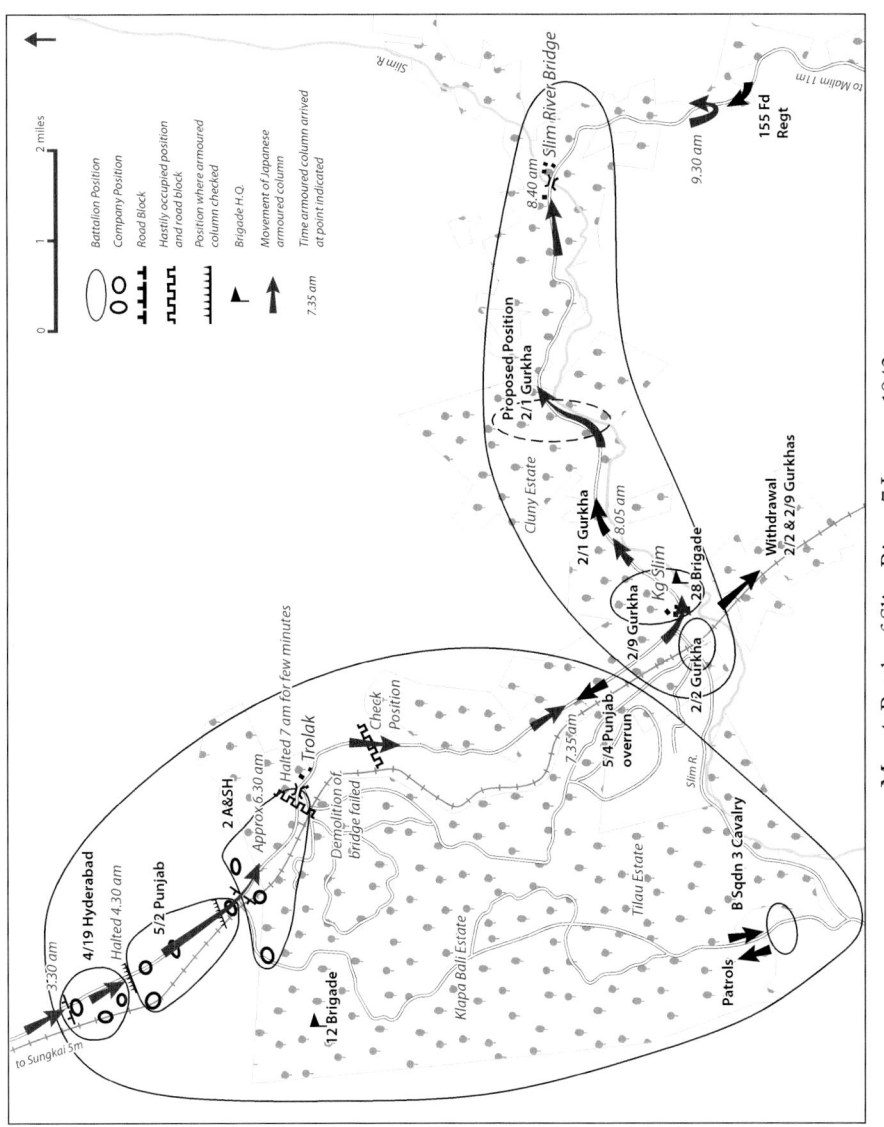

Map 4 Battle of Slim River, 7 January 1942.

in Malaya. The fighting quickly revealed how badly organised, trained and equipped the Indian troops were for war in the jungle. Bewildered by the jungle and the Japanese, morale amongst poorly trained Indian troops plummeted. In contrast, the confident battle hardened IJA appeared 'at home' in the jungle.

Some successful actions were fought by jungle-trained troops. The Argylls' first action at the Battle of Grik Road on 19 December showed the importance of jungle training in Malaya. The Argylls defended in depth and undertook aggressive encircling patrols. When they took Sumpitan, the battalion had advanced 36 miles in five hours. Stewart noted that when the Japanese were attacked they bunched. When the Argylls finally had to withdraw due to the weight of Japanese forces, it was again a fighting withdrawal using ambushes and encirclement.[58]

The Indian Army never recovered from this early defeat in Northern Malaya, and quickly fell back down the peninsula. At the Battle of Slim River on 7 January, once again tanks were decisive and went through the best-trained brigades of 11th Indian Division. The Trolak position was held by 12th Indian Infantry Brigade, now commanded by Stewart, but the sad reality was that individual units were depleted for example the 5th/2nd Punjabis were exhausted with low morale and had lost fifty percent of its fighting efficiency. The battalion and its parent brigade had withdrawn 176 miles in three weeks. The 28th Indian Infantry Brigade held the Slim River position, 6.5 miles south of Trolak. Both brigades were very short of anti-tank weapons. Stewart selected the area due to its favourable terrain. The Japanese tanks attacked at 3am on 7 January 1942, they broke through the first defensive line held by the 4/19th Hyderabads and were upon the 5/2nd Punjabis by 4.30am, and by 6.30am in the area defended by the Argylls and captured Trolak. The Japanese tanks continued for the intact bridge at Slim river which they took after driving through the units of 28th Indian Infantry Brigade. In this battle Stewart's tactics were at fault, due to bad positioning and the lack of anti-tank weapons and anti-tank mines, his exhausted and depleted brigade could not prevent the Japanese from smashing right through it. Although Stewart's concept of filleting had been shown to be successful, but on this occasion by the enemy.[59] This defeat meant that the Japanese were able to take Kuala Lumpar unopposed. The 11th Indian Division had been destroyed and General Wavell, ABDA Commander, ordered Percival to bring the remnants back to Johore.

The Japanese reached Johore Bahru at the foot of the Malay peninsula on 31 January 1942. The remaining uncommitted reinforcements on Singapore Island were 44th Indian Brigade, part of the recently-formed 17th Indian Division, and Indian and Australian replacements who had arrived between 22-24 January respectively, and the

---

58 See Stewart, pp. 29-47.
59 See K. D. Bhargava & K. N. V. Sastri, *Campaigns in South-East Asia 1941-1942* (New Delhi: Pentagon Press, 2012), pp. 214-222. See also Louis Allen, *Singapore 1941-1942* (London: Davis-Poynter, 1977), p. 53; Warren, pp. 129-145 and Deakin and Webb, 'The Malayan Campaign', pp. 56-58.

rest of 18th Division which arrived on 29 January. All these troops needed training (some lacked even basic training) and they had no chance to acclimatise. They were nevertheless deployed in the front line of coastal defence. The III Corps took over the northern area; the Australians were on the west with 44th Indian Infantry Brigade and the Singapore Fortress troops under Major General Keith Simmons, comprising two Malaya Infantry Brigades and the Singapore Straits Volunteer Force. The only reserve force were the remnants of 12th and 6th/15th Indian Infantry Brigades.[60] The Japanese, under heavy artillery cover, attacked the Australian forces on 10 February and slowly advanced onto the island where, through the breakdown of communications, shortage of water, fuel, ammunition and general chaos, General Percival surrendered on 15 February. The defence of Singapore Island had lasted just fifteen days, finally crumbling when the Japanese captured the water supply. The defeat was one of the worst in British history with about 130,000 Commonwealth troops being taken prisoner. Churchill described it as 'the worst disaster and largest capitulation in history'.[61] Numbers vary considerably for the number of Indian troops captured but it is generally thought about 65,000 with 20,000 joining the Indian National Army and the remainder enduring captivity in New Guinea, New Britain and Bougainville.[62]

Lessons from Malaya

The disastrous Malayan campaign was a shocking defeat for British arms. It was carefully analysed and it quickly became apparent that 'milking' was a fundamental problem affecting all Indian units. GHQ India were also eager to discern lessons for troops in Burma and those under training. Early lessons were incorporated into a revised edition of *MTP* No. 9 (India) in January 1942. This training manual discussed the Japanese infiltration, outflanking tactics and the use of local disguise by the Japanese forces, which made it very difficult for Indian troops to recognise them. The Japanese troops travelled lightly and made good use of tanks, which had previously been discounted by Malaya Command as they had been seen as unsuitable for the terrain. It remarked on

---

60   The 6th and 15th Indian Infantry Brigades had combined forces to form the 6th/15th Indian Infantry Brigade on 22 December 1941 at Ipoh.
61   Winston S. Churchill, *The Second World War: 7. The Onslaught of Japan* (London: Cassell, 1964), p. 81.
62   See Raghavan, *India's War*, p. 283. See also Chandar S. Sundaram, 'The Indian National Army, 1942-1946: A Circumstantial Force' in Daniel P. Marston and Chandar S. Sundaram (eds.), *A Military History of India and South Asia* (Wesport, Connecticut: Praeger, 2007), pp. 123-130. For those Indian soldiers that did not join the INA and remained as prisoners of war see Peter Stanley, "Great in adversity": Indian prisoners of war in New Guinea' *Journal of the Australian War Memorial*, (November 2002) www.awm.gov.au/journal/j37/indians.asp accessed 29 October 2012; G. J. Douds, 'The Men Who Never Were: Indian POWs in the Second World War', *South Asia*, Vol. 27, No. 2, August 2004, pp. 182-216 and John Baptist Crasta, *Eaten by the Japanese: The Memoir of an Unknown Indian Prisoner of War*, (New York: The Invisible Man Press, 2013).

the use of Japanese snipers who used chained dogs to give warning of any approaching enemy. It maintained that the main defence against these Japanese tactics and ruses in the jungle was defence in depth, more mobile and less heavily laden troops, good fire discipline, withdrawal and immediate counterattacking.[63]

The early lessons from Malaya were also incorporated into the *AITM* series that was used in India to disseminate the latest tactical lessons and training information. *AITM* No. 14 published in February 1942 reiterated the general lessons from Malaya, such as keeping equipment to a minimum, a single light machine gun per platoon, the issuing of rifles or Thompson submachine guns to all soldiers, good fire discipline, frontal attacks only as fixing operations and immediate counterattacks. The example of the Argylls' action at Grik Road was cited, where the Japanese became a herd once they lost the initiative, showing that the Argylls' training methods were successful. It demonstrated that static defence was inappropriate in the jungle and that defence in depth was essential to prevent any encircling movements. At Grik, for example, the Argylls' operated at a depth of eight or nine miles. Accordingly, the ratio of casualties was five to one in the Argylls' favour, the high proportion of dead Japanese 'owing to the close range at which they sustained minor tactical defeat and the number of successful ambushes'.[64] *AITM* No. 15 attributed the three most important lessons from Malaya as being the passing on of information, patrolling, and high physical fitness and discipline. Areas where specialised training were seen as lacking were road discipline, anti-aircraft small arms defence, anti-tank defence, concealment and the lack of offensive spirit. There was little mention of jungle training, but rather a general need for the toughening up of troops.[65]

The British High Command made an immediate effort to learn from the debacle in Malaya and pass on training suggestions by ensuring that trained and experienced officers and specialists were evacuated. General Wavell, C-in-C ABDA, wrote in the foreword of Colonel Stewart's battalion history published in 1947:

> If all units in Malaya had been trained and led with the same foresight and imagination as Brigadier Stewart showed in the training of his battalion, the story of the campaign would have been different. It was the realisation of this that led me to order Brigadier Stewart's return to India, after his battalion and his brigade had both practically ceased to exist, to impart his knowledge and ideas to units in India preparing for the return match with the Japanese.[66]

---

63 See *MTP* No. 9 (India): *Notes on Forest Warfare*, 2nd edition, January 1942, pp. 21-23, IOR, L/MIL/17/5/2250.
64 See *AITM* No. 14, Jan-Feb 1942, pp. 12, 16-17, IOR, L/MIL/17/5/2240.
65 See *AITM* No. 15, March-April 1942, p. 2, IOR, L/MIL/17/5/2240.
66 Stewart, *Thin Red Line*, p. VI.

On 12 February, Stewart was evacuated to India with three other Argylls, Major Angus Rose, Captain David Wilson and Company Sergeant Major Arthur Bing.[67] En route Stewart also imparted his knowledge to the Australians in Java and on the voyage to Ceylon. Indeed, it is generally accepted by Australian and British historians that it was Stewart's experience, rather than General Gordon Bennett, which helped to advance the development of jungle warfare doctrine in the Australian Army.[68] It was following consultation with Stewart that the Australians produced a pamphlet on Japanese tactics in Malaya that was distributed throughout the Australian Army.

Specialist knowledge possessed by the Argylls on their return to India was passed on through lecture tours. Stewart also made a radio broadcast about the campaign to build up morale. Major William Alston, Senior Instructor of the Tactical School at Poona, recorded that when Stewart and Rose visited 'they ran a very useful model demonstration and exercise for the staff of the school, which became the basis of our teaching for the rest of the time I was there'.[69] Major Richard Storry, another evacuee from Singapore, attended a lecture by Stewart at the Intelligence School at Karachi:

> The lecture was a most outspoken, in parts bitter indictment of the higher planning & conduct of operations in Malaya. Mistakes of strategy & tactics were analysed, Jap methods described and Col Stewart's own theories of counteracting them explained. It was a merciless post-mortem which impressed us all. This lecture Stewart gave, I heard, up & down India that Spring 1942. Later he was one of those who directed the training of units for operations in Burma; so much, I think, is owed to him.[70]

Following the completion of the lecture tours in India, the evacuated Argylls made up No. 6, GHQ Training Team, who organised training exercises and lectures for 14th Indian Division and 2nd Division based on their experience.[71] Apart from Stewart, the

---

67 See Wilson, *Sum of Things*, p. 80.
68 See L. Wigmore, *The Japanese Thrust* (Canberra: Australian War Memorial, 1957), p. 443, n. 6. See also A. B. Lodge, *The Fall of General Gordon Bennett* (Sydney: Allen & Unwin, 1986), pp. 214-215; John Moremon, 'Most Deadly Jungle Fighters? Australian infantry in Malaya and Papua, 1941-43' (Unpublished BA thesis, Sydney, 1992), pp. 36-38 and Tim Moreman, 'The Jungle, the Japanese and the Australian Army: Learning the lessons of New Guinea, 1942-1944 (Unpublished paper, 2001), pp. 6-7.
69 W. H. Alston, 'My Day and Age': The Memoirs of William Lowry Alston at one time a British Officer in H. M. Indian Army 1917-1947 (Unpublished Memoir), Vol. 7, chapter 3, NAM, 8005-151. See also Major David Rissik, 'Forgotten Front' (Unpublished Memoir), p. 13, IWM, 91/8/1.
70 Major G. R. Storry, 'Service with the Intelligence Corps in India and Burma March 1942 – May 1943', (Unpublished Memoir, 1946-47), IWM 01/34/2, 6/10.
71 See HQ 14th Indian Division War Diary May 1942, TNA, WO 172/467, Jungle Warfare Courses, 11th July 1942, TNA, WO 172/448 and Co-ordinating Conference – Comilla, 30 April 1942, TNA, WO 172/467. See also Wilson, *Sum of Things*, pp. 84, 88-89.

other Argylls remained in India to instruct. Rose was in the training team until 1943 and then set up the Jungle Warfare Training Centre at Raiwala, before commanding a battalion of King's Own Scottish Borderers in Burma.[72] Captain Wilson and CSM Bing became chief instructors at 2nd Division's Battle School at Poona.[73] On Stewart's return to the UK, his report on the lessons from Malaya was reprinted for use by the UK Home Forces.[74] He highlighted the importance of training and tactics, but it 'remained of secondary consideration with commanders and staff and with most units'.[75] He continued:

> Jungle War requires the highest degree of skill of any type of war. This was easy to see during training. Quality always wins and wins incredibly. It takes three months before a man ceases to be a liability and six months before he is effective. This statement is from actual experience. Jungle war is a war of very highly-trained specialists, where the actual man and minor infantry tactics are dominant. This fact was never appreciated.[76]

Stewart was back in the Far East by 1944, when he was appointed Brigadier General Staff 11th Army Group responsible for training. Tuker wrote after the war that the troops trained along the lines of the Malaya Command training pamphlet rather than GHQ India's *MTP* No. 9 and the *AITMs* but this is a case of being wise after the event.[77]

Several other officers who had fought in the campaign also wrote detailed reports pinpointing the lessons of the campaign. Brigadier Carpendale of 28th Indian Infantry Brigade was another officer evacuated from Singapore and his findings also noted the importance of jungle training.[78] However neither Stewart nor Carpendale were promoted after Malaya and did not hold field command again, probably due to the

---

72 See *Indian Army List* (April 1943). 2nd GSO DMT's Training Team.
73 See Moffat and McCormack, *Moon over Malaya*, pp. 133, 145, 194 & 197. See also Augustus Muir, *The First of Foot: The History of the Royal Scots (The Royal Regiment)* (Edinburgh: Royal Scots History Committee, 1961), p. 154 and Wilson, *Sum of Things*, pp. 96-97. See also Jungle Warfare Courses, 11 July 1942, TNA, WO 172/448. Rose and Wilson as part of No. 6 GHQ Training Team gave a series of lectures to 2nd Division on 14-15 June 1942.
74 See Lt. Col. Stewart, Lessons from the Malayan Campaign, TNA, WO 203/6462 and Lt. Col. I. M. Stewart, Report on Malayan Campaign, 19 September 1942, TNA, WO 106/2613. See also *Military Training Pamphlet* No. 52. *Forest, Bush, and Jungle Warfare Against a Modern Enemy* (August, 1942) and *Notes from Theatres of War* No. 5: Far East (May, 1942), IWM.
75 Stewart, Lessons from the Malayan Campaign, p. 1.
76 Ibid., p. 4.
77 See Tuker, *Pattern of War*, pp. 65-66. See also letter from Tuker to the editor of the *Daily Telegraph*, 15 March 1967, *Tuker Mss.*, IWM, 71/21/7/4.
78 See Brigadier W. Carpendale, Report on Operations of 11 Indian Division in Kedah and Perak, IOR, L/WS/1/192.

disastrous Slim River battle. Thus although both were good trainers their leadership in battle was lacking.[79]

Conclusion

The majority of reports on Malaya were drawn up for Major H. P. Thomas, who prepared a detailed and influential report for the C-in-C India during the early Summer of 1942. In this process he also interviewed over one hundred officers. His findings stated that it was unlikely 'that an exact and detailed account will ever be available owing to the destruction of official records prior to capitulation'. He noted that there was no specialised training for jungle warfare but went on to outline various causes for the defeat: 'In conjunction with other serious disadvantages, including inferiority in numbers, and lack of air support, weakness in training was little short of disastrous'. This in combination with the lack of direction from Malaya Command about doctrine was directly responsible for the poor standard of training. Moreover, he stressed that important lessons were learnt from the disastrous defeat and Thomas commented that the 'tactical lessons have already been embodied in various pamphlets'.[80] All the reports from Malaya hammered home the importance of appropriate minor tactics and training for jungle fighting. These were instrumental for the development of Indian Army jungle warfare doctrine.

In conclusion, the Australian, British and Indian Armies all learnt lessons from the campaign in Malaya and Ian Stewart was instrumental in this process for all three armies. Relevant doctrine, training pamphlets and training instructions were available to the Indian Army formations in Malaya such as 9th and 11th Indian Divisions and 12th, 28th Indian Infantry Brigade. The main obstacle was the expansion of the Indian Army which meant that these units were continually being 'milked'. Those brigades that came as reinforcements such as 44th and 45th Indian Infantry Brigades had little basic training and what they had undertaken was for open warfare and had very little opportunity for acclimatisation. This in addition to the time spent building defences was the main problem and therefore there was no time for realistic training.

---

79 See Major General D. K. Palit, *The Campaign in Malaya* (Dehra Dun: The English Book Depot, 1989), pp. 89-90.
80 See Report drawn up by Major H. P. Thomas OBE, I.A., New Delhi, 30 May 1942, TNA, WO 106/25741.

6

Jungle Warfare: Burma, 1942-44

The Burma campaign of 1942-45 has been called and continues to be called the 'Forgotten War' and the reconquering 14th Army, the 'Forgotten Army' in the UK. However a huge bibliography has been produced on both the campaign and 14th Army since the end of the Second World War. The second edition of *The Burma Campaign Memorial Library: Descriptive Catalogue and Bibliography* published in 2001 listed 1,034 publications on the Burma campaign.[1] Since then almost a book a year on this theatre of war has been published as well as memoirs, regimental and battle histories.[2] Thus, it can now be stated as Graham Dunlop has aptly put: 'the campaign

---

1   See Gordon Graham and Frank Cole (compilers), *Burma Campaign Memorial Library* (London: School of Oriental and African Studies, 2001).
2   A selection of more recent historical studies includes: Julian Thompson, *The Imperial War Museum Book of the War in Burma* (London: Sidgwick & Jackson, 2002); Daniel Marston, *Phoenix from the Ashes: The Indian Army in the Burma Campaign* (Westport, Connecticut: Praeger, 2003); Christopher Bayly and Tim Harper, *Forgotten Armies: The Fall of British Asia, 1941-1945* (London: Allen Lane, 2004); Jon Latimer, *Burma: The Forgotten War* (London: John Murray, 2004); T. R. Moreman, *The Jungle, the Japanese and the British Commonwealth Armies at War, 1941-45: Fighting Methods, Doctrine and Training for Jungle Warfare* (London: Frank Cass, 2005); Robert Lyman, *The Generals: From Defeat to Victory, Leadership in Asia, 1941-45* (London: Constable, 2008) and Graham Dunlop, *Military Economics, Culture and Logistics in the Burma Campaign, 1942-45* (London: Pickering & Chatto, 2009); Fergal Keane, *Road of Bones: The Siege of Kohima 1944* (London Harper Press, 2010); Alan Warren, *Burma 1942: The Road from Rangoon to Mandalay* (London: Continuum, 2011). The most recent books are James Holland's *Burma '44: The Battle that turned Britain's War in the East* (London: Bantam, 2016) about the Battle of the Admin Box, Hemant Singh Katoch's *The Battlefields of Imphal* (London: Routledge, 2016) and Kaushik Roy's *Sepoys against the Rising Sun: The Indian Army in the Far East and South-East Asia, 1941-45* (Leiden: Brill, 2016) that also covers the South East Asian campaigns in Malaya and Borneo as well as the Burma campaign. Memoirs and regimental histories include John Randle's *Battle Tales from Burma* (Barnsley, South Yorkshire: Pen & Sword, 2004); Terence R. Molloy (ed.), *The Silchar Track* (Cambridgeshire: Melrose Books, 2006), R. E. S. Tanner and D. A. Tanner, *Burma 1942: Memories of a Retreat: The diary of Ralph*

in Burma is anything but forgotten. A wealth of historical literature, professional, technical, academic and popular, has been published since the end of the war and still continues to be written prodigiously'.[3] Although this body of work largely remains focused on the British experience rather than that of the Commonwealth troops. Indeed no volume exists that looks at the Burma campaign in equal measure from the point of view of the three main allies: American, British and Commonwealth (African and Indian troops), Chinese forces as well as nationalist forces such as the Indian National Army, the Burma Defence Army under Aung Sang Sun and the Japanese occupation forces.

This chapter will chart the lack of training for jungle warfare that was apparent in the Retreat from Burma in 1942 and the lessons learned from both that campaign and the disastrous First Arakan. These lessons were instigated by the Infantry Committee in June 1943 that included a clear jungle warfare doctrine that was disseminated by the training divisions, schools and centres across India that was instrumental in the later successful battles in the Arakan and at Kohima and Imphal.

The problems of fighting in the jungle in Burma had been previously studied and practised by paramilitary units. The paramilitary forces in Burma comprised the Burma Military Police (BMP), the Burma Frontier Force and the Burma Auxiliary Force. The BMP had a long tradition of maintaining internal security and in this role had been involved in jungle warfare against irregular tribesmen since 1896. Lessons were encapsulated in a training manual produced in 1902, which was revised in the 1920s.[4] However, there is little to suggest that these lessons were adopted in the Indian Army, but the experience was disseminated by word of mouth among BMP officers who were Indian Army officers on temporary loan to the Burma Army.[5]

The Retreat from Burma

The garrison in Burma in 1941 comprised two regular battalions from the British Army, namely the 2nd Battalion, the Gloucester Regiment and the 2nd Battalion, the King's Own Yorkshire Light Infantry as well as the Burma Rifles.[6] They were

---

Tanner, *KOYLI* (Stroud, Gloucestershire: The History Press, 2009) and Leslie Edwards, *Kohima: The Furthest Battle* (Stroud: History Press, 2009).

3   Dunlop, *Military Economics*, p. 5.
4   See Captain A. W. Taylor, *Jungle Warfare: the conduct of small expeditions in the jungles and hilly tracts of Burma, and a system of drill and musketry instruction connected therewith, for the use of officers of the Burma Military Police* (Rangoon, 1902). Reprinted as Captain J. W. Young, *Manual of Jungle Warfare for the Officers of the Burma Military Police* (Rangoon, 1928). See also Captain J. W. Young, 'Notes on Jungle Warfare', *JUSII*, Vol. LVIII, No. 251, April, 1928, pp. 338-363.
5   See Moreman, '"Small Wars" and "Imperial Policing"', pp. 112, 120-122.
6   For the state of training and the lack of equipment in both the Gloucesters and the KOYLI see Terence Dillon, *Rangoon to Kohima* (RHQ: Gloucestershire Regiment, nd), pp. 18-19 and Tanner & Tanner, *Burma 1942: Memories of a Retreat*, pp. 50-52, 55-56

reinforced by 13th Indian Infantry Brigade in April 1941 and 16th Indian Infantry Brigade in November that together formed the nucleus of 1st Burma Division. Brigadier John Jones, CO 16th Indian Infantry Brigade, wrote: 'Of the three battalions in the brigade none had been longer in it than 6 weeks. None of the battalions had carried out higher training of any sort during the year'. As for jungle training, 'no one had any experience of jungle, except a few senior officers whose experience was confined to '*Shikar*''.[7] Lieutenant General Thomas Hutton, Burma Army Commander, commented on the state of 1st Burma Division: 'It was never a Division in the real sense of the word and had few ancillary units except one or two Mountain Batteries. Its composition was frequently changed'.[8]

The 17th Indian Division was also destined for Burma. However, the division's standard of general training was poor. In December 1941, Brigadier 'Punch' Cowan, officiating as DMT, had agreed with the CO, Brigadier (Acting Major General) John Smyth VC, that the division needed a further six weeks' training once it had arrived in Iraq, where it was originally earmarked. In the event, two of its brigades, the 44th and 45th, were nevertheless sent to Malaya as the military situation deteriorated there.[9] Thus, all that was sent to Burma of the original division was one brigade, the 46th, and the divisional HQ. As Lieutenant John Randle of 7/10th Baluch Regiment, in 46th Indian Infantry Brigade, wrote in his memoir, all of the training undertaken in India was for open warfare.[10] Indeed once the battalion had arrived in Rangoon, the battalion CO, Major Jerry Dyer, asked the GSO1 (Training) at Burma Command about training areas, only to be told 'you can't do much training here, it's all bloody jungle!'[11] As Tim Moreman has pointed out copies of the second edition of *MTP* No. 9 *Notes on Forest Warfare* were sent to Burma but it is difficult to gauge how widely dispersed and used the pamphlet actually was.[12]

The 17th Indian Division was strengthened after war broke out, by the attachment of 48th Indian Brigade and 2nd Burma Brigade. However, very little jungle training

respectively. For a breakdown of the individual nine battalions of the Burma Rifles, organisation and their lack of training see Major General J. D. Lunt, 'The Burma Rifles', *Journal of the Society for Army Historical Research*, Vol. LXXVI, No. 307, Autumn 1998, pp. 202-207. See also Jeffreys, *British Army in the Far East*, pp. 43-45.

7   Major-General S. Woodburn Kirby, *War Against Japan*, Vol. II (London: HMSO, 1958), pp. 440-441.
8   Lieutenant General Sir Thomas Hutton, 'Rangoon 1941-42: A Personal Record', p. 19, IWM, 99/73/1. See also Davies, 'Small Green Men', pp. 108-109.
9   See Hutton, 'Rangoon 1941-42: A Personal Record', pp. 18-20, IWM, 99/73/1. See also Raymond Callahan, *Burma 1942-45* (London: Davis Poynter, 1978), pp. 32, 35-36.
10 John Randle, *Battle Tales from Burma* (Barnsley: Pen & Sword, 2004), p. 1. See also C. R. L. Coubrough, *Memories of a Perpetual Second Lieutenant* (self-published, 2000), p. 9 and Daniel Marston, 'The War in Burma, 1942-1945: The 7/10th Baluch Experience', Kaushik Roy (ed.), *The Indian Army in the Two World Wars* (Leiden: Brill, 2012), p. 256.
11 Quoted in Randle, *Battle Tales*, p. 5.
12 Moreman, *Jungle*, p. 36.

had been undertaken by the incoming units nor as a formation. The defending forces were later reinforced by the battle-hardened 7th Armoured Brigade from the Middle East and 63rd Indian Infantry Brigade. The armoured brigade found the terrain could slow them up and therefore were not quite as effective as it had been hoped. Thus as Lieutenant Colonel William Abraham noted in his diary in his role as liaison officer from Middle East Command: 'In the jungle the Japs had complete moral ascendancy...our troops, especially 17 Div., were NOT in a good enough state for offensive action or for anything more than static defence in open country'.[13]

On 20 January 1942 the Japanese 15th Army, comprising 33rd and 55th Divisions, invaded Burma. The invading forces continually outflanked the British and Indian units in the jungle. Once the retreating forces reached the vital bridge over the River Sittang, only a hundred miles from Rangoon, Smyth and Brigadier Noel Hugh-Jones, CO 48th Indian Infantry Brigade, prematurely blew the bridge before two brigades of 17th Indian Division were able to cross.[14] Most of the Gurkha troops could not swim with large numbers becoming casualties or being taken prisoner. With the significant loss of manpower and equipment, the defending forces were outnumbered and under-equipped for the remainder of the campaign, even with reinforcements. Resulting in the disastrous and longest retreat in British military history.[15] However, there were successful actions during the retreat, such as that of the 48th Indian Infantry Brigade at Kokkogawa on 12 April 1942 which resulted in a significant Japanese reverse. The brigade had a large percentage of regular well-trained Gurkha soldiers who prior to Burma had had recent experience on the North West Frontier in contrast to other Indian brigades in Burma. The new brigade commander, Brigadier Ronnie Cameron, adopted an all-round defence in the jungle with artillery and tank support, the formation repelled the Japanese diversionary attacks. An efficient and well-trained formation

13 Diary of visit as liaison officer, 4-8 March 1942 in the Papers of Major General Sir William Ernest Victor Abraham on microfilm, Centre of South Asian Studies, Cambridge.
14 A decision that continued to haunt Hugh-Jones who drowned himself in 1952.
15 For a recent detailed history of the campaign based on secondary sources, see Warren, *Burma, 1941*. See also Marston, *Phoenix from the Ashes*, chapter 3, Moreman, *Jungle*, pp. 35-45. For the experience of the civilian retreat that included a large number of Indian evacuees, see Michael D. Leigh, *The Evacuation of Civilians from Burma: Analysing the 1942 Colonial Disaster* (London: Bloomsbury, 2014). A modern re-assessment of the campaign based on primary sources is much needed. It is worth noting that all the army commanders at the initial stages of the Japanese invasion: Hutton, Percival and Stilwell were all staff officers with no experience of field command and this is demonstrated in their conduct of operations. Stilwell and the remnants of 38th Chinese Division retreated to India rather than China. They underwent training at Ramgarh and fought extremely well under Stilwell's command later in Northern Burma, but the divisional commander, Major General Sun Li-jen, was never again trusted by Chiang Kai-shek.

had proved it could adapt to jungle warfare even after being in almost continuous action for months and again proved it at Kyaukse.[16]

The lessons of the Retreat from Burma were studied in India. It was generally acknowledged that failure in Burma was due in large amount to a lack of training in jungle warfare. As Lieutenant General Hutton, GOC Burma, commented in his Despatch:

> As regards the British and Indian Army units, the jungle has never, whether in India or Burma, been regarded as "a good training area". In the former this was understandable at a period when practically all the troops were earmarked for Mid-East. In Burma it was incomprehensible. Jungle warfare was obviously inevitable if Burma were attacked and it is well-known to require a very high standard of training.[17]

Hutton also noted that too much reliance had been placed on motor transport rather than the pack transport needed for jungle warfare, but the lack of jungle training was a 'very important factor' in the retreat.[18] On the Indian Army, in particular, he wrote: 'Its efficiency depended on long training, complete confidence in its British and Indian Officers and expertise in the use of its weapons and equipment. Given these conditions it was magnificent but lacking them it was no match for the Japanese or indeed any other trained army'.[19]

The 17th Indian Division under the command of Major General 'Punch' Cowan, who had replaced Smyth as commanding officer after the disastrous Sittang Bridge, established a committee led by Brigadier Ronnie Cameron together with divisional battalion commanders with the role of identifying new training, tactics and equipment needed to fight successfully in the jungle. The resulting Cameron Report stated that training in the jungle was of vital importance 'so that movement and control in it becomes second nature'. Weapons such as *dhahs*, an Indian knife, were essential for clearing jungle undergrowth and firearms had to be kept clean due to the problems of jamming in the moist jungle atmosphere that hastened rust and corrosion. The report highlighted the value of the 2-inch mortar and the range of the 3-inch mortar, although the latter was less portable with tanks viewed as good for both morale and close support of the infantry. Most importantly the report concluded that all arms of

---

16   See Kirby, *War Against Japan*, pp. 232-239. See also Warren, *Burma 1942*, pp. 206, 216-218. For Kyaukse see Bisheshwar Prasad, *The Retreat from Burma* (India & Pakistan: Combined Inter-Services Historical Section, 1954), pp. 314-421.
17   Lieutenant General T. J. Hutton, 'Operations in Burma from 27th December to 5th March, 1942', *Supplement to the London Gazette*, 5 March 1948, p. 1694.
18   Ibid., p. 1695.
19   Hutton, 'Rangoon 1941-1942', p. 55.

combat were to be jungle trained as 'all units in jungle warfare must be responsible for their own protection'.[20]

Jungle Training, 1942

After the Retreat from Burma, the Military Training Directorate made efforts to learn from the experiences of fighting in the jungle. All the lessons from Malaya and Burma were encapsulated into the third edition of the jungle warfare training pamphlet *MTP No. 9 Jungle Warfare* published in August 1942. It was considerably larger than the first edition, with an increase from eleven to seventy-three pages and now had a distribution of 45,000 copies to all the officers of the Indian and British Armies. It stressed that the Japanese were not 'supermen' and that 'our better trained troops, British, Australian, Indian and Gurkha, have proved this more than once'.[21] The third edition included a section on Japanese tactical methods which were described at length but were summed up in the four words: 'mobility, speed, infiltration and encirclement'.[22] There were sections on attack and defence for all arms against Japanese tactics, ambushes, patrols, administrative problems, minor tactics and training. For attack, encircling and filleting were the two suggested methods and aggressive patrols and ambushes were to be used in both attack and defence. The idea of the defensive boxes were adapted from the 'box doctrine' developed in North Africa:

> Our boxes will, therefore, be placed astride the enemy's lines of approach. They must be made as strong as possible artificially-with wire, mines, booby traps, automatic fire, etc. – in order to economize men. They must be fully stocked to withstand a siege. They must be in depth along the L. of C. so that if the enemy by-passes the first he will bump the second and so on, and so that he can be squeezed between them by counter-attack from each side.[23]

It was stressed that as the jungle was alien to nearly all the fighting troops they needed practical training in it. Training was divided into four areas of jungle craft: map reading and the use of the compass to find one's way in the jungle; concealment; jungle lore; and use of weapons to achieve the maximum effect. These lessons had all been learnt in the disastrous campaigns in Malaya and Burma where compasses had often been in very short supply and the few maps available were out of date. However

---

20 Lessons of the Burma Campaign, April-May 1942, TNA, WO 203/5716. See also Ian Lyall Grant and Kazuo Tamayama, *Burma 1942: The Japanese Invasion* (Chichester: Zampi Press, 1999), p. 323.
21 *MTP (India)* No. 9, *Jungle Warfare* 3rd Edition, August 1942, p. 2, IOR, L/MIL/17/5/2250.
22 Ibid., p. 5.
23 Ibid., p. 26. See also French, *Raising Churchill's Army*, pp. 219-220.

the pamphlet perpetuated the myth that Japanese were short-sighted, and its concealment hints were taken from 'Scouting for Boys'.[24]

Some progress was made in disseminating jungle warfare doctrine and implementing appropriate training, especially with the publication of this new edition of *MTP* No. 9. However, this was still insufficient according to some officers, Lieutenant Cooper of the 9th Battalion, Border Regiment commented: 'Some good pamphlets were beginning to arrive, but Jungle Warfare was still very much in its experimental stages and 'Bungle Warfare' still seemed to most people a better description of our efforts'.[25] The problem seemed to be the failure to take heed of lessons in the pamphlets and put them into practice in training. Thus, more notice and practical application of *MTP* No. 9 was necessary for the jungle warfare training to succeed.

As in other theatres, training was directed by the pamphlets produced by GHQ India that provided the doctrine that was disseminated to the individual divisions, largely initially through training teams and then through training instructions produced within the division. For instance, the 3/9th Gurkhas in 26th Indian Division and the 2/1st Punjab Regiment and 47th Indian Infantry Brigade in 14th Indian Division, all underwent jungle training under the guidance of Lieutenant Colonel Arthur Cumming VC, a veteran of the Malayan Campaign, along with Captain Ishar Singh and Lieutenant Hussein Khan and a specialist training team.[26] In addition, No. 6 Training Team led by Major Angus Rose visited 14th Indian Division and at a Co-ordinating Conference held within the formation in April 1942 the proof copy of *MTP* No. 9 was brought to the attention of the attending officers.[27] At the beginning of June the division undertook a divisional TEWT and Major A.D. Firth, along with Major Robin Parry, established and ran a Jungle Warfare School at Comilla.[28] Although no training instructions were ever produced in the division, training teams visited, a jungle warfare divisional school was set up, the current doctrine for jungle warfare was available to officers, training with other arms was undertaken and the lessons from the Cameron Report were absorbed.[29]

However, in 17th Indian Division, after their experience in Burma, it was very quickly realised that training was of vital importance and training instructions were issued accordingly. The first priority was the training of new recruits that were drafted into the division. Thus the initial page of the first divisional training instructions was

---

24 See *MTP* No. 9, pp. 49-50. See also Moreman, *Jungle*, pp. 56-58.
25 Raymond Cooper, *B Company: One Man's War in Burma 1942-1944* (London: Dobson, 1978), p. 33.
26 See Stevens, *9th Gurkha Rifles*, p. 215 and Moreman, *Jungle*, pp. 50, 60, 226 note 22.
27 See Co-ordinating Conference, Comilla, 30 April 1942, TNA, WO 172/467.
28 See 14th Indian Division T.E.W.T. No.1, 29 May 1942, TNA, WO 172/467 and Brigadier A. D. Firth, 'The Retreat from Burma, an account of an officer who was with 2nd Battalion the Duke of Wellington's Regiment throughout', p. 7, IWM, 99/48/1.
29 See Extracts from the Cameron Report on the Burma Campaign in the War Diary of 14th Indian Division War Diary, 1942, TNA, WO 171/467.

dedicated to drill, saluting, general turn out and discipline but it noted that training also needed to be realistic as:

> The new draft will not know the jungle. They will feel lost and confused – if not actually frightened of it. They must be taught to get used to it and use it to their advantage. They must learn to differentiate between the real and artificial noises (which must be laid on). In the final stages of this training live SAA will be used to accustom recruits to the confused feeling of all round fire especially on a jungle road or in a village.[30]

Thus the new drafts would become acclimatised to the jungle conditions. The instruction noted the importance of junior officer leadership and the need for collective training in fitness, 'busting' road blocks, patrolling and getting used to the jungle. A second training instruction issued in June 1942 stated that there was now enough jungle training literature and the division just had to get on with it. This literature consisted of the Cameron Report, the Malaya report, *Japanese Tactical Methods* pamphlet and the *AITM's*.[31] *Japanese Tactical Methods* was produced by Colonel Francis Brink of the US Army and then published in South West Pacific Command in February 1942. It was reprinted, under the orders of Wavell, in India in March 1942. It looked at the characteristics of the Japanese Army with regards to tactics, equipment and armament. It proved very useful in both the Pacific and South East Asia theatres. The sections on tactics and movement noted the use of infiltration that had proved so successful against the British and Commonwealth forces across the region.[32] Five more training instructions were produced by the division in 1942 covering such subjects as standardisation and the detection and removal of mines and booby traps.[33] Standardisation across the division ensured 'that troops who had not had the time to carry out long and full training, can react by force of habit to deal with any normal situation in the field'.[34] 23rd Indian Division, commanded by Savory, were also based in Assam in 1942 but learnt 'on the job' as no training instructions were issued in the division but they did undertake joint exercises with 17th Indian Division.[35] Thus as *Fauji Akhbar* claimed there was a 'New Training – New Spirit' where lessons had been

---

30 17 Indian Division Training Instruction No. 1, 4 June 1942, TNA, WO 172/475.
31 See 17 Indian Division Training Instruction No. 2, 24 June 1942, TNA, WO 172/475. See also Moreman, *Jungle*, p. 60 and Marston, *Phoenix from the Ashes*, pp. 82-83.
32 See *Japanese Tactical Methods: Characteristics of Japanese Operations* (GHQ: India, 1942), IWM.
33 See Training Instruction No. 3, 'Standardizations', 8 July 1942, Training Instruction No. 4, 'Further Standardizations', 13 July 1942 and Training Instructions No. 7 'Detection and Removal of Mines and Booby Traps', 19 November 1942, TNA, WO 172/475.
34 Training Instruction No. 3, 8 July 1942, TNA, WO 172/475.
35 See War Diary of 23rd Indian Division, 1942, TNA, WO 172/501. See also Marston, *Phoenix from the Ashes*, p. 83 and Moreman, *Jungle*, p. 61.

learned from the fighting in the Retreat from Burma whereby troops did not rely on fixed defences or MT rather mobility was of the utmost importance which 'all makes for keenness and efficiency and it is obvious there is a new offensive spirit'.[36]

The Army in India was unable to concentrate entirely on preparing for jungle warfare, as the strategic situation meant that GHQ India also provided troops during the early years of the war for campaigns in the Middle East and North Africa.[37] There was also substantial civil unrest in India during this period and many battalions were assigned to internal security duties. The Cripps Mission and the resultant 'Quit India' movement of which the August Crisis of 1942 was the most serious meant that 57 infantry battalions were needed to deal with the disturbances that increased to 105 battalions deployed by April–May 1943. Much of the trouble occurred in the Eastern Army's province and thus training for the war against the Japanese was delayed. Airfield construction, factory production of arms, clothing and equipment were similarly retarded.[38] In addition, there was the problems of the food crisis and the monsoon of 1942 that was followed by a terrible malaria epidemic on the lines of communication to units in North East India that doubled in numbers by 1943.[39] There were also disturbances by the Hurs, a Muslim sect in Sind, and a lashkar (tribal war party) influenced by the Fakir of Ipi creating problems on the North West Frontier. 59 Indian Army battalions and 8 British battalions were based on the NWF in 1942 and 57 British and Indian battalions and four armoured car regiments the following year.[40] Thus large numbers of troops were engaged on the NWF, internal security, with the famine and health crises also having an important impact that meant large numbers of troops were therefore unable to train in jungle warfare. Although surprisingly this did not affect recruitment and indeed became an added incentive for enlisting nor did it produce much dissent within the Indian Army.[41]

The First Arakan

The First Arakan campaign of September 1942–March 1943 and the ensuing Japanese counteroffensive was yet again a dismal failure with defeat inflicted on the British and Indian troops by a numerically-inferior force. Raymond Callahan

---

36 'New Training – New Spirit', *Fauji Akhbar*, Vol. XX, No. 30, 25 July 1942, p. 9.
37 See chapter 3.
38 See Brown, *Modern India*, p. 314. See also Voigt, *India in the Second World War*, p. 166.
39 See Voigt, *India in the Second World War*, pp. 153 Lieutenant-Colonel B. L. Raina, *Official History of the Indian Armed Forces in the Second World War 1939-1945: Medical Services: Medicine, Surgery and Pathology* (India & Pakistan: Combined Inter-Services Historical Section, 1955), p. 257.
40 See Jacobsen, *Modernization of the Indian Army*, p. 118, Moreman, *Frontier Warfare*, p. 179 and Kirby, *The War Against Japan* Vol. III, p. 27.
41 See Voigt, pp. 167-168. See also Bayly & Harper, *Forgotten Armies*, p. 196.

has described it as 'perhaps the worst managed British military effort of the war'.[42] It was the first time that British and Indian forces came up against the defensive strength of the IJA. The Japanese bunkers appeared indestructible. Each one usually consisted of a small heavily-fortified post holding ten men, positioned accordingly to protect a neighbouring bunker often on reverse slopes. However, shelling did inflict casualties on the enemy in the bunkers. As a result the Japanese left one sentry in the bunker while the rest of the platoon hid in nearby caves during the Allied bombardments. Once the shelling lifted the Japanese reoccupied the bunker to repel the imminent attack.[43]

By March 1943 morale was generally low, with some units, such as the 1/15th Punjab Regiment having been in continuous action for five months. Long periods in action without relief and the resulting low morale showed 'the need for relief of units so that they do not become exhausted by continuous contact with the enemy and by the very severe physical conditions'.[44] The lack of any decisive victorious action over the Japanese forces did little to improve morale. Troops were exhausted and 'browned off' and generally demoralised by the jungle and the disastrous campaign in the Arakan with British troops, in particular, thinking that they are taking part in a "forgotten" campaign in which no one in authority was very interested.[45] Similarly disease sorely undermined both morale and combat effectiveness and urgently needed addressing. The casualty rate had reached over 10, 000 a week by June 1943 and over half of these were due to malaria.[46] Compounded by the problems of the length of time and the numerous changes of transport involved in getting the wounded and sick back to the base hospitals.

A careful study of the campaign was made and of the lessons learned by officers who had fought listing positive and negative lessons.[47] Wavell and Lieutenant General Irwin, Eastern Army Commander, attributed the failure down to poor regimental

---

42   Callahan, *Burma*, p. 59. See also Jeffreys, *British Army in the Far East*, pp. 39-42, Marston, *Phoenix from the Ashes*, pp. 86-91, Moreman, *Jungle*, pp. 64-75.
43   See Private Takeo Kawakami, 'Donbaik' in Kazuo Tamayama and John Nunneley (eds.), *Tales by Japanese Soldiers of the Burma Campaign 1942-1945* (London: Cassell, 2000), pp. 124-125 and Tim Moreman, '"Debunking the Bunker": From Donbaik to Razabil, January 1943-March 1944' in Jeffreys & Rose (eds.), *The Indian Army, 1939-47*, pp. 108-134.
44   Court of Enquiry into the Evacuation of Maungdaw, *Tuker Mss.*, IWM, 71/4/3/2.
45   See Report on Visit to Maungdaw Front 4/5/43 - 9/5/43 by a Liaison Officer from HQ 15 Corps, Papers of Lieutenant General Noel Irwin, *Irwin Mss.*, IWM, P139.
46   See Field Marshal Viscount Wavell, 'Operations in the India Command, from 1st January, 1943 to 20th June 1943', *Supplement to The London Gazette*, 20 April 1948, p. 2518.
47   See Report on Visit to Maungdaw Front 4/5/43 - 9/5/43 by a Liaison Officer from HQ 15 Corps, *Irwin Mss.*, IWM, P139. See also Court of Enquiry into the evacuation of Maungdaw, *Tuker Mss.*, IWM, 71/4/3/2, and Notes on lessons from Operations in Arakan, report by Commander 71 Indian Infantry Brigade, TNA, WO 203/1167.

command and the lack of time for training.[48] This, in fact, reflected rather badly on themselves rather than on their subordinates. Indeed with Wavell's reputation as a trainer it was surprising it took him so long to comprehend the importance of training in the jungle.[49] This situation was not helped by Wavell's continued underestimation of the Japanese Army which he still saw in terms that were common prior to the Japanese invasion of South East Asia. Equally his perception of the Indian Army was that of the 'unmilked' divisions in North Africa and therefore he could not understand why the Indian Army could not defeat the Japanese.

The Arakan campaign had been a tactical failure. Repeated attacks on a narrow front against the bunkers had proved disastrous at an early stage, and the encircling tactics employed by the Japanese at the end of the campaign had again proved decisive. The importance of artillery, tank or air support was shown in attacks against entrenched fortified positions.[50] Patrolling was seen as being of paramount importance in both attack and defence and defences had to be secure.[51] The outstanding failure in the campaign noted by most reports was the overall low level of training and the very low standard of the training of reinforcements. Large numbers were needed but were arriving from regimental depots with little basic training let alone jungle warfare training and a longer period of training was therefore needed for both basic training and training in jungle warfare.[52] According to a Court of enquiry on the evacuation of Maungdaw, 'almost all the unsteadiness and drop in morale can be attributed to the low standard of reinforcements' and 'that one and all considered the fault lay in training and lack of training, i.e. troops being sent to a theatre for which they had no practical preparation whatever, together with a large percentage of almost raw recruits'.[53]

Jungle Training, 1943

The lack of experience of fighting in the jungles of South East Asia together with the rapid expansion of the Indian Armed Forces was largely responsible for the disastrous defeats in Malaya, Burma and the First Arakan in the Far Eastern theatre.[54] A change at the highest level was instigated by Churchill.[55] Most significantly, Wavell was appointed Viceroy of India to be replaced by the return of General Claude Auchinleck as C-in-C India in June 1943 and operational control for campaigns was

---

48 See Letter from Wavell to Irwin, 25 March 1943 and Letter from Irwin to Wavell, 20 April 1943, *Irwin Mss.*, IWM, P139.
49 See Hutton, 'Rangoon 1941-42', p. 74, IWM 99/73/1.
50 See ibid., p. 357.
51 See Notes on lessons from operations in Arakan, TNA, WO 203/1167.
52 See Formation of the Training Divisions in India, IOR, L/WS/1/1364.
53 Court of Enquiry into the evacuation of Maungdaw, *Tuker Mss.*, IWM, 71/4/3/2.
54 See 'India at War', p. 144, *Corbett Mss.*, CAC, CORB 3/28.
55 See Callahan, *Churchill and his Generals*, pp. 194-195.

now to be conducted by the newly appointed Supreme Allied Commander in South East Asia, Lord Louis Mountbatten. As a result of these changes and the disastrous early campaigns against the Japanese, GHQ India made some important changes in senior staff officers and frontline commanders to improve military effectiveness. The Arakan failure brought about the dismissal of Irwin who was replaced by Lieutenant General Sir George Giffard, a veteran of the bush fighting in East Africa during the First World War.[56] Later that year General Slim was appointed as 14th Army Commander and a range of experienced divisional commanders were also appointed such as Major Generals Frank Messervy and 'Pete' Rees, commanding 7th and 19th Indian Divisions respectively, both of whom had not fared well in North Africa but were to become very distinguished divisional commanders in the Burma campaign.[57]

At the same time changes were made in the training structure as the C-in-C India had initially appointed Major General J. Bruce-Scott, former GOC 1st Burma Division, as Inspector of Infantry to address infantry training after the Retreat from Burma. However, his experiences had exhausted him and rendered him ineffectual in his new role. After the First Arakan, he was replaced by Major General Reginald Savory who had commanded 23rd Indian Division in Assam. Savory was 'given wide powers over training, organisation, arms and equipment, [and] played a critical role for the rest of the war'.[58] In his own words: 'I spent most of my time, not only visiting the training establishments, but also infantry units throughout India. I also made regular trips to the front, so as to acquaint myself with conditions at the time and apply the lessons learnt'.[59] He also learnt from other theatres in this new role, when he established the infantry liaison letters in December 1943 that included lessons learned in both South East Asia and the South West Pacific Area.[60]

The appointments of Auchinleck, Savory and Slim were an important factor in the eventual defeat of the Japanese. As Raymond Callahan has commented: 'It helped of course that the key figures in Indian military affairs were, for the first time in the war, all drawn from the Indian Army and thus understood the traditions and ways of the Indian Army'.[61] In direct contrast to the situation at AHQ India during the First World War where the majority of senior officers were British service.[62]

56 See Lewin, *Slim*, p. 124. See also Malcolm Page, *A History of the King's African Rifles and East African Forces* (Barnsley: Pen & Sword, 1998), pp. 173-175.
57 See Callahan, *Churchill and his Generals*, p. 270, note 90. See also Callahan, 'Were the "Sepoy Generals" Any Good?', pp. 310-312 and Jeffreys, 'Slim's Welsh General', pp. 147-160.
58 Callahan, *Burma*, p. 98.
59 Letter from Lieutenant General Reginald Savory to Professor Raymond Callahan, 24 October, 1976, *Savory Mss.*, NAM, 7603-93-71A.
60 See Roy, *Sepoys Against the Rising Sun*, pp. 228-233.
61 Raymond Callahan, 'The Jungle, the Japanese and the Sepoy' (Unpublished Paper), p. 7.
62 See chapter 1.

The defeats in South East Asia had highlighted the importance of infantry in jungle warfare with the result that Wavell convened the Infantry Committee in June 1943 with a brief to improve the standard of British and Indian infantry. The Committee was chaired by Major General Roland Richardson, Deputy Chief of the General Staff, and included Major General Roland Inskip who was later appointed Inspector of Training Centres, Major General John Grover, GOC 2nd Division, Major General Cecil Toovey, Deputy Adjutant General, and Major General H. L. 'Taffy' Davies who had been chief of staff to Generals Hutton and Slim during the Retreat from Burma and had recently been appointed GOC 25th Indian Division. The Committee studied the problem for two weeks. The defeats in Burma and Malaya were blamed on the 'milking' and expansion of the Indian Army, the failure to recognise the importance of infantry in battle, the lack of basic training and experienced leadership, the fighting on two fronts, the lack of collective training as formations, prolonged periods of contact with the enemy, the problems of providing trained reinforcements, the problem of malaria and the lack of resources.[63] Although it is important to note as Raymond Callahan has wisely pointed out that 'no overhaul of doctrine would have a fighting chance of having an impact on training... until the core issue of open-ended expansion was confronted'.[64] Expansion was brought to an end in 1943 due to Churchill's distrust of the Indian Army that ironically was a major factor in the revival of the army for the remainder of the war.

The Infantry Committee's solution was the thorough training of recruits followed by a period of jungle training for both British and Indian troops. Regimental Training Centres were unable to deal with all training needs. For example, the 13th Frontier Force Rifles had 14 active battalions organised, equipped and armed in six different ways. The committee accepted the DMT's proposal that training divisions be established to teach jungle warfare after basic training. All Indian troops and British reinforcements would now undergo two months jungle training under designated training divisions.[65] The need for a definitive jungle warfare doctrine with battle drills that recruits and trained soldiers could all follow across India was also highlighted.[66] The committee also recommended collective training, the training with other arms and the RAF, concluding that few units 'can yet be said to be fully efficient in jungle warfare'.[67]

---

63 See Report of Infantry Committee 1943, 1st-14th June, pp. 1, 3, IOR, L/WS/1/1371.
64 Raymond Callahan, *Triumph at Imphal-Kohima* (Lawrence, Kansas: University Press of Kansas, forthcoming 2017), p. 91. I'm very grateful to Ray Callahan for allowing me to both read and reference from his forthcoming work.
65 See Report of Infantry Committee, p. 16.
66 See Report of Infantry Committee, p. 8.
67 Ibid., p. 25. See also Jeffreys, pp. 15-16, Marston, pp. 95-97 and Moreman, pp. 80-84.

Jungle Warfare doctrine

The campaigns in Malaya, Burma and First Arakan had showed that *MTP* No. 5 on *Extensive Warfare, MTP* No. 9 and the existing training material were insufficient for jungle warfare training as the manuals did not fully address new tactical problems such as bunkers. It was not until after the First Arakan that the *AITM*s included regular sections on jungle warfare and specific training for warfare in this terrain. In conjunction with the different editions of *MTP* No. 9 the steady development of thinking on jungle warfare from 1940 onwards is demonstrated. Although it had become apparent that the training pamphlets such as *MTP* No. 14 (India) were not being put into effect.[68] However, in accordance with the directives from GHQ India the *AITM*'s gave increasing coverage to jungle warfare from *AITM* No. 20 onwards published in April 1943. There were sections on jungle lore, lessons from exercises and operations and jungle warfare minor tactics. One example of which was the need for soldiers to work in pairs or threes, harking back to 'a certain Gurkha Regiment' where soldiers were punished if found alone. An essential part of Tuker's training of his Gurkha regiment during the 1930s.[69]

As with the infantry liaison letters, *AITM* No. 21 assimilated lessons from the American and Australian experiences in the South West Pacific campaign where the myth of the 'Japanese superman' had also been evident. It noted the importance of leadership with an American officer stating: 'I have had to get rid of 25 officers because they just weren't leaders. I had to make the Battalion commander weed out the poor leaders. Or junior leaders were finding out that they must know more about their men'. Good junior leadership was essential in jungle warfare as on patrol; officers, VCOs and NCOs needed to make decisions on the spot without referral to the command chain as direct command and control in the jungle was very difficult. Similarly in the South West Pacific, individual training and training in night fighting were emphasized. As the individual often had to act on his own and night training accustomed soldiers to the jungle noises with an Australian officer remarking 'Our fellows have had the best results with surprise night attacks without fire until the last moment, the Jap does not relish it when we are on top, his morale cracks…'.[70] The pamphlet also stressed the importance of anti-mosquito drill which had been understood after the early defeat in Burma but had not been rigorously enforced during the Arakan debacle. Tents and shelters were sprayed before morning parade and all men were ordered to apply the anti-mosquito cream before leaving the tent. At evening parade, all men were inspected by the officer in charge to make sure the cream had been applied and then the tents would be sprayed inside and out.[71]

---

68 See *AITM* No. 20, April 1943, Appendix D, p. 21, IOR, L/MIL/15/5/2240.
69 See *AITM* No. 20, April 1943, pp. 11-12, 19-28, IOR, L/MIL/17/5/2240.
70 *AITM* No. 21, June 1943, Appendix B, pp. 42-46, IOR, L/MIL/15/5/2240.
71 See ibid., pp. 20-21.

In September 1943, the Military Training Directorate produced a comprehensive jungle warfare doctrine with the publication of 80,000 copies of the fourth edition of *MTP* No. 9 (India), *The Jungle Book*. The new edition doubled the circulation of the previous editions of *MTP* No. 9 and, as Auchinleck later commented, it 'passed on the latest knowledge on jungle fighting to every officer and all British NCO's'.[72] The aim was to help commanding officers train their units in the specialised fighting methods needed to beat the IJA in the jungle, stating: 'In principle there is nothing new in jungle warfare, but the environment of the jungle is new to many of our troops. Special training is therefore necessary to accustom them to jungle conditions and to teach them jungle methods'.[73] Listing the examples of jungle craft, physical fitness, good marksmanship and decentralised control as the necessary attributes that needed addressing in jungle warfare training. It had a new format that according to Auchinleck was to be different from the usual dull training manuals and was intended to popularise training.[74] It therefore included photographs and cartoons for the first time in order to make it more appealing to officers and men.

The training manual assimilated all the lessons from the previous editions of *MTP* No. 9, the *AITM*s and included lessons from the First Arakan and the American and Australian experiences of fighting the Japanese in the Pacific. In the section on the infantry, it reiterated the importance of this arm as the most important in the jungle. It noted the need for thorough training in the use of rifles, bayonets, grenades, automatic weapons and mortars in the jungle and the importance of fire control.[75] The major change was on countering Japanese bunker defences. It suggested the employment of previously underused anti-tank weapons for the infantry and co-operation with the other arms as essential in bunker busting. The artillery could provide barrage fire on a narrow front, stating that lifts of a hundred yards every three minutes were needed in average jungle and a slower rate in thicker jungle. As well as aircraft and tanks that could be of equal value in support of infantry, particularly against bunkers. As in previous editions of *MTP* No. 9, there were sections on attack, defence and ambushes. The section on patrolling had increased, while the chapter on withdrawal had been reduced to an emphatic: "THERE WILL BE NO WITHDRAWAL".[76] *The Jungle Book* covered all the lessons that had been learnt since 1941 and as a result the individual sections were very thorough. The training manual was used by the Indian Army for the remainder of the Second World War. It was by no means perfect, however, and was meant to be added to and improved upon. A later *AITM* commented that the notes in *The Jungle Book* were excellent notes but they needed to be amplified as the

---

72 Report by General Sir Claude J. E. Auchinleck covering the period 16 November 1943-31 May 1944, TNA, WO 203/2669A.
73 See *MTP* No. 9 (India), *The Jungle Book*, 4th edition, (September 1943), p. 1. IOR, L/MIL/17/5/2250.
74 See Report by General Sir Claude J. E. Auchinleck, TNA, WO, 203/2669A.
75 See *The Jungle Book*, p. 4.
76 See *The Jungle Book*, pp. 6, 12-13, 21.

result of battle experience.[77] Colonel John Cross, a jungle warfare expert, has more recently commented:

> I pay my respects to the unknown authors of *The Jungle Book*, the military training pamphlet that the Indian Army produced in September 1943. It reflected the improvement of morale in the Army after its blistering defeats in 1942 and was the first attempt to portray conventional British military thinking for jungle warfare.[78]

Indeed, *The Jungle Book* later formed the basis for two War Office manuals in 1944-45, demonstrating that it was the Indian Army who pioneered jungle warfare doctrine for the British Army.[79] *The Jungle Book* together with the other ancillary training manuals became the focus for the dissemination of doctrine in India for all the units and formations preparing for jungle warfare in Burma.

Training Divisions

The main impetus for training in India was now for jungle warfare, overseen by the C-in-C, General Sir Claude Auchinleck, who implemented the proposals of the Infantry Committee and the DMT.[80] 14th and 39th Indian Divisions were chosen as the training divisions and were withdrawn from front line duty to reorganise. The 14th Division had served on the North East Frontier during 1942 and fought in the First Arakan. It was now based at Chhindwara. The 39th stationed at Saharanpur, formerly 1st Burma Division, had been involved in the Retreat from Burma and had been training for jungle warfare for six months.[81] British infantry reinforcements were trained in jungle warfare by 52nd Brigade at Budni in Bhopal State, after basic training with the 13th Battalion, The Sherwood Foresters, at Jubbulpore.[82] The

---

77 See *AITM* No. 24, March 1944, p. 11, IOR, L/MIL/17/5/2240. See also 7th Indian Div Comd's Operational Notes No. 5, 14/1/44, Papers of General Sir Frank Messervy, *Messervy Mss.*, LHCMA, 5/5.
78 Cross, p. 59. See also Jeffreys, pp. 17-18, Marston, 98, 104-109, Moreman, pp. 104-105.
79 See War Office. *Military Training Pamphlet* No. 51, *Preparation for Warfare in the Far East*, June 1945 2nd edition and *Military Training Pamphlet* No. 52, *Warfare in the Far East*, December 1944, IWM.
80 See Despatch by General Sir Claude J. E. Auchinleck, 21st June 1943 - 1st Nov 1943, p. 1, TNA, WO 203/4204. See also Moreman, pp. 84-86.
81 See Deedes, *Historical Record of the Royal Garwhal Rifles*, p. 108. See also Formation of the Training Divisions in India, IOR, L/WS/1/1364.
82 See Field Marshal Sir Claude J. E. Auchinleck, 'Operations in the Indo-Burma Theatre based on India from 21 June to 15 November 1943', *Second Supplement to the London Gazette*, 27 April 1948, p. 28.

training divisions started taking recruits from the beginning of December 1943 and the 52nd British Brigade by mid-December.[83]

The 39th Indian (Training) Division was established in August 1943 and comprised 106th, 113th and 115th Indian Infantry Brigades and commanded by Major General Frank Moore. The 115th Brigade consisted of the amalgamated 14th, 29th, 38th, 56th and 7/10th Gurkha battalions. For instance, the 38th Gurkha Rifles were made up from the 3rd and 8th Gurkha Rifles, under the command of Lieutenant Colonel W. R. J. Spittle.[84] Major S. C. S. Pickford was the training major for this new battalion. Despite having no previous experience of the jungle, a hurried attempt was made to learn, before the first recruits arrived, by carrying out extensive patrols in the Siwalik Hills. Lessons learnt included the difficulty of marching to compass bearings and the importance of physical fitness. Pickford realised that once the jungle and the climate had been overcome, the Japanese would be 'no problem'. His training programme proved highly effective and was later adopted by the whole division.[85] Similarly the 9th Battalion, 16th Punjab Regiment served in 39th Training Division, of which the regimental historian commented: 'All the active battalions were deeply indebted to the Ninth for the imaginative, sound and tough training it gave to their recruits'.[86] According to the divisional CO, the formation 'carried out a difficult and arduous task with a success that was proved in all the jungles and on every battlefield, from Imphal to Rangoon'.[87]

The 14th Indian Division was commanded by Major General Arthur 'Tiger' Curtis who had served in both the Retreat from Burma and the First Arakan. However, only a few officers in the division had battle experience against the Japanese. Some instructors were sent from serving battalions, but units rarely sent their best men and it took three months to train them.[88] Not only infantry, but all arms underwent jungle training as it was such an alien environment to all soldiers. British gunners,

---

83 See Auchinleck, Despatch, Appendix No. 18, p. 71.
84 See Lieutenant Colonel H. J. Huxford, *History of the 8th Gurkha Rifles 1824-149* (Aldershot: Gale & Polden, 1954), pp. 283-286 and Barclay, *3rd Queen Alexandra's Own Gurkha Rifles*, pp. 246-253.
85 See S. C. S. Pickford, *Destination Rangoon* (Denbigh, Clywd: Gee & Son, 1989), pp. 183-197.
86 Lawford and Catto, *Solah Punjab*, p. 280.
87 Major General F. M. Moore, 'The 39th Training Division in the Second World War' in Condon, *Frontier Force Regiment*, p. 588.
88 See Report 14 Indian Division Jul 1943-Nov 1945, pp. 1-2, *Curtis Mss.*, IWM, P140. See also Jeffreys, pp. 42-43. Captain Bill Jeffrey was desperate to the leave the training division and joined the Chindits. He wrote: 'On leave, therefore, we were considering ways and means of escape, for we had no wish to be left in Chhindwara commanding training batteries until the end of the war. To join Wingate's Special Force seemed to be the best course, for he alone seemed to have the power to persuade GHQ to transfer officers from such units as ours.' W. F. Jeffrey, *Sunbeams like Swords* (London: Hodder & Stoughton, 1950), p. 11.

engineers and signallers were also trained in 14th Indian Division. The emphasis was on individual and section training for the infantry, whereas the other arms concentrated on weapons training. For example, the training division had one Indian field regiment, one Indian anti-tank regiment and one light anti-aircraft regiment for the Indian artillery with the 'main job of these regiments is to give two months troop training to recruits from training centres before they are sent to units'. Although some went to holding batteries in the reinforcement camps before joining their units. For British gunners it was a refresher course after the voyage out to India. Indian officers went there from the RA Depot at Deolali and the various OTS.[89] Infantry recruits, including officers and NCOs, were trained at section and platoon level by a representative training battalion from their regiment within the two training divisions.

Liaison visits between the new training divisions and the regimental centres were introduced and 'most Centre Commanders made considerable alterations in certain aspects of training in their centres as a result of their visits'.[90] There were also visits from officers to lecture on operational lessons from Burma and other experts such as Jim Corbett, who was an expert in tracking and killing man-eating tigers in the Indian jungles. He was commissioned as a lieutenant colonel to instruct the men of the two training divisions in jungle lore.[91] He lectured on tracking, edible plants, how to differentiate poisonous snakes and the way to make a friend of the jungle.[92] His book, *Man-Eaters of Kumaon*, was recommended reading in the training division and was translated into Roman Urdu by GHQ India. It described some of Corbett's experiences of tracking down tigers in the jungle. It was thought that valuable lessons of jungle lore could be learnt and then applied to operations against the Japanese.[93] The most important reading material were the *AITM*'s and *The Jungle Book* where the important passages were highlighted in order to cut down on the amount of reading that officers had to undertake in the gruelling training regime, as the divisional report stated:

> Officers had little time for study or even to read important pamphlets issued from higher authority. The issue of paper was kept down to essential limits and all pamphlets, circulars and directives were suitably marked in coloured pencil by Div HQ. This enabled officers to concentrate on those points that concerned them, and saved some reading.[94]

---

89 See Chief of the General Staff, Reorganisation of Artillery, 19 July 1943, pp. 1, 5-6, *Dimoline Mss.*, IWM 73/40/1. The units were the 10th Indian Field Regiment, Indian Artillery, 16th Indian AT Regt. and 14th LAA Regt.
90 14th Indian Division Report, p. 9.
91 See Alston, chapter 37. See also Moore, '39th Training Division', pp. 588-589.
92 See Martin Booth, *Carpet Sahib: A Life of Jim Corbett* (London: Constable, 1986), pp. 224-225.
93 See 14th Indian Division Report, pp. 16-17.
94 Ibid., p. 17.

When the Brigadier Infantry visited the division in May 1945 he reported that 'I found a sound, well thought out training and administrative programme constantly supervised by senior commanders, imparted by keen and painstaking instructors to a physically fit, alert and cheerful body of trainees'. His visit showed that lessons had been learned from the fighting in Burma and the ensuing doctrine was promulgated: 'Thought, planning and rehearsal has resulted in doctrine and lessons from the front being presented in a practical and interesting manner'.[95]

The training divisions made a very important contribution to defeating the IJA in Burma in 1944-45. For instance, 16th (Training) Battalion of the Punjab Regiment, of 55th Infantry Brigade in 14th Indian Division, sent 1,957 trained soldiers to the 1st, 2nd, 3rd, 5th, 14th and 15th Battalions of the regiment.[96] As the regimental historian wrote: 'The 16th's role may have been unspectacular, but it was none the less essential, for it contributed very largely to the ultimate collapse of the Japanese in Burma'.[97] Officers were given practice in command and control, medical officers and administrative units were also trained in jungle warfare.[98] These training divisions were seen as 'a revolution in training policy and practice and proved their worth in the successes that followed'.[99] Although they were really a continuation of the practice in infantry regiments of using training battalions but for a specific terrain and type of warfare. The training battalions had been instituted in 1921 as a permanent depot with one training company for each of the battalions in the regiment.[100]

Jungle Warfare Schools

Auchinleck ensured that jungle warfare training formed the main focus of all training carried out by units, formations and at training schools and establishments throughout India. For example, the syllabus for the Tactical School now included large sections dealing with jungle training where officers 'learnt the latest tactical doctrine and were exercised in the co-operation of all arms'.[101]

The Jungle Warfare School at Comilla initially run by 14th Indian Division moved to Sevoke near Darjeeling in Northern Bihar in 1943. Those officers who attended were now capable of instructing their battalions in jungle warfare skills when they returned to their units. It was still run by Major Parry of the 2/5th Gurkha Rifles and Major Firth of the Duke of Wellington's Regiment, both of whom had fought in

---

95   Ibid., pp. 25-25b.
96   See Major Mohammed Ibrahim Qureshi, *History of the Punjab Regiment 1759-1956* (Aldershot: Gale & Polden, 1958), pp. 419-421.
97   Qureshi, *Punjab Regiment*, p. 421.
98   See 'India at War', p. 235, *Corbett Mss.*, CAC CORB 3/28.
99   'India at War', p. 139, *Corbett Mss.*, CAC CORB 3/28. See also Prasad, *Expansion*, p. 72 and Moreman, pp. 92-94.
100 See chapter 1.
101 Letter from Savory to Callahan, 24 October 1976, *Savory Mss.*, NAM, 7603-93-71A.

the Retreat from Burma and therefore the training 'embodied all the ideas on jungle fighting learnt by 17th Division during its retreat through Burma and in later fighting with the Japanese in the Chin Hills'.[102] Each course lasted for 15 days and demonstrated new tactics required for jungle warfare to British, Indian officers and other ranks. The course not only covered jungle training but also included a period of battle inoculation to accustom those attending to the noise and confusion of battle.[103] The syllabus included patrolling, living off the land, fire control, minor tactics, preparation of road blocks and other obstacles, house to house fighting, camouflage, use of small craft, explosives, booby traps and jungle lore. It finished with a three day course in the jungle which was 'a first class test for endurance and quickwittedness on which our lives were soon to depend'.[104] Lessons learnt at the school were meant to be put into practice, once the students returned to their units. However, according to *AITM* No. 22, commenting on the Jungle Warfare course at Sevoke, this was not always the case, stating: 'The School's teaching MUST be absorbed, by using students as unit instructors on their return'. The biggest problem was that VCOs and NCOs were still having difficulty with fire control in the jungle and were very wary of the terrain that few of them had encountered before. Other criticisms included weak compass work and that students were 'surprised by the physical and mental strain imposed upon them in the jungle'. It was also perceived that the contents of the course were not being absorbed by the parent units, who failed to take advantage of men trained as instructors at GHQ Jungle Warfare Schools.[105] Due to the demand for places on the course, a second jungle warfare school was opened at Shimoga with the first course starting on 29 November 1943.[106] Its remit included training jungle warfare instructors for both the Indian and British Armies. Captain Peter Collister's comments on the instructors showed how seriously the training was taken by those attending it: 'The centre was mainly staffed by extroverted heroes of the Arakan fighting, clad in jungle greens, festooned with bandoliers and grenades'.[107] Both schools taught the diverse uses of bamboo, with bamboo used to make anything from *bashas* to cooking utensils with jungle lore taught by Captain Edgar Peacock who had been a forest officer in Burma prior to the war.[108]

The existing Jungle Warfare Training Centre at Raiwala Bara, near Dehra Dun in Central Command, was initially set up by Major Angus Rose in December 1942 to

---

102   Cooper, *B Company*, p. 38.
103   See letter from Captain C. A. Morris, 14 August 1943, Papers of Captain C. A. Morris, *Morris Mss.*, IWM 99/22/1.
104   DMT India's liaison letter No. 11, 18 June 1943, IOR, L/WS/1/1302.
105   *AITM* No. 22, August 1943, pp. 15-16, IOR, L/MIL/15/4/2240.
106   See Calder, 'From Sloth belt to Springboard', p. 84.
107   Captain Peter Collister, 'Then a Soldier', (Unpublished Memoir), p. 175, IWM, 83/40/1.
108   See Captain C. A. Morris, letter, 14 August 1943, *Morris Mss.*, IWM 99/22/1 and John Henslow, *A Sapper in the Forgotten Army* (Petersfield: self-published, 1986), p. 59. See also Jeffreys, pp. 72-73.

train Indian reinforcements destined for Eastern Army, but it had never functioned properly in its assigned role. Following the formation of the training divisions it took on the role of training complete units or cadres in jungle warfare skills and moved to the Gudalur area in February 1944.[109] For example, two battalions of the newly formed 50th Indian Parachute Brigade commanded by Brigadier Hope Thomson were trained at Raiwala in late 1943. Eric Nield wrote the 153rd Gurkha Parachute Battalion history and served with them. He commented:

> The chief instructor at the school was Major James of the Middlesex Regiment. He had served with "V" Force and had gone through the Burma Retreat and so was full of excellent ideas. I think that we didn't frankly believe a great deal of what he taught us, as none of it was mentioned in any infantry training manuals. It is difficult for anyone who has not served in the jungle to appreciate that feeling of isolation which comes over one, and the training necessary to make individuals confident of finding their way about and maintaining themselves in thick undergrowth, if necessary, for days at a time.[110]

The training had three stages, the first week consisted of drills for jungle manoeuvres and different types of ambush. The second week was training schemes for all-day and all-night training. The final week comprised two separate two day exercises. Overall, the training proved invaluable when the battalion and the brigade were caught up in the fighting at Sangshak in March 1944.[111] Auchinleck anticipated that the reorganisation of the training schools and the new training divisions would, 'go far to improve the individual efficiency of reinforcements, particularly in jungle warfare, both of junior officers and other ranks'.[112]

Training the 5th and 7th Indian Divisions

Collective training in 14th Army was also carried out, shown by the examples of the 5th and 7th Indian Divisions. Slim was insistent on thorough training by all his formations. The 5th Indian Division commenced training in June 1943 at Chas, Bihar, and then moved to Lohardya, Ranchi, where it trained for fighting in the jungles of Burma. The Division was already battle-hardened after its experiences in the Western Desert

---

109 See Auchinleck's Despatch, pp. 27-28. See also DMT India's liaison letters, IOR, L/WS/1/1302, Calder, 'From Sloth belt to Springboard', p. 91-92 and Moreman, pp. 95-97.
110 Eric Nield, *With Pegasus in India: the story of 153 Gurkha Parachute Battalion* (Singapore, Jay Birch (printer, nd.), p. 51.
111 Ibid., pp. 59-69. See also Harry Seaman, *The Battle at Sangshak* (London: Leo Cooper, 1989) and Barkawi, *Soldiers of Empire*, pp. 364-371 for the interesting story of the historiography of the battle with the historian Louis Allen, the veterans of 50th Brigade and Brigadier Hope Thomson.
112 Connell, *Auchinleck*, p. 763.

and the Middle East, but had to adapt to jungle warfare conditions. A new series of training instructions starting with Training Instruction No. 1 (India) were produced. The first one stated: 'This division has now to train for operations of a character different to which it has been accustomed and to train quickly, hence every lesson must have a specific object and be practical'.[113] As they were training before the issue of *The Jungle Book*, the division was relying on the earlier edition of *MTP* No. 9 *The Jungle Warfare* published in August 1942 calling it 'our Bible for jungle tactics'.[114] A very thorough set of training instructions were issued, with instructions as a result of GOC's conferences were again produced by the division, before going into action in the Arakan. Even after action, weekly newsletters were produced by the division with the aim of informing the reinforcement camp of the division's activities with news of training and the lessons learnt.[115] The division also acquired jungle-experienced units such as the 27th Mountain Regiment who had spent the last five months in the Arakan and the 123rd Indian Infantry Brigade, that included the 2/1st Punjabis and the 1/17th Dogras who had both fought in the First Arakan. These veterans of the First Arakan also helped train the division in jungle warfare.[116] The new brigade commander of the 161st Indian Infantry Brigade was Brigadier Dermot Warren who had been GSO1 in 14th Indian Division. Training was undertaken in co-operation with air support and tanks which was seen as the key to jungle warfare tactics in addition to 'aggressive patrolling'.[117]

The 7th Indian Division moved to the Chhindwara area in January 1943 and was one of the first formations to embark on jungle training. The training team attached to the division by GHQ was led by Lieutenant Colonel Marindin, who had participated in the Retreat from Burma, with jungle lore taught by Captain Edgar Peacock.[118] There were exercises in co-operation with artillery, mortars and medium machine guns, called 'Blitz' tactics. From May to September the division carried out training in co-operation with the artillery and the 25th Dragoons, Royal Armoured Corps.[119] Notes were produced within the division to learn the lessons from the Arakan that had been approved by the DMT.[120] The 7th Indian Division recognized particular points for training that needed to be improved that included reconnaissance patrols and defensive positions during the night as well as all round defence during the day, the immediate digging in once a

---

113 5th Indian Division Training Instruction No. 1 (India), 16 July 1943, TNA WO 172/1936.
114 Ibid.
115 See 5th Indian Division weekly Newsletter No. 1, 3 Jan. 1944, TNA, WO 172/4278. See also Brett-James, *Ball of Fire*, pp. 249-253.
116 Lieutenant Colonel G. H. Cree, IWM, SA 10469.
117 See Brett-James, *Ball of Fire*, pp. 250-253. See also Moreman, pp. 111-114.
118 See Roberts, *Golden Arrow*, pp. 11-12. See also Geraldine Peacock, *The Life of a Jungle Walla: Reminiscences in the Life of Lt. Col. E. H. Peacock DSO MC* (Ilfracoombe, Devon: Stockwell, 1958), pp. 63-64.
119 See Roberts, *Golden Arrow*, p. 14. See also Huxford, *8th Gurkha Rifles*, p. 231.
120 See The Division in Advance to Contact (Supported by Tanks), 28 June 1943, TNA, WO 172/1943.

position had been taken and the use of strong fighting patrols. In attack, the usefulness of the doctrine encapsulated in *The Jungle Book* was re-emphasised, stating: 'These notes are excellent' and that they were clearly based on experience gained during the First Arakan. Although the division only had a few advance copies with at least one copy at each brigade HQ. The divisional notes mentioned the need for all commanding officers to study the training manual before the next attack. However, it also showed that the doctrine continually needed updating. For example, in the section on consolidation of the objective, it was recognized that 'The doctrine that the first wave should go right through to the objective is sound' but that a loss of control in the attack was almost inevitable. Thus it was recommended that command and control needed to be quickly regained to which the divisional report gave the following example: 'There was an outstanding lesson on this point when the Donbaik position was attacked by us on 18 February. We gained both objectives, raggedly, but failed in the consolidation for the reasons explained. Much good work and great gallantry was accordingly wasted'.[121] Training continued with two patrols sent out every day, with a fighting patrol sent out every other day and an ambush patrol was taken alternately with another company.[122] Even in a relatively-quiet sector, troops had little chance to rest. Such small-scale encounters helped build confidence and eliminate the Japanese 'supermen' myth. Both 5th and 7th Indian Divisions also underwent training in co-operation with the Royal Air Force for air supply.[123]

British formations in India tended to learn their own lessons and instigate training not based on GHQ India doctrine, although 2nd Division had a training team from 17th Indian Division and had such men as David Wilson who had fought under Ian Stewart in Malaya to help direct training.[124] Similarly received opinion is the Chindits (3rd Indian Division) under Major General Orde Wingate didn't learn from GHQ India. However, training instructions were produced within the formation and copies were sent to the DMT and GHQ India.[125]

Thus, GHQ India, the training divisions, training within 14th Army's divisions and the new doctrine of jungle warfare encapsulated in *The Jungle Book,* provided a basis for uniformly jungle trained troops ready to defeat the enemy, and 'not just a single enemy but several – the terrain, the climate, the diseases and the Japanese'.[126]

---

121 7th Indian Division Commander's Operational Notes No. 5, 15 November 1943, TNA, WO 172/1943 and *Messervy Mss.*, LCMHA, 5/5.
122 See Geoffrey Evans and Anthony Brett-James, *Imphal: A Flower on Lofty Heights* (London: Macmillan, 1962), p. 54.
123 See Field Marshal Sir William Slim, *Defeat into Victory* (London: Cassell, 1956), p. 146.
124 See Wilson, *The Sum of Things*, p. 102. See also Callahan, *Triumph at Imphal-Kohima*, pp. 160-162.
125 See Training Instructions produced for 3rd Indian Division, Papers of Major General Orde Wingate, IWM, OCW104.
126 G. W. Robertson, *The Rose and the Arrow* (136th Field Regiment Old Comrades Association, 1986), p. 152.

Fighting in the Jungle, 1944

Both 5th and 7th Indian Divisions learnt from their experience of fighting in the 2nd Battle of Arakan. They used infantry and tank co-operation tactics, originally developed at Ranchi and refined at Razabil, in counterattacks against the Japanese.[127] On 12 February 1944, Artillery Hill was subjected to a daylight attack by the Japanese. It was defended by the 24th Anti-Aircraft and Anti-Tank Regiment acting as infantry. The enemy hid in the jungle and took the position by surprise. A counterattack by the West Yorkshires was unsuccessful, so two troops of 'C' Squadron, 25th Dragoons were deployed firing high explosive shells to clear the jungle undergrowth. When the tanks were at a reasonably close distance, solid shot was used to loosen the earth around Japanese bunkers and then high explosive shells were used to destroy them. Finally, when the tanks were within 100 to 300 yards, they fired their machine guns over the crest, allowing the infantry to advance without the threat of shell splinters. The infantry advanced to within 15 yards of the Japanese position before attacking with grenades and bayonets and capturing the hill. This action marked 'the beginnings of the new technique in tank and infantry co-operation, which in months to come was to prove decisive against Japanese suicide squads fighting from positions tunnelled into jungle-covered hillsides'.[128]

The Battle of the Admin Box and the defence of similar boxes occupied by the remainder of 5th and 7th Indian Divisions heralded the turning point of the Burma campaign. This was the first time the Japanese had been defeated in the jungle by British and Indian troops. The myth of the Japanese superman was truly destroyed which was a huge boost to the morale of the 14th Army. As Anthony Irwin has commented: 'For the first time in Burma we had stood and fought the Jap and the Jungle and beaten both. To me the defeat of the jungle is the more important, and the defeat over the superman complex'.[129] It also raised the confidence of the civilian populations in India and Britain in the ability of 14th Army to defeat the Japanese in Burma.[130] Jungle training and new defensive tactics had proved effective, not only by the infantry, but also by administrative troops trained to fight in the jungle.

After the 2nd Arakan there was time for the divisions to learn from the campaign as Messervy stated in his first training directive: 'Now that the Division is coming into reserve after 7 months in the line the opportunity will be taken to polish up certain lines of training which need constant attention' such as weapons training, drill

---

127 See Roberts, *Golden Arrow*, p. 14; Brett-James, *Report My Signals*, p. 253; Slim, *Defeat into Victory*, p. 146 and Moreman, *Jungle*, pp. 114-117.
128 Roberts, *Golden Arrow*, pp. 83-84. See also Tom Grounds, *Some Letters from Burma: The Story of the 25th Dragoons at War* (Tunbridge Wells: Parapress, 1994), pp. 113-114 and John Leyin, *Tell Them of Us: The Forgotten Army - Burma* (Stanford-le-Hope, Essex: self-publised, 2000).
129 Anthony Irwin, *Burmese Outpost* (London; Collins, 1945), p. 127.
130 See Kirby, *War Against Japan*, Vol. III, p. 152.

and preparation of defences for monsoon garrisons.[131] In addition each brigade within the division was to set up a committee to study the lessons of the campaign. The establishing paper asked for comments on the principles in the training manuals, the *AITM*s, divisional operational and training notes with particular reference to patrolling, ambushes, night operations and generally attack and defence.[132]

This growing ascendancy over the Japanese on the jungle battlefield was re-emphasised when the IJA made its main attack, Operation 'U-GO', later that spring. Its prime objective was the speedy capture of Imphal by 15th Army, under General Renya Mutaguchi, to forestall the imminent Allied invasion of Burma.[133] The advance of the Japanese 33rd and 15th Divisions began on 9 March. To the north, 31st Division was assigned the objective of Kohima in order to cut the Dimapur-Imphal road. This Japanese offensive had been expected, but not quite so soon, leaving the defending troops spread out over a wide area: 17th Indian Division was in the Tiddim area, 50th Indian Parachute Brigade at Kohima, one brigade of 23rd Indian Division near Ukhrul and 20th Indian Division in the Kabaw Valley. They all had to withdraw in order to concentrate under IV Corps on the Imphal Plain to prevent Japanese infiltration. This withdrawal of large numbers of troops was in stark contrast to the early defeats of the British and Commonwealth Armies in the Far East, as they were carefully conducted tactical fighting withdrawals rather than pell-mell retreats. The 17th Indian Division, still commanded by Major General 'Punch' Cowan, was not ordered to withdraw, however, until 13 March and as a result were cut off by the rapid Japanese advance. The 33rd Japanese Division marched against 17th Indian Division and 20th Indian Division, and two brigades of 23rd Indian Division were called in to help the 17th retreat along the Tiddim Road. In addition, Slim ordered the transfer of formations from the Arakan front to ensure overwhelming superiority on the Imphal Plain. After their successes in the Arakan, both 5th and 7th Indian Divisions travelled by air and train to the Imphal and Dimapur area. Slim's plan was to let the Japanese forces get to the edge of the Imphal plain and then destroy them with mobile strike forces supported by artillery, armour and air support.

The historiography of this campaign continues unabatedly in favour of the fighting at Kohima where the majority of British troops such as the 4th Battalion, the Royal West Kent Regiment and 2nd British Division fought. Imphal, where the majority of defending troops were Indian Army, has largely been ignored as the last good history of Imphal was written in 1962.[134] This bias towards Kohima with little mention of the

---

131 7th Indian Division Commander's Training Directive No. 1, 5 April 1944, TNA, WO 172/4290.
132 See Lessons from Operations, 7 April 1944, TNA, WO 172/4290.
133 See Louis Allen, 'Mutaguchi Renya and the Invasion of India, 1944' in Brian Bond (ed.), *Fallen Stars: Eleven Studies of Twentieth Century Military Disasters* (London: Brassey's, 1991), pp. 215-239.
134 See Evans and Brett-James, *Imphal*. In contrast to the books on Kohima, for example: Arthur Campbell, *The Siege: A Story from Kohima* (London: Allen & Unwin, 1956); John

Indian Army started with the publication of the Winston Churchill's memoirs with only two pages devoted to the battles of Kohima and Imphal and of these only one on Imphal.[135] As Raymond Callahan has pointed out Churchill's low opinion of the Indian Army has affected the subsequent historiography of both the Indian Army but also the Battles of Kohima and Imphal.[136]

The advancing 31st Japanese Division was held up by two battalions of 50th Parachute Brigade at Ukhrul and Sangshak, giving the garrison at Kohima essential time to build up their inadequate defences. The Kohima area was less densely covered by jungle than the previous battleground in the Arakan, being 5000 feet above sea level surrounded by cultivated terraces, with jungle-clad hills further away. The 161st Brigade was sent into action immediately, with orders to protect Kohima and keep the vital supply route to Dimapur open. The 4th Royal West Kent Regiment, together with a battery of the 24th Mountain Regiment and the 2nd Field Company, Indian Engineers, joined the garrison of mainly non-combatants or exhausted units retreating from the Chindwin River. The garrison consisted of about a thousand men, commanded by Colonel Hugh Richards, with the remains of the Assam Regiment, detachments of the paramilitary Assam Rifles, the Burma Regiment plus troops from the reinforcement camp, non-combatant troops who had not been evacuated, and a battalion of untrained Nepalese State Forces. The Japanese attacked Kohima on 4 April. Indeed if General Sato and 31st Division had bypassed Kohima, they would have probably taken the lightly defended Dimapur, which was the base and railhead for the whole central front and thus of strategic importance, but his orders were to march on Kohima which he doggedly adhered to. The remainder of 161st Indian Infantry Brigade were two miles away at Jotsoma, from where the formation provided decisive artillery support to the garrison, protected by the two infantry battalions, as the battery with the garrison was too restricted in space to use their guns and therefore acted as observation posts with wireless communication. One target was hit by 3,500 rounds in the space of five hours.

Colvin, *No Ordinary Men: The Story of the Battle of Kohima* (London: Leo Cooper, 1995); Edwards, *Kohima*; Keane, *Road of Bones*; John McCann, *Echoes of Kohima* (Oldham: self-published, 1989) and Arthur Swinson, *Kohima* (London: Cassell, 1966). This is remedied by the publication of Raymond Callahan's *Triumph at Imphal-Kohima* next year and Hemant Singh Katoch's *The Battlefields of Imphal*.

135 See Winston Churchill, *The Second World War: Vol. V: Closing the Ring* (London: Cassell, 1952).

136 See Raymond Callahan, 'Did Winston Matter? Churchill and the Indian Army, 1940-45' in Alan Jeffreys and Patrick Rose (eds.), *The Indian Army, 1939-47: Experience and Development* (Farnham: Ashgate, 2012), pp. 57-67. See also Catherine Wilson, 'Responsible History? Churchill's Portrayal of the Indian Army in the Second World War', *Ex Historica*, Vol. 4, 2012, pp. 96-124 and Cat Wilson, *Churchill on the Far East in the Second World War: Hiding the History of the 'Special Relationship'* (Basingstoke: Palgrave, 2014).

By mid-April the general situation looked bleak but nevertheless Mountbatten, Slim and General Geoffrey Scoones, IV Corps Commander, were not discouraged by the existing state of affairs as large scale reinforcements were already on their way and coupled with air supremacy, the air supply of formations could go ahead as planned. As Slim had requested, the transfer of XXXIII Corps: comprising 2nd Division, 268th Indian Infantry Brigade and 2 tank regiments, from the other side of India, joined the fighting. The plan was to open up the Dimapur-Kohima-Imphal road and join forces with IV Corps with an immediate objective of relieving 161st Brigade and the garrison at Kohima. However, the Japanese had taken most of Kohima with the defenders grouped around the Deputy Commissioner's bungalow and tennis court on Garrison Hill. Supplies were air-dropped by parachutes but due to the very small drop zone often fell into Japanese hands with the RAF also providing support with canon-fire and pin-point bombing. The siege was over on 18 April when the road was cleared by the 1/1st Punjab Regiment and the wounded and non-combatants were evacuated. The defenders had seen off 25 Japanese attacks in fourteen days although the siege was only fourteen days out of a total of 64 that it took to defeat the Japanese at Kohima. The garrison was finally relieved by 6th Brigade of 2nd Division. General Giffard, C-in-C, 11th Army Group, saw this early defence of Kohima as the turning point in the Japanese attack.[137] A mixed group of trained and untrained troops successfully held off two Japanese regiments, the equivalent of two brigades, showing that training and morale were much better than the previous year. Lieutenant John Henslow, an officer in Queen Victoria's Own Madras Sappers and Miners, serving in 421st Indian Field Company part of the relieving force at Kohima commented: 'What confronted me was something that reminded me of the pictures of the battle of the Somme, a landscape of shell holes and truncated trees'.[138] The fighting at Kohima continued and it took 2nd Division and 33rd Brigade until June to clear the area of Japanese troops, who held on in their bunkers and defensive positions.[139]

Fighting around Imphal continued during this period at considerable intensity. The historian, Jon Latimer, commented that:

> Imphal was an extremely untidy battle, in no conventional form such as Alamein, lasting from the end of March until mid-June, during which hundreds of chance encounters, ambushes, forward attacks and desperate defences occurred that cannot be charted, and never will be.[140]

---

137 General Sir George Giffard, Operations in Burma and North-East India from 16th November, 1943 to 22nd June, 1944, *Supplement to The London Gazette*, 13 March 1948, p. 1360.
138 Henslow, *A Sapper in the Forgotten Army*, p. 75.
139 See Roberts, *Golden Arrow*, chapter 13.
140 Latimer, *Burma*, p. 272.

The 33rd Japanese Division was still fighting 17th Indian Division to the southwest of Imphal at Bishenpur, together with a brigade of 20th Indian Division. The rest of 20th Division was at Shenam and 5th Indian Division at Ukhrul was up against the Japanese 15th Division with 23rd Indian Division in reserve.[141] The Japanese came closest to success on 6 April when they captured the commanding heights around Nunshigum, which overlooked Imphal. This was the nearest the IJA would get to Imphal. It was taken from a detachment of the 3/9th Jats, but the remainder of the battalion retook it later that day. On 11 April the Japanese retook the position. The allied counterattack came two days later, when the hill was bombarded by dive-bombers, fighter-bombers and artillery. The hill was retaken in a famous action by the 3rd Carabiniers and a battalion of the 1/17th Dogras, when all the officers had become casualties and the attack was led by NCOs.[142] This action demonstrated that the use of initiative and junior leadership learnt during training proved effective at Nunshigum. Thus despite the best efforts of the Japanese, the basic plan of concentrating IV Corps in the Imphal Plain had been carried out without losing either 17th or 20th Indian Divisions. Scoones now had 17th, 20th, 23rd and 5th Indian Divisions under his command demonstrating that the battle was largely fought by the Indian Army. Due to manpower problems the British Army was rather depleted by mid-1944 with most British infantry battalions in theatre being 18 % below war establishment.[143] For example, the 1st Battalion of the Northamptonshire Regiment in 20th Indian Division had only three companies of about 82 men each when they attacked Kyaukchaw in January 1944.[144] In June 1944 23rd Indian Division had only one British infantry unit and one British artillery unit, almost making it an all Indian Army formation that would have been unheard of at the beginning of the war.[145]

In May the counter-offensive plan for IV Corps was to attack Ukhrul and for 17th Indian Division to cut the Tiddim Road to the rear of 33rd Japanese Division. After regrouping Scoones used 5th and 23rd Indian Divisions for the counter-offensive

---

141 See Brett-James, *Report My Signals*, pp. 322-355. See also Ian Lyall Grant, *Burma: The Turning Point: The Seven Battles on the Tiddim Road* (Chichester: Zampi Press, 1993) and A. J. Doulton, *The Fighting Cock: Being the History of the 23rd Indian Division 1942-1947* (Aldershot: Gale & Polden, 1951).
142 See Lieutenant-Colonel L. B. Oatts, *I Serve: Regimental History of the 3rd Carabiniers (Prince of Wales's Dragoon Guards)* (Norwich: Jarrold (printer), 1966), pp. 263-267 and Arthur Freer, *Nunshigum: On the Road to Mandalay* (Durham: Pentland Press, 1995).
143 See John Peaty, 'The Chindits and Special Forces Manpower', *The British Army Review*, No. 128, Winter 2001-02, p. 56.
144 See S. N. Prasad, *The Reconquest of Burma: Volume I: June 1942-June 1944* (India & Pakistan: Combined Inter-Services Historical Section, 1958), p. 167.
145 See Doulton, *Fighting Cock*, pp. 306-307. See also Chris Kempton, *'Loyalty and Honour': The Indian Army September 1939-August 1947: Part I: Divisions* (Milton Keynes: Military Press, 2003), pp. 118-120. In the order of battle the units were the 1st Battalion, the Seaforth Highlanders and the 158th Field Regiment, Royal Artillery in which the author's great uncle, George Currie, served with throughout the Second World War.

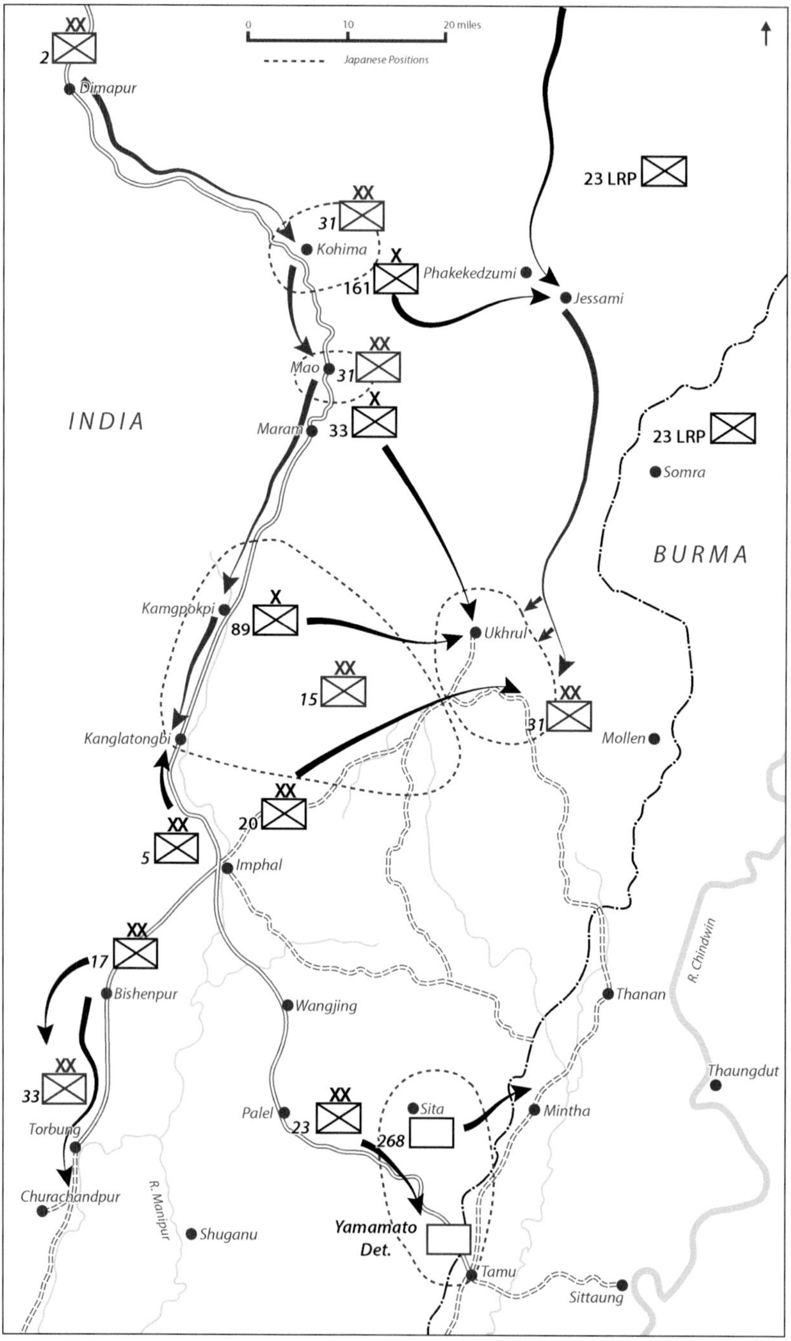

Map 5 The Counter-offensive at Kohima and Imphal, June–July 1944.

against the Japanese forces, 5th Indian Division (along with 89th Brigade of 7th Indian Division) advanced ten miles up the Imphal-Kohima road, 20th Indian Division held the hills of Crete West and Scraggy and pushed 23 miles along the track to Ukhrul until they were relieved by the 23rd Indian Division, who pushed the Japanese out of the Shenan Area. The 17th Indian Division got the better of the Japanese 33rd Division, against whom they had fought in the 1942 retreat. On the night of 5/6 June British soldiers of 2nd Division met up with troops of 5th Indian Division, 29 miles north of Imphal at Milestone 109. As General 'Bill' Slim wrote in his memoir: 'The Imphal-Kohima battle, the first decisive battle of the Burma campaign, was not yet over, but it was won'.[146] Although the Japanese forces refused to admit defeat and when the order was finally given to 15th Army to retreat to the Chindwin on 9 July, the 15th and 31st Divisions were in complete disarray, only 33rd Division kept its cohesion as a fighting force.

The battles of Imphal and Kohima depended on air supply and the retention of the airfields at Imphal and Palel. Allied air superiority was maintained by short Spitfire fighters and long range fighters, Mustangs and Lightnings. During April, transport squadrons provided continuous air supply to IV Corps, which received a daily average of nearly 500 tons of supplies. The RAF together with the USAAF and the Indian Air Force (IAF) were instrumental in winning the battles of Kohima and Imphal. For example, air defence of Imphal was conducted by a day to day strength of seven squadrons: eighteen from the RAF and three from the IAF.[147] In addition the training divisions and reinforcement camps had proved successful by providing trained reinforcements for the 14th Army and thus the divisions were kept 'at a proper state of efficiency'.[148] Casualty and malaria casualty rates in particular were considerably lower due to both the enforced anti-malarial discipline and casualty evacuation measures brought in. For example in the first half of 1944, 24,000 casualties were evacuated by air from all fronts.[149]

During the battles of Kohima and Imphal, the British and Indian Armies inflicted a crushing defeat on the IJA. There were 53,505 casualties in the Japanese 15th Army whose overall strength had been 84,280, in contrast to 16,700 casualties in

---

146 Slim, *Defeat into Victory*, p. 346.
147 See Peter Preston-Hough, *Commanding Far Eastern Skies: A Critical Analysis of the Royal Air Force Superiority Campaign in India, Burma and Malaya 1941-1945* (Solihull: Helion, 2015), pp. 200-230. See Probert, *Forgotten Air Force*; Gerald A. White Jr., 'Manna from Heaven: Development of aerial re-supply by the Royal Air Force and Indian Army in India and Burma 1942-1943', *RAF Historical Society Journal*, Issue 58, April/May 2104, pp. 115-127 and also his unit history of USAAF unit air-dropping supplies in Burma, *The Great Snafu Fleet: 1st Combat Cargo/344th Airdrom/326th Troop Carrier Squadron in World War II's CBI Theater* (self-published, 2000).
148 General Sir George Giffard, 'Operations in Burma and North-East India from 16th November, 1943 to 22nd June, 1944', *Supplement to The London Gazette*, 13 March 1951, p. 1368.
149 See ibid., p. 1369.

178   Approach to Battle

the Commonwealth forces. In addition, the 14th Army had captured 100 guns and 20 tanks.[150] Slim commented in a letter to his friend, Lieutenant Colonel H. R. K. Gibbs, that 'there is no doubt about it that the old Fourteenth Army has given him [the Japanese] the biggest defeat he has ever had in his whole history'.[151] The fighting bore out the importance of jungle training as well as air superiority, organised logistics and good leadership. It showed what resolute jungle-trained troops, with confidence in themselves and their leaders, could achieve in battle. The actions at Kohima and Imphal demonstrated the successful use of infiltration tactics and aggressive patrolling when fighting in dense jungle against the IJA. It showed the benefits of tank, artillery and air co-operation and demonstrated the resolve of support units, all of which was made possible with thorough jungle training. Even though the jungle was a difficult environment, it was no longer one that caused alarm or fear among Indian troops. The soldiers of the 14th Army had grown considerably in confidence and were no longer afraid of this environment or the Japanese, and they displayed increasing battlefield effectiveness with aggressive tactics in both defence and attack.[152]

Conclusion

By mid-1944 in Burma, India and Ceylon, Auchinleck had command of the Indian Army, Mountbatten operational control of the South East Asia Command with Slim commanding the 14th Army. Thus the command structure was now clearly defined in the theatre and allowed GHQ India to concentrate on training. The 14th Army was by no means perfect by the summer of 1944, but now had the upper hand over the Japanese. The 7th Indian Division's 2nd Training Instruction commented:

> Although we have now behind us 10 months of operational experience, that does not mean that we are by any means perfect in battle. On the contrary, the wastage in junior leaders and the absorptions of a large number of reinforcements have decreased out battle efficiency. But, with that experience to guide us, we can now in a comparatively short time not only regain the efficiency of last autumn but greatly – surpass it.[153]

Thus the division needed to study and analyse the lessons from the Arakan, Imphal and Kohima and apply them to training. This was achieved through company training, the training of junior leaders and individual training. Company training was through discussions on cloth or sand models, TEWTS and exercises. The training

---

150   See Kirby, *War Against Japan*, Vol. III, p. 372.
151   Letter from General W. Slim to Lieutenant Colonel H. R. K. Gibbs, 15 August 1944, IWM, Misc. 54 item 824.
152   See Marston, *Phoenix from the Ashes*, pp. 138-156, Moreman, *Jungle*, pp. 124-142.
153   7th Indian Division Training Instruction No. 2, 3 July 1944, TNA, WO 172/4290.

of junior leaders was a priority as 'at present needs most attention. In battle success depends more than on any other factor on the courage, initiative, cunning and skill of section and platoon commanders'. This training would be through cadre courses using a demonstration platoon and individual training ranging from weapon training to field hygiene and was recorded in every company. The instruction also mentioned the need for physical fitness, drill and night work.[154] VCOs and NCOs were instrumental as leaders in the jungle, shown by the members of the Frontier Force Rifles such as Jemadar Ram Gul, Naik Jagat Ram and Havildar Punjab Singh reported in *Fauji Akhbar*:

> Naik Jagat Ram, a Dogra, of Kangra district, recently ambushed a party of enemy at night on a track 20 miles from his patrol base and killed 18 with a shower of grenades.
> Havildar Punjab Singh, of Jammu district, pleaded for a chance to take out a patrol before being posted to a job where there was not much opportunity for action. He had just returned from a 50-mile patrol lasting five days…
> Another patrol led by Jemadar Ram Gul, a Pathan, of Kohat district, lay in wait for 24 hours from a position over-looking the Tiddim Road before he and his men swooped down on an enemy convoy scattering them with a shower of grenades.[155]

As after the Arakan at brigade level but cut short due to the fighting in Assam, tactical discussions were to take place every Wednesday to discuss patrolling, ambushes, attack, defence and for the next phase of fighting to look at river crossings.[156] The 4/8th Gurkha Rifles and 89th Brigade listed the lessons learnt from the recent fighting. Patrolling was seen as instrumental and the basis for all tactics in the jungle. The battalion and the brigade reiterated the importance of using a patrol order card, described in *AITM* No. 25 as both a reminder to the patrol commander of the main points to cover in their patrol and as the accompanying patrol report proforma. It was suggested that they should be used by all divisions and the proforma was 'exceedingly useful, as a patrol leader on his return is a tired man, and such a proforma will save him time and help his memory'.[157] Although the formation did not agree that reconnaissance patrols should be not more than two or three men and an officer that had previously been written up in *AITM* No. 25. They believed that a

154 Ibid.
155 'Exploits of the "Tiger" Patrols', *Fauji Akhbar*, Vol. XXII, No. 23, 3 June 1944, p. 13.
156 See 7th Indian Division Training Instruction No. 3, 25 July 1944, TNA, WO 172/4290.
157 Lessons from Operations, 10 September 1944, p. 3, TNA, WO 172/4290 and *Messervy Mss.*, LCHMA, 5/15. See also *AITM* No. 25, pp. 67-68, IOR, L/MIL/17/5/2240; Patrick Davis, *A Child at Arms* (London: Hutchinson, 1970), pp. 62-63, 89-90; Scott Gilmore, *A Connecticut Yankee in the 8th Gurkha Rifles* (London: Brassey's, 1995), p. 163 and Marston, *Phoenix from the Ashes*, pp. 174, 202.

patrol needed at least one 'get-away man' and probably two in the jungle or at night, thus a patrol should comprise four men and an officer.[158] Thus the doctrine was being continually added to through battle experience and was only meant as a guide and not a dogma that had to be adhered to. There were also particular lessons from the attack and capture of Ukhrul such as the necessity for village fighting battle drill, the value of snipers, observation posts for 3-inch mortars, periscopes when troops were pinned to the ground and the value of slit trenches. Although the slit trenches needed to be carefully sited away from trees and bushes which were useless against artillery fire and caused more casualties and the need to stay in the slit trenches after a Japanese bombardment was noted due to the fact Japanese gunners often returned to shell the same position.[159]

Thus 14th Army prepared for the next phase of the fighting and absorbed the lessons of the recent operations.[160] In training terms after the initial fighting in the jungle, formations and units underwent retraining for the plains of Burma. In 1944-45 new training pamphlets were still being produced such as the *Battle Bulletins* whose object was 'to publish first hand reports received from troops in the forward areas'.[161] *Battle Bulletin* No. 5, for example, was published in October 1944 with sections on the attacks on Jail Hill at Kohima and crossing the Gargliano in Italy, lessons learned in the problems of infantry-tank co-operation and the experiences of other Allied Armies such as the Australians in New Guinea.[162] As Scott Gilmore, 4/8th Gurkhas, commented: 'we read the manuals, which by now were thick on the table, packed with advice won from two years of campaigning in Burma and the Pacific'.[163]

The victory in Burma was achieved by the Indian Army supported by the British, East and West African forces. The American and Chinese forces were also instrumental with the fighting in Northern Burma, alongside the combined air forces of the Royal Air Force, the United States Army Air Force and the Indian Air Force, as well as the second Chindit Operation. In conclusion training, doctrine, improved logistics, air supply, medical advances and health discipline, artillery, tank and air support, high morale and good leadership were all essential in the Indian Army for the defeat of the Japanese forces at Kohima and Imphal. In addition, equipment was no longer in short supply in SEAC by the Summer of 1944, in contrast to the previous low priority accorded to this theatre.

---

158 See ibid., p. 3 and *AITM* No. 25, p. 2, IOR, L/MIL/17/5/2240.
159 Ibid., p. 3. See also Marston, *Phoenix from the Ashes*, pp. 172-174, Moreman, *Jungle*, pp. 144-160.
160 See K. W. Cooper, *The Little Men: A Platoon's Epic Fight in the Burma Campaign* (London: Robert Hale, 1992), p. 20. Cooper served with the 1st Battalion, the Border Regiment in 20th Indian Division. He was given the job of training reinforcement NCOs for the future.
161 See List of GS Training publications 1945, p. 5, IOR, L/MIL/17/5/2199.
162 See *Battle Bulletin* No. 5, October 1944, Gurkha Museum.
163 Gilmore, *A Connecticut Yankee in the 8th Gurkha Rifles*, p. 173.

7

Training in India at the end of the Second World War

The training organisation in India was vast by 1945. The Indian Army had not only trained for jungle warfare but also for air-mobile operations, amphibious operations and for the open warfare in the central plains of Burma in the next phases for the war.[1] Together with formations in Burma, lessons continued to be learned through training instructions issued within the divisions. By this time it was largely the Indian Army fighting in Burma together with the East and West African Divisions due to the shortage of British manpower available.

In 1942, Southern Army had become an operational command due to formations undertaking training but also for the defence of Southern India. The XXXIII Corps took over the battlecraft school at Chingleput, originally set up by 19th Indian Division, that meant all formations and units such as 25th Indian Division attended. The 19th Indian Division undertook training in this period due to the threat of invasion, 'All forms of collective training had therefore to be practiced at once. Although emphasis was placed on company and battalion training, at least once a fortnight each brigade was required to carry out a brigade exercise, with particularly stress on mobility'. The 19th and 25th Indian Divisions also undertook a number of exercises, For example, Exercise Trump 1 was set up in early March 1943 by XXXIII Corps, under Lieutenant General Philip Christison, whereby 19th Division fought a defensive delaying action and 25th Division trained in the approach march and attack. Exercise Barge in August was the biggest exercise undertaken in India where XXXIII Corps followed the events of the 4th Mysore War. Then at the end of the year both divisions moved to Malabar and Nilgiri to undertake jungle warfare training. In

---

1   For air-mobile operations training material see Army/Air Operations Pamphlet No. 5 (Indian), *Maintenance by Air (Provisional)*, 1945 and Army/Air Operations Pamphlet No. 6 (India) *Air transported Operations (Provisional)* 1944. Both prepared under the joint direction of H.E. Commander-in-Chief in India and the Allied Air Commander-in-Chief South East Asia and then reprinted by the War Office, IOR, L/MIL/5/2242. See also *Military Training Pamphlet* No. 8 (India) *Air Forces in Support of the Army* Parts 1, 2 & 5, IOR/MIL/5/2249 & Part 5 IWM, K.79/1909.

December 1943, 19th Indian Division undertook the first large scale jungle training, Exercise Malabar, where the division fought and maintained itself on one road in the jungle. Similarly, 25th Indian Division undertook Exercise Wynad where the divisions attacked a bunker position and then also maintained itself on one road in the jungle.[2] By December 1943 19th Indian Division had completed its jungle training at Coimbatore and 25th Indian Division was training at Mysore.[3]

The 19th Indian Division was the best trained division in the Indian Army having undergone training for two years prior to joining IV Corps on the Imphal Plain in October 1944. It was the first standardized division capable of fighting in the roles that had previously been undertaken by differing divisional organisations.[4] General Sir George Giffard due to limited resources and the need to increase efficiency had decided that Airborne, Assault, Armoured, Light, Mechanical Transport and Animal and Mechanical Transport Divisions would be standardized to a become a Standard Division capable of jungle fighting, operations involving transportation by air, amphibious operations and open warfare.[5] This was demonstrated by 19th Indian Division which was very successful in Burma, taking Mandalay in Slim's audacious plan Operation 'Extended Capital'. The division epitomized the new professionalism of the Indian Army capable of adjusting to all forms of warfare from jungle warfare in Imphal to the open warfare on the central plains, the crossing of the River Irrawaddy and the brutal fighting in Mandalay.

After the taking of Mandalay, the first divisional training instruction was produced in May 1945, as the division had a period of rest in May and the time to re-learn the importance of patrolling, training with tanks and polish up battle drills. There was a whole section on junior leadership where officers needed to practice the appreciation of verbal and written orders, co-ordination of all arms as well as administrative essentials such as anti-malarial discipline. In addition every officer in the division had to write up a paper each month on three subjects which were a narrative of any action the officer had been involved in. Secondly the three most important lessons for future operations and a sketch map of the action.[6] The divisional commander, 'Pete' Rees trained 19th Indian Division hard and the division continued to learn the lessons from each phase of fighting, it proved to be one of the most effective fighting formations in Burma.[7] The Indian Army achieved 'The Last and Greatest Victory of the British

---

2 Calder, 'From Sloth belt to Springboard', pp. 27, 33, 39, 48, 57, 60, 75, 80, 87-88.
3 See Auchinleck, Despatch, Appendix No. 18, p. 71. See also Davies, 'Small Green Men', pp. 127-130.
4 See Developments in Infantry Organization 1939-1944, *Savory Mss.*, NAM, 7603-93-69.
5 See General Sir George Giffard, 'Operations in Burma and North East India from 16 November 1943 to 22 June 1944', *Supplement to the London Gazette*, 19 March 1951, pp. 1366-1367. See also Jeffreys, *British Army*, pp. 21-24.
6 See 19th Indian Division Training Instruction, No. 1, May 1945, TNA WO, 172/6996.
7 See Jeffreys, 'Slim's Welsh General', pp. 154-159. See also Marston, *Phoenix from the Ashes*, pp. 181-199 and Moreman, *Jungle*, pp. 182-197.

Indian Army' with Operation 'Extended Capital' and the recapture of Rangoon in May 1945.[8]

Combined Operations Training

Southern Army was also the base for combined operations training. A Combined Training Centre at Kharakvasla was set up in 1941, coming under the direction of 36th Indian Division in 1942. In June 1942 a combined operations and intelligence centre manned by HQ Southern Army, HQ 225th Group RAF and naval officers was established at Kumara Park, Bangalore. Then in July 1943 Madh Island, north of Bombay, was selected as the new Combined Training Centre and established in September with 6th Brigade of 2nd Division the first formation to attend. The other brigades in 2nd Division along with 29th Independent Brigade underwent training at Madh as they were to be the assault brigade groups. They were to be followed by 19th and 25th Indian Divisions to be trained as the follow through divisions and therefore trained in wetshod landings.[9] As there was insufficient Royal Indian Naval (RIN) personnel to man the necessary landing craft for combined operations, three Indian Army battalions were transferred to the RIN. These men were trained at a new Landing Craft Training School, HMIS Hamla, at Manapam set up on 1 January 1943. Due to the monsoon from June to October at Madh, another centre was set up at Cocanada in October 1943 and much later another at Karakvasla, but there were insufficient officers as instructional staff.[10]

Combined operations training relied heavily on the British experience in Europe. Majors G. D. Upson, 5/2nd Punjab Regiment, and H. L. Boultbee, 7th Light Cavalry, attended training courses in the UK. Copies of all the training material was requested for the DMT. Reports such as 'Report of Committee on Beach Organisation', 13 November 1943, 'Role of Amphibious Divisions South East Asia', 14 November 1943 and 'Working of a Beach Group', 3 May 1944 were sent out to India. The first draft of Combined Operations pamphlet 'Amphibian Vehicles, Operation, Control and Maintenance' was sent out to GHQ India at the request of Major Upson.[11]

Major General Alec Lee was appointed Major General Combined Operations Training in December 1942, after coming out from the UK. In 1943 training was

---

8   See Graham Dunlop, 'The Recapture of Rangoon, 1945: The Last and Greatest Victory of the British Indian Army' in Jeffreys and Rose (eds.), *The Indian Army, 1939-1947*, pp. 138-155.
9   See Beyts, *The King's Salt*, p. 27. He commanded the 3rd Bn, 6th Rajputana Rifles and later took over 62nd Indian Infantry Brigade in 1945 in 19th Indian Division.
10 See Calder, 'From Sloth belt to Springboard', pp. 19, 40, 43, 48, 50, 56-57, 81. See also Auchinleck, 'Operations in the Indo-Burma Theatre based on India from 21 June to 15 November 1943', *Second Supplement to the London Gazette*, 27 April 1948, p. 2668 and Training Combined Operations, IOR, L/WS/1/787.
11 See Training Combined Operations, IOR, L/WS/1/787.

184 Approach to Battle

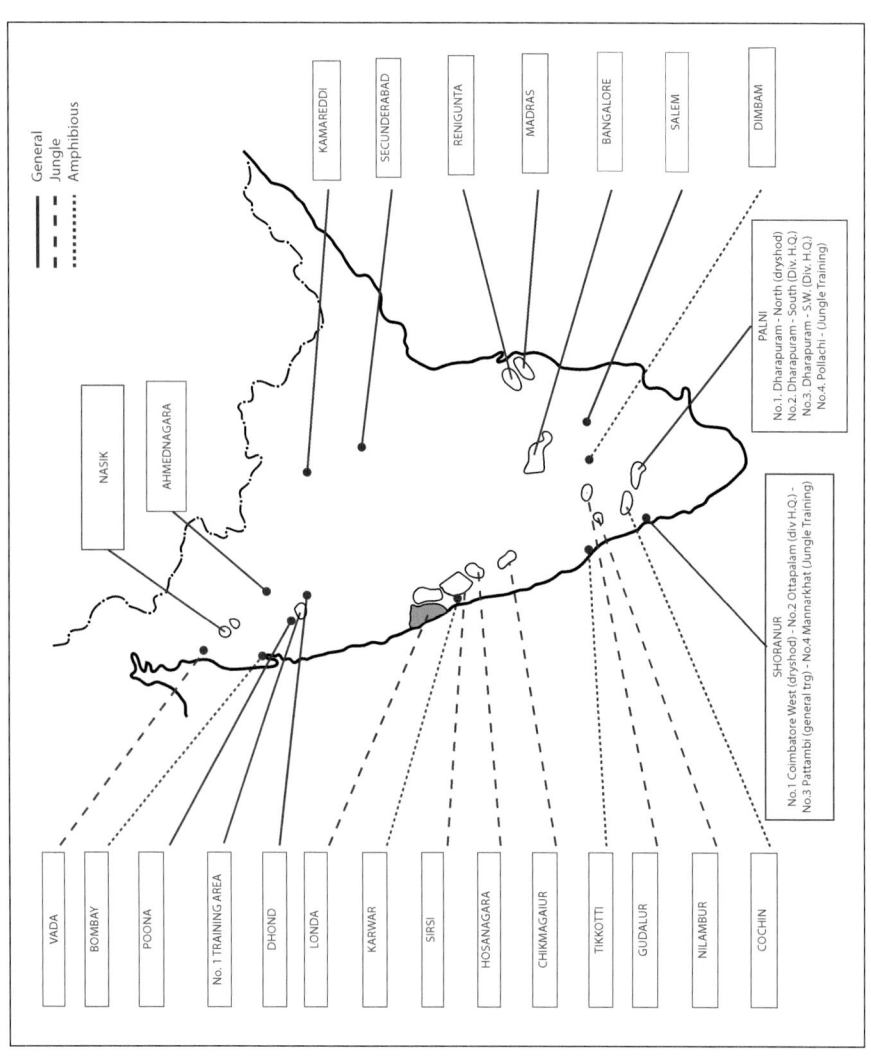

Map 6 Training areas in Southern Army, 1944-45.

organised under the newly formed Directorate of Combined Operations that was responsible for the training of two Indian infantry divisions, an Indian beach group and an Indian brigade. In addition a combined operations mobile staff school toured and instructed staff at 11th Army Group.[12] Thirty eight combined operations pamphlets, including some specifically produced for India, were issued to units at the Combined Training Centres.[13] In May 1944 GHQ India set up 'Formation Training' under Major General Lee with two training wings for 'higher training in amphibious and jungle warfare' for formations under GHQ India but were available for use by SEAC. The headquarters was responsible for drafting training programmes, administration of exercises and the provision of resources in conjunction with the divisions and HQ Southern Army.

However, this new structure did not work as it muddied the waters in the command structure between GHQ India, SEAC and Southern Army as 'Formation Training' was the responsibility of divisional commanding officers guided by directives from the DMT with the exception of amphibious operations which was under the Director of Combined Operations. Thus the army commander who had previously had responsibility for the training of formations in Southern Army, except amphibious training, had no responsibility for training once divisions had been assigned to SEAC. In addition, Formation Training had no specialist advisers such as for artillery or engineers and quite often the Major General Formation Training was junior and had less experience than the divisional commanders. The result was 'Formation Training' was abolished in June 1944 and the training wings became the more familiar training teams, for example 'B' Wing became No. 2 Training Team. Once again the army commander was responsible for all training bar the Combined Training Centres. Thus even in the later stages in the war, new training initiatives were adopted but if they did not work were quite quickly terminated.

At the same time in June 1944 the responsibility for some training schools and establishments were delegated to army commanders. Category 'A' establishments remained under the control of the DMT whereas the majority of schools came under 'B' and were administered by the army commander with the exception of allotting places and instructors. By 1945 Southern Army had ten jungle training areas, six amphibious and eleven general training establishments.[14] At the same time combined operations training of XXXIV Corps was top priority for the planned reconquest of Singapore and Malaya, for instance 23rd Indian Division undertook training in November 1944, although Operation 'Zipper' took place in September 1945, after the Japanese surrender.

12   See 'India at War', pp. 139-140, 235-236, *Corbett Mss.*, CAC, CORB 3/28. See also Training Combined Operations, IOR, L/WS/1/787.
13   See List of GS Training publications 1945, pp. 20-22, IOR, L/MIL/17/5/2199. See for example *Combined Operations Pamphlet* No. 42 Supplement No.1 (India) *Brigade Group Dryshod Exercises 1944* (Delhi, 1944), IWM, K.97/241.
14   See Calder, 'From Sloth belt to Springboard', pp. 101-102, 109A.

Military Training Directorate

A new DMT was appointed in May 1943, Major General Edward Gurdon, a British service officer. A month later he commented on how the standards of infantry training had deteriorated after the First Arakan:

> I have stepped into a proper hornets nest and the whole training of the infantry out here is now being reorganised. The standard of training recruits and reinforcements has been disgracefully low ... I have now demanded 10 months basic and 2 months post recruit training, which of course is having immediate and big repercussions.[15]

The DMT understood the need to get back to a higher standard of training within the army. One of which was through battle drill as there was a tradition of using battle drill in the Indian Army since pre-1914 for fighting on the North West Frontier campaigns.[16] Tarak Barkawi has described drill as 'simultaneously training, practice and ritual'.[17] The directorate produced a training pamphlet laying down battle drills for section, platoons and companies for jungle warfare which was produced during the Summer of 1943 to complement *MTP* No. 9 *The Jungle Book*. In contrast to battle drill in the UK, where it was thought it would stifle initiative, it was aimed at the Indian soldiers since 'every private soldier must now be something of a tactician' and battle drill would help develop the initiative of the soldiers.[18] This was demonstrated in the field as shown by a report produced by the 4/8th Gurkha Rifles that commented on the lessons learned in recent operations in 1944, stating that:

> The teaching of battle drill will pay a handsome dividend every time. Every man does at least know what action he has to take under any circumstances and why, and with the knowledge he can work out any adaptations necessary. It therefore ensures that every man will do something based on sound training instinctively.[19]

---

15 Letter from Major General Edward T. L. Gurdon to Brigadier Gordon Thompson, War Office, May 1943, IOR, L/WS/1/766.
16 See Moreman, *Frontier Warfare*, pp. 42-53 and for the importance of drill see Barkawi, *Soldiers of Empire*, pp. 180-183, 213-217.
17 Barkawi, *Soldiers of Empire*, p. 213.
18 The Instructors' Handbook on Fieldcraft and Battle Drill (India), pp. 4-5, IWM. See also Battle Drill for Thick Jungle 1943, IOR, L/MIL/17/5/2236. See Harrison Place, pp. 40-62 and Tim Harrison Place, 'Lionel Wigram, Battle Drill and the British Army in the Second World War', *War in History*, Vol. 7, No. 4, 2000, pp. 442-462.
19 Lessons from Operations 4/8GR No. 01/326 of 10 September 1944, TNA, WO 72/4290 and *Messervy Mss.*, LCHMA, 5/15.

The battalion understood the need for battle drill and demanded that all officers and NCOs knew the battle drill laid down in *Battle Drill for Thick Jungle 1943* and *AITM*s 24 and 25 before they joined their unit.[20]

In addition to the Australian and American experiences of fighting the Japanese in the Pacific used in the *AITM*s and *MTP* No. 9, in April 1943 Colonel Forster, on the British Army Staff at Washington, was made responsible for gathering information about jungle warfare equipment for India Command and the resulting information was distributed to India Command, the War Office and Australia Command.[21] In August 1943 the first of many jungle warfare liaison letters passed between India Command and the Australian Military Forces, which later included the War Office in its circulation along with the New Zealand and US Commands and War Office Monthly Training Reports were circulated to India with material on both mountain and jungle warfare.[22] In addition, fifty Indian Army officers were sent to Australia. There they attended the Jungle Warfare School at Canungra and were then attached to fighting units in New Guinea. On their return to India some became instructors and others rejoined their units.[23] In November a senior Australian officer, Brigadier Lloyd, who had fought in New Guinea and had been the Commandant of the Australian Tactical school, was loaned to India Command for six months, during which time he visited and lectured to the 14th Army and Jungle Warfare Schools such as at Shimoga.[24] The DMT Australia toured training establishments in February 1945 and twenty Canadian officers toured India Command, various schools and training establishments and had been attached to units in Burma.[25]

The War Office set up the 220 Military Mission in June 1943 in order to look into the equipment and organisation to defeat the Japanese. It was led by Major General John 'Tubby' Lethbridge who visited the USA, India, South West Pacific and Australia to study the problems of jungle warfare. The Mission's report was published in March 1944 but the recommendations were only really put into practice for British troops coming out from Europe after the end of the war with Nazi Germany.[26] After completion of the report, Lethbridge returned to the Burma to take up the post of

---

20 See ibid.
21 See Liaison Letter No. 11, 18 June 1943. IOR, L/WS/1/1302.
22 See Jungle Warfare – Training 11/10/43 – 11/3/44, TNA, WO 106/4708. See also DMT's Monthly Training Report, IOR, L/WS/1/764.
23 See Auchinleck, Despatch, 21 June 1943-15 November 1943, p. 2667. See also, James R. Allen, *In the Trade of War* (Tunbridge Wells: Parapress, 1994), p. 61 and an unpublished paper by Tim Moreman, 'The Jungle, the Japanese and the Australian Army: Learning the Lessons of New Guinea, 1942-44'.
24 See Liaison Letter No. 13, 7 October 1943, IOR, L/WS/1/1302.
25 DMT's Monthly Liaison Letter No. 2, February 1945, IOR, L/WS/1/766.
26 See 220 Military Mission Report, 25 March 1944, TNA, WO 203/5250 and Major-General J. S. Lethbridge Papers, LHCMA. See also Lieutenant Colonel D. J. C. Wiseman, *The Second World War 1939-1945 Army: Special Weapons and types of Warfare* (London: HMSO, 1952), pp. 283-297.

Chief of Staff to Slim when Major General Steve Irwin left 14th Army to become Commandant of the Staff College at Quetta.[27]

The Military Training Directorate staff more than doubled between 1944 and 1945 and had increased from three sections in 1940 to ten by September 1945.[28] Some functions such as the editorial team of *Fauji Akhbar* had been transferred to the Public Relations Directorate in 1944.[29] In 1945 the new Director of Military Training was Major General Donald Bateman and the Directorate was responsible for all training apart from medical and combined operations training.[30] The original three sections were for training schools and establishments, higher training and training publications and individual training and control of the training schools. In 1943 there were eight sections that also included one for soldier's individual training and one for war diaries and the history of the Burma campaign. Three new sections had been set up for languages, education and films respectively.[31] Although education passed to the Adjutant General's Branch in 1944, the directorate was further expanded in August 1944 to include the technical training of animal transport and supply branches of the RIASC, military training of services such as Provost, Clerks, Indian Pioneer Corps, Transport, Veterinary, Remounts and Canteens, and WAC (I). Then in 1945 responsibility for training in the armoured corps, artillery and signals was also transferred to the directorate meaning that there was ten sections by the end of the war with 64 officers.[32]

Training pamphlets continued to be written and produced. The third edition of *MTP* No. 16 (India) *Platoon Leading in Frontier Warfare* was published in 1945, updated as a result of Tuker's Frontier Committee. Although there are very few pamphlets that authorship can be ascertained. One exception is *A Lecture to Infantry Officers on Man Management* that was written by Major General Reginald Savory whilst he was Inspector of Infantry. Two copies per company in all arms were distributed throughout India. The object was to train and keep men mentally and physically fit for battle and maintain this through and after action. He wrote that the greatest commandment was that: 'A well-trained man knows that he is a better man than the

---

27 Slim wrote in *Defeat into Victory*, p. 387: 'I was again very fortunate as I was able to get in his place Brigadier 'Tubby' Lethbridge, a Sapper who combined the typical clear-headedness of an engineer with a broad humanity that made him a pleasure to work with or under…The experience he had gained during a long visit to the Australian Army in New Guinea made the conditions of our war familiar to him.'
28 See Prasad, *Expansion*, pp. 307, 509.
29 See ibid., p. 318.
30 See 'India at War', p. 324, *Corbett Mss.*, CAC, CORB 3/28.
31 For films see 'Fade Out', 'Military Training Films (India) – A Retrospect', *JUSII* Vol. LXXIV, No. 315, April 1944, pp. 171-176. New training films listed in DMT's Monthly Liaison Letter No. 6, July 1945, IOR, L/WS/1/766 include 'Infantry and Tank Co-operation' and 'Driving Film for the Public'.
32 DMT's Monthly Liaison Letter No. 6, July 1945, IOR, L/WS/1/766. See also Prasad, *Expansion*, pp. 306-307, 509.

enemy and that makes him mentally fit for battle'. The pamphlet noted the need to relieve boredom, maintain good relations between officers and men, maintain discipline, as well as keeping a soldier mentally fit through: leave, comfort, saluting, turn-out, mail and pay. For physical fitness, Savory recommended: bringing troops fresh to the battlefield, anti-malaria discipline, efficient evacuation of the wounded, maintenance in battle and battle discipline. Followed by a period of recovery after battle.[33] These were all lessons that Savory had learnt in command ranging from the 1930s, the North and East African campaigns and commanding 23rd Indian Division on the Assam border before becoming Inspector of Infantry in 1943. He asked Ian Stewart for his opinion on the training pamphlet who remarked that 'It is really admirable, and I got quite excited when I found all my pet points coming out!'[34]

By 1945, there were 920 training pamphlets listed by GHQ India, although those listed included both those produced by GHQ India and War Office manuals reprinted in India.[35] These were available across India at training schools and establishments as well as divisional and brigade headquarters and the library at GHQ India which was staffed by a member of the Military Training Directorate.[36] The value of the training manuals were paramount as one post-war commentator has remarked in the *Journal of the United Service Institution of India*:

> An important point in training that must not be omitted is that of the value of training literature. Well-written and illustrated booklets are of immense value, especially during the period of expansion of the forces. In the past, training manuals have had little appeal to other then the military scholar; in fact they have been so ably condensed that a non-military trained mind would have difficulty in following them. Let the future military literature be therefore of a more vivid character, and more on the line of the various military pamphlets and published during the late war.[37]

The threat posed by malaria had clear training implications that were also addressed by India Command. For example, a medical school of jungle warfare was set up in July 1943 by 26th Indian Division in the Arakan and was attended by officers from all the other divisions based in North East India. Medical advances had ensured that malaria could be contained through insecticides, anti-malarial discipline and mepracrine,

---

33   Major General R. A. Savory, *A Lecture to Infantry Officers on Man Management* (Delhi: Chief of the General Satff (India), June 1944), *Savory Mss.*, NAM 7603-93-69.
34   Letter from Ian Stewart to Savory, *Savory Mss.*, NAM, 7603-93-69.
35   See List of GS Training publications 1945, IOR, L/MIL/17/5/2199. See also Reorganisation of the Army and Air Force in India, 1945, Vol. 2, pp. 98-99, IOR, L/WS/2/77.
36   See *Defence Headquarters* (New Delhi: War Department, 1945), p. 74.
37   Huelin, 'Was our Pre-War Training Wrong?', p. 386.

although casualties remained a problem.[38] Medical officers were being trained in anti-malarial measures by October and anti-malarial works sections were set up to counter the problems in Assam by improving drainage. Anti-malarial discipline was strictly enforced and, by late 1943, these measures had proved to be largely successful. Malaria rates were also high in jungle warfare training areas. To combat this a policy was adopted whereby training should be restricted to non-malarial areas in Northern India where the malaria season was short. In the centres that could not be relocated, such as the Jungle Warfare Training School at Managade in Mysore, a malaria control system was enforced. Malaria casualties in forward areas was now treated at the Malarial Forward Treatment Units and thus the unit and lines of communication were less affected by malaria casualties.[39]

However, some training establishments were slower to adapt their syllabi. As late as October 1944 the Staff College at Quetta did not treat jungle warfare as a separate subject, as shown in the Commandant's words: 'the conditions and limitations imposed by jungle are studied in each series dealing with an operation of war'.[40] Captain H. R. C. Pettigrew and Captain Walter Walker both taught at Quetta, however, and used their experiences of the Retreat from Burma as the basis for their lectures, as well as Major General Stephen Irwin, Slim's Chief of Staff in 14th Army, becoming Commandant in late 1944.[41] Charles MacFetridge remembered a sudden change of emphasis mid-term at Quetta in 1943 from the Western Desert to Burma, and from TEWTs to Jungle Exercises Without Trees. As he wryly commented: 'A year after the Japanese had reached its North-East Frontier, the Indian Army was at last concentrating on the war in Burma'.[42]

38 See Mark Harrison, 'Medicine and the Culture of Command: the Case of Malaria Control in the British Army during the two World Wars', *Medical History*, Vol. 40, No. 4, October 1996, pp. 447-452.
39 See Lieutenant-General N. Wilson, Medical Situation in India Command, 20th December 1943, IOR, L/WS/1/1324; M. K, Afridi, 'Malaria Control' in Lieutenant Colonel B. L. Raina (ed.), *Official History of the Indian Armed Forces in the Second World War 1939-1945: Medical Services: Preventive Medicine (Nutrition, Malaria Control and Prevention of Disease)* (India & Pakistan: Combined Inter-Services Historical Section, 1961), pp. 253-430. See also Mark Harrison, *Medicine & Victory: British Military Medicine in the Second World War* (Oxford: OUP, 2004), pp. 213-221 and John Baty, *Surgeon in the Jungle War* (London: Kimber, 1979), pp. 78-79.
40 Morale Reports, Aug, Sep & Oct 1944, IOR, L/WS/1/761.
41 See Pettigrew, 'It Seemed Very Ordinary', p. 147-148, IWM, 84/29/1. See also Tom Pocock, *Fighting General: The Public and Private Campaigns of General Sir Walter Walker* (London: Collins, 1973), p. 61 and General Sir Walter Walker, *Fighting On* (London: New Millenium, 1997), pp. 64-65 and Slim, *Defeat into Victory*, p. 387.
42 Charles MacFetridge, 'The Indian Army in Burma: A Personal Reminiscence' in David Smurthwaite (ed.), *The Forgotten War: British Army in the Far East 1941-1945* (London: NAM, 1992), p. 62.

Education

Educational training for the Indian Army made significant advances during the war, with support from Auchinleck. The Education school at Belgaum was increased and four regional schools were also established in order to teach Urdu and English to the large numbers of Indian recruits. By 1942, three thousand instructors were recruited.[43] In Middle East Command under Auchinleck, an education officer with three teams comprising a British officer, a subedar and four jemadars were sent in 1942 to act as mobile schools to train instructors.[44]

The Directorate of Welfare and Amenities was set up under the Adjutant General's Branch in November 1942.[45] The Education section that later became the Directorate of Army Education produced a large number of pamphlets specifically for British and Indian troops in India, following the example of the British Army.[46] The directorate produced *The Welfare Education Handbook* that established wartime educational policy within the army. It was brought out under the auspices of Wavell, where he stated in the preface:

> Welfare Education is an integral part of the Army's training and their attitude towards it should be one of understanding and enthusiasm. If this training is undertaken in the right spirit officers will become better leaders, their men better soldiers and all will emerge the better citizens for their service in the Army.[47]

Thus the soldier needed to be aware of what he was fighting for, that would in turn improve morale. At the same time the Morale Committee was set up in 1943 and reports were produced.[48] The aims of the educational directorate in India were to focus on the necessity of fighting Japan, show the importance of India in the global war, inculcate a spirit of responsible citizenship as well as keep British soldiers in touch with developments in the UK but also maintain the confidence between British and Indian troops. The pamphlet reiterated the principle that education was now an integral part of training for both British and Indian troops.

---

43 See White, *Army Education*, p. 145.
44 See Wayper, *Mars and Minerva*, p. 175
45 See Prasad, *Expansion*, p. 374.
46 For British Army education during the Second World War, see S. P. Mackenzie, *Politics and Military Morale: Current Affairs and Citizenship Education in the British Army 1914-1950* (Oxford: Clarendon Press, 1992), p. 57-173 and Jeremy A. Crang, *The British Army and the People's War 1939-1945* (Manchester: Manchester University Press, 2000), pp. 114-131.
47 *The Welfare Education Handbook: A Manual designed for the guidance of all officers in the conduct of talks and dscussions on "Current Affairs"*. (New Delhi: Directorate of Welfare & Amenities, GHQ India, 1943), preface. IOR, L/MIL/17/5/2331.
48 See Morale Committee, 1943-1945, IOR, L/WS/1/1375.

Later in 1943 Auchinleck was responsible for a concerted effort in education, partly as the Infantry Committee had estimated that 82% of infantry recruits to the Indian Army were illiterate.[49] When he had been C-in-C Middle East he had noticed the importance of education that was being carried out exclusively for British troops. He wrote to Wavell impressing the need for this to be extended to Indian troops stating:

> My last point is the need for preparing the Indian soldier for the post-war period. Service in the Middle East, and contact with men of other nations, has developed and changed the Indian soldier's outlook. I consider it is of the utmost importance that this awakened interest be guided into channels which will be useful to the men themselves, to India and India's interest in good and stable government.[50]

As a result the Directorate of Army Education produced the pamphlet *Wartime Education for Indian Troops* in 1944. This pamphlet encapsulated the doctrine for educating Indian soldiers during the war. Educational policy was divided into primary and wartime education. Primary was a continuation of the pre-war educational training slightly modified to suit wartime conditions. Wartime education was largely based on the experience of the British Army. Pamphlets such as *Current Affairs* were amended for Indian troops with versions in English and Urdu. The object was to explain to the Indian soldier what, where and why the war was being fought. For example, the version of *Current Affairs Monthly* No. 4 *Why we are Fighting* produced for Indian Troops in 1944. The pamphlet addressed the reasons for the Second World War and why it was relevant to India and Indian troops. The aim was for platoon commanders to get their men to discuss the ideas, each part contained a quiz, a summary and a series of talking points. The junior leader led the questions and summary and helped the men discuss the talking points in 'Josh' groups.[51] The main sections in *Current Affairs* No. 4 were on fighting to save India from invasion as well as rescue China and South East Asia from Japanese domination. It also stressed that India was 'fighting to safeguard our Indian way of life, to remain free to worship God as we please, to trade as we please and with whom we please'.[52] The last two reasons for fighting were to prevent future aggression and for a better India that was 'clean, healthy, educated and prosperous'.[53]

---

49 See Report of the Infantry Committee, IOR, L/WS/1/1371.
50 Directorate of Army Education, Adjutant General's Branch, GHQ India, *Wartime Education for Indian Troops* (New Delhi: GHQ India, 1944), p. 2.
51 'Josh' means pep, spirit or enthusiasm in Urdu. See Barkawi, *Soldiers of Empire*, pp. 344-345.
52 Directorate of Army Education, Adjutant General's Branch, GHQ India, *Current Affairs* No. 4 (I.T.) New Series. October 1944. *Why we are Fighting* (New Delhi: GHQ India, 1944), p. 2.
53 Ibid., p. 5.

Although the pamphlets were based on those for British troops they were re-written for Indian troops in both English and Roman Urdu. In comparing *Current Affairs* No. 42 (B.T.) *Burma during the War* (June 1945) and *Current Affairs* No. 11 (I.T.) *Burma during the War* (May 1945). The version for Indian troops uses the same method of quiz, summary and a series of talking points whereas the version for British troops is much more matter of fact. Although most of the text is similar explaining the geography, culture and politics of Burma as well as the success of the recent campaigns. The main difference was Britain's relationship with Burma in the pamphlet for British troops and the Indian version highlighted the large amount of Indians who had lived and worked in the country before the Japanese invasion, a large percentage of whom had evacuated in 1942.[54]

The four main series of pamphlets were *Current Affairs (Indian Troops)*, *Winning the Peace (Taraqqi ke Usul)*, *The Illustrated Review* all issued monthly and *Map Review* issued fortnightly. *Winning the Peace* had a similar format to *Current Affairs* with a summary, talking points and a quiz after the discussion as they dealt with historical subjects such as the history of India and the British Empire.[55] The series was geared towards the soldier as an individual in Indian society and prepare him for the post-war world. Both *Winning the Peace* and *Current Affairs* were meant for leading discussions by the officer, VCO or NCO. Copies were also placed in the unit information room so that soldiers could read them with one issue per thirty men. *Map Review* was two-sided, one side was a map of the world showing all that had happened in the last fortnight and the other had a featured side with a map or picture connected with a topical subject or aspect of regimental life or training that could be used by the platoon commander as the basis of a talk. *The Illustrated Review* had pictures, articles and stories in Urdu, Hindi, Telegu and Tamil that would be of general interest and was more of recreational value than educational. All of them were issued in English and Urdu with the *Map Review* and *Illustrated Review* proving very popular with Indian troops.[56] However as *Wartime Education for Indian Troops* suggested there was little new in the education programme, it just had a much higher degree of importance than previously as it was really a continuation of citizenship and general knowledge of the pre-war education syllabus but had become a lower priority due to the expansion of

---

54 See Directorate of Army Education, *Current Affairs* No. 42 (B.T.) *Burma during the War* (June 1945) and *Current Affairs* No. 11 (I.T.) *Burma during the War* (May 1945) (New Delhi, GHQ India, 1945). See also *Current Affairs* Nos. 32, 35-36, 39, 41, 43-45, 47-48 & 51, IOR, L/MIL/5/2306.

55 See Directorate of Army Education (India), Adjutant General's Branch, GHQ India, *Winning the Peace Taraqqi ke Usul: India through the Ages* – II (November, 1944), (New Delhi, GHQ India, 1944), IWM.

56 See *Wartime Education for Indian Troops* (GHQ India, Directorate of Army Education, 1944), pp. 3-4 and *Wartime Education for British Troops* (GHQ India, Directorate of Army Education, 1944), p. 6. See also Waypers, p. 175 and William Arthur, '"The Padang, the Sahib and the Sepoy": The Role of the Indian Army in Malaya, 1945-6', (Unpublished DPhil thesis, Oxford University, 2014), chapter 1.

the Indian Army in the early years of the war as well as the low educational standards of recruits. The pamphlet summed up that primary education was the educational training needed by the soldier to perform his given role and wartime education was 'the mental basis of morale and the intellectual preparation for peace'.[57]

By the end of the war the syllabus of the Indian Army Special Certificate of Education was completely re-written and accepted by a large number of Indian universities as the equivalent of the matriculation examination. In 1945 new Basic methods of instruction were adopted for the teaching of English.[58] In the UK, Basic Education Centres had been set up across the country staffed by AEC personnel who instructed a six week course of reading and writing based a pamphlet entitled *English Parade* that had improved reading and spelling ages by a couple of years.[59] Agriculture was a consistent factor in both pre-war and wartime education as a large percentage of soldiers were recruited from farming communities in the Punjab and as the war progressed from across India.

As in the pre-war Indian Army, each unit had an officer and a VCO to organise education and help train the platoon commanders to lead discussion sessions. For example, each infantry battalion would have a Wartime Education Committee comprising the commanding officer, the second-in-command, company commanders as well as the subadar major which would decide what education activities would be cascaded down to platoon commanders with the education officer and VCO on hand to provide help or advice. The education officers, in turn, were trained at the Army School of Education and supported by local AEC officers, who could lecture themselves but also bring in civilian experts on subjects like history and agriculture. There was also a Current Affairs School in Shillong in Eastern Command.[60] The pamphlets provided the basis of the discussions either starting or ending with a quiz depending on the complexity of the subject. The pamphlet *Wartime Education for Indian Troops* stated:

> The ideal is balanced discussion: the expression of reasonable opinion and arguments based on knowledge and not on prejudiced opinion. In no circumstances has a man the right to express personal and possibly prejudiced opinions that will inflame passions: that criticise the acts of his own OR Allied Governments: or that reflect unfavourably on the action of commanders.[61]

Other methods of promulgating education included dramatic productions, music recitals, poetry readings, hobbies and handicrafts and there were also touring

---

57 *Wartime Education for Indian Troops*, p. 5.
58 Liaison Letter No. 1, 5 April 1946 between Director of Education GHQ and Director of Education War Office, IOR, L/WS/1/1753.
59 See Crang, *British Army and the People's War*, p. 126.
60 See Liaison Letter No. 1, 5 April 1946.
61 *Wartime Education for Indian Troops*, p. 12.

parties.⁶² Although education officers had to be mindful of religious and cultural differences between the British and Indian soldiers. In the different wings of the Army Education School for example, leatherwork that proved so popular with British troops was unthinkable to Hindu soldiers and indeed handicrafts such as leatherwork and woodwork were looked down up by caste conscious Indian soldiers.⁶³ It was also recommended that the unit information room contained a small reference library including such publications as *Whitaker's Almanac*, atlases, dictionaries, encyclopaedias and books on India, Indian villages and agriculture. Other journals produced by the Inter Services Public Relations Directorate such as *Weekly Commentary* and *Indian Information* were recommended.

In addition, the Indian soldiers' fortnightly newspaper, *Fauji Akhbar* was popular with soldiers and was reported and staffed by mainly civilian Indians. It was highly illustrated, covering news of Indian personnel in all theatres, all services, with news from across India ranging from agriculture, training and education to pictures of the most popular Indian movie actresses.⁶⁴ In an article entitled 'Training for War and Peace' in the newspaper, journalists visited the Armoured, Royal Indian Army Service Corps, Indian Army Medical Corps and Observer Corps training establishments in India. It was noted that education played a large role in the training as a high standard was required to operate a tank or armoured car. The article commented of the training centre for the Indian Army Medical Corps:

> Education includes Roman-Urdu, Mathematics and (in the case of the better educated recruit) English. Considerable attention is paid to "Welfare Education" which aims at making the recruit a better citizen than he was before joining the Army, and includes lectures and demonstrations on such subjects as village cleanliness, care of crops, care of cattle, etc., soil erosion, litigation, and international affairs, including the cause and course of the war, etc.⁶⁵

Wartime education continued during field operations with *Current Affairs* and *Winning the Peace* sent to all units in South East Asia Command. The only materials needed for the discussion groups were a blackboard and chalk with the back of a lorry proving a good substitute for a blackboard.⁶⁶ Major Burnett produced his own broadsheet in 268th Indian Infantry Brigade as he felt *Fauji Akhbar* was insufficient and too general. He saw that British troops 'were confident, self-assured and assumed inherent superiority, which contrasted with the quiet diffidence of the Indian *jawan*.

---

62 See Liaison Letter No. 1, 5 April 1946.
63 See Geoffrey Treese, *Laughter at the Door* (London: Macmillan, 1974), p. 126.
64 See run of *Fauji Akhbar* 1939-1935 held in IWM. For example a series of articles on citizenship were published see Vol. XXII, No. 34, 19 August 1944.
65 *Fauji Akhbar*, Vol. XXII, No. 20, 3 May 1944, p. 27.
66 See *Army in India Training Memorandum* No. 28, June 1945, p. 32, IOR, L/MIL/17/2/2240.

He wrote: 'I felt that part of this assurance derived from the fact that they were better informed than their Indian counter-parts'.[67] Although short lived, it was his attempt to keep his troops in touch with what was happening in the war.

Educational training continued after the war even though the Current Affairs School and the six mobile education training teams were disbanded.[68] For instance at battalion level, the 7/2nd Punjab Regiment whilst in Malaya produced a training instruction that stated: 'Due to active conditions the standard of education in the battalion is low. Constant supervision by officers will be necessary to see that the standard is raised quickly by good teaching methods'.[69] Education training was initiated for demobilisation with schemes set up in the Punjab, Bombay and Madras for soldiers wanting employment as civilian teachers. Other provinces had similar schemes but the pay offered was not enough to tempt service personnel.[70] For all those troops with more than two months to serve, fifteen periods per week were reserved for education with compulsory subjects for discussion based on *Current Affairs* and *Winning the Peace* such as the principles of rural and urban development and citizenship. Optional subjects included learning English for the Indian Army English certificate (along Basic lines) or English up to the standard of the Special Certificate. Civilian instructors needed to be drafted in due to the large numbers set for demobilisation and extra textbooks in citizenship, rural and urban development were ordered and made available to troops.

The success of both the primary and the wartime education initiatives were cemented by the establishment of the Indian Army Education Corps in February 1946.[71] By 1946 there were Vocational Training Centres in each unit that were largely educational and provided that an Indian soldier passed his ordinary vernacular examinations in his unit he could progress through the Regimental Centre right up until university matriculation level. Regimental Training Centres were also made responsible for the civilianisation of soldiers in direct contrast to their wartime role for both technical and educational purposes. In addition three more King George Royal Indian Schools were formed in 1946 for about three hundred pupils and efforts were made to improve conditions such as hospital and educational facilities for the wives and daughters of soldiers in unit lines.[72]

---

67 Major F. T. Burnett, 'Keeping up with the Hunt: The Story of 268 Indian Infantry Brigade' (Unpublished Memoir), p. 65, IWM.
68 See Liaison Letter No. 2, 1 May 1946, IOR, L/WS/1753.
69 7/2nd Punjab (Recce) Training Instruction No. 1, 25 February 1946, TNA, WO 172/10232.
70 See Liaison Letter No. 2, 1 May 1946, IOR, L/WS/1753.
71 See Liaison Letter No. 1, 5 April 1946, IOR, L/WS/1753.
72 See Education British and Indian Troops Welfare Notes: Education, IOR, L/WS/1/823.

Willcox Committee

The Reorganisation Committee, otherwise known as the Willcox Committee, was set up by Auchinleck in November 1944 to look at India's defence requirements after the war. In the previous year, Auchinleck had toured throughout India inspecting about 500 units of the three armed forces as well as the civilian war effort in factories, munition works and shipbuilding yards.[73] He noted the value of sport such as boxing for training, remarking, 'this sport produces a comradeship and friendliness between all ranks which cuts across any outworn ideas of segregation or aloofness as between officer and man'.[74] In particular the committee looked at the expansion of the Indian Armed Forces and included a number of sections on training with reference to the experience of the war. The committee was chaired by Lieutenant General Henry Willcox along with Brigadier William Thompson, Brigadier Kodandera Cariappa, Brigadier Enoch Powell, Air Commodore Edgar Kingston-McCloughry, RAF and Commander E. C. Streatfeild-James, RIN. Willcox had been GOC Central Command since 1942. Central Command had been responsible for much of the training in India and although British Service, he had also been the senior instructor at Quetta (1936-38) and therefore had an excellent overview of training in India both before and during the war as well as a spell as Inspector of Infantry in the British Army at the beginning of the war. Brigadier Thompson had been Senior Instructor at the IMA (1937-40) and was BGS, War Staff, India Office (1942-44), Brigadier Cariappa became the first Indian C-in-C in 1948, Enoch Powell who had been Professor of Greek at Sydney University before the war, joined the British Army and came to India in 1943 as secretary to a joint inter-service committee, India and South East Asia Commands and then Assistant Director in the General Staff Branch, GHQ India. According to Philip Mason, a member of the Indian Civil Service, Auchinleck appointed Powell as he wanted someone with a good brain but who was also not a professional soldier.[75]

The Report was published in 1945 with a large number of recommendations with training as an important part. The Regimental Training Centres were seen as a successful concept and 'that recruit training is most economically and efficiently carried out at the centres'.[76] Similarly the training divisions were praised and recommended for continuation. Reservists were recommended for staffing expanded OTS as well as reinforcement camps with the report stating:

---

73 See 'C-in-C's Tribute to India's War Effort', *Fauji Akhbar*, Vol. XXII, No. 52, 26 December 1944, p. 11.
74 See 'Boxing tends to develop Character: Gen. Auchinleck emphasises value of sport in training of our Jawans', *Fauji Akhbar*, Vol. XX11, No. 52, 26 December 1944, p. 5.
75 See Philip Mason, *A Shaft of Sunlight: Memories of Varied Life* (London: Andre Deutsch, 1978), p. 197.
76 See Reorganisation of the Army and Air Force in India, 1945, Vol. 1, p. 37, IOR, L/WS/2/77.

Further, it should be a recognized duty of the Military Training Directorate in peace to maintain complete plans to accommodate two training divisions in suitable areas and provide on mobilization for officers' training schools with a capacity of about 150 per cent of the total officer strength of the peacetime army, that is, 100 per cent for the first phase of expansion plus 50 per cent for wastage during the second year.[77]

The report wasn't entirely uncritical of the training structure during the war. For example, it was recommended that the School of Engineering should be responsible for all instruction in military engineering, except recruit training, as the previous three centres of Sapper and Miner groups meant that there was no centralized doctrine. The Frontier Warfare School at Kakul was established in 1941 to train inexperienced units on Frontier duty but after the war when Indian Army units resumed tours of the NWF the need for the school was seen as unnecessary. The need for army air liaison officers were noted and air co-operation would need to become an integral part of training at both the Tactical School and Staff College. The importance of combined operations and the need for a centre where formations could be trained with a tri-service staff that could also research and experiment with combined operations equipment for Indian conditions was seen as necessary.

The report suggested that training centres and regimental centres be co-located wherever possible. For example in the Indian Armoured Corps, recruit training was undertaken at Lucknow, the Armoured Corps School was at Ferozepore, the Tank School was at Babina and the AFV School and OTS were at Ahmednagar. Major Barrow commanded a wing of the Tank School from 1943 until 1945 with 1000 men under his command and about 100 to 150 tanks training all Armoured Corps recruits to a high standard of tank driving and maintenance. Lucknow, Ferozepore and Babina were seen as unsuitable climatically with Lucknow and Ferozepore also unsuitable as a training ground and accommodation respectively. The report suggested that IAC Training Centre and AFV School be situated at Ahmednagar near the Corps with two thirds of the IAC based near Poona, with the 'proximity to one another of the training establishments and the formations will be of benefit on both sides'. This actually occurred in 1948 after Independence with the establishment of the Armoured Corps Centre and School that trained recruits, young officers and had instructor wings, according to Major General Sandhu the new establishment was so successful it remained intact until the 1970s.[78] Similarly the report suggested that the IAVC Training Centre and the Veterinary School at Ambala should be also joined by the Animal Training Centre which was at Jullundur.[79]

---

77   Ibid., p. 43.
78   Reorganisation of the Army and Air Force in India, p. 270. See also Sandhu, *Indian Armour*, pp. 256-257.
79   See ibid., pp. 251, 253-4, 255-256, 270, 273.

The report listed 75 training schools and establishments in India that included the Staff College, Combined Training Centre, Tactical School, Corps schools, Army Schools and Training Centres for both regimental and Corps. This list did not include the wartime schools such as those set up for jungle warfare, frontier warfare and combined operations.[80] The schools were reduced after the war but twenty two remained in the current form, thirteen continued to fulfil some operational or training requirement, such as No. 3 GHQ Training Team to meet special training requirements. Four schools were reduced by fifty per cent until their roles could be fulfilled by unit commanders and then would be disbanded and fourteen were to be disbanded.[81] Thus demonstrating that by 1945 India had a huge number of training establishments and schools that were instrumental in training large numbers of officers and men for the eventual victory in the War against Japan.

Officer Training

Initially most of the British cadet officers were civilians residing in India but by 1942 they either came from volunteers from Officer Cadet Training Units (OCTU) in the UK, British other ranks who had been recommended for the OCTU or passed the War Office Selection Board or through the schoolboy cadet scheme.[82] By mid-1943 about 200 other ranks became cadet officers per month but this had decreased to a hundred by 1944. At the same time the Directorate of Selection of Personnel was set up and very quickly was successful in recruiting officers of sufficient calibre. At the same time, Indian cadets were in the region of a hundred and sixty a month.[83] The district interview boards used at the beginning of the war had limited success as large numbers of cadets continued to drop out of the OTS so the system was centralized under GHQ. The system adopted was taken from the British Army selection system with the use of psychological testing in order for the cadets to be directed towards the job the individual was most suited.[84] Those candidates who failed the selection board could attend the Kitchener Inter-Services Pre-Cadet College at Nowgong, established in November 1944. They trained for five months to develop the necessary

---

80 See Reorganisation of the Army and Air Force in India, 1945, Vol. 2, pp. 98-99, IOR, L/WS/2/77.
81 See Training Schools India – Reduction of GHQ Schools and Courses, September 1945, IOR, L/WS/1/789.
82 See Precis for talk to WO Lecturers by General Lockhart, December 1942, *Lockhart Mss.*, NAM, 8310-154-30.
83 See Prasad, *Expansion*, p. 101.
84 See Supplement to *The London Gazette* 29 April 1948, Operations in the Indo-Burma Theatre based in India from 21 June 1943 – 15 November 1943, by Field Marshal Sir Claude J. E. Auchinleck, p. 2666. For the development and experience of the War Office Selection Board in the British Army see Crang, *British Army and the People's War*, chapter 2.

skills to develop initiative, personality, self confidence, physical fitness and increase knowledge of English in order to apply as an officer cadet for a second time.[85]

The cadet scheme in Britain was mainly recruited through public schools.[86] Prospective cadets could apply aged seventeen and half years old, sometimes interviewed and then would enlist in the Royal Scots aged eighteen, when they could embark for India to join an OTS and eventually become an ECO.[87] Retired Indian Army officers were attached to Army Home Commands as GSO1 Liaison Officers to lecture at schools in their areas and select cadets. The first cadets left the UK in September 1941 and by May 1945 about a thousand had gone to India with these cadets being praised by an OTS commandant as good officer material.[88] Alternatively cadets also volunteered after similar lectures at the pre-OCTU at Wrotham, Kent, and some were put down on the 'Pink List' (draft for the Indian Army) without their knowledge.[89] The Great Central Hotel at Marylebone Station was the base for the Indian Army Selection Board, then cadets enlisted in the Royal Scots until 1943 and later the Queen's Royal Regiment (West Surrey) as the training detachment for the Indian Army based at Invicta Lines, Maidstone.[90] They trained under a joint Queen's Regiment/ Royal West Kent Regiment Primary Training Wing for six weeks basic training, then twelve weeks infantry training with an Indian Army holding Company at No. 13 Infantry Training Centre, commanded by Indian Army officers, and one week at the pre-OCTU at Wrotham. After embarkation leave, cadets assembled again at the Great Central Hotel, which was a transit camp and marched to a railway station for a train to Liverpool or Glasgow where they embarked for a troopship to India.

Denis Wood was interviewed by Colonel Alan Auret, a retired Indian Army officer working as the Indian Army Liaison Officer for HQ Western Command, in May 1944. He attended the Indian Army Selection Board and was offered a cadetship in August 1944. His basic training was six weeks with No. 63 Primary Training Wing at Victoria Barracks in Maidstone and then he joined the Indian Army Holding Company ('F' Company), No. 13 Infantry Training Centre at Invicta Lines at Maidstone for 12 weeks infantry training, the detachment was commanded by Major Jimmy Arkell of

---

85 See 'New Training College for Potential Officers', *Fauji Akhbar*, Vol. XXIII, No. 5, 30 January 1945, p. 10.
86 See John Shipster, *Mist on the Rice-fields: A Soldier's story of the Burma Campaign and the Korean War* (Barnsley: Pen & Sword, 2000), p. 15. See also Prasad, *Expansion*, pp. 103-104.
87 See Precis for talk to WO Lecturers by General Lockhart, December 1942, *Lockhart Mss.*, NAM, 8310-154-30.
88 See Prasad, *Expansion*, pp. 103-104.
89 See John Irwin, 'A Royal Engineer at OTS Mhow, India, 1944', *Journal of the Society for Army Historical Research*, Vol. 78, No. 316, (2000), p. 291. See also Major Ian Gibb, 'A Walk in the Forest' (Unpublished Memoir), p. 2, IWM, 86/3/1; Davis, *A Child at Arms*, p. 2; Capt. Peter Gorb, 'My Phoney War 1939-1948: A Memoir' (Unpublished Memoir, 2005), p. 10, IWM, 06/39/1.
90 See Davis, *A Child at Arms*, p. 2. Also e-mail correspondence with Major Jim Vickers, 20 June 2012 and Lieutenant Colonel Alastair Rose, 23 June 2012.

the 5th Royal Gurkha Rifles. Training consisted of drill, fieldcraft, weapon training, PT, route-marching, bivouacking and cooking in pairs and a ten mile timed march in full battle order. He attended OTS Bangalore undertaking the elementary Urdu examination for which cadets received Rs 100 reward as well as learning about man management and the staple employment of the Indian Army as aid to the civil power where cadets were instructed in the need to take Indian Army Form D-908, amongst other subjects.[91] The three main themes in training at Bangalore were military, sport for teamwork and administration for writing reports and military law.[92]

Views of the training at the OTS were mixed with Patrick Davis commenting in 1943 that 'Mhow taught me nothing new about infantry tactics at section level and we had few chances to practice with a platoon or company', he continued '…I am left with a conviction that much of the instruction was unnecessarily out of date and some of it near to comedy'.[93] This seems to be a common view of OTS Mhow, in particular.[94] However, more realistic training progressed in the last couple of years of the war with Captain Taylor commenting on his fellow officer cadets at Mhow in late 1944 '…they are a grand crowd, chosen, in modern style, for their abilities. The only trouble is that they are all so keen that the standard they set is pretty stiff and takes some keeping up with'.[95] Major Gibb attended Mhow in early 1945 stating that 'Our demonstration platoon was dressed as Japanese soldiers and our tactical manoeuvres were designed specifically to fight the Japanese in Burma'.[96] The school had improved under the command of Brigadier H. Shuker from 1942 until June 1945 who had experimented on both the administrative and training side in his time as commandant.[97] He met reporters from *Fauji Akhbar* in early in 1945 explaining that:

> The main object of the training…was to instil and foster in the cadets the qualities of leadership, initiative, courage, resource and individuality and thereby to transform them into able and efficient officers. All cadets, Indian and British, are treated alike, All have to undergo the same discipline and the same exacting training, work together and mess together.[98]

---

91   See unpublished memoir of enlistment and training by Colonel D. R. Wood, 23 February 2011, written up for the author and deposited in the IWM. See also Desmond McDougall, 'Memoirs of an Indian Army E.C.O.' (Unpublished Memoir), pp. 6-13, 30-43, copy sent to the author.
92   See McDougall, 'Memoirs of an Indian Army E.C.O.', p. 35.
93   Davis, *A Child at Arms*, p. 11.
94   See Paul Byron Norris, *Willingly to War 1939-1945* (London: BACSA, 2004), p. 23 and Shipster, *Mist*, p. 16.
95   Captain L. M. Taylor, 'Forgotten Diary' (Unpublished Memoir), p. 232, IWM, 87/38/2.
96   Gibb, 'A Walk in the Forest', p. 11.
97   See *Officers' Training School Mhow Magazine*, No. 8, June 1945, pp. 3-6. I'm grateful to Emma Kay for a copy of this journal.
98   *Fauji Akhbar*, Vol. XIII, No.7, 13 February 1945, p. 10.

Training now lasted nine months, the first two of which was elementary comprising drill and exercise, the next five consisted of weapon training, leadership, security and learning the essentials of jungle warfare through mock battles and assault courses. At the same time discussion groups were fostered for the intellectual development of the cadets as well as language skills. The OTS had theatres and cinemas and were often remembered for the dramatic productions undertaken whilst a cadet.[99]

After the OTS infantry officers joined the training divisions, although those joining individual corps would attend a period of extra training with their corps. In 1943 the cadet wing of the Fighting Vehicle School was detached to form the Armoured Corps Officers' Training School (ACOTS). Once officer cadets had completed 16 weeks at the OTS they spent 32 weeks at the ACOTS learning about driving and maintenance of soft vehicles and AFV, gunnery, wireless and tactical training as crew commanders.[100] Officers for the RIASC spent three months at the RIASC School at Kakul before joining their unit. In 1945 Kakul became an OTS for cadets earmarked for the RIASC. The cadets spent only eight weeks at the OTS if they were already in the army or sixteen weeks from civilian life and then spent a period of between 22-26 weeks covering both basic and technical training.[101]

The OTS and the IMA were essential to the war effort, as Pradeep Barua has stated about the IMA equally applies to all the OTS:

> The IMA proved invaluable to the British war effort in the Southern hemisphere. Without the academy's invaluable work in churning out Emergency Commissioned Officers (ECO's), it is doubtful if the Indian Army could have maintained the massive formations it had on the Burma Front.[102]

The OTS meant that there was a huge increase in the amount of officers generally and Indian officers in particular who numbered 15,540 by the end of the war. General officer training continued after the OTS with Major General Roland Inskip, the Inspector of Training Centres, running a course on tactics, administration, staff work, culture and history.[103] Officer training adapted as in early 1945, the weapon training, teaching of Urdu, administrative training, map reading and command of troops of officer cadets was deemed unsatisfactory. With the result that cadets went straight to the training divisions from the OTS, rather than the regimental centres, where specialist staff carried out instruction for officers. They spent four months with the training division, concentrating on drill, physical training, the learning of Urdu and administration for the first month, section and platoon training in jungle

---

99 See ibid., pp. 10, 20.
100 See Sandhu, *Indian Armour*, p. 34.
101 See Moharir, *History of the Army Service Corps*, pp. 137-139. See also Sydney Bolt, *Pseudo Sahib* (Aylesbeare, Devon: Hardinge Simpole, 2007), pp. 41, 55.
102 Barua, *Army Officer Corps*, p. 50.
103 See Elliot, *A Memoir of India*, pp. 30-31.

warfare for the next two months and the final month commanding troops in holding companies.[104]

Regimental Training Centres

Even with the 'Quit India' movement, the Bengal Famine and other internal security issues, recruitment for the Indian Army was not really affected during the war, in the 2nd Punjab Regiment for instance, the training battalion had 1, 629 recruits in 1942, 1, 265 in 1943 and 971 in 1944 per year.[105] In the 1st Punjab Regiment, the Training Battalion raised seven new battalions and as the regimental historian stated: 'That the Training Battalion was able to do this successfully says much for the basic soundness of the organisation of 1922 and for the devoted efforts of all who served with it during the war'. In July 1942, the Training Battalions were designated Training Centres and in 1943 Major General Roland Inskip was appointed to the new position of Inspector of Training Centres, in order to help the DMT, and he made a tour of all the centres to improve standards. For instance, the Training Centre, 1st Punjab Regiment was visited in 1943 by most other training centres because of its high standards of jungle warfare training and its mock-up jungle and these ideas were later circulated.[106] The centres were centralized with the establishment of the Centres Organization on 1 April 1943. The Centres now came under the control of GHQ India with an HQ that included specialist staff. They were renamed Regimental Centres and provided general training and holding battalions for the regiments and the commanding officer of each centre was upgraded to a colonel. In the 16th Punjab Regiment 15,070 recruits passed through the Regimental Training Centre during the war.[107]

The training for *jawans* lasted for between six to nine months, depending on the time during the war and the individual regiment with the ideal length seen as nine months and by the end of the war training lasted at most Regimental Training Centres for between eight and nine months.[108] The training was meant to instill pride for the unit, weapons training, a grounding in fieldcraft and produce disciplined soldiers. For the first couple of weeks, a recruit underwent pre-basic training which was meant to get the recruit used to the regiment, the routine, understand regimental tradition, an introduction to drill and instill the idea that he is fighting for his family. According to the Recruits Training Syllabus for the 15th Punjab Regimental Centre, these first two weeks were very important: 'Success can only be obtained by the VCO and Instructors exercising the personal touch and personal interest in each man'.[109] The centres not

---

104 See DMT's Monthly Liaison Letter No. 2, February 1945, IOR, L/WS/1/766.
105 See Lawford and Catto, *Solah Punjab*, p. 280 and Betham and Geary, *The Golden Galley*, p. 301.
106 See Qureshi, *First Punjab Regiment*, pp. 275-278.
107 See Huxford, *8th Gurkha Rifles*, p. 276 and Lawford and Catto, *Solah Punjab,* p. 280.
108 See Auchinleck, Despatch, 21 June 1943-15 November 1943, p. 2667.
109 15th Punjab Regimental Centre, Recruits Training Syllabus 1945, p. 6. Author's collection.

only increased in numbers throughout the war but also in size, the 15th Punjab Regimental Centre increased its total size by an extra 1.5 miles with new ranges and assault courses. The administrative staff remained fairly constant in the centre but had a high turnover of instructors and new recruits. The centres were inspected regularly by senior officers such as Major General Roland Inskip, the Inspector of Training Centres and the C-in-C India, General Sir Claude Auchinleck.[110] Brigadier G. A. L. Farwell visited the centre just before Christmas 1944 commenting:

> The most marked impression which I got from my visit was that the whole Centre was very much alive and all the men there, V.C.Os., N.C.Os., recruits and boys were all very much on their toes. I had heard that things there were not altogether satisfactory or up to the standard we expect, but I am very glad to be able to say that, even if this had been true in the past, it is not so now.[111]

In the RTC of the 14th Punjab Regiment, equipment and weapons were extremely short in 1942 with thirty recruits training with one Vickers Berthier gun and the centre was mainly staffed by ECOs. The Vickers Berthier were replaced by Bren guns, staffed by officers recovering from wounds and retired VCOs as well as officers with recent experience of fighting. As with all Indian Army regiments it was unsurprising that the regimental yearbook commented that the recruits at the 14th Punjab RTC were the best trained in the training division and out of twelve training centres.[112] However, as Gerald Elliott, who spent two years as instructor at the Frontier Force Rifles Centre at Abbottabad, has pointed out about the training in the centres: 'Our training was little more than preliminary conditioning and our sepoys needed far more to fit them for taking on the Japs in Burma'.[113]

Corps Centres improved in the same period, the IAVC set up an OTS in 1944 where 79 RAVC officers and 74 IAVC officers were trained. Colonel George Barnett who had been Commandant of the IAVC since 1942 wrote that by 1944 the Centre had 'better instructors, intensified training, with fewer recruits had combined to establish a centre very different from the shambles of 1943'.[114] The centre also put on courses for sowar dressers who looked after horses, mules, donkeys, camels, buffaloes

---

110 See 15th Punjab Regimental Centre Newsletter 1944, pp. 2-3, IWM. See also 'C-in-C's Tour of the Frontier: Intensive Training of Units', *Fauji Akhbar*, Vol. XXII, No. 3, 15 January 1944; 'C-in-C visits Jungle Training Units', *Fauji Akhbar*, Vol. XXII, No. 28, 8 July 1944 and 'Baluch Regt. Training Centre', *Fauji Akhbar*, Vol. XXII, No. 15, 8 April 1944, p. 18.
111 See 15th Punjab Regimental Centre Newsletter November 1944-February 1945, p. 2, IWM.
112 See 14th Punjab Regiment Yearbook, Nineteenth Issue, 1945, pp. 50-56.
113 Elliot, *A Memoir of India*, p. 21.
114 Harfield, 'The IAVC Centre, Ambala during World War II', p. 55.

and cattle as well as animal first aid and farrier courses.[115] 2073 recruits passed through the centre and at the end of the war it took on the role of training men in agriculture prior to demobilization. When the Centre was inspected by GOC Lahore District in 1946, he commented: 'An excellent Centre in every way. No special problems. Man-management of a very high order. I hope that officers from Area HQ when visiting Ambala will not fail to look round this Centre which is in many respects a model for all…'.[116] Similarly in the RIASC the MT training battalions were expanded re-named Training Centres with their companies as training battalions in May 1942. By 1944 there were ten MT Training Centres for recruits and eight MT Training Groups that were responsible for the training of units. Conditions within the training centres dramatically improved, at the MT Training Centre in Southern Army there were regular concert parties, a dramatic society, a cinema, daily and weekly newspapers in English, Urdu, Tamil, Telugu and Malayalam and a radio for the use of cadets. In addition there was a sports stadium for wrestling and boxing matches and the centre grew its own vegetables with any surplus sold to the government, relatives could stay in the camp with free food and lodging for three days and a 'Petitions Committee' met once a week to consider complaints and requests from the cadets.[117] The VCO school for supply training at Bareilly was expanded due to its very high standards of training, to include training for VCOs to all branches of the RIASC but due to the difficulty in sparing students only one course from all branches took place.[118] This was the first training school entirely for VCOs in the history of the Indian Army.[119]

In the 3rd Gurkha Regimental Centre, training pamphlets in Roman Gurkali were produced for instructors.[120] The standing orders listed the most important subjects to be taught to the Gurkha recruits with included work, cleanliness, smartness, knowledge of the history of the regiment, discipline, energy, initiative, weapons training, fieldcraft and demonstrations.[121] In the Gurkha Regimental Centres recruits undertook a thirty mile march before joining the 38th Gurkha Rifles, the training battalion in the training division. Once in the 38th Gurkha Rifles, the recruits continued to undertake route marches of thirty miles and before joining their battalion they would do a six day patrol with a daily distance of ten miles in hot weather and fifteen in cold over open and jungle country.[122] In the 2nd King Edward's Own Gurkha Rifles

---

115 See 'Veterinary Officers' Training Centre', *Fauji Akhbar*, Vol. XXII, No. 16, 15 April 1944, p. 22.
116 Quoted in Harfield, 'The IAVC Centre, Ambala during World War II', p. 57.
117 See *Fauji Akhbar*, Vol. XXIII, No.1, 2 January 1945, p. 11.
118 See Moharir, *History of the Army Service Corps*, pp. 132-133, 136, 139-140, Appendix D.
119 See Creese, '*Swords Trembling in their Scabbards*', p. 167.
120 See Driving Ka Drill [Driving Instructions] (Dehra Dun, A.V. Pres, 1943) and 3rd Gurkha Regimental Centre, Standing Orders (Dehra Dun, A.V. Press, 1942), Gurkha Museum
121 Ibid. Standing Orders.
122 See Lessons from Operations. Copy of 4/8GR No. 01/326 of 10 September 1944, TNA, WO 72/4290.

the RTC developed over the period of the war with the centre established in 1940 from the joining of the two training companies of the 1st and 2nd Battalions of the regiment. Within three months of it forming there were 3,000 recruits in the RTC. Then it was reorganised into four training companies with a strength of over 800 in each company. This was extended to six training companies and then formed into three training battalions and RTC HQ. The HQ was responsible for dealing with administration, 'A' Battalion consisted of two companies that undertook advanced training for trained recruits and a specialist company for training signallers, drivers and mortarmen. 'B' and 'C' Battalions also had two companies that both trained new recruits and there was a cadre for training instructors and young officers. As with other RTCs, pensioners and reservists had to be called up to instruct due to the vast expansion of the centre and equipment was scarce with only four light machine guns and 250 rifles to go round 3,000 recruits in 1940. At the beginning of the war the staff of the RTC comprised three British and ten Gurkha officers and by 1945 there were 45 British and about 80 Gurkha officers with 250 British officers and about 10,000 men passing through the centre.[123]

The impact of the RTCs on the wider war was very important, As Michael Calvert has written in his memoir:

> Therefore, by 1943, India itself had little left, and very great credit is due to the so-called Colonel Blimps in the depots and training centres of India who kept their faith in the Indian Army during its nadir and raised it eventually from a demoralized, unstable wreck in 1943 to its position at the end of 1944 and 1945, when it probably had the highest morale and offensive spirit of any army in the world.[124]

Once the recruit had finished at the RTC, he would then spend two months on jungle warfare in the training divisions and then recruits were sent to the reinforcement camps, where training was continued until they could join their battalions. The rest and reinforcement camps were reorganised under Colonel Gradige. They had been set up in April 1943 on the example of those in the Middle East and were designed to hold and train 3,000 troops. The instructors were from India, often with little experience of frontline conditions, and ratios of instructors to troops were very low with little direction for training, all resulting in poor morale and cases of ill-discipline. After August 1943, each camp was allocated to a particular division, with twelve Reinforcement Camps for 14th Army each with two British and eight Indian

---

123 See Denis Wood, 'The Indian Army Officer Corps and the training of the Indian Army 1939-47', 2 April 2011, pp. 5-6, written up for the author and a copy deposited in the IWM.
124 Michael Calvert, *Prisoners of Hope* (London: Jonathan Cape, 1952), p. 86.

sections and realistic training was undertaken and discipline restored.[125] In December 1943, the GSOII of 7th Indian Division visited 27 Reinforcement Camp to find that training was based upon divisional training, battle inoculation was used and reinforcements usually spent little time in the camp, usually only a few days and not more than a month.[126] According to General George Giffard 'Training staffs are available in each camp to keep reinforcements at a proper state of efficiency'.[127]

Conclusion

In conclusion by 1945, India had a vast training organisation administered by the Military Training Directorate with a relatively small staff that was responsible for all training in the Indian Army with the exception of education and combined operations. The directorate had issued or reprinted over 900 training pamphlets ranging from jungle warfare, combined operations to physical training and engineering publications. It oversaw over a hundred training schools and establishments across India. The directorate and the training establishments were run by officers that had experienced warfare in North and East Africa, Italy and Burma.

A large number of officers had fought together at both the Battle of Keren and in Burma and had also attended or been instructors in training establishments before and during the war. For example, Colonel Geoffrey Beyts (later Brigadier) joined the infantry branch of the directorate in 1945. He had served in Burma and was putting this experience towards updating the infantry training manuals.[128] Lieutenant Pillai (later Brigadier) escaped from Singapore and returned to India where he became an instructor at the Jungle Warfare School.[129] Captain Monty Palit (later Major General) attended the Tactical School at Poona in 1942, commanded by Major General Steve Irwin, and was asked to be an instructor, an appointment that was the turning point in his career and where he became 'a fully trained professional, tactically competent to handle units of all-arms'.[130] They inculcated a professionalism within the Indian Army during the war and also passed this on to the next generation of Indian officers after Partition in 1947. This is demonstrated by Geoffrey Beyts who commanded the Junior Leader's wing of the Infantry School at Mhow where cadets from OTS Bangalore

---

125   See Brigadier J. H. Gradige, 'How the Fourteenth Army was Reinforced', *JUSII*, Vol. LXXV, No. 321, October 1945, pp. 452-453. See also 'India at War', p. 226. *Corbett Mss.*, CAC, CORB 3/28 and Slim, pp. 190-191.
126   See Visit of GSO II to 27 Reinforcement Camp 22 December 1943, 26 December 1943, TNA, WO 172/1943.
127   Giffard, 'Operations in Burma and North East India from 16 November 1943 to 22 June 1944', p. 1368.
128   See Beyts, *King's Salt*, p. 31.
129   See Brigadier M. M. Pillai, *Three Thousand Miles to Freedom* (New Delhi: Lancer Publications, 2009).
130   Major General D. K. Palit, *Musings and Memories* Volume 1 (New Delhi: Palit & Palit in association with Lancer Publications, 2004), p. 162.

were now trained for three months before gaining their commissions, he then took over the whole Infantry School until 1948.[131] Brigadier Francis Ingall took up the post of Commandant of the Pakistan Military Academy until 1950 and the IMA was headed up by Brigadier Barltrop, an inveterate trainer who had brought the 3rd Gurkha Training Centre to a very high standard. He brought together a good team of British and Indian officers for the academy to re-open for the first intake of Indian cadets in February 1946.[132]

Thus doctrine was produced within the directorate through training pamphlets and memoranda and disseminated by formations fighting in Malaya, North Africa, Italy and Burma through the issuing of training instructions at divisional, brigade and battalion level. Nearly all Indian Army divisions issued training instructions with very few exceptions. Similarly this structure was inherited in the post-Independence Indian Army that were also issuing training pamphlets and memoranda in a very similar format until the 1960s.

---

131 See Beyts, *King's Salt*, pp. 32-33.
132 See Francis Ingall, *The Last of the Bengal Lancers* (London: Leo Cooper, 1988), pp. 114-145 and Lieutenant General Sir James Wilson, *Unusual Undertakings: A Military Memoir* (London: Leo Cooper, 2002), pp. 128-136.

Conclusion

During the Second World War, India was a vital source of men, money and supply. It was the base for operations in both the Middle East and South East Asia. Defence expenditure was at its highest in 1944-45 at Rs. 896.16 crores, of which half was actually chargeable to India. In addition India provided £286.5 million worth of materials for the war effort, mainly ordnance, textiles and clothing. The Indian Army increased from 205,058 in October 1939 to 2,251,050 in July 1945.[1] It had been transformed from an Imperial Policing force in 1939 to a modern professional and national army in 1945 contributing enormously to the Allied cause. Lieutenant Colonel Ronald Neep commented in his unpublished memoir 'From Bugle to Hooter', that on meeting up in Rangoon with his regiment, the Sikh Regiment, after having been a prisoner of war for three years:

> I then had to meet their colonel. In came a young man of about twenty five or twenty six years old – a real winner. I mentally compared him with the Commanding Officers I had known at the beginning of the war; many over fifty years old and really past command and I realised a big change had taken place in the Army while I had been away.[2]

This was possible largely due to the development of training and a culture of professionalism in the officer corps from the 1930s onwards. Officers such as Generals Bateman, Briggs, Corbett, Cowan, Messervy, Rees, Savory and Tuker either taught in training establishments, worked in the Military Training Directorate or issued training instructions within their formations, not forgetting Generals Auchinleck and Slim who supported and encouraged this professional military culture. This generation of pre-war officers were instrumental in training the Indian Army during the Second World War and inculcating the importance of training to the next generation of Indian Army officers. Thus, the Indian Army developed an institutionalised training framework which helped foster a professional military identity among both

---

1 See Brown, *Modern India*, p. 309.
2 Lieutenant Colonel Ronald Neep, '"From Bugle to Hooter": being some casual memories as told by an ordinary Edwardian' (Unpublished Memoir) lent to the author, p. 95.

its officers and soldiers. This was achieved by both continuity and adaptation.³ The continuity comprised the use of training battalions and training establishments which were in existence in the 1920s, in combination with training instructions and training memoranda that were issued in the 1930s, both at regimental and AHQ level. These were all developed during the war into new training centres and schools as the army expanded, as well as training teams and divisions. The Military Training Directorate was responsible for the doctrine produced in the training pamphlets and memoranda, which filtered down to division, brigade and even battalion level through training instructions. This was demonstrated by the experience of 4th, 5th, 8th and 10th Indian Divisions in the Mediterranean and Middle East and nearly all the Indian divisions fighting in Burma. Moreover, it was not just a top down process as doctrine and training adapted from the bottom up also. This idea of a 'learning institution' had permeated throughout the Indian Army by 1945. All the Indian divisions were continually learning the lessons and adapting to the campaigns that they were engaged in.

However, this was not true of all armies by the end of the Second World War. As Gerald Elliott has suggested in his memoir, that it would be taking his loyalty too far by claiming the Indian Army was a better fighting organisation than the British Army due to its 'careful training and better leadership'.⁴ This training organisation and learning culture was certainly not so apparent in the British Army, although it is very difficult to compare the volunteer professional Indian Army of 1945 to the very different organisation of the conscripted citizen British Army during the Second World War.

The effectiveness of training stuttered at the beginning of the war due to firstly, the expansion of the Indian Army and secondly, the fact that the Indian Army was under-equipped and unready to fight a modern army. Thus progress in training the Indian Army was retarded for the first years of war. Once the training structure was expanded and training manuals were published to unprecedented levels under the direction of the Military Training Directorate, the Indian Army not only led the way in training for jungle and mountain warfare but also created a huge training organisation within India for all forms of warfare. Training underpinned the raising of morale of the Indian Army as a whole from 1943 onwards and particularly in the Burma campaign. This development within the Indian Army was instrumental in the crushing defeat of the IJA in Burma and made an important contribution to the Italian campaign. As Vice Admiral Mountbatten, Supreme Allied Commander South East Asia, wrote in his report to the Combined Chiefs of Staff, Auchinleck and India Command 'could hardly have done more for me'.⁵ Although it is important to

---

3   See Roy, *Sepoys Against the Rising Sun*, p. 399.
4   Elliot, *A Memoir of India*, p. 16.
5   Vice Admiral The Earl Mountbatten of Burma, *Report to the Combined Chiefs of Staff by the Supreme Allied Commander South-East Asia 1943-1945* (London: HMSO, 1951), p. 214.

note that India Command, with no operational command, was allowed to build up this training organisation undisturbed.

The late Christopher Bayly has argued convincingly that by 1945 the Indian Army had become a national army, even if politically neutral. This developed after 1943 when unit-led discussion or 'Josh' groups were encouraged by Auchinleck and GHQ India to discuss political questions, underpinned by pamphlets such as *Current Affairs*. It had become essential to keep Indian troops well informed regarding current affairs and junior officers were forbidden to denounce Gandhi, Nehru or other members of the Congress party, being regarded as national leaders by the soldiers.[6] However this process of educating the army had essentially begun in the 1920s with the establishment of the Army Education School at Belgaum and had further developed during the 1930s at both unit and Army Headquarters level. This continued throughout the war, bar a short a lapse at the beginning due to the rapid expansion of the Indian Army, with an added impetus in 1943 due to the example of the British Army, spearheaded in India by Auchinleck. Thus the increasing importance of education in the Indian Army was a gradual process that was essential for training from the 1920s onwards, making it a truly national army, recruited from all over India by 1945.

This book opens with a quotation from Tuker and hence seems fitting to finish with his thoughts on the importance of the Directorate of Military Training. Even though the directorate had increased in size and the CO was promoted to the rank of major general during the war, Tuker felt it needed to be even bigger and commanded by a lieutenant general as the directorate never appeared strong enough nor the DMT senior enough. For instance, he remembered that as DMT, he was never able to get a commitment from the Director of Military Operations as to which theatre a formation was being sent to and therefore had no operational directive on which to base training upon.[7] In an article on the training in the post-war army, Tuker noted that pre-war 'the opportunity to obtain instruction was there; seniors did try to teach their juniors to the best of their ability'.[8] He suggested a number of reforms in his paper such as a bigger cadre of officers and an adequate training grant. Tuker hoped his paper would provoke thought on the subject and concluded:

> We have got to realise that conditions for us are not the same as those for the army at Home. We must go our own way in many respects. Our training must teach our officers independence of thought, based on scientific military education.

---

6   See C. A. Bayly, '"The Nation Within": British India at War, 1939-1947' in Raziuddin Aquil and Kaushik Roy (eds.), *Warfare, Religion, and Society in Indian History* (Delhi: Manohar, 2012), 299-300.
7   See letter from Tuker to Major General Stanley Woodburn Kirby, 15 September 1965, *Tuker Mss.*, IWM 71/21/7/4.
8   'Auspex', 'Officers' Training in the Post-War Army', p. 126, *Tuker Mss.*, IWM, 71/21/5/1.

> Finally, let us remember that if our tactical technique remains the same for two years, then it is probably out of date. New methods, perhaps new weapons, are needed to get it up to date and keep it there.[9]

This was achieved in India at the end of the Second World War with the Indian Army leading the way for training and tactics for both mountain and jungle warfare and a continually updated doctrine, with an emphasis on the initiative of junior officers, being encouraged. Thus by Tuker's very high standards, the Indian Army had built on the existing pre-war training structure and developed and adapted to fight successfully in the Mediterranean and South East Asian theatres. As he wrote in a letter in 1946 to the future first C-in-C of Independent India, General (later Field Marshal) Carippa: 'It was always my job during this last war to show the whole world that India's Army was the greatest on any battlefield. It is pretty certain, from what one has read since, that we have succeeded in showing this'.[10]

---

9   Ibid., p. 131.
10 Letter from Tuker to Cariappa, 11 January 1946, Private Papers of Field Marshal K. M. Cariappa, NAI, Part 1 Group 1S No.1-161.

Biographical Notes

Field Marshal Sir Claude Auchinleck (1884-1981)
Auchinleck was commissioned into the 62nd Punjabi Regiment in 1904. He saw service in Egypt, Aden and Mesopotamia during the First World War and Kurdistan after the war. He was an instructor at Staff College, Quetta, 1930-32 and was made Deputy Chief of the General Staff in India in 1936. In 1939 he was made commander of IV Corps in the UK and then went to Norway in 1940 as C-in-C Land Forces. He then commanded V Corps and Southern Command in quick succession before returning to India as C-in-C in late 1940. He was C-in-C Middle East, 1941-42 and C-in-C India again until 1947.

Major General Donald Bateman (1901-1969)
Bateman was gazetted into the 10th Baluch Regiment in 1920. He served on the North West Frontier in the interwar period. During the Second World War he was GSO1 in 4th Indian Division and was responsible for writing some of the divisional training instructions. He was the first Commandant of the Middle East Training Centre. Then he commanded 5th Indian Infantry Brigade in Tunisia and Italy, 1942-44. He became Director of Military Training in late 1944 until 1947. He retired in 1948 as commander of the Bombay Area.

Lieutenant General Sir Noel Beresford-Pierse (1887-1953)
Beresford-Pierse was commissioned into the Royal Artillery in 1907 and served in Egypt, Mesopotamia and France during the First World War. He was an instructor at the Senior Officers' School, Belgaum, 1936-38. He was in command of the artillery in 4th Indian Division from 1938 and later commanded the Division in 1940 at the Battles of Sidi Barrani and Keren. He was made commander of Western Desert Force in 1941. In 1941 he was briefly GOC Sudan before becoming commanding Southern Command until the end of the war. He retired in 1947.

Field Marshal Kodandera Cariappa (1900-1994)
Cariappa, nicknamed Kipper, was in the first cohort of Indian officers to be commissioned after the First World War at Daly Cadet College, Indore in 1919. He joined the 2nd Battalion, 88th Carnatic Infantry but quickly transferred to the 2nd

Battalion, 125th Napier's Rifles who served in Mesopotamia. He joined the 17th Dogra Regiment and served in Waziristan. In 1932 he was the first Indian officer to attend the Staff College at Quetta. At the beginning of the Second World War he was Brigade Major in 20th Indian Infantry Brigade. In 1941, he became Deputy Assistant Quartermaster General in 10th Indian Division in Iraq. In March 1942 he was second-in-command of the 16th/7th Rajput Battalion and the following month he was promoted to Lieutenant Colonel and commanded the battalion. Again, he was the first Indian officer to command a battalion. In 1943 he was appointed Assistant Quarter Master General in Eastern Command, then the same post in 26th Indian Division before being promoted to Brigadier on 1 November 1944 when he served on Willcox's Reorganisation Committee. In November 1945 he commanded Bannu Frontier Brigade in Waziristan. In 1947 he attended the Imperial Defence College, then Deputy Chief of the General Staff, followed by command of Eastern Command. Then in 1949 he was the first Indian officer to become C-in-C India. He retired in 1953.

Lieutenant General Thomas Corbett (1888-1981)
Corbett joined Hodson's Horse in 1908. During the First World War he served on the Western Front. In 1930 he transferred to the 2nd Lancers (Gardner's Horse). He was an instructor at the Staff College at Quetta during the 1930s and in January 1940 he was appointed Brigadier, Cavalry at AHQ and oversaw the mechanisation of the cavalry regiments. He briefly commanded 1st Indian Armoured Division, then 4th Indian Corps in Iraq before being appointed Chief of the General Staff to General Auchinleck, C-in-C Middle East. He was dismissed along with Auchinleck in the 'Cairo Purge' of August 1942. He briefly commanded 7th Indian Division and retired in 1943. He headed up the Indian Historical Section until the end of the war.

Major General David 'Punch' Cowan (1896-1983)
Cowan was commissioned into the Argyll and Sutherland Highlanders in 1915 and transferred to the 6th Gurkha Rifles in 1917. He was one of the initial instructors at the Indian Military Academy, 1932-34, Deputy Director of Military Training 1941 and officiating DMT in 1942. He assumed command of 17th Indian Division after the disastrous blowing up of the Sittang Bridge. He commanded the division until the recapture of Rangoon in 1945. He was made commander of the British-Indian Division of the Allied Occupation Force in Japan, 1945-46 and retired in 1947.

Major General Alfred Curtis (1894-1971)
Curtis was gazetted into the Sikh Regiment in 1915 and saw service on the North West Frontier and Mesopotamia during the First World War. During the Second World War he commanded 13th Indian Infantry Brigade in the Retreat from Burma. He was appointed commanding officer for 14th Indian Division in 1943 and was instrumental in making it an effective training division for the remainder of the war. He retired in 1948.

Major General James Elliott (1898-1990)
Elliott joined the 1st Punjab Regiment in 1922. He was an instructor at the Staff College, Quetta, 1935-37 and moved to the Directorate of Military Training in 1938. During the Second World War he was the Director of Military Training, 1942-43. He was Deputy Welfare General, 1945-46 and then Deputy Military Secretary to the Defence Committee, India in 1947, retiring the following year. He wrote a number of books on India and the Indian Army including *The Story of the Indian Army 1939-1945* (1965).

Major General Edward Gurdon (1896-1959)
Gurdon was commissioned into the East Yorkshire Regiment in 1914, transferring to the Rifle Brigade the following year. Most of his First World War Service was in East Africa. He was an instructor at Camberley from 1937 until 1940. He commanded the 1st Battalion the Black Watch in British Expeditionary Force in 1940. In 1941 he was appointed BGS IV Corps in Burma, followed by a brief period as a District Commander and BGS Eastern Army in India. In 1943 he was made Director of Military Training in India until 1944. He retired from the British Army in 1948 having commanded a division in the British Army of the Rhine.

Lieutenant General Sir Thomas Hutton (1890-1981)
Hutton was commissioned into the Royal Artillery in 1909 and saw service in France and Italy during the First World War. Most of his interwar service was in the War Office. He was appointed Deputy Chief of the General Staff, AHQ India, in 1940 and promoted to Chief of the General Staff the following year. In 1941 he was appointed GOC Burma and in command of the early disasters of the Retreat from Burma, until replaced by General Alexander. In 1941 he was created Secretary of the War Resources and Reconstruction Committee in India and retired in 1944.

Major General Roland Inskip (1885-1971)
Inskip was gazetted into the 13th Frontier Force Rifles in 1908. He served in France, Mesopotamia and Palestine during the First World War and the North West Frontier in the interwar period. He was a district commander in India, 1939-41 and GOC Ceylon, 1941-42, after which he retired. However he was re-employed at GHQ India as Inspector of Training Centres, 1943-45, was Chief of the Bhopal State Forces, 1946-47 and retired again.

Major General Wilfrid Lloyd (1896-1944)
Lloyd was commissioned in the King's Shropshire Light Infantry in 1914 and transferred to the Indian Army in 1917. He served with the Kumaon Rifles on the North West Frontier and commanded the 4th/19th Hyderabad Regiment, 1936-39. During the Second War, he commanded 5th Indian Infantry Brigade, 1940-41 and became Director of Military Training for a few months, 1941-42. Followed by command of

14th Indian Division in the First Arakan and 10th Indian Division in Egypt where he died in a motor accident in Cairo.

General Sir Frank Messervy (1893-1974)
Messervy served with Hodson's Horse during the First World War and later on the North West Frontier. He acted as an instructor at the Staff College, Quetta from 1934 until 1937. During the Second World War he commanded Gazelle Force at Keren, 4th Indian Division, 1st Armoured Division and 7th Armoured Division in the Western Desert. He escaped from the Germans when his headquarters were overrun by impersonating an officer's batman. He took over command of 7th Indian Division and was instrumental in the Battle of the Admin Box and the defence of Kohima. He was known as 'General Frank' within the division. He was promoted to command IV Corps in December 1944. He was GOC Malaya in 1946, commanded Northern Command, 1946-47 and became the first C-in-C of the Pakistan Army in 1947, retiring the next year.

Lieutenant General Arthur Percival (1887-1966)
Percival was commissioned into the Essex Regiment during the First World War and saw service in France. He later served in North Russia and Ireland. He served in Nigeria from 1925-29, was on the instructing staff at Camerley in 1932 and was a staff officer in Malaya, 1936-38. During the Second World War he was briefly BGS I Corps, commanded 43rd (Wessex) Division, Assistant CIGS and then commanded 44th (Home Counties) Division. Then in April 1941 he was appointed GOC Malaya. After the Fall of Singapore in February 1942 he spent three years as a Far East Prisoner of War. He retired in 1946.

Major General Thomas 'Pete' Rees (1898-1959)
Rees was born in Holton Road, Barry in South Wales, the son of a Baptist minister. He was commissioned into the 73rd Carnatic in 1915 and transferred to the 125th (Napier's) Rifles serving in Mesopotamia and Palestine. Between the wars he served in Waziristan and on the North West Frontier and was an instructor at the Royal Military College, Sandhurst from 1928 until 1930. He commanded the 3rd Battalion, 6th Rajput Rifles in 1939 on the North West Frontier. He served as GSO1 with 4th Indian Division in North Africa, commanded 10th Indian Infantry Brigade at Keren and briefly commanded 10th Indian Division in Iraq and North Africa. His most successful period as a commander was with 19th Indian Division which recaptured Mandalay in Operation 'Extended Capital'. He then commanded 4th Indian Division in 1945 and subsequently had the difficult task commanding the Punjab Boundary Force during the transfer of power in 1947. He retired from the army in 1948.

Major General Denys Reid (1897-1970)
Reid was commissioned into the Seaforth Highlanders in 1915 and served in France during the First World War. He transferred to the 5th Mahratta Light Infantry

after the war. He commanded the regiment's 3rd Battalion, 1940-41 and was Commander of 29th Indian Infantry Brigade in North Africa, 1941-42. He was taken prisoner in Tobruk in June 1942 and released from captivity in 1943. He was made GOC 10th Indian Division and led the division throughout the Italian campaign. He retired in 1947.

Lieutenant General Sir Dudley 'Pasha' Russell (1896-1978)
Russell was gazetted into the 13th Frontier Force Rifles in 1917 and served in Palestine during the First World War. During the Second World War he commanded the 6th Battalion, Frontier Force Rifles and served as a staff officer with 5th Indian Division. Commander of 5th Indian Infantry Brigade in Cyrenaica in 1942 and appointed GOC 8th Indian Infantry Division in January 1943, he led the division throughout the Italian campaign. He was GOC Delhi and East Punjab Command in 1947 and Chief British Adviser to the Indian Army from 1948 until his retirement in 1954.

Lieutenant General Sir Reginald Savory (1894-1980)
Savory was gazetted into the 11th Sikh Regiment in 1915. He served in the Gallipoli campaign and in Egypt in the First World War. After the war he served in the newly introduced training battalion of the Sikh Regiment and spent time at the Indian Wing of the Army School of Education. He saw service in Siberia, Kurdistan, Iraq and Waziristan in the interwar period and was an instructor at the Indian Military Academy, Dehra Dun, 1932-34. During the Second World War he commanded 11th Indian Infantry Brigade in North Africa and at Keren, 1940-41. He was briefly GOC Eritrea before returning to India as GOC 23rd Indian Division. In 1943 he was made Director of Infantry, India, followed by GOC Persia and Iraq Command, 1945-46. He retired as Adjutant General, India in 1948.

Field Marshal Sir William Slim (1891-1970)
Slim served with the Royal Warwickshire Regiment during the Gallipoli campaign where he was badly wounded. On recovery he transferred to the West India Regiment. He served at Army Headquarters in Delhi in 1918 and transferred to the 1st/6th Gurkha Rifles in 1920. He was an instructor at the Staff College, Camberley and attended the Imperial Defence College during the 1930s and was commandant of the Senior Officers' School in 1939. During the Second World War he commanded 10th Indian Infantry Brigade at Keren, 10th Indian Division in Iraq, Burcorps in the Retreat from Burma and XV Corps in 1942. He was commander of 14th Army in 1943 from whence he rightly achieved recognition as one of the best army commanders of the war for such operations as Extended Capital. He became C-in-C Allied Land Forces, South East Asia in August 1946, Commandant of the Imperial Defence College in 1946, Chief of the Imperial General Staff, 1949-52 and Governor General of Australia, 1952-60. His book,

Defeat into Victory, is one of the best memoirs to be written by an army commander during the twentieth century.

Lieutenant General Sir Francis 'Gertie' Tuker (1894-1967)
Tuker joined the 1st/2nd (King Edward VII's Own) Gurkha Rifles in 1914. He served throughout the First World War in Mesopotamia and on the North West Frontier and Persia, 1919-21. He commanded his regiment, 1937-39 and was made Director of Military Training, 1940-41. He was appointed GOC 4th Indian Division in 1942, serving with the division in the desert with 8th Army, in Tunisia with 1st Army and Italy before falling ill with rheumatoid arthritis in 1944. Once partially recovered he chaired the Frontier Committee, 1944, became GOC Ceylon in 1945 and commanded Eastern Command, 1946-47. He retired from the Indian Army in 1948. His important publications include: *Approach to Battle* (1963) a study of the 8th Army in North Africa, *Pattern of War* and *While Memory Serves* (1949) covering the last two years of the Indian Army before Partition.

Field Marshal Archibald Wavell (1883-1950)
Wavell was commissioned into the Black Watch and saw service in the South African War. In the First World War he served in France, South Russia and Palestine. He commanded 2nd Division in 1935, then became C-in-C Southern Command in 1938 and C-in-C Middle East in 1939 just before the outbreak of war. He was replaced as C-in-C Middle East by General Auchinleck in 1941 and took his job as C-in-C India. Wavell was appointed Viceroy of India in 1943 to be replaced by Lord Mountbatten in 1946.

Lieutenant General Sir Henry Willcox (1889-1968)
Willcox was commissioned into the Sherwood Foresters in 1912 and served in France and Palestine during the First World War. He was an instructor at Staff College, Quetta, 1937-38. Nicknamed 'Ulysses', he was Inspector of Infantry at the War Office at the beginning of the Second World War and briefly commanded 42nd (East Lancashire) Division. He was posted out to India to take up the new role commanding Central Command in 1942 and was the chairman of the Indian Army Reorganisation Committee in 1944. He retired in 1946.

Bibliography

Primary Sources

Official Documents
War of 1939 to 1945 Military Headquarters Military Missions, TNO, WO 106
War of 1939 to 1945 War Diaries, TNA, WO 169, 172, 204
Military Department Library, BL, IOR, L/MIL/17
War Staff Series Files 1921-1950, BL, IOR, L/WS/1

Private Papers
Papers of Major General Sir William Abraham, Centre of South Asian Studies, Cambridge
Papers of Field Marshal Sir Claude Auchinleck, John Rylands Special Collections, AUC
Papers of Major B. E. Barrow, IWM
Papers of Major General Donald Bateman, IWM, 72/117/2
Papers of Major General Raymond Briggs, IWM, 99/1/2
Papers of Field Marshal K. M. Cariappa, NAI
Papers of Brigadier Harold Charrington, LCHMA
Papers of Lieutenant General Thomas Corbett, CAC, CORB
Papers of Lieutenant J. R. Cottle, IWM, 67/289/1
Papers of Major General Alfred Curtis, IWM, P140
Papers of Brigadier H. K. Dimoline, IWM, 73/40/1
Papers of Lieutenant Colonel B. K. Dymott, IWM, 67/264/1
Papers of Lieutenant General Sir Geoffrey Evans, IWM, P309
Papers of Brigadier A. D. Firth, IWM, 99/48/1
Papers of Lieutenant Colonel J. Frith, NAM, 7306-121
Papers of General D. D. Gracey, LHCMA
Papers of Lieutenant General Sir Lewis Heath, IWM, LMH
Papers of Lieutenant General Sir Thomas Hutton, LHCMA
Papers of Major General A. W. W. Holworthy, IWM, 91/40/2
Papers of Lieutenant General N. M. S. Irwin, IWM, P139
Papers of Major General B. W. Key, IWM, P456

Papers of Major General J. S. Lethbridge, LHCMA
Papers of General Sir Rob Lockhart, NAM, 8310-154-25
Papers of Major General Lewis Owen Lyne, IWM, 71/2/5
Papers of General Sir Frank Messervy, LHCMA
Papers of Captain C. A. Morris, IWM, 99/22/1
Papers of General Arthur Percival, IWM, P16-27
Papers of Captain of V. P. Sams, IWM, 05/02/1
Papers of Lieutenant General Reginald Savory, NAM, 7603-93-71A
Papers of Brigadier Sir John Smyth VC, IWM
Papers of Major G. R. Storry, IWM, 01/34/2
Papers of Lieutenant General Sir Francis Tuker, IWM, 71/21/74
Papers of Brigadier David Wilson, IWM

Unpublished Memoirs
W. H. Alston, 'My Day and Age: the Memoirs of William Lowry Alston at one time a British Officer in H. M. Indian Army 1917-1947', NAM, 8005-151.
Major F. T. Burnett, 'Keeping up with the Hunt: The Story of 268 Indian Infantry Brigade', IWM.
Lieutenant Colonel R. S. M. Calder, 'From Sloth belt to Springboard being a brief account of the activities of Southern Command India during World War II', NAM, 8209-14.
Captain Peter Collister, 'Then a Soldier', IWM, 82/15/1.
Major General H. L. Davies, '"Small Green Men": An Autobiography', IWM, 08/120/1.
Lieutenant Colonel C. C. Deakin and Major G. M. S Webb, 'The Malayan Campaign, 1941-42: Accounts of the part played by the 5th Battalion, 2nd Punjab Regiment', NAM, 6509-14.
Major General J. G. Elliott, 'Unpublished manuscript on the Battle of Keren', IWM, Misc 952.
Brigadier A.D. Firth, 'The Retreat from Burma, an account of an officer who was with the 2nd Battalion the Duke of Wellington's Regiment throughout', IWM, 99/48/1.
Major Ian Gibb, 'A Walk in the Forest', IWM, 86/3/1.
Major Peter Gorb, 'My Phoney War 1939-1948: A Memoir', IWM, 06/39/1.
Lieutenant General Sir Thomas Hutton, 'Rangoon 1941-42: A Personal Record', IWM, 99/73/1.
Captain Peter Gordon Kendall, 'The War Years 1939-1945', IWM, 02/32/1.
Desmond McDougall, 'Memoirs of an Indian Army E.C.O.' copy sent to the author.
Lieutenant Colonel Ronald Neep, ' "From Bugle to Hooter": being some casual memories as told by an ordinary Edwardian', copy lent to the author.
Colonel H. R. C. Pettigrew, 'It seemed very ordinary': Memoirs of Sixteen Years in the Indian Army 1932-1947', IWM, 84/29/1.
Major David Rissik, 'Forgotten Front', IWM, 91/81/1.

Captain E. L. G. Stones, 'Indian Reminiscences of Professor E. L. G. Stones, as a cadet and then an officer in the Royal Corps of Signals (1941-45)', IWM, 85/52/1.
Major G. R. Storry, 'Service with the Intelligence Corps in India and Burma March 1942-May 1943', IWM, 01/34/2.
Captain L. M. Taylor, 'Forgotten Diary', IWM, 87/38/2.
Brigadier F. H. Vinden, 'By Chance a Soldier', IWM, 96/36/1.

Journals
Fauji Akhbar, IWM
15th Punjab Regimental Centre Newsletter, IWM
14th Punjab Regiment Yearbook, IWM
Supplements to *The London Gazette*
The Manchester Guardian
Officers Training School Mhow Magazine

Interviews
Interview of Field Marshal Sir Claude Auchinleck with Charles Allen for the BBC, 1974, IWM, 4902
Ralph Robert Griffith, IWM, 18467
Interview of Lieutenant General B. M. Kaul with Professor Stephen Cohen, 19 December 1964
Muhammad Ismail Khan, IWM, 117448
Lieutenant Colonel Donald Jeffrey Lear, IWM, 23225
Interview of General Sir Frank Messervy with Professor Stephen Cohen, 28 November 1963
Interview of Brigadier Alan McPherson with Professor Stephen Cohen, 18 November 1963
Interview of Brigadier C. J. C. Molony with Professor Stephen Cohen, 14 September 1963
Interview with Brigadier John Stephenson with Professor Stephen Cohen, 3 December 1963
Brigadier David Wilson, IWM, 20456

Secondary Sources

Lieutenant Colonel M. G. Abhyankar, *Valor Enshrined: A History of the Maratha Light Infantry 1768-1947* (New Delhi: Orient Longman, 1971).
James R. Allen, *In the Trade of War* (Tunbridge Wells: Parapress, 1994).
Louis Allen, *Burma: The Longest War 1941-1945* (London: Dent, 1984).
—— *Singapore 1941-1942* (London: Davis-Poynter, 1977).
Alan Allport, *Browned Off and Bloody-Minded: The British Soldier goes to War, 1939-1945* (New Haven: Yale University Press, 2015).

Anon., *The Army in India and its Evolution* (Calcutta: Superintendent Government Printing, India, 1924).
Anon., *Defence Headquarters* (New Delhi: War Department, 1945).
Anon., *History of the 5th Royal Gurkha Rifles (Frontier Force) Vol. II 1929-1947* (Aldershot: Gale & Polden, 1956).
Anon., *Indian Military Almanac* (Delhi: General Staff, 1929).
Anon., *Statistics of the Military Effort of the British Empire during the Great War 1914-1920* (London: HMSO, 1922).
Anon., *The Tiger Triumphs* (Delhi: HMSO for the Government of India, 1946).
AHQ Information Bureau, *A Summary of Information for the Benefit of War Block and other officers of the Indian Army* (Simla: Government of India Press, 1936).
Major General Rafiuddin Ahmed, *History of the Baloch Regiment 1939-1956* (Uckfield, East Sussex: Naval & Military Press, nd.),
Simon Anglim, *Orde Wingate and the Brtish Army, 1922-1944* (London: Pickering & Chatto, 2010).
Sekhar Bandyopadhyay, *From Plassey to Partition and After: A History of Modern India* (New Delhi: Orient Blackswan, 2015).
Tarak Barkawi, *Soldiers of Empire: Rethinking Army, Society and Battle with the British Indian Army in the Asia-Pacific Wars* (Cambridge: CUP, forthcoming 2017).
Niall Barr, *Pendulum of War: The Three Battles of El Alamein* (London: Jonathan Cape, 2004).
Christopher Bayly and Tim Harper, *Forgotten Armies: The Fall of British Asia, 1941-1945* (London: Allen Lane, 2004).
Brigadier C. N. Barclay (editor), *The Regimental History of the 3rd Queen Alexandra's Own Gurkha Rifles Vol. II 1927-1947* (London: William Clowes & Sons, 1953).
A.J. Barker, *Eritrea 1941* (London: Faber & Faber, 1966).
Pradeep Barua, *The Army Officer Corps and Military Modernisation in Later Colonial India* (Hull: University of Hull Press, 1999).
John Baty, *Surgeon in the Jungle War* (London: Kimber, 1979).
Jim Beach (editor), *SS 135 The Division in Attack – 1918*, reprinted as *SCSI Occasional Paper No. 53* (Shrivenham: Strategic and Combat Studies Institute, 2008).
Lieutenant Colonel Sir Geoffrey Betham and Major H. V. R. Geary, *The Golden Galley: The Story of the Second Punjab Regiment 1761-1947* (Oxford: 2nd Punjab Regiment Officers' Association, 1956).
Brigadier G. H. B Beyts, *The King's Salt* (self-published, 1996).
K. D. Bhargava and K.N.V. Sastri, *Campaigns in South East Asia 1941-42* (New Delhi: Pentagon Press, 2012).
Major P. C. Bharucha, *Official History of the Indian Armed Forces in the Second World War 1939-1945: The North African Campaign 1940-43* (India & Pakistan: Combined Inter-Services Historical Section, 1956).
Carel Birkby, *It's a Long Way to Addis* (London: Frederick Muller, 1942).
Jonathan Boff, *Winning and Losing on the Western Front: The British Third Army and the Death of Germany in 1918* (Cambridge: CUP, 2012).

Sydney Bolt, *Pseudo Sahib* (Aylesbeare, Devon: Hardinge Simpole, 2007).
Brian Bond, *British Military Policy between the Two World Wars* (Oxford: Clarendon Press, 1980).
—— *The Unquiet Western Front: Britain's Role in Literature and History* (Cambridge, CUP, 2002).
Lieutenant Colonel J. R. Booth and Lieutenant Colonel J. B. Hobbs, *Ninth Battalion, Fourteenth Punjab Regiment* (Cardiff: Western Mail, 1948).
Martin Booth, *Carpet Sahib: A Life of Jim Corbett* (London: Constable, 1989).
Romen Bose, *Singapore at War* (Singapore: Marshall Cavendish, 2012).
Anthony Brett-James, *Ball of Fire: The Fifth Indian Division in the Second World War* (Aldershot: Gale & Polden, 1951).
—— *Report My Signals* (London: Hennel Locke Ltd., 1948).
Rupert Brooke, *The Collected Poems of Rupert Brooke: With a Memoir* (London: Sidgwick & Jackson, 1918).
Judith M. Brown, *Modern India: The Origins of an Asian Democracy* (Delhi: OUP, 1985).
John Buckley, *Monty's Men: The British Army and the Liberation of Europe, 1944-45* (New Haven: Yale University Press, 2014).
Raymond Callahan, *Burma 1942-1945* (London: Davis-Poynter, 1978).
—— *Churchill and his Generals* (Lawrence, Kansas: University Press of Kansas, 2007).
—— *The East India Company and Army Reform, 1783-1798* (Cambridge, Massachusetts: Harvard University Press, 1972).
—— *Triumph at Imphal-Kohima* (Lawrence, Kansas: University Press of Kansas, forthcoming 2017).
—— *The Worst Disaster: The Fall of Singapore* (Newark: University of Delaware Press, 1977).
Michael Calvert, *Prisoners of Hope* (London: Jonathan Cape, 1952).
Arthur Campbell, *The Siege: A Story from Kohima* (London: Allen & Unwin, 1956).
Michael Carver, *Dilemmas of the Desert War: The Libyan Campaign 1940-1942* (Staplehurst, Kent: Spellmount, 2002).
Captain Philip Spencer Chapman, *Citizenship in India* (Bombay: OUP, 1923).
David Chandler (editor), *The Oxford Illustrated History of the British Army* (Oxford: OUP, 1994).
Winston Churchill, *The Second World War* (London: Cassell, 1948-54).
Ong Chit Chung, *Operation Matador* (Singapore: Times Academic Press, 1997).
Robert M. Citino, *The Path to Blitzkrieg: Doctrine and Training in the German Army, 1920-1939* (Mechanicsburg, PA: Stacpoole Books, 2008).
A.H. Clarke and W. Clarke, *History of the Royal West African Frontier Force* (Aldershot: Gale & Polden, 1964).
Peter Cochrane, *Charlie Company: In Service with C Company 2nd Queen's Own Cameron Highlanders 1940-1944* (London: Chatto & Windus, 1977).
Stephen Cohen, *The Indian Army* (Delhi: OUP, 1991).
Nigel Collett, *The Butcher of Amritsar: General Reginald Dyer* (London: Hambledon, 2005).

Brigadier General J. J. Collyer, *The South Africans with General Smuts in German East Africa 1916* (Pretoria: Government of South Africa, 1939).
John Colvin, *No Ordinary Men: The Story of the Battle of Kohima* (London: Leo Cooper, 1995).
Brigadier W. E. H. Condon, *The Frontier Force Regiment* (Aldershot: Gale & Polden, 1962).
John Connell, *Auchinleck* (London: Cassell, 1959).
Allan Converse, *Armies of Empire: 9th Australian Division and 50th Division in Battle, 1939-1945* (Cambridge: CUP, 2011).
K. W. Cooper, *The Little Men: A Platoon's Epic Fight in the Burma Campaign* (London: Robert Hale, 1992).
Raymond Cooper, *B Company: One Man's War in Burma 1942-1944* (London: Dobson, 1978).
Justin J. Corfield, *A Bibliography of the Literature Relating to the Malayan Campaign and the Japanese Period in Malaya, Singapore and Northern Borneo* (Hull: University of Hull Centre for South East Asian Studies, Bibliography and Literature Series Paper No.5, 1988).
Justin and Robin Corfield, *The Fall of Singapore* (Richmond, Australia: Hardie Grant Books, 2012).
C. R. L. Coubrough, *Memories of a Perpetual Second Lieutenant* (self-published, 2000).
Jeremy A. Crang, *The British Army and the People's War 1939-1945* (Manchester: Manchester University Press, 2000).
John Baptist Crasta, *Eaten by the Japanese: The Memoir of an Unknown Indian Prisoner of War* (New York: The Invisible Man Press, 2013).
Michael Creese, *'Swords Trembling in their Scabbards': The Changing Status of Indian Officers within the Indian Army, 1757-1947* (Solihull: Helion, 2015).
J. P. Cross, *Jungle Warfare* (Barnsley: Pen & Sword, 2008).
W. E. Crosskill, *The Two Thousand Mile War* (London: Robert Hale, 1980).
Patrick Davis, *A Child at Arms* (London: Hutchinson, 1970).
Alex Danchev and Daniel Todman (editors), *Field Marshal Lord Alanbrooke: War Diaries 1939-1945* (London: Weidenfeld & Nicolson, 2001).
Lieutenant General Sir Ralph B. Deedes, *Historical Record of the Royal Garwhal Rifles Vol. II 1923-1947* (Dehra Dun: Army Press, nd.).
Anirudh Deshpande, *British Military Policy in India, 1900-1945* (New Delhi: Manohar, 2005).
Terence Dillon, *Rangoon to Kohima* (RHQ: Gloucestershire Regiment, nd.).
R. A. Doughty, *The Seeds of Disaster: The Development of French Army Doctrine, 1919-1939* (Mechanicsburg, PA: Stacpoole Books, 2014).
A. J. Doulton, *The Fighting Cock: Being the History of the 23rd Indian Division* (Aldershot: Gale & Polden, 1951).
Graham Dunlop, *Military Economics, Culture and Logistics in the Burma Campaign, 1941-1945* (London: Pickering & Chatto, 2009).
David Edgerton, *Britain's War Machine* (London: Penguin, 2012).

Jill Edwards (editor), *El Alamein and the Struggle for North Africa: International Perspectives from the Twenty-first Century* (Cairo: The American University in Cairo Press, 2012).
Leslie Edwards, *Kohima: The Furthest Battle* (Stroud: History Press, 2009).
Modris Eksteins, *Rites of Spring: The Great War and the Birth of the Modern Age* (London: Bantam Press, 1989).
DeWitt C. Ellinwood, Jr., *Between Two Worlds: A Rajput Officer in the Indian Army, 1905-1921: Based on the Diary of Amar Singh of Jaipur* (Lanham, Maryland: Hamilton Books, 2005).
Gerald Elliot, *A Memoir of India* (self-published, 2014).
Major General J. G. Elliott, *A Roll of Honour 1939-1945* (London: Cassell, 1965).
—— *Field Sports in India 1800-1947* (London: Gentry Books, 1973).
Geoffrey Evans, *The Desert and the Jungle* (London: Kimber, 1959).
Geoffrey Evans and Anthony Brett-James, *Imphal: A Flower on Lofty Heights* (London: Macmillan, 1962).
Brian P. Farrell, *The Defence and Fall of Singapore* (Stroud: Tempus, 2005).
Brian P. Farrell and Garth Pratten, *Malaya 1942* (Canberra: Army History Unit, 2009).
Jonathan Fennell, *Combat and Morale in the North African Campaign* (Cambridge: CUP, 2011).
David Fraser, *We Shall Shock Them: The British Army in the Second World War* (London: Hodder & Stoughton, 1983).
George MacDonald Fraser, *Quartered Safe Out Here* (London: Harvill, 1992).
Arthur Freer, *Nunshigum: On the Road to Mandalay* (Durham: Pentland Press, 1995).
David French, *Raising Churchill's Army: The British Army and the War against Germany 1919-1945* (Oxford: OUP, 2000).
John Gaylor, *Sons of John Company: The Indian & Pakistani Armies 1903-1991* (Tunbridge Wells: Parapress, 1996).
Sir Andrew Gilchrist, *Malaya 1941: The Fall of a Fighting Empire* (London: Robert Hale, 1992).
Scott Gilmore, *A Connecticut Yankee in the 8th Gurkha Rifles* (London: Brassey's, 1995).
Michael Glover, *An Improvised War: The Ethiopian War 1940-41* (London: Leo Cooper, 1987).
Ian Gooderson, *A Hard Way to Make a War: The Allied Campaign in Italy in the Second World War* (London: Conway, 2008).
Gordon Graham and Frank Cole (compilers), *Burma Campaign Memorial Library* (London: School of Oriental and African Studies, 2001).
Ian Lyall Grant, *Burma: The Turning Point: The Seven Battles on the Tiddim Road* (Chichester: Zampi Press, 1993).
Ian Lyall Grant and Kazuo Tamayama, *Burma 1942: The Japanese Invasion* (Chichester: Zampi Press, 1999).
Robert Graves, *Goodbye to All That* (London: Cassell, 1929).
Lavinia Green, *Chink: A Biography* (London: Macmillan, 1989).

Jeffrey Grey (editor), *The Last Word? Essays on Official History in the United States and British Commonwealth* (Westport, Connecticut: Praeger, 2003).
Paddy Griffiths, *World War II Desert Tactics* (Oxford: Osprey, 2008).
Tom Grounds, *Some Letters from Burma: The Story of the 25th Dragoons at War* (Tunbridge Wells: Parapress, 1994).
Charles Gwynn, *Imperial Policing* (London: Macmillan, 1934).
Andrew Hargreaves, Patrick Rose and Matthew Ford (editors), *Allied Fighting Effectiveness in North Africa and Italy, 1942-1945* (Leiden: Brill, 2014).
Glyn Harper and John Tonkin-Covell, *The Battles of Monte Cassino: The Campaign and its Controversies* (Auckland: Allen & Unwin, 2013).
A.M. L. Harrison, *History of 11th Indian Division in Malaya* (Unpublished history).
Richard Head and Tony McClenaghan, *The Maharaja's Paltans: A History of the Indian State Forces (1888-1948)* (New Delhi: Manohar, 2013).
Lieutenant Colonel M. C. A. Henniker, *Memoirs of a Junior Officer* (London: Blackwoods, 1951).
John Henslow, *A Sapper in the Forgotten Army* (Petersfield, self-published, 1986).
John Archibald Hislop, *A Soldier's Story: From the Khyber Pass to the Jungles of Burma: The Memoir of a British Officer in the Indian Army 1933-1947* (New Haven, East Sussex: New Haven Publishing, 2010).
James Holland, *Burma '44: The Battle that turned Britain's War in the East* (London: Bantam, 2016).
Michael Howard, *The Causes of War* (London: Unwin, 1984).
Lieutenant Colonel H. J. Huxford, *History of the 8th Gurkha Rifles 1824-1949* (Aldershot: Gale & Polden, 1954).
Samuel Hynes, *A War Imagined: The First World War and English Culture* (London: Bodley Head, 1990).
Francis Ingall, *The Last of the Bengal Lancers* (London: Leo Cooper, 1988).
Anthony Irwin, *Burmese Outpost* (London: Collins, 1945).
Ashley Jackson, *The British Empire and the Second World War* (London: Hambledon Continuum, 2006).
—— *Distant Drums: The role of the Colonies in British Imperial Warfare* (Brighton: Sussex Academic Press, 2010).
—— *Mad Dogs and Englishmen: A Grand Tour of the British Empire at its Height 1850-1950* (London: Quercus, 2009).
W. G. F. Jackson, *The Mediterranean and Middle East Vol. VI: Victory in the Mediterranean Part I, 1st April to 4th June* (London: HMSO, 1984).
W. F. Jeffrey, *Sunbeams like Swords* (London: Hodder & Stoughton, 1950).
Alan Jeffreys, *British Army in the Far East 1941-45* (Oxford: Osprey, 2005).
Alan Jeffreys and Patrick Rose (editors), *The Indian Army, 1939-47: Experience and Development* (Farnham: Ashgate, 2012).
Rob Johnson (editor), *The British Indian Army: Virtue and Necessity* (Newcastle: Cambridge Scholars Publishing, 2014).

Raghu Karnad, *Furthest Field: An Indian Story of the Second World War* (London: William Collins, 2015).
Lieutenant General B. M. Kaul, *The Untold Story* (Bombay: Allied Publishers, 1967).
Fergal Keane, *Road of Bones* (London: Harper Press, 2010).
Chris Kempton, *'Loyalty & Honour': The Indian Army September 1939 – August 1947* (Milton Keynes: The Military Press, 2003).
Yasmin Khan, *The Raj at War: A People's History of India's Second World War* (London: Bodley Head, 2015).
Anthony King, *The Combat Solider: Infantry Tactics and Cohesion in the Twentieth and Twenty-First Centuries* (Oxford: OUP, 2014).
Clifford Kinvig, *Scapegoat: General Percival of Singapore* (London: Brassey's, 1996).
Major General S. Woodburn Kirby, *Singapore: The Chain of Disaster* (London: Cassell, 1971).
—— *History of the Second World War: War Against Japan* (London: HMSO, 1957-69), Vols. 1-5.
James Kitchen, *The British Imperial Army in the Middle East: Morale and Military Identity in the Sinai and Palestine Campaigns* (London: Bloomsbury, 2014).
Hemant Singh Katoch, *The Battlefields of Imphal: The Second World War and North East India* (London: Routledge, 2016).
Apurba Kundu, *Militarism in India: The Army and Civil Society in Consensus* (London: I. B. Taurus, 1998).
Brian Lavery, *Hostilities Only: Training the Wartime Royal Navy* (London: National Martime Museum, 2004).
Lieutenant Colonel J. P. Lawford & Major W. E. Catto, *Solah Punjab: The History of the 16th Punjab Regiment* (Aldershot: Gale & Polden, 1967).
Michael D. Leigh, *The Evacuation of Civilians from Burma: Analysing the 1942 Colonial Disaster* (London: Bloomsbury, 2014).
Ronald Lewin, *Slim the Standardbearer* (Ware: Wordsworth, 1999).
John Leyin, *Tell Them of Us: The Forgotten Army – Burma* (Stanford-le-Hope, Essex, self-published, 2000).
Nick Lloyd, *The Amritsar Massacre: The Untold Story of the One Fateful Day* (London: I. B. Taurus, 2011).
Michael LoCicero, Ross Mahoney & Stuart Mitchell (editors), *A Military Transformed? Adaptation and Innovation in the British Military, 1792-1945* (Solihull: Helion, 2014).
A.B. Lodge, *The Fall of General Gordon Bennett* (Sydney: Allen & Unwin, 1986).
Robert Lyman, *First Victory: Britain's Forgotten Struggle in the Middle East, 1941* (London: Constable, 2006).
—— *The Generals: From Defeat to Victory, Leadership in Asia, 1941-45* (London: Constable, 2008).
J. F. MacDonald, *Abyssinian Adventure* (London: Cassell, 1957).
Colonel J. N. Mackay, *History of 7th Duke of Edinburgh's Own Gurkha Rifles* (London: William Blackwood & Sons, 1962).

Compton Mackenzie, *Eastern Epic* (London: Chatto & Windus, 1951).
S. P. Mackenzie, *Politics and Military Morale: Current Affairs and Citizenship Education in the British Army 1914-1950* (Oxford: Clarendon Press, 1992).
Lieutenant Colonel Tony Mains, *Sandhurst to the Khyber 1932-1940* (Durham: The Memoir Club, 1999).
Daniel Marston, *The Indian Army and the End of the Raj* (Cambridge: CUP, 2014).
—— *Phoenix from the Ashes* (Westport, Connecticut: Praeger, 2003).
Daniel Marston and Chandar Sundaram (editors), *A Military History of India and South Asia* (Westport: Praeger, 2007).
Bob Maslen-Jones, *Outrageous Fortune* (Caithness, Scotland: Whittles Publishing, 2006).
Philip Mason, *A Matter of Honour* (London: Jonathan Cape, 1974).
—— *A Shaft of Sunlight: Memories of a Varied Life* (London: Andre Deutsch, 1978).
Tony Mason and Eliza Reidi, *Sport and the Military: The British Armed Forces 1880-1960* (Cambridge: CUP, 2010).
John Masters, *Bugles and a Tiger* (London: Michael Joseph, 1956).
—— *The Road Past Mandalay* (London: Michael Joseph, 1961).
Henry Maule, *Spearhead General: The Epic Story of General Sir Frank Messervy and his Men in Eritrea, North Africa and Burma* (London: Odhams Press, 1961).
R. M. Maxwell, *Villiers-Stuart goes to War* (Edinburgh: Pentland Press, 1990).
Spike Mays, *Fall Out the Officers* (London: Eyre & Spottiswoode, 1969).
John McCann, *Echoes of Kohima* (Oldham, self-published, 1989).
Lieutenant General S. L. Menezes, *Fidelity and Honour: The Indian Army from the Seventeenth to the Twenty-first Century* (New Delhi: OUP, 1999).
Rana Mitter, *China's War with Japan, 1937-1945: The Struggle for Survival* (London: Penguin, 2014).
Jonathan Moffatt & Audrey Holmes McCormack, *Moon over Malaya: A Tale of the Argylls and Marines* (Glasgow: Coombe Publishing, 1999).
Brigadier V. J. Moharir, *History of the Army Service (1939-1945)* (New Delhi: Sterling Publishers, 1979).
Terence R. Molloy (editor), *The Silchar Track* (Cambridgeshire: Melrose Books, 2006).
R. J. Moore, *Churchill, Cripps, and India, 1939-1945* (Oxford: Clarendon Press, 1979).
Tim Moreman, *The Army in India and the Development of Frontier Warfare, 1849-1947* (Basingstoke: Macmillan, 1998).
—— *The Jungle, the Japanese and the British Commonwealth Armies at War, 1941-45* (London: Frank Cass, 2005).
Joseph Moretz, *Thinking Wisely, Planning Boldly: The Higher Education and Training of Royal Navy Officers, 1919-1939* (Solihull: Helion, 2015).
George Morton-Jack, *The Indian Army on the Western Front: India's Expeditionary Force to France and Belgium in the First World War* (Cambridge: CUP, 2014).
Vice Admiral The Earl Mountbatten of Burma, *Report to the Combined Chiefs of Staff by the Supreme Allied Commander South East Asia 1943-1945* (London: HMSO, 1951).

Augustus Muir, *The First of Foot: The History of the Royal Scots (The Royal Regiment)* (Edinburgh: Royal Scots History Committee, 1961).
Mohammed Musa, *Jawan to General: Recollections of a Pakistani Soldier* (Karachi: East and West Publishing Company, 1984).
Major General Partap Narain, *Subedar to Field Marshal* (New Delhi: Manas Publications, 1999).
Eric Nield, *With Pegasus in India: The Story of the 153 Gurkha Parachute Battalion* (Singapore: Jay Birch (printer) nd.)
Paul Byron Norris, *Willingly to War 1939-1945* (London: BACSA, 2004).
Lieutenant Colonel L.B. Oatts, *I Serve: Regimental History of the 3rd Carabiniers (Prince of Wales's Dragoon Guards)* (Norwich: Jarrold (printed), 1966).
William O. Odom, *After the Trenches: The Transformation of the US Army, 1918-1939* (Texas A & M University Press, 2008).
David Omissi, *The Sepoy and the Raj* (London: Macmillan, 1994).
Neil Orpen, *East African & Abyssinian Campaigns* (Cape Town: Purnell, 1968).
Richard Overy, *Why the Allies Won* (London: Pimlico, 1995).
Malcolm Page, *A History of the King's African Rifles and East African Forces* (Barnsley: Pen & Sword, 1998).
Dharm Pal, *Campaign in Italy, 1943-45* (Delhi: Combined Inter-Services Historical Section, 1960).
—— *Campaign in Western Asia* (New Delhi: Pentagon Press, 2012).
Major General D. K. Palit, *The Campaign in Malaya* (Dehra Dun: The English Book Depot, 1989).
—— *Musings and Memories Vol. 1* (New Delhi: Palit & Palit in association with Lancer Publications, 2004).
Michael Paris, *Warrior Nation: Images of War in British Popular Culture, 1850-2000* (London: Reaktion Books, 2000).
Major General Sher Ali Pataudi, *The Story of Soldiering and Politics in India and Pakistan* (Pakistan: Syed Mobin Mahmud & Co., 1988).
Geraldine Peacock, *The Life of a Jungle Walla: Reminiscences in the Life of Lt. Col. E. H. Peacock DSO MC* (Ilfracoombe, Devon: Stockwell, 1958).
Mark Peattie, Edward Drea and Hans van de Ven (editors), *The Battle for China: Essays on the Military History of the Sino-Japanese War of 1937-1945* (Stanford: Stanford University Press, 2011).
Lieutenant General A. E. Percival, *The War in Malaya* (London: Eyre & Spottiswoode, 1949).
F. W. Perry, *The Commonwealth Armies: Manpower and Organisation in Two World Wars* (Manchester: MUP, 1988).
S. C. S. Pickford, *Destination Rangoon* (Denbigh, Clywd: Gee & Son, 1989).
Brigadier M. M. Pillai, *Three Thousand Miles to Freedom* (New Delhi: Lancer Publications, 2009).
Major General I. S. O. Playfair, *The Mediterranean and Middle East: Vol. 1: The Early Successes against Italy* (London: HMSO, 1954).

Timothy Harrison Place, *Military Training in the British Army, 1940-1944* (London: Frank Cass, 2000).
Tom Pocock, *Fighting General: The Public and Private Campaigns of General Sir Walter Walker* (London: Collins, 1997).
Douglas Porch, *Hitler's Mediterranean Gamble: The North African and Mediterranean Campaigns in World War II* (London: Weidenfeld & Nicolson, 2004).
Bisheshwar Prasad, *Defence of India: Policy and Plans* (India & Pakistan: Combined Inter-Services Historical Section, 1963).
—— *East African Campaign 1940-41* (India & Pakistan: Combined Inter-Services Historical Section, 1963).
—— *The Retreat from Burma* (India & Pakistan: Combined Inter-Services Historical Section, 1954).
Sri Nandan Prasad, *Official History of the Indian Armed Forces in the Second World War: Expansion of the Armed Forces and Defence Organisation 1939-45* (India & Pakistan: Combined Inter-Services Historical Section, 1956).
—— *The Reconquest of Burma Vol. I June 1942-June 1944* (India & Pakistan: Combined Inter-Services Historical Section, 1958).
John Prenderghast, *Prender's Progress: A Soldier in India, 1931-1947* (London: Cassell, 1979).
Peter Preston-Hough, *Commanding Far Eastern Skies: A Critical Analysis of the Royal Air Force Superiority Campaign in India, Burma and Malaya 1941-1945* (Solihull: Helion, 2015).
Henry Probert, *The Forgotten Air Force in the War against Japan, 1941-1945* (London: Brassey's, 1995).
Major Mohammed Ibrahim Qureshi, *History of the Punjab Regiment 1759-1956* (Aldershot: Gale & Polden, 1958).
Srinath Raghavan, *India's war: The Making of South Asia 1939-1945* (London: Allen Lane, 2016).
Lieutenant Colonel B. L. Raina, *Official History of the Indian Armed Forces in the Second World War 1939-1945: Medical Services: Medicine, Surgery and Pathology* (India & Pakistan: Combined Inter-Services Historical Section, 1955).
—— *Official History of the Indian Armed Forces in the Second World War 1939-1945: Medical Services: Preventive Medicine (Nutrition, Malaria Control and Prevention of Disease* (India & Pakistan: Combined Inter-Services Historical Section, 1961).
John Randle, *Battle Tales from Burma* (Barnsley: Pen & Sword, 2004).
Major General Indar Jit Rikhye, *Trumpets and Tumults* (New Delhi: Manohar, 2004).
Erich Maria Remarque, *All Quiet on the Western Front* (London: Putnam, 1929).
David Reynolds, *The Long Shadow: The Great War and the Twentieth Century* (London: Simon & Schuster, 2013).
Charles Richardson, *From Churchill's Secret Circle to the BBC: The Biography of Lieutenant General Sir Ian Jacob* (London: Brassey's, 1991).
Brigadier M. R. Roberts, *Golden Arrow: The Story of the 7th Indian Division* (Aldershot: Gale & Polden, 1952).

G. W. Robertson, *The Rose and the Arrow* (136th Field Regiment Old Comrades Association, 1986).
Angus Rose, *Who Dies Fighting* (London: Right Book Club, 1944).
Kaushik Roy, *India and World War II: War, Armed Forces, and Society, 1939-45* (New Delhi: OUP, 2016).
—— *The Army in British India: From Colonial Warfare to Total War 1857-1947* (London: Bloomsbury, 2013).
—— *The Indian Army in the Two World Wars* (editor), (Leiden: Brill, 2012).
—— *The Oxford Companion to Modern Warfare in India* (New Delhi: OUP, 2009).
—— *Sepoys against the Rising Sun: The Indian Army in the Far East and South-East Asia, 1941-45* (Leiden: Brill, 2016).
—— (editor), *War and Society in Colonial India 1807-1945* (New Delhi: OUP, 2006).
S. H. Rudolph, L. I. Rudolph with Mohan Singh Kanota, *Reversing the Gaze: Amar Singh's Diary, A Colonial Subject's Narrative of Imperial India* (Boulder, Colorado: Westview Press, 2002).
Denis Russell-Roberts, *My Own War in Malaya* (Privately published, nd.).
Harry Seaman, *The Battle at Sangshak* (London: Leo Cooper, 1989).
Lieutenant Colonel J. L. Scoullar, *Official History of New Zealand in the Second World War 1939-45: Battle for Egypt: The Summer of 1942* (Wellington: War History Branch, 1955).
John Shipster, *Mist on the Rice-fields: A Soldier's story of the Burma Campaign and the Korean War* (Barnsley: Pen & Sword, 2000).
Major General Gurcharn Singh Sandu, *The Indian Armour: History of the Indian Armoured Corps (1941-1971)* (New Delhi: Vision Books, 1987).
Siegfried Sassoon, *Memoirs of an Infantry Officer* (London: Faber & Faber, 1930).
Peter Schifferle, *America's School for War: Fort Leavenworth, Officer Education, and Victory in World War II* (Lawrence: University Press of Kansas, 2010).
Colonel L. W. Shakespeare, *History of the Assam Rifles* (London: Macmillan, 1929).
Lieutenant Colonel Gautam Sharma, *Nationalisation of the Indian Army* (New Delhi: Allied Publishers, 1996).
Robin Sharp, *The Life of an E.C.O. in India* (Bishop Auckland: Pentland Press, 1994).
Gary Sheffield, *The Chief: Douglas Haig and the British Army* (London: Aurum Press, 2011).
Sierra Leone Battalion Royal West African Frontier Force, *Bush Warfare* (Freetown: Sierra Leone Battalion, 1938).
Ivan Simson, *Singapore: Too Little, Too Late: Some Aspects of the Malayan Disaster in 1942* (London: Leo Cooper, 1970).
Lieutenant Harbakhsh Singh, *In the Line of Duty: A Soldier Remembers* (Delhi: Lancer Publications, 2000).
Brigadier Jasbir Singh, *Escape from Singapore* (New Delhi: Lancer Publications, 2010).
Major General V. K. Singh, *Leadership in the Indian Army* (New Delhi: Sage, 2005).
B. P. N. Sinha and Sunil Chandra, *Valour and Wisdom: Genesis and Growth of the Indian Military Academy* (New Delhi: Oxford & IBH Publishing Co., 1992).

General Sir Andrew Skeen, *Lessons in Imperial Rule: Instructions for British Infantrymen on the Indian Frontier* (Barnsley: Frontline Books, 2008).
Field Marshal Sir William Slim, *Defeat into Victory* (London: Cassell, 1956).
—— *Unofficial History* (Barnsley: Pen & Sword reprint, 2008).
Edward Smalley, *The British Expeditionary Force, 1939-40* (Basingstoke: Palgrave Macmillan, 2015).
Nick Smart, *Biographical Dictionary of British Generals of the Second World War* (Barnsley: Pen & Sword, 2005).
E. D. Smith, *Even the Brave Falter* (London: Robert Hale, 1978).
Peter Stanley, *Die in Battle, Do not Despair: The Indians on Gallipoli, 1915* (Solihull: Helion, 2015).
—— *White Mutiny: British Military Culture in India 1825-1875* (London: Hurst, 1998).
Lieutenant Colonel G. R. Stevens, *Fourth Indian Division* (Toronto: McLaren, nd.).
—— *The 9th Gurkha Rifles Vol. 2 1937-1947* (9th Gurkha Rifles Regimental Association, 1953).
—— *History of the 2nd King Edward VII's Own Goorkha Rifles (The Sirmoor Rifles) Vol. III 1921-1948* (Aldershot: Gale & Polden, 1952).
Andrew Stewart, *The First Victory: The Second World War and the East African Campaign* (New Haven: Yale University Press, 2016).
Brigadier I. M. Stewart, *The Thin Red Line: 2nd Argylls in Malaya* (London: Nelson, 1947).
Matthias Strohn, *The German Army and the Defence of the Reich: Military Doctrine and the Conduct of the Defensive Battle 1918-1939* (Cambridge: CUP, 2011).
Arthur Swinson, *Kohima* (London: Cassell, 1966).
Kazuo Tamayama and John Nunneley, *Tales by Japanese Soldiers of the Burma Campaign 1942-1945* (London: Cassell, 2000).
R. E. S. Tanner and D. A. Tanner, *Burma 1942: Memories of a Retreat: The diary of Ralph Tanner, KOYLI* (Stroud: History Press, 2009).
Captain A. W. Taylor, *Jungle Warfare: the Conduct of small expeditions in the jungles an hilly tracts of Burma, and a system of drill musketry instruction connected therewith, for the use of officers of the Burma Military Police* (Rangoon, 1902).
Julian Thompson, *The Imperial War Museum Book of the War in Burma* (London: Sidgwick & Jackson, 2002).
Richard Tolson, *A Soldier Poet: Letters and Poems of an English Officer 1938-1952* (Oxford: Tolson Publications, 2009).
Daniel Todman, *Britain's War: Into Battle 1937-1941* (London: Allen Lane, 2016).
—— *The Great War: Myth and Memory* (London: Hambledon, 2005).
Geoffrey Treese, *Laughter at the Door* (London: Macmillan, 1974).
Lieutenant General Sir Francis Tuker, *Approach to Battle: A Commentary Eighth Army, November 1941 to May 1943* (London: Cassell, 1963).
—— *The Pattern of War* (London: Cassell, 1948).
Kristian Coates Ulrichsen, *The First World War in the Middle East* (London: Hurst, 2014).

Lieutenant General S. D. Verma, *To Serve with Honour* (Privately published, 1988).
General G. L. Verney, *The Desert Rats: The History of the 7th Armoured Division 1938 to 1945* (London: Hutchinson, 1954).
Colonel J. P. Villiers-Stuart, *Letters of a Once Punjab Frontier Force Officer to his Nephew giving his Ideas on Fighting on the North West Frontier and in Afghanistan* (London: Sifton Praed, 1925).
Johannes H. Voigt, *India in the Second World War* (New Jersey: Humanities Press, 1988).
General Sir Walter Walker, *Fighting On* (London: New Millenium, 1997).
Philip Warner, *Auchinleck: The Lonely Soldier* (London: Buchan & Enright, 1981).
Alan Warren, *Burma 1942: The Road from Rangoon to Mandalay* (London: Continuum, 2011).
—— *Singapore 1942* (London: Hambledon, 2002).
—— *Waziristan, the Faqir of Ipi and the Indian Army* (Karachi: OUP, 2000).
General Sir Archibald Wavell, *Generally Speaking* (London: Macmillan, 1946).
Leslie Wayper, *Mars and Minerva: A History of Army Education* (Winchester: Royal Army Educational Corps Association, 2004).
Colonel A. C. T. White, *The Story of Army Education 1643-1963* (London: Harrap, 1963).
Gerald A. White Jr., *The Great Snafu Fleet: 1st Combat Cargo/344th Airdrom/326th Troop Carrier Squadron in World War II's CBI Theater* (self-published, 2000).
L. Wigmore, *The Japanese Thrust* (Canberra: Australian War Memorial, 1957).
Steven I. Wilkinson, *Army and Nation: The Military and Indian Democracy since Independence* (Cambridge, Massachusetts: Harvard University Press, 2015).
General Sir James Willcocks, *The Romance of Soldiering and Sport* (London: Cassell, 1925).
Cat Wilson, *Churchill on the Far East in the Second World War: Hiding the History of the 'Special Relationship'* (Basingstoke: Palgrave, 2014).
David Wilson, *The Sum of Things* (Staplehurst: Spellmount, 2001).
General Sir James Wilson, *Unusual Undertakings: A Military Memoir* (London: Leo Cooper, 2002).
Lieutenant Colonel D. J. C. Wiseman, *The Second World War 1939-1945 Army: Special Weapons and Types of Warfare* (London: HMSO, 1952).
Francis Yeats Brown, *Bengal Lancer* (London: Anthony Mott, 1984).
Captain J. W. Young, *Manual of Jungle Warfare of the Officers of the Burma Military Police* (Rangoon, 1928).

Articles

Louis Allen, 'Mutaguchi Renya and the Invasion of India, 1944' in Brian Bond (editor), *Fallen Stars: Eleven Studies of Twentieth Century Military Disasters* (London: Brassey's, 1991).

"An Infantry Soldier", 'Collective Training in a Battalion', *JUSII*, Vol. LX, No. 259, April 1930.

Duncan Anderson, 'The Very Model of a Modern Manoeuvrist General: William Slim and the Exercise of High Command in Burma' in Gary Sheffield and Geoffrey Till (editors), *Challenges of High Command in the Twentieth Century* (Camberley: Strategic and Combat Studies Institute, 1999).

C. T. Atkinson, 'The Expansion of the Indian Army' in Sir Charles Lucas (editor), *The Empire at War* (London: Humphrey Milford & Oxford University Press, 1926).

C. A. Bayly, ' "The Nation Within": British India at War, 1939-1947' in Raziuddin Aquil and Kaushik Roy (editors), *Warfare, Religion, and Society in Indian History* (Delhi: Manohar, 2012).

"Beknut", 'Collective Training in a Battalion – A Criticism', *JUSII*, Vol. LX, No. 261, October 1930.

Tarak Barkawi, 'Culture and Combat in the Colonies: The Indian Army in the Second World War', *Journal of Contemporary History*, Vol. 14, No. 2, April 2006.

—— 'Peoples, Homelands, and Wars? Ethnicity, the Military, and Battle among British Imperial Forces in the War against Japan', *Comparative Studies in Society and History*, Vol, 24, No. 1, 2004.

Antony Best, 'This Probably Over-Valued Military Power: British Intelligence and Whitehall's Perception of Japan, 1939-1941', *Intelligence and National Security*, Vol. 12, No. 3, July 1997.

Sanjoy Bhattacharya, 'British Military Information Management Techniques and the South Asian Soldier: Eastern India during the Second World War', *Modern Asian Studies*, Vol. 34, No. 2, May 2000.

Brian Bond, 'British Anti-War Writers and their Critics' in Hugh Cecil and Peter Liddle (editors), *Facing Armageddon: The First World War Experienced* (London: Leo Cooper, 1996).

John M. Bourne, 'The East India Company's Military Seminary, Addiscombe, 1809-1858', *Journal of the Army Society of Historical Research*, Vol. 57, No. 232, Winter 1979.

Andrew N. Buchanan, 'The War Crisis and the Decolonization of India, December 1941-September 1942: A Political and Military Dilemma', *Global War Studies*, Vol. 8, No. 2, 2011.

John Buckley and Gary Sheffield, 'The British Army in the era of Haig and Montgomery', *Journal of the Royal United Service Institution*, Vol. 159, No. 4, 2014.

Raymond Callahan, 'Did Winston Matter? Churchill and the Indian Army, 1940-45' in Alan Jeffreys and Patrick Rose (editors), *The Indian Army: Experience and Development* (Farnham: Ashgate, 2012).

—— 'Servants of the Raj: The Jacob Family in India, 1817-1926', *Journal of the Society of Army Historical Research*, Vol. 56, No. 225, Spring 1978.

—— 'Were the 'Sepoy Generals' Any Good? A reappraisal of the British-Indian Army's High Command in the Second World War' in Kaushik Roy (editor), *War and Society in Colonial India 1807-1945* (New Delhi: OUP, 2009).

Lucio Ceva, 'The North African Campaign 1940-43: A Reconsideration', *Journal of Strategic Studies*, Vol. 13, No. 1, 1990.
Major B. H. Chappel, 'Indian Cavalry Reorganization, 1937', *JUSII*, Vol. LXVII, No. 287, April 1937.
Brigadier L. P. Collins, 'The Indian Military Academy', *JUSII*, Vol. LXIV, No. 277, October 1934.
Captain H. L. Davies, 'Military Intelligence in Tribal Warfare on the North West Frontier of India', *JUSII*, No. 272, July 1933.
Lieutenant Colonel E. R. S. Dons, 'The New Infantry Training, 1937', *JUSII*, Vol. LXVII, No. 293, October 1938.
G. J. Douds, 'The Men Who Never Were: Indian POWs in the Second World War', *South Asia*, Vol. 27, No. 2, August 2004.
Captain H. C. Duncan, 'The Principles of Training', *JUSII*, Vol. LX, No. 260, July 1930.
Jonathan Fennell, 'Courage and Cowardice in the North African Campaign: The Eighth Army and Defeat in the Summer of 1942', *War in History*, Vol. 20, No. 1, 2013.
Graham Dunlop, 'The Recapture of Rangoon, 1945: The Last and Greatest Victory of the British Indian Army' in Alan Jeffreys and Patrick Rose (editors), *The Indian Army: Experience and Development* (Farnham: Ashgate, 2012).
'Fade Out', 'Military Training Films (India) – A Retrospect', *JUSII*, Vol. LXXIV, No. 315, April 1944.
John Ferris, 'Worthy of Some Better Enemy? The British estimate of the Imperial Japanese Army, 1919-41 and the Fall of Singapore', *Canadian Journal of History*, Vol. XXVII, August 1993.
David French, 'Colonel Blimp and the British Army: British Divisional Commanders in the War Against Germany, 1939-1945', *English Historical Review*, Vol. III, No. 444, November 1996.
—— 'Doctrine and Organisation in the British Army, 1919-1932', *Historical Journal*, Vol. 44, No. 2, 2002.
Robert T. Foley, 'Dumb donkeys or cunning foxes? Learning in the British and German Armies during the Great War', *International Affairs*, Vol. 90, No. 2, 2014.
Captain M. C. T. Gompertz, 'The New Infantry Training, Vol. II', *JUSII*, Vol. LXII, No. 267, April 1932.
John Gooch, 'Military Doctrine and Military History' in John Gooch (editor), *The Origins of Contemporary Doctrine* (Camberley: Strategic & Combat Studies Institute, 1997).
Ian Gooderson, 'Assimilating Urban Battle Experience – The Canadians at Ortona', *Canadian Military Journal*, Winter 2007-08.
Brigadier J. H. Gradige, 'How the Fourteenth Army was Reinforced', *JUSII*, Vol. XXV, No. 321, October 1945.

Partha Saratha Gupta, 'The Debate on Indianisation 1918-1939' in Partha Saratha Gupta and Anirudh Deshpande (editors), *The British Raj and the Armed Forces 1857-1939* (Delhi: OUP, 2002).

Alan Harefield, 'The IAVC Centre, Ambala during World War II', *Durbar: Journal of the Indian Military Historical Society*, Vol. 12, No. 2, Summer 1995.

Mark Harrison, 'Medicine and the Culture of Command: the Case of Malaria Control in the British Army during two World Wars', *Medical History*, Vol. 40, No. 4, October 1996.

T. A. Heathcote, 'The Army of British India' in David Chandler (editor), *The Oxford Illustrated History of the British Army* (Oxford: OUP, 1994).

Lieutenant Colonel W. H. Huelin, 'Was Our Pre-War Training Wrong?', *Journal of the United Service Institution of India*, Vol. LXXVI, No. 325, October 1946.

John Irwin, 'A Royal Engineer at OTS Mhow, India, 1944', *Journal of the Society for Army Historical Research*, Vol. 78, No. 316, 2000.

Major General F. A. M. B. Jenkins, 'Some Lessons from the Italian Campaign', *JUSII*, Vol. LXXIV, No. 314, January 1944.

Keith Jeffrey, 'An English Barrack in the Oriental Seas? India in the aftermath of the Great War', *Modern Asian Studies*, Vol. 15, No. 3, 1981.

—— 'The Eastern Arc of Empire: A Strategic View 1850-1950', *Journal of Strategic Studies*, Vol. 5, No. 4, December 1982.

Alan Jeffreys, 'Military Education in the Indian Army, 1920-1946' in Doug Delaney and Rob Engen (editors), *Military Education in the British Empire (1858-1948)* (University of British Columbia Press, forthcoming 2017).

—— 'The Officer Corps and the training of the Indian Army with Special Reference to Lieutenant-General Francis Tuker' in Kaushik Roy (editor) *The Indian Army in the two World Wars* (Leiden: Brill, 2011).

—— 'The Indian Army in Malayan Campaign, 1941-1942' in Rob Johnson (editor), *The Indian Armies* (Newcastle: Cambridge Scholars Press, 2014).

—— 'Indian Army Training for the Italian Campaign and Lessons Learnt' in Andrew Hargreaves, Patrick Rose and Matthew Ford (editors), *Allied Fighting Effectiveness in North Africa and Italy, 1942-45* (Leiden: Brill, 2014).

—— 'Slim's Welsh General: Major General 'Pete' Rees in the Burma Campaign', *Transactions of the Honourable Society of Cymmrodorion*, Vol. 12, 2006.

—— 'Training the Indian Army' in Ashley Jackson (editor) 'New research on the British Empire and the Second World War' in *Global War Studies*, Vol. 7, No. 2, 2010.

—— 'Training the Indian Army, 1939-1945' in Alan Jeffreys & Patrick Rose (editors) *The Indian Army, 1939-1947* (Farnham: Ashgate, 2012).

—— 'Training the Troops: The Indian Army in Egypt, Eritrea and Libya, 1940-42' in Jill Edwards (editor), *El Alamein and the Struggle for North Africa: International Perspectives from the Twenty-first Century* (Cairo: American University in Cairo Press, 2012).

Indivar Kamtekar, 'A Different War Dance: State and Class in India 1939-1945', *Past and Present*, No. 176.
Gyanesh Kudaisya, '"In Aid of Civil Power": The Colonial Army in Northern India, c.1919-42', *Journal of Imperial and Commonwealth History*, Vol. 32, No. 1, January 2004.
Nick Lloyd, 'The Amritsar Massacre and the minimum force debate', *Small Wars and Insurgencies*, Vol. 21, No. 2, June 2010.
Major General J. D. Lunt, 'The Burma Rifles', *Journal of the Society for Army Historical Research*, Vol. LXXVI, No. 307, Autumn 1998.
Charles MacFetridge, 'The Indian Army in Burma: A Personal Reminiscence' in David Smurthwaite (editor), *The Forgotten War: British Army in the Far East 1941-1945* (London: National Army Museum, 1992).
John M. Mackenzie, 'The Popular Culture of Empire in Britain' in Judith M. Brown and Wm. Roger Louis (editors), *The Oxford History of the British Empire: Volume IV: The Twentieth Century* (Oxford: OUP, 1999).
Chris Mann, 'The Battle of Wadi Akarit, 6 April 1943: 4th Indian Division and its Place in 8th Army' in Alan Jeffreys and Patrick Rose (editors), *The Indian Army, 1939-47: Experience and Development* (Farnham: Ashgate, 2012).
—— 'Failures in Command and Control: The Experience of 4th Indian Division at the Second Battle of Cassino, February 1944' in Andrew Hargreaves, Patrick Rose and Matthew Ford (editors), *Allied Fighting Effectiveness in North Africa and Italy, 1942-1945* (Leiden: Brill, 2014).
Daniel Marston, 'A Force Transformed: The Indian Army and the Second World War' in Daniel Marston and Chandar Sundaram (editors), *A Military History of India and South Asia* (Wesport: Praeger, 2007).
—— 'The War in Burma, 1942-1945: The 7/10th Baluch Experience' in Kaushik Roy (editor), *The Indian Army in the Two World Wars* (Leiden: Brill, 2012).
Cesar Campiani Maximiano, 'Learning on the Job: Training the Brazilians for Combat on the Gothic Line' in Andrew Hargreaves, Patrick Rose and Matthew Ford (editors), *Allied Fighting Effectiveness in North Africa and Italy, 1942-1945* (Leiden: Brill, 2014).
Major N. I. Mitchell-Carruthers, 'Annual Training', *JUSII*, Vol. LVII, No. 253, October 1928.
Brian Montgomery, 'Change: The Indian Army before the demise of our Indian Empire in 1947', *Imperial War Museum Review*, No. 3, 1988.
Tim Moreman, '"Debunking the Bunker": Donbaik to Razabil, January 1943-March 1944' in Alan Jeffreys and Patrick Rose (editors), *The Indian Army, 1939-47* (Farnham: Ashgate, 2012).
—— 'From the Desert Sands to the Burmese Jungle: The Indian Army and the lessons of North Africa, September 1939-November 1942' in Kaushik Roy (editor), *The Indian Army in Two World Wars* (Leiden: Brill, 2011).

—— 'Lord Kitchener, the General Staff and the Army in India, 1902-14' in David French and Brian Holden Reid (editors), *The British General Staff: Reform and Innovation c. 1890-1939* (London: Frank Cass, 2002).

—— '"Small Wars and Imperial Policing": The British Army and the Theory and Practice of Land Warfare in the British Empire, 1919-1939', *Journal of Strategic Studies*, Vol. 9, No. 4, 1996.

George Orwell, 'The Lion and Unicorn: Part 1: England Your England' in *Orwell's England* (London: Penguin, 2001).

John Peaty, 'The Chindits and Special Forces Manpower', *The British Army Review*, No, 128, Winter 2001-02.

Major A. E. Percival, 'The West African Frontier Force', *Army Quarterly*, Vol. XV, No. 1, October 1927.

Tim Harrison Place, 'Lionel Wigram, Battle Drill and the British Army in the Second World War', *War in History*, Vol. 7, No. 4, 2000.

Srinath Raghavan, 'Protecting the Raj: The Army in India and Internal Security c.1919-1939', *Small Wars and Insurgencies*, Vol. 21, No. 2, June 2010.

P. E. Razzell, 'Social Origins of Officers in the Indian and British Home Army: 1758-1962', *British Journal of Sociology*, Vol. 14, No. 3, September 1963.

Jeffrey Richards, 'Boys Own Empire: Feature Films and Imperialism in the 1930s' in John M. Mackenzie (editor), *Imperialism and Popular Culture* (Manchester: Manchester University Press, 1986).

Simon Robbins, 'The right way to play the game: the ethos of the British High Command in the First World War', *Imperial War Museum Review*, No. 6.

Major M. R. Roberts, 'Object!', *JUSII*, Vol. LXVII, No. 288, July 1937.

Patrick Rose, 'Indian Army Command Culture and the North West Frontier, 1919-1939' in Alan Jeffreys and Patrick Rose (editors), *The Indian Army, 1939-47: Experience and Development* (Farnham: Ashgate, 2012).

Kaushik Roy, 'Discipline and Morale of the African, British and Indian Army units in Burma and India during World War II: July 1943 to August 1945', *Modern Asian Studies*, Vol. 44, No. 6, April 2010.

—— (editor) 'Expansion and deployment of the Indian Army during World War II: 1939-45', *Journal of the Society for Army Historical Research*, Vol. 88, No. 55, Autumn 2010.

—— 'Military Loyalty in the Colonial Context: A Case Study of the Indian Army during World War II', *Journal of Military History*, Vol. 73, No. 2, April 2009.

Lieutenant Colonel G. B. Scott, 'The Training of a Battalion in the Indian Army', *JUSII*, Vol. LVI, No. 243, April 1926.

Simon Shoul, 'Soldiers, Riot Control and Aid to the Civil Power in India, Egypt and Palestine, 1919-1939', *Journal of Army Historical Research*, Vol. 86, No. 346, Summer 2008.

Major A. L. Skinner, 'Annual Training – Another View', *JUSII*, Vol. LX, No. 258, January 1930.

Peter Stanley, ' "Great in Adversity": Indian prisoners of war in New Guinea', *Journal of the Australian War Memorial*, November 2002.

—— '"The Part We Played in This Show": Australians and El Alamein' in Jill Edwards (editor), *El Alamein and the Struggle for North Africa: International Perspectives from the Twenty-first Century* (Cairo: The American University in Cairo Press, 2012).

Captain T. H. L. Stebbing, 'King George's Royal Indian Military Schools', *JUSII*, Vol. LXVI, No. 282, January 1936.

Andrew Stewart, ' "Speed and dash": The British Commonwealth's Campaign in East Africa, 1940-41', *Global War Studies*, Vol. 7, No. 2, 2010.

Craig Stockings, 'An Abundance of Riches: Training & Sustaining the Second AIF in First Libyan Campaign, North Africa, 1940-41' in Peter Dennis & Jeffrey Grey (editors), *Riase, Train and Sustain: Delivering Land Combat Power* (Canberra: Australian Military History Publications, 2010).

Hew Strachan. 'Training, Morale and Modern War', *Journal of Contemporary History*, Vol. 41, No. 2, 2006.

Chandar S. Sundaram, 'The Indian National Army, 1942-1946: A Circumstantial Force' in Daniel P. Marston and Chandar S. Sundaram (editors), *A Military History of India and South Asia* (Westport: Praeger, 2007).

—— 'Seditious Letters and Steel Helmets: Disaffection among Indian Troops in Singapore and Hong Kong, 1940-1, and the formation of the Indian National Army' in Kaushik Roy (editor), *War and Society in Colonial India 1807-1945* (New Delhi: OUP, 2006).

——'"Treated with Scant Attention": The Imperial Cadet Corps, Indian Nobles, and Anglo-Indian Policy, 1897-1917', *Journal of Military History*, Vol. 77, January 2013.

Captain C. W. Toovey, 'The Training of the Indian Platoon Commander', *JUSII*, Vol. LVII, No. 247, April 1927.

'Auspex' (pseudonym for F. S. Tuker), 'A Matrimonial Tangle (or Mountains and Machine Guns)', *JUSII*, Vol. LXII, No. 272, July 1933.

Major General F. S. Tuker, 'The Preparation of Infantry for Battle', *Army Quarterly*, Vol. XLIX, No. 1, October 1944.

Ian van der Waag, 'Contested Histories: Official History and the South African Military in the Twentieth Century' in Jeffrey Grey (editor), *The Last Word? Essays on Official History in the United States and British Commonwealth* (Westport, Connecticut: Praeger, 2003).

Alan Warren, 'The Indian Army and the Fall of Singapore' in Brian Farell & Sandy Hunter (editors), *Sixty Years On: The Fall of Singapore Revisited* (Singapore: Eastern Universities, 2003).

Gerald A. White Jr., 'Manna from Heaven: Development of aerial re-supply by the Royal Air Force and Indian Army in India and Burma 1942-1943', *RAF Historical Society Journal*, Issue 58, April/May 2104.

Alexander Wilson, 'Mechanisation and the Test of Battle: The Indian Calvary, 1939-41' in Rob Johnson (editor), *The British Indian Army: Virtue and Necessity* (Newcastle: Cambridge Scholars Publishing, 2014).

Catherine Wilson, 'Responsible History? Churchill's Portrayal of the Indian Army in the Second World War', *Ex Historica*, Vol. 4, 2012.

Captain J. W. Young, 'Notes on Jungle Warfare', *JUSII*, Vol. LVIII, No. 251, April 1928.

Theses and unpublished papers

William Arthur, '"The Padang, the Sahib and the Sepoy": The Role of the Indian Army in Malaya, 1945-6' (Oxford University: DPhil thesis, 2014).

Raymond Callahan, 'The Jungle, the Japanese and the Sepoy' (Unpublished paper for the New Military History of South Asia Conference, Cambridge, 15-17 July 1997).

Mark Cook, 'Evaluating the Learning Curve: The 38th (Welsh) Division on the Western Front 1916-1918' (University of Birmingham: MPhil thesis, 2005).

Vipul Dutta, 'The Making and Un-making of Indian Armed Forces Institutions, 1940-1950' presented at the India and the Second World War Workshop at Kellogg College, Oxford University on 17 January 2013 as part of the British Empire at War Research Group.

Alistair Geddes, 'Major General Arthur Solly Flood, GHQ and Tactical Training in the BEF, 1916-1918' (University of Birmingham: MA Dissertation, 2007).

Mark H. Jacobsen, 'The Modernisation of the Indian Army, 1925-39' (Irvine: University of California PhD thesis, 1979).

Tim Moreman, 'The Jungle, the Japanese and the Australian Army: Learning the lessons of New Guinea, 1942-1944' (Unpublished paper, 2001).

John Moremon, 'Most Deadly Jungle Fighters? Australian Infantry in Malaya and Papua, 1941-43' (Sydney University: BA Dissertation, 1992).

Patrick Rose, 'British Army Command Culture 1939-1945: A Comparative Study of British Eighth and Fourteenth Armies' (KCL University: PhD thesis, 2008).

Colonel D. R. Wood, 'The Indian Army Officer Corps and the training of the Indian Army 1939-47', 2 April 2011 based on the author's experiences written up for the author and a copy deposited in the IWM.

Index

Index of People

Alexander, Field Marshal Harold, 120, 127, 215
Auchinleck, Field Marshal Sir Claude, xiv, 29, 32, 35, 51-52, 60, 65, 71-73, 87, 89, 94, 96-97, 101, 106, 129, 158-159, 162-164, 166, 168, 178, 182-183, 187, 191-192, 197, 199, 203-204, 209-211, 213-214, 218-219, 221, 224, 233

Barker, Colonel Arthur, 111-112
Barrow, Major B. E., 28, 48, 219
Bateman, Major General Donald, 93-95, 106, 116, 119, 128, 188, 209, 213, 219
Bennett, General Gordon, 145, 227
Beresford-Peirse, Major General Sir Noel, 79, 90, 93
Beyts, Colonel Geoffrey, 44, 207-208
Bing, Company Sergeant Major Arthur, 145-146
Briggs, Major General Harold, 98, 107, 114, 116, 209, 219

Cameron, Brigadier Ronnie, 151-152
Carpendale, Brigadier W. S., 139, 146
Churchill, Winston, xi, xv, xx, xxiii, 28, 32, 46, 55, 94-95, 106, 132, 143, 153, 158-160, 173, 223, 225, 228, 230, 233-234, 240
Cochrane, Lieutenant Peter, 32, 92, 109, 120, 223
Collins, Brigadier Lionel Peter, 46-47
Collister, Captain Peter, 167, 220

Corbett, Major General Tom, xxi, 32, 36-37, 43, 48, 50-52, 56, 79-80, 82-87, 89, 106-107, 158, 165-166, 185, 188, 207, 209, 214, 219, 223
Cowan, Major General David 'Punch', 46-47, 51-52, 58, 150, 152, 172, 209, 214
Cunningham, General Alan, 94, 111

Davies, Major General Henry 'Taffy', 51, 72, 81-82, 160
Davis, Patrick, 179, 201, 224
Deakin, Lieutenant Colonel C. C., 136, 220
Dimoline, Brigadier Harry, 103-105, 117-118, 122, 124, 128, 165, 219
Dorman-Smith, Brigadier Eric, 35, 58
Duncan, Captain H. C., xvii, 41-42, 52, 234-235

Elliott, Gerald, 204, 210
Elliott, Major General James 'Jim', xxi, 115
Evans, Lieutenant General Sir Geoffrey, 90, 92, 112, 170, 219, 225

Firth, Major A. D., 154, 166

Gandhi, Mohandas K., 55, 211
Giffard, Lieutenant General Sir George, 159, 174, 177, 182, 207
Gilmore, Scott, 179-180, 225

241

Gurdon, Major General Edward, 186, 215

Hartley, General Sir Alan, 51, 97, 105, 118
Heath, Major General Sir Lewis 'Piggy', 114-116, 130
Holworthy, Major General Alan, 103, 119, 123, 126, 219
Hutton, Lieutenant General Sir Thomas, 58, 83, 150-152, 158, 160, 215, 219-220

Ingall, Brigadier Francis, 44, 208, 226
Inskip, Major General Roland, 160, 202-204, 215
Irwin, Major General Stephen, 157-159, 171, 188, 190, 200, 207, 219, 226, 236

Kaul, Lieutenant General B. M., 45, 51, 221, 227
Kitchener, Lord, 27, 30-31, 46, 76, 199, 238
Kirby, Major General Stanley Woodburn, xxi, 131, 134-135, 139, 150, 152, 156, 171, 178, 211, 227

Le Fleming Major, 46-47
Le Marchand, Colonel Frank, 61, 120, 128
Lee, Major General Alec, 183, 185
Lethbridge, Major General John 'Tubby', 187-188, 220
Lloyd, Brigadier Wilfrid, 92, 112, 116, 187
Lyne, Major General Lewis Owen, xxiv, 220

MacFetridge, Charles, 190, 237
Mackenzie, Compton, xxi, 116, 228
McPherson, Brigadier Alan, 53, 221
Mains, Lieutenant Colonel Tony, 44-45, 228
Messervy, General Sir Frank, 29, 32, 94-95, 111, 114-116, 159, 163, 170-171, 179, 186, 209, 216, 220-221, 228
Montgomery, Field Marshal Sir Bernard, xxiii-xxiv, 28-29, 97, 107, 117, 234, 237
Montgomery, Colonel Brian, 29, 61
Mountbatten, Lord Louis, 159, 174, 178, 210, 218, 228

Musa, General Mohammed, 46, 47
Mutaguchi, General Renya, 172, 234

Neep, Lieutenant Colonel Ronald, 209, 220

O'Connor, General Richard, 89, 92

Parry, Major Robin, 154, 166
Pataudi, Major General Sher Ali, 45, 229
Peacock, Captain Edgar, 167, 169
Percival, Lieutenant General Arthur, 64, 130-131, 137-138, 140, 142-143, 151, 216, 220, 227, 229, 238
Pettigrew, Colonel H. R. C., 69-70, 190
Pickford, Major S. C. S., 164, 229
Prasad, Bisheshwar, xxi, 37, 152, 230

Rawlinson, Field Marshal Henry, 34, 76
Rees, Lieutenant Colonel Thomas 'Pete', 51-52, 90, 93, 107, 114, 116, 118, 159, 182, 209, 216, 236
Reid, Major General Denys, 114, 116, 118, 126, 216
Rose, Major Angus, 133, 145-146, 154, 167
Russell, Major General Dudley 'Pasha', 116, 118, 121, 124-125, 135, 217, 231
Russell-Roberts, Denis, 135, 231

Savory, Lieutenant General Reginald, xiii-xiv, 38-40, 46-48, 50-52, 92-93, 116, 155, 159, 166, 182, 188-189, 209, 217, 220
Scoones, General Geoffrey, 51, 174-175
Singh, Amar, 43, 225, 231
Singh, Lieutenant General Harbakhsh, 47, 231
Skeen, General Andrew, 31, 60, 232
Slim, Field Marshal Sir William 'Bill', x, xiii-xiv, xvi, 31, 51-52, 60, 88, 107, 116, 118, 141-142, 147, 159-160, 168, 170-172, 174, 177-178, 182, 188, 190, 207, 209, 217, 227, 232, 234, 236
Smyth, Brigadier John, 105, 150-152, 220
Solly-Flood, Major General Arthur, xxiii, 31

Index   243

Stewart, Brigadier Ian 'Mad', 136-137, 139, 142, 144-147, 170, 189, 232
Stones, Captain E. L. G., 69-70, 221

Toovey, Major General Cecil, 40, 160, 239
Tuker, Lieutenant General Sir Francis 'Gertie', xix, 48-49, 51-52, 56, 58-59, 63, 66-67, 75, 77, 80, 88, 94-98, 102-103, 105, 107, 117-118, 123, 128-129, 146, 157-158, 161, 188, 209, 211-212, 218, 220, 232, 236, 239

Verma, Lieutenant General S. D., 45, 87, 233
Villiers-Stuart, Brigadier General William, 31, 60, 228, 233

Vinden, Brigadier F. H. 'Jo', 131, 221

Walker, General Sir Walter, 45, 190, 230, 233
Warren, Alan, xxii, 35, 44, 130, 135, 148, 233, 239
Wavell, Field Marshal Archibald, 76, 79, 90, 94, 108, 111, 115, 142, 144, 155, 157-158, 160, 191-192, 218, 233
Willcox, General Henry 'Ulysses', 79, 197, 214, 218
Wilson, Captain David, 132-133, 138, 145-146, 170, 220-221, 233
Wilson, Major General Sir Roger, 56-57
Wingate, Major General Orde, xxiv, 111, 170
Wood, Colonel Denis, xv-xvi, 200, 206

Index of Places

Addiscombe, 43, 234
Afghanistan, 56, 60, 233
Africa, i, xvi, xix, 30, 37, 64, 78, 81, 89, 93, 96, 98, 105, 107, 111, 114, 116-118, 123, 131, 133, 136, 153, 156, 159, 207, 215-218, 224-226, 228, 236-237, 239
Ahmednagar, 41, 77, 82-83, 198
Ajmer, 41, 76
Amabala, 44, 77
Armoured Fighting Vehicles (AFV) School, 82-83, 198
Arakan, xiii, 149, 156-159, 161-164, 167, 169-173, 178-179, 186, 189, 216
Army School of Education, 36, 39-40, 49, 75, 77, 194-195, 211, 217
Army School of Physical Training, 41, 77
Assam, 63, 155, 159, 179, 189-190
Australia, xvii, 130, 187, 217, 224

Babina, 83, 198
Bangalore, 44, 68, 70-71, 77, 183, 201, 208
Bardia, 93-94
Belgaum, 36, 39-40, 45, 67-70, 77, 107, 191, 211, 213
Bengal, 27, 33, 44, 203, 208, 226, 233

Bihar, 166, 168
Bishenpur, 175-176
Bombay, 27, 40, 45, 77, 82, 183, 196, 213, 223, 227
Brig's Peak, 112, 114
Burma, ix, xi, xviii-xx, 30, 32, 37, 47, 52, 64, 78, 111, 114, 116, 128-129, 132-133, 143, 145-146, 148-154, 156-161, 163-169, 171-175, 177-178, 180-183, 187-188, 190, 193, 199-202, 204, 207, 214-215, 217, 220-221, 223-228, 230-234, 236-239

Cairo, 87, 98, 214, 216, 225, 237, 239
Calcutta (Kolkata), xv, xviii, xxii, 30, 40, 43, 58, 222
Camberley, xxiii, 34, 46, 52, 215, 217, 234-235
Cameron Ridge, 112, 114-115
Cassino, 32, 123-124, 126-127, 226, 237
Ceylon, 145, 178, 215, 218
Chhindwara, 76, 163-164, 169
China, 151, 192, 228-229
Chindwin River, 173, 176-177
Combined Training Centre, 121, 183, 199
Comilla, 145, 154, 166

Cyprus, 97-98, 105, 122
Cyrenaica, 92, 94-95, 217

Dehra Dun, 45-46, 122, 147, 167, 205, 217, 224, 229
Deir-el-Shein, x, xvi, 89, 99-100, 103, 108
Delhi, 31, 118, 217
Deolali, 71, 77, 165
Dimapur, 172-174
Dologorodoc, 114-115
Donbaik, 157, 170, 237

Egypt, 30-31, 37, 59, 74, 89-90, 93, 101, 107, 213, 216-217, 231, 236, 238
El Alamein, xvi, 89, 95, 98-99, 101-103, 107, 117, 174, 222, 225, 236, 239
Equitation School, 41, 77
Eritrea, 65, 94, 98, 107, 109-112, 114-115, 117, 217, 222, 228, 236

Ferozepore, 76, 83, 198

Gallipoli, iv, 30, 217, 232
Gazala, 98, 107
Gothic Line, 32, 125-129, 237
Greece, 65, 126

Haifa, 58, 88
Halfaya, 88, 93-94
Hong Kong, 37, 136, 239

Imperial Defence College (IDC), xii, 51-52, 214, 217
Imphal, x, 148-149, 160, 164, 170, 172-178, 180, 182, 223, 225, 227
Indian Armoured Corps Training Centre (IACTC), xii, 83-84, 88, 198
Indian Army Ordnance Corps (IAOC) Training Centre, 68, 77
Indian Cavalry Training Centre, 84-85
Indian Military Academy (IMA), xii, 40, 46-47, 68-70, 75, 77, 107, 197, 202, 208, 214, 217, 232, 235
Indore, 35, 44, 76, 213
Iraq, 66, 78, 87-88, 98-99, 105, 118, 150, 214, 216-217

Italy, i, xvi, xix, 90, 107, 109, 111, 115-116, 118, 120, 122-124, 126, 128-129, 180, 207, 213, 215, 218, 225-226, 229, 236-237

Japan, xxi-xxii, 140, 143, 150, 152, 156, 171, 178, 191, 199, 214, 227-228, 230, 234
Jhelum, 41, 76
Johore, 133, 136, 142
Jubbulpore, 68, 77, 163
Jullundur, 41, 76, 198
Jungle Warfare School, 146, 154, 166-167, 187, 190, 207

Kakul, 48, 61, 71, 77, 198, 202
Karachi, 35, 37, 145, 229, 233
Karakvasla, 78, 183
Kassala, 111, 114
Kenya, 110-111
Keren, x, 88, 93-94, 103, 110-117, 119, 129-130, 207, 213, 216-217, 220
King George's Royal Indian Military School, 41, 76, 196, 239
Kirkee, 68, 77
Kohima, x, 148-149, 160, 170, 172-174, 176-178, 180, 216, 223-225, 228, 232
Kota Bahru, 135, 140

Lebanon, 119-120, 123
Libya, 107, 236
Lucknow, 83, 198

Madras, 27, 34, 57, 77, 174, 196
Malaya, ix, xiii, xvii, xxii, 37, 63-64, 78, 105, 116, 130-140, 142-148, 150, 153-155, 158, 160-161, 170, 177, 185, 193, 196, 207, 216, 224-226, 228-232, 240
Mandalay, xxiv, 32, 148, 175, 182, 216, 225, 228, 233
Maungdaw, 157-158
Mediterranean, xix, 75, 90, 115, 119, 125, 210, 212, 226, 229-230
Mesopotamia, 30, 213-216, 218
Middle East, i, xvii, xix, 30-31, 55, 64, 75, 82, 87-90, 92, 94, 96, 98, 101, 104-108,

115-117, 119, 125, 127, 135, 138, 151, 156, 169, 191-192, 206, 209-210, 213-214, 218, 226-227, 229, 233
Middle East Staff School, 104, 119
Middle East Training Centre, 106, 117, 119, 213
Mount Sanchil, 112, 114
Mount Zeban, 112, 114
Mountain Warfare School, 31, 119-121, 123
Muttra, 39, 85
Mysore, 182, 190

New Guinea, 143, 145, 180, 187-188, 238, 240
New Zealand, 37, 94, 98, 101, 105, 127, 187, 231
Nibeiwa, 90, 92-93
North East Frontier, 132, 163
North West Frontier (NWF), i, xii, xxv, 30, 33, 35-36, 43-44, 53, 59-62, 64, 79, 109-111, 115, 117, 128, 132, 139, 151, 156, 186, 198, 213-216, 218, 233, 238
Nunshigum, 175, 225

Officer Training School (OTS) Bangalore, 68, 70-71, 73, 201, 208
Officer Training School (OTS) Mhow, 68, 70-71, 77, 200-201, 208, 221, 236
Omar, 94-95
Ortona, 123, 236

Pachmarhi, 41, 77, 83
Pacific, 155, 159, 161-162, 180, 187, 222
Pakistan, xxi, 27-28, 36-37, 45-47, 99, 110, 129, 152, 156, 175, 190, 208, 216, 222, 229-230
Palestine, 30, 59, 64, 97, 106, 122, 215-218, 227, 238
Persia, 118, 217-218
Peshawar, 60, 82
Poona, 32, 77-78, 85, 145-146, 198, 207
Punjab, 57, 194, 196

Quetta, 29, 34, 44-46, 50-51, 77, 83, 188, 190, 197, 213-216, 218

Raiwala, 146, 167-168
Ranchi, 168, 171
Rangoon, 148-152, 158, 164, 183, 209, 214, 220, 224, 229, 232-233, 235
Razabil, 157, 171, 237
Roorkee, 48, 68
Royal Armoured Corps (RAC) School, xi, 87-88, 198, 202
Royal Military College, 43, 216
Ruweisat Ridge, 98-99

Sandhurst, 34, 43-46, 48, 216, 228
Sangshak, 168, 173, 231
School of Artillery, 48, 71, 77
School of Weapon Training and Mechanisation, 77, 83
Senior Officers' School, xxiv, 41, 45, 51-52, 67, 77, 213, 217
Sevoke, 166-167
Shimoga, 167, 187
Sialkot, 73, 86
Sicily, 118, 121-122
Sidi Barrani, x, 32, 86, 89-94, 107, 111, 118, 213
Signal School, 41, 77
Singapore, xxii, 37, 64, 130-131, 133, 135-137, 139-140, 142-143, 145-146, 168, 185, 207, 216, 221, 223-225, 227, 229, 231, 233, 235, 239
Sittang Bridge, 152, 214
Small Arms School, 41, 77, 83
Sollum, 93-94, 107

Tactical School, 77, 145, 166, 187, 198-199, 207
Tiddim, 172, 175, 179, 225
Tobruk, 94, 99, 217
Tummar East, 90, 92
Tummar West, 90, 92

Ukhrul, 172-173, 175, 177, 180

Waziristan, 35, 42, 44, 48-49, 82-83, 132, 214, 216-217, 233
Western Desert, 96-97, 168, 190, 216

Index of Military Formations & Units

11th Army Group, 146, 174, 185

Eastern Army, 156-157, 168, 215
1st Army, 89, 118, 218
8th/Eighth Army, xix, 46, 89, 94-95, 97, 101, 103, 107-108, 117, 126, 218
14th/Fourteenth Army, 116, 148, 159, 168, 170-171, 177-178, 180, 187-188, 190, 206, 217

III Indian Corps, 116, 130, 140, 143
IV Corps, 116, 172, 174-175, 177, 182, 214-216
V Corps, 118, 126, 213
XXXIII Indian Corps, 174, 181

1st Armoured Division, 79, 85-87, 95, 104, 216
1st Burma Division, 150, 159, 163
2nd British Division, 145-146, 160, 170, 172, 174, 177, 183, 218
2nd New Zealand Division, 94, 98, 105
4th Indian Division, xix, 65, 89-90, 92-98, 102-104, 106-107, 110-112, 114-129, 210, 213, 216, 218
5th Indian Division, 65, 89, 98, 102, 107, 110-111, 114, 116, 130, 168-172, 175, 177, 210, 217
7th Armoured Division, 89-90, 93-94, 98, 116, 216
7th Indian Division, 79, 105, 116, 159, 163, 168-172, 177-179, 207, 214, 216
8th Indian Division, 78, 89, 116, 118, 121-125, 128-129, 210, 217
9th Australian Division, 98, 105-106
9th Indian Division, 130, 134, 140, 147
10th Indian Division, 88-89, 102, 107, 116, 118, 122, 126-129, 210, 214, 216-217
11th Indian Division, 130, 135, 139-140, 142, 147
14th Indian Division, 116, 145, 154, 163-166, 169, 214, 216
17th Indian Division, 78, 142, 150-152, 154-155, 167, 170, 172, 175, 177, 214

19th Indian Division, 78, 116, 159, 181-183, 216
20th Indian Division, 53, 172, 175, 177, 180
23rd Indian Division, 116, 155, 159, 172, 175, 177, 185, 189, 217
25th Indian Division, 81, 160, 181-183
26th Indian Division, 154, 189, 214
39th Indian (Training) Division, 76, 163-165
51st (Highland) Division, 102, 105-106

5th Indian Infantry Brigade, 89, 92, 102, 107, 112, 114, 116, 119, 121, 125, 128, 213, 215, 217
6th Brigade, 174, 183
7th Indian Infantry Brigade, 94, 102-103, 114, 120, 126
9th Indian Infantry Brigade, 114-116
10th Indian Infantry Brigade, 50, 114-116, 126, 216-217
11th Indian Infantry Brigade, 32, 89-90, 92-94, 112, 114, 116, 120, 126, 217
12th Indian Infantry Brigade, xvi, 130, 136, 138-139, 142-143, 147
13th Indian Infantry Brigade, 150, 214
17th Indian Infantry Brigade, 124-125
18th Indian Infantry Brigade, xvi, 89, 99-102, 108
19th Indian Infantry Brigade, 78, 124
20th Indian Infantry Brigade, 126, 214
22nd Guards Brigade, 94, 101
28th Indian Infantry Brigade, xvi, 139-140, 142, 146-147
29th Indian Infantry Brigade, 114, 217
43rd (Gurkha) Lorried Brigade, 125-127
44th Indian Infantry Brigade, 142-143, 147, 150
45th Indian Infantry Brigade, 147, 150
48th Indian Infantry Brigade, 150-151
50th Indian Parachute Brigade, 168, 172-173
52nd Brigade, 163-164
89th Indian Infantry Brigade, 177, 179

161st Indian Infantry Brigade, 102, 169, 173-174
268th Indian Infantry Brigade, 174, 195

Argyll and Sutherland Highlanders, 2nd Battalion, 78, 132, 136-137, 139, 142, 144-146
Baluch Regiment, 3/10th, 118, 126
Burma Military Police, 132, 149
Burma Rifles, 149-150
Cameron Highlanders, 2nd Queen's Own, 32, 88, 92, 94, 112, 114
Central India Horse, 50, 83
Cypriot Mule Company, 110, 114
Dogras, 1/17th, 114, 169, 175
Dragoons, 25th 169, 171
Duke of Connaught's Own Bombay Lancers, 82-83
East India Company, 27-28, 43
Essex Regiment, 99, 101-102
Frontier Force Regiment, 118, 125
Frontier Force Rifles, 41, 114, 160, 179, 204, 215, 217
Gardner's Horse *see* Lancers (Gardner's Horse), 2nd
Gordon Highlanders, 131, 137
Gurkha Rifles (The Sirmoor Rifles), 2nd King Edward VII's Own, 48-49, 63, 73, 205, 218
Gurkhas Rifles, 3rd 99,101
Gurkha Rifles, 5th, 166, 201
Gurkha Rifles, 6th, 214, 217
Gurkha Rifles, 8th, 164, 179-180, 186
Gurkha Rifles, 38th, 164, 205
Hodson's Horse, 29, 214, 216
Hyderabad Regiment, 4/19th, 34, 136, 142, 215
Lancers (Gardner's Horse), 2nd, 50, 214
Light Cavalry, 7th, 85, 183
Light Cavalry, 16th, 34, 85
Mahratta Light Infantry, 34, 77, 114, 116, 216
Prince Of Wales's Own Cavalry, 14th *see* Scinde Horse
Punjab Regiment, 1st, 34, 92, 95, 112, 154, 169,174, 203, 215

Punjab Regiment, 2nd, 73, 136, 142, 183, 196, 203
Punjab Regiment, 14th, 57, 166, 204
Punjab Regiment, 15th, 125, 157, 203-204
Punjab Regiment, 16th, 73, 136, 164, 166, 203
Rajputana Rifles, 92, 112, 183
Royal Fusiliers, 1st Battalion, 92, 112
Royal Tank Regiment, 7th, 90, 92
Royal West African Frontier Force, 110, 138
Royal West Kent Regiment, 92, 172-173
Scinde Horse (14th Prince Of Wales's Own Cavalry), 28, 48, 82-83
Sherwood Foresters, 163, 218
Sikhs, 11th, 47, 50, 99, 101-102, 112, 135, 217
Skinner's Horse, 50, 83
West India Regiment, 31, 217
West Yorkshires, 114, 171

Army Education Corps (AEC), 40, 46, 75, 194, 196
British Army, xxiii-xxv, 28, 30-31, 34-35, 41-44, 52, 61-62, 67, 69, 72, 81-82, 86, 110, 132, 137, 149, 163, 175, 187, 191-192, 197, 199, 210-211, 215
British Expeditionary Force, xxiii, 90, 215
Central Command, 79, 167, 197, 218
Gazelle Force, 111-112, 116, 216
GHQ India, i, xix, xxv, 49, 58, 62-63, 70, 77, 82-83, 86-89, 95-96, 104, 116, 120-121, 133, 143, 146, 154, 156, 159, 161, 165, 170, 178, 183, 185, 189, 197, 203, 211, 215
Gurkha Training Centre, 3rd, 205, 208
Indian Air Force, 177, 180
Indian Armoured Corps, 57, 82-84, 87-88, 198
Indian Army Ordnance Corps (IAOC), 37, 58, 68, 77, 79
Indian Engineers, 68, 173
Indian Pioneer Corps, 78, 188
Indian State Forces, xii, 43, 46, 76, 118
Indian Territorial Force, 57, 68

Malaya Command, 63, 131, 133-134, 136-139, 143, 146-147
Middle East Command, 82, 88, 151, 191
North Force, 114-115
Northern Command, 50, 61, 79-80, 216
Officer Cadet Training Unit (OCTU), 137, 199-200
Royal Air Force (RAF), xvii, 41, 60, 65, 84-85, 88, 106, 111, 134, 140, 160, 170, 174, 177, 180, 183, 197
Royal Armoured Corps (RAC), 87-88, 169
Royal Artillery (RA), 28, 99, 103-104, 165, 175, 213, 215
Royal Australian Air Force, xvii, 136, 140
Royal Indian Army Service Corps (RIASC), 37, 57, 71, 74, 77, 79, 83, 188, 195, 202, 205
Royal Indian Navy (RIN), 183, 197
Royal Tank Corps, 77, 82
South East Asia Command (SEAC), 178, 180, 185, 195, 197

Southern Army, HQ, 78, 183, 185
Southern Command, 77-80, 106, 213, 218
Sudan Defence Force, 110-111
Training Team, No. 2, 78, 103, 185
Training Team, No. 6, 145, 154
United States Army Air Force (USAAF), 177, 180
Veterinary Corps, 37, 74
Western Desert Force, 89, 92-94, 213

Imperial Japanese Army (IJA), 133, 139-140, 142, 155, 157-158, 162, 166, 172, 175, 177-178, 210
Indian National Army, 143, 149

15th Army (Japanese), 151, 172, 177

15th Division (Japanese), 172, 175, 177
31st Division (Japanese), 172-173
33rd Division (Japanese), 151, 172, 175, 177

Index of General & Miscellaneous Terms

First Arakan Campaign, xiii, 149, 156, 158-159, 161-164, 169-170, 186, 216
Third Afghan War, 32, 42

A Lecture to Infantry Officers on Man Management, 188-189
Amritsar Massacre, 59, 227, 237
Army Council, 62, 105

Battles:
  Admin Box, 148, 171, 216
  El Alamein, 89, 98
  Grik Road, 142, 144
  Keren, x, 93, 110, 112-113, 115-116, 129-130, 207, 220
  Sidi Barrani, x, 86, 89, 91, 93
  Slim River, x, xvi, 141-142, 147
  Wadi Akarit, 117, 237

Burma Campaign, xiii, xix, xxii, 105, 107, 148-149, 153-154, 157, 159, 171, 177, 180, 188, 200, 210, 224-225, 231-232, 236

Cameron Report, 152, 154-155
Chatfield Committee, 36, 54
Combined operations training, 78, 118, 120, 183, 185, 188
Congress Party, 55, 211

Defence of India, xxi, 35, 230
Desert warfare, ix, 53, 78, 81, 89-90, 97-99, 102, 134, 138-139
Directorate of Army Education, 191-193

East African Campaign, 110, 132-133, 189, 230, 232
East India Company, 27-28, 43

Index   249

Fauji Akhbar, 56-57, 59, 68, 71, 76, 79, 119, 155-156, 179, 188, 195, 197, 200-201, 204-205, 221
Field Service Pocket Book (*FSPB*), 30, 61-62, 134
Field Service Regulations Vol. II, 30, 42, 62-63, 70, 132
'filleting', 137, 142, 153
Formation Training, 50-51, 78, 94, 135, 185
Frontier warfare, 42, 60-61, 64, 70, 79, 116, 129, 156, 186, 188, 198-199, 228

Government of India, xxi, 33, 35, 37, 40, 77, 97, 124, 222

Jungle warfare, ix, xxiv, 63, 70, 78, 105, 111, 130-139, 145-149, 152-154, 156, 158, 160-163, 166-170, 181-182, 185-187, 189-190, 199, 202-203, 206-207, 212, 224, 232-233, 240

Malayan Campaign, 130, 135-136, 140, 142-143, 146, 154, 220, 224, 236
Middle East Training Pamphlet No. 10, 90, 92
Military Training Directorate (Directorate of Military Training), i, xiv, 58, 62, 67-68, 74, 80, 83, 87, 153, 162, 186, 188-189, 198, 207, 209-211, 215
'milking', 56, 84, 135, 137-138, 143, 160
Mohmand Campaign, 42, 72
Mountain warfare, i, ix, xvi, xxv, 31, 41, 64-65, 80, 96, 98, 109-112, 114-124, 126-129, 210
MTP No. 5 (India) *Notes on Training for Extensive Warfare 1940*, 64, 85, 161
MTP No. 6 (India) *The Support of Land Forces by Aircraft in Tribal Warfare on the Western Frontier of India 1940*, 60-61, 79
MTP No. 7 (India) *Extensive Warfare (Notes on Warfare in Mountainous Country between Modern Forces in Eastern Theatres) 1940*, 64-65, 96, 109, 117
MTP No. 9 (India), 63-64, 133, 143-144, 146, 150, 153-154, 161-163, 165, 169-170, 186-187

MTP No. 14 (India) on *Infantry Section Leading*, 64-65, 88, 161
MTP No. 16 (India) *Platoon Leading in Frontier Warfare*, 61, 188
MTP No. 23 *Operations*, Part I, *General Principles, Fighting Troops and their Characteristics and Army Training Memoranda No. 24*, 62, 84
MTP No. 33 *Training in Field Craft and Elementary Tactics*, 62, 65, 75
Mutiny, 27-29, 232

North African Campaign, 89, 93, 99, 102, 105, 108, 122, 222, 225, 235
Notes on Forest Warfare, 63, 133, 144, 150

Operations:
 'Battleaxe', 93-94, 108
 'Crusader', 94-96, 98, 104-105
 'Extended Capital', 182-183
 'Matador', 131, 140, 223
 'Supercharge', 102, 107

Partition, 44, 129, 208, 218, 222
Public Relations Directorate, 188, 195

'Quit India', 156, 203

Retreat from Burma, 149, 152-154, 156, 159-160, 163-164, 167-169, 190, 214-215, 217, 220, 230

Tactical Exercises Without Troops (TEWTS), xii, 45, 51, 60, 68, 78, 85-86, 89, 154, 178, 190
Tactical Notes for Malaya, 63, 133, 139
Tribal warfare, 51, 61, 64, 79, 235
Tunisian Campaign, 105, 117-118

War Office, xxiv, 29-30, 34-35, 41-43, 51, 53, 56, 59, 61-62, 66-67, 70, 75, 78, 84, 87, 128, 131, 138, 163, 181, 186-187, 189, 194, 199, 215, 218
Wartime Education for Indian Troops, 192-194
Winning the Peace, 193, 195-196